Together *till the End*

Together *till the End*

A Blueprint for Successful Marriage

Lehlohonolo Lucas Mazindo

PARTRIDGE
A Penguin Random House Company

ISBN:	Softcover	978-1-4828-2552-7
	eBook	978-1-4828-2551-0

Print information available on the last page.

To order additional copies of this book, contact
Toll Free 0800 990 914 (South Africa)
+44 20 3014 3997 (outside South Africa)
orders.africa@partridgepublishing.com

www.partridgepublishing.com/africa

Contents

Foreword vii
Preface ix
1. Introduction 1
2. The Biblical Origin of Marriage 6
3. Marriage Implications 25
4. Preparation for Marriage 37
   4.1 Why People Get Married 40
   4.2 Choosing a Life Partner 54
   4.3 Courtship 60
   4.4 Marital Expectations 65
5. Fusion of Two Different Entities 72
   5.1 Gender Differences 75
   5.2 Differing Family Backgrounds 98
   5.3 Different Personalities 101
   5.4 Diverse Abilities 110
6. *"Forsaking All Others"* – Get Your Priorities Right 114
7. *"For Better or Worse"* – Stages of Marriage 122
8. *"For Richer or Poorer"* – Financial Matters 131
9. Sex in Marriage 136
10. *"To Love and to Cherish"* – Romance in Marriage 153
11. Children in Marriage 165
12. The In-Laws – *Part of the Package* 181
13. Marriage and Technology 193
14. Baggage from the Past 198
15. Essential Values in Marriage 206
   15.1 Love 206
   15.2 Tolerance 209

15.3 Faithfulness and Trust....210
15.4 Mutual Fulfilment....211
15.5 Mutual Understanding....213
15.6 Mutual Empowerment....214
15.7 Intimacy....214
15.8 Respect....215
15.9 Devotion....216
15.10 Transparency....217
15.11 Companionship....218
15.12 Forgiveness....219
16. Communication in Marriage....222
17. Love Languages in Marriage....237
18. Temperament Issues....248
19. *"Happily Ever After"* – Happiness in Marriage....274
20. Marriage Must be Managed....289
21. *"In Sickness and in Health"* – Illnesses in Marriage....297
22. Marriage Killers....303
22.1 Infidelity....303
22.2 Confinement....305
22.3 Domestic Violence....306
22.4 Addictions....311
22.5 Selfishness....314
22.6 Destructive Criticisms....316
22.7 Sarcasm....318
22.8 External Interferences....319
22.9 Pride....320
22.10 Excessive Jealousy and Insecurities....321
23. Marital Conflict....325
24. *"To Have and to Hold... Till Death Do Us Part"* – The Truth About Divorce....333
25. Count Yourself In....341
26. Marriage: A Type for Eternity....345
References....349

Foreword

Lehlohonolo Lucas Mazindo started working at Families South Africa (FAMSA) Welkom after finishing his studies in Psychology. From the onset it was obvious that this young man has a passion for life in general, but specifically for making a real difference in people's lives. Working in rural areas, taking services to the communities, he had the opportunity to put words into practice. And so it was, many lives were touched and changed for the better.

At FAMSA we believe that the family is the basis of the greater community. If we just look at all the social ills that exist in our communities today, we have to agree that our communities are not healthy. Looking deeper at this issue, we will realize that families are suffering. This is due to multiple challenges in our society and both internal and external threats that are present.

One of these threats/challenges is the breakdown of marriages. It has become far too easy to end a marriage. Usually not taking into consideration the effect it has on everyone involved. We are living in an era of "quick fixes". Couples are somehow not willing to work out their differences within the marriage, but would rather give up on the marriage – not realizing the long-term effects of a divorce.

This book is a valuable tool for all couples who are thinking of marriage, already married (for any length of time) or going through a difficult period in their relationships – or anyone for that matter, who wants to gain information and skills regarding a healthy marriage/relationship.

FAMSA Welkom is very proud to have played a part in Mr. Mazindo's journey which has culminated in the writing of this book. We believe that this book will have a positive impact on the lives of all people who will take the opportunity to read it.

Coba Swart
Senior Social Worker
Director: Families South Africa – Welkom

Preface

The world today is harshly confronted by the rapidly increasing social problems. Crime, prostitution, rape, teenage pregnancy, dropping out of school, homelessness, suicide, juvenile delinquency, alcohol and drug addiction, wickedness, violence, peer pressure, sexually transmitted infections, moral degeneration, gansterism, hatred, sexual promiscuity; all these and more can be traced back to dysfunctional families and broken marriages. If marriages are not healthy, families will be dysfunctional; and the whole community will suffer. The governments spend billions of dollars trying to fix the problems facing their nations; and still there is no solution, because they address the symptoms and leave the core of the problem unattended. If they could spend more money and resources on strengthening marriages, they would reduce many social problems tremendously. It takes less money and resources to build strong marriages than it does to deal with the consequences of broken marriages.

As a professional counsellor, I very often meet a lot of teenagers and young adults with behaviour problems. When I get to the core of their problems, I usually discover that there is something wrong at home. Some teenagers are looking at the wrong places for the love they are not getting at home. Some feel guilty for the violence that is always taking place between their parents; others are angry because their parents are going or have gone through divorce, and they find themselves caught in the middle. Some are resentful of their fathers who were never there for them; and others are carrying the horrible scars of being physically and emotionally abused by their step-parents and relatives who preyed on them like vultures while their parents were busy afflicting each other. Some learnt to hurt other people by observing how their parents hurt each other. As sociologists rightfully put it, *socialisation begins at home.* Whatever the children learn in their homes, they practice in their societies. Healthy marriage is the foundation of healthy homes, and healthy homes produce healthy individuals, who then constitute healthy communities.

Marriage is a divine gift from God. He designed it for mankind so that they may enjoy the ultimate expressions of love. He also instituted it to typify the nature of our relationship with Christ. No human relationship is more valuable before God than marriage; because marriage illustrates the passion of His only begotten Son Jesus Christ for His people. Regrettably, people in the twenty first century are gradually losing faith in marriage. Some make the flawed conclusions that marriage is no longer relevant. However, marriage is as relevant as life itself; and it is still God's best idea for humanity. What makes marriage miserable to many couples is that they violate the principles that God has set up to enable them to enjoy their marriages. Even the most useful devices can be deadly if not operated according to the manufacturer's instructions. Marriage was created by God; therefore, it can only succeed if it is managed according His principles.

This book was written to share godly principles that will help you make your marriage a success. Inside this book are truths that will challenge your usual way of thinking and give you a whole new perspective on marriage and life. You will also discover psychological insights that will help you gain deeper understanding of human behaviour and how it affects marriage and life in general. This book was written for the reader as well, not only for the reader's partner. Therefore, as you read it, read it for yourself; and encourage your spouse to read it for themselves. It will empower you as you read it; and it will empower your spouse as they read it. The primary purpose for this book is to help you build a successful marriage through the application of godly principles. Not only will this message empower you to build a successful marriage; it will also help you grow personally.

This book carries the real message for real people; addressing real problems by helping you find real solutions. The message in this book is relevant to our everyday lives, and it is aimed to be on *TIME* – Transformational, Informative, Motivational and Empowering. As you read, you will discover the truth that will not only strengthen your relationships; but also liberate you psychologically and spiritually. Some of the truths in this book may be hard to ingest, but they will help you find true happiness in your marriage and life in general. They may feel unpleasant when you read them; but they will give you power to transform your marriage when you practice them. Marriage was not built to fail; and with this book my primary goal is to help you grow stronger in your marriage so that you and your spouse can live happily *together till the end.*

1

Introduction

In this busy world, life seems to be moving on a fast lane. People seek to achieve more in less time and with less effort. Convenience has become every person's obsession. Everything seems to be done in a hurry. Companies make big profits out of creating instant products. We have instant yeast, instant coffee, instant porridge, instant messaging and many other instant products that were designed to help people shortcut significant processes in pursuit of success. We are rapidly moving away from valuable practices such as enrolling at universities for full qualifications and opt for short courses instead. Even universities are starting to introduce short courses in order to accommodate this generation of people who seem to be pursuing convenience at the expense of quality.

We spend most of our time on internet and newspapers trying to look for opportunities to get rich instantly while we sit in the comfort of our homes, lose weight quickly with less or no effort, get the perfect body in less than six weeks without working out, and any other simple ways to achieve success with no sweat. The general principles of success are being breached in the process of trying to achieve a lot at low cost. Day by day innovations are being made in desperate attempts to help people blink their dreams into reality. Countries are making lots of money through lottery because it promises instant and effortless riches.

Our growing obsession for instant products robs us off the valuable lessons we could learn in the process. It steals away the valuable experiences that could make us stronger and wiser. As a result a lot of people stumble into the success they cannot sustain. They lay hold of the things they cannot keep, because they have not allowed time and process to teach them valuable principles of retention. The pursuit of instant success denies them time to make proper preparations for the very things they are so desperately running after, and this causes them to lose the sense of permanence in their achievements. They achieve it all instantaneously and lose it all soon afterwards.

Unfortunately, people seem to be following the same approach in as far as marriage is concerned. They settle for instant attractions, instant dates, instant marriage, instant divorce, and instant remarriage; and before they know it, they are all alone confronted by debilitating effects of the damage they suffered in their short-lived marriages. Eventually they make faulty conclusions that marriage no longer exists, or that marriage is an 'awful' experience. Marital success cannot be achieved through quick fixes and love portions; it requires a great deal of time, effort, preparation and commitment.

When you log into the internet or read the news papers, you come across the advertisements of products and tips that promise to help you improve your marital relationship instantly. You apply the given tips or products in your relationship and find yourself dealing with more disappointment, confusion and frustration, and you wonder if you can ever be happy in your marriage. Eventually you lose faith in marriage instead of losing faith in the products they advertised. Remember, most of those people are not as interested in the success of your marriage as they are in getting their hands on your hard-earned money. People who are truly interested in the success of your marriage will tell you the truth, and the truth is that marriage takes time to develop, and it requires your full commitment.

The increasing love for instant gratification in the modern society has instilled in many people the irresistible passion for pleasure. Countless numbers of people embrace pleasure and forsake significant values such as discipline, patience, perseverance, love and commitment. They do everything in their power to avoid anything that requires them to stay in the course. They remain committed to the relationship for as long as it gives them pleasure and forsake it as soon as they find another one that promises to give more pleasure.

The media at the same time is playing the role of magnifying pleasure over commitment. Movies display marriage as a boring life of chores and routines, while extra-marital relationships are presented as extremely pleasurable. They exhibit fornication and adultery as more fun and pleasurable than the love scenes that take place between married couples, which are always interrupted by phone calls, children showing up with sad faces, or landlords with eviction notices. Movies, soaps and dramas are always about falling in love and never about staying in love. As a matter of fact most movies end at the beginnings of love relationships; how those relationships will be sustained is left for viewers to figure out.

Now more than ever, many people all over the world have lost faith in marriage because they faced a lot of disappointments therein. The rate of divorce seems to be increasing day by day. This leads to an increasing number of people avoiding marriage even when they are in stable relationships. They resort to new arrangements such as cohabitation because it is more instant and convenient, and it does not require lifelong commitment. Sex is no longer kept within the perimeters of marriage as God designed it, and this leads to more and more children being born out of wedlock and raised by single parents.

The loss of faith in marriage and the avoidance thereof puts marriage under the threat of extinction like dinosaurs. The general acceptance of pre-marital or casual sex and cohabitation by the society makes marriage appear obsolete. Marriage in the modern society, like rhinos and elephants, is gradually becoming an endangered institution. The gradual shifting of marriage towards the backseat gives rise to the question: Is marriage approaching a dead end? The answer to this question is a big *NO!* Marriage was instituted by God to be a permanent relationship, and everything God has established continues to survive even under severe threats of extermination.

Science has it that water does not have the shape or colour of its own; rather, it takes the shape and colour of its container. Same applies with marriage; it is shaped by the personalities, characters, habits, choices, decisions, values and attitudes of the people involved. As a matter of fact, marriage is a good thing, because everything that God created is good. God ordained marriage to be enjoyed, not to be endured. The choices that we make and the decisions that we take are the main reasons why many people remain unhappy in the union that was designed for their pleasure. Marriage, like electricity, if not operated according to its basic laws and principles, can be very dangerous; people might get shocked, and hearts might be broken.

The reason why marriage turns sour is because people are not giving themselves enough time to learn the principles that will help them keep it alive. They are too quick to marry, and too quick to divorce. They don't stay long enough to learn from their experiences. They quickly forsake their current marriage to pursue a 'different' one; then they perpetuate the same habits and practices that led to the failure of the previous marriage. They continually run away from the experience that would teach them to build successful marriages. No matter how powerful the advices you receive concerning marriage, some lessons are best learned through experience, and each time you walk away after every unpleasant experience, you deny yourself the valuable lessons on the principles that will help you retain your marriage.

Marital relationships, like finger prints, are unique; no two relationships are the same. What works in one marital relationship may not work in the other. Therefore, much as it is vital to get as many advices as possible regarding marriage, it is equally significant that you open your heart to learn new lessons from your own marriage. No marriage is flawless. We all make mistakes and fail sometimes; but we can use those mistakes and failures to strengthen our marriages by deriving lessons from them. Mistakes and failures are good lesson-carriers. When you make a mistake and become aware of it, you experience the feelings of guilt and remorse, which are very unpleasant feelings. But soon afterwards, you learn never to make that mistake again, and that also helps you to avoid reliving the unpleasant experiences of guilt and remorse.

Sometimes in marriage it is okay to give yourself permission to fail and make mistakes; but at the same time you should be prepared to face the consequences thereof. Many people deny their mistakes because they are afraid of the consequences; nevertheless, even if you can deny the mistake, you cannot deny its consequences. Instead of denying your mistake and being defensive about it, acknowledge it and make a commitment to learn from it, and avoid making that mistake again. The genius who invented the light bulb, Thomas Edison, when asked about his thousand times failure in creating a light bulb, he answered: "I have not failed a thousand times; I have successfully discovered a thousand ways that don't work". This should be our attitude in marriage. We should not regard a mistake as failure, but as a successful discovery of what does not work in marriage until we discover what works. Most important to remember is that failure is not the opposite of success; it is part of it.

The delusion regarding ourselves thinking that we are flawless super-beings causes us to expect too much from each other within marital relationships, and this increases our levels of disappointment, frustration and discouragement each time we or our partners make mistakes. The truth is that no marriage is immune from error because no human being is perfect. One other thing that makes it hard to admit our mistakes is that our partners punish us profusely for them and give us no room for improvement. Condemning our partners for their mistakes instead of lovingly correcting them causes them to develop denial and defensiveness; and this denies them a valuable opportunity to learn from their mistakes, and it thus impairs their personal growth. A forgiving and supportive attitude is therefore essential if a marriage is to grow.

There is no need to give up on marriage; it is still one of the best and greatest institutions God has ever created. You cannot quit driving your car just because there are road accidents; you just have to adhere to the rules of road safety and be more careful when you drive. In the same way, you cannot give up on marriage just because people get hurt in marital relationships; you just have to adhere to the principles and continue to learn creative ways to make it work. In this material we will be exploring general concepts around marriage and learn practical ways to increase the rate of success in our marriages. I therefore advise that as you learn new lessons from this material, make a commitment to find ways to apply them in your marriage, ensuring that you modify them to suit the peculiarities of your own marital relationship.

2

The Biblical Origin of Marriage

It would be extremely difficult for me to communicate about marriage without making a specific reference to the Bible because marriage was instituted by God, and He has given us the Bible as the manual to guide us as we navigate through life. It is in the Bible that we can discover the purpose and origin of marriage. It all began in the Book of Genesis 2:18-24, when God out of his observation of Adam's loneliness saw the necessity to make for him a helper comparable to him. Out of His observation, God concluded that it is not good for a man to be alone, and He decided to make for him a suitable companion to be his wife (Genesis 2:18).

As we read the Book of Genesis 2:21-24, we learn that God caused Adam to fall into deep sleep and took out a rib from him to create a woman; then He brought her to him and woke him up. When Adam opened his eyes and awoke from his deep sleep, he saw a woman and knew that she was the one – the bone of his bones and the flesh of his flesh. The fact that God created a woman with a rib of her husband implies that part of the husband will be in his wife, and part of the wife will be in her husband; and this means that when people get married, they become one entity. However, this does not mean they are identical. God made them different from each other, not to *compete* with each other, but to *complement* each other.

Verse 24 of the second chapter in the Book of Genesis outlines one of the essential laws in marriage – the law of *leaving* and *cleaving. Therefore a man shall leave his father and mother and be joined to his wife, and they shall become one flesh* (Genesis 2:24). Take note that this is not just an instruction; it is a *law* – a principle. An instruction can be disobeyed or ignored; even though the consequences thereof cannot be ignored. For example, you can choose to infringe traffic rules and exceed the speed limit, even though you cannot ignore the traffic fine or possible incarceration. The example of the law will be the law of gravity. Gravity keeps you on the ground whether you like it or not, and you have no option to disobey or ignore it. If you jump up, gravity will pull you down no matter how bad you want to disobey it and stay off the ground. Therefore, the law of leaving and cleaving cannot be ignored or disobeyed. If you can't *leave* your parents, you can't *cleave* to your wife.

The law of marriage does not allow a man to cling to both his parents and his wife; he must *leave* the parents and *cleave* to the wife. Marriage cannot be successful when a man insists on squeezing his parents into the relationship. Leaving means not only to evacuate the house where you used to stay with your parents; it also means they cannot interfere with the decisions made in your marriage. Parents also may not interfere with the marital relationships of their children unless they are invited by mutual consent of both partners to intervene in whatever situation they may need their help in. In other words, when it comes to the affairs within their children's marriage, parents should intervene not by intrusion, but by invitation.

God created a human being as a social being. He created him with an inherent need to love and be loved. Therefore for a human being, relationships are essential for survival. Of all human relationships, the most significant is marital relationship. There is no human relationship greater than this. Even God Himself honours marriage so much that He uses it figuratively to illustrate our relationship with Him. The Bible regards the Lord Jesus Christ as the Bridegroom and His church as the bride (Revelation 21:2; 9-10). The Apostle Paul in His letter to the church of Ephesus instructed husbands to love their wives as Christ loves the church, and wives to submit to their husbands as the church submits to Christ (Ephesians 5:22-33).

From the Scriptures referred to above we can learn that we cannot truly understand marriage before we understand Christ's relationship with His church. The Bible teaches us that a husband is to his wife as Christ is to His church, and a wife is to her husband as the church is to Christ. This is the perfect order of marriage. From this illustration we learn that the most important relationship is our relationship with the Lord Jesus Christ; secondary to that is our relationship with our spouses. One of the many reasons why most marriages fail is because the people involved have neglected the most important relationship, the personal relationship with Christ – the Source and Sustainer of everything.

Husbands cannot love their wives enough if they do not have the personal experience of the love of Christ for them, and wives cannot submit totally to their husbands if they have not learnt to submit themselves wholly to Christ. A husband is the head of his wife just as Christ is the Head of His church. Failure to apply this truth very often results in marital failure. God is not sexist; He is a loving Father who never requires from us His children what He has not given us the inherent ability and grace to carry out, and He always instructs us with our best interest at heart. He is not putting anyone at an advantage over the other; He is only bringing balance and order into this divine relationship called marriage.

Wives, submit to your own husbands, as to the Lord. For the husband is the head of the wife, as also Christ is Head of the church; and He is the Saviour of the body. Therefore, just as the church is subject to Christ, so let the wives be to their own husbands in everything (Ephesians 5:22-24). God is the One who created us, and He knows us more than we know ourselves. One thing to always remember is that God loves his people, and whatever He instructs us to do, He knows it will bring forth nothing but great success to us. Therefore, this instruction was given to wives for the benefit of their marriages. God created a man with an inherent need to be respected, and a man's ego responds positively to praise and compliment. Nothing moves the heart of a man more than a woman who submits to him and acknowledges him as head over her.

In the corporate world today, women continue to rise to top management positions in government and private institutions. Their positions obviously give them authority over many men who work under their supervision. Does it mean that a woman should subject herself to the men who are supposed to take instructions from her? The answer is NO! In this case all men who are under the leadership of a woman in the work or business environment must submit to her. *Bondservants, be obedient to those who are your masters according to the flesh, with fear and trembling, in sincerity of heart, as to Christ; not with eyeservice, as men-pleasers, but as bondservants of Christ, doing the will of God from the heart, with goodwill doing service, as to the Lord, and not to men* (Ephesians 6:5-7). The corporate word for bondservant in the modern world is employee or subordinate.

A bondservant or subordinate can be a man or woman, and the Apostle Paul in the Scripture referred to above commands subordinates to obey their supervisors as to Christ. In the work or business environment, a man should play a submissive role to his supervisor or employer, even if that supervisor or employer is a woman. Women should therefore not compromise their leadership roles in the work environment and subject themselves to the men they are supposed to lead. The instruction is very clear: "*Wives,* submit to your *own husbands...*" A specific context applies to this instruction, a context of marriage. This instruction should not be misinterpreted. It does not instruct women to submit to men; it instructs wives to submit to their husbands.

I have observed chaotic situations where wives submit themselves more to other women's husbands than to their own, especially in the Christian environment where wives submit more to their pastors than they do to their own husbands. That is not the order of God. Not only is it ungodly for a wife to submit more to any other man than to her own husband, it is also unhealthy for the marriage. A man is a territorial species, he hates competing for his wife's attention with any another man; it is harmful to his nature. A husband is jealous for his wife just as Christ is for His church. Jesus is not pleased when His church heeds the voices of any other gods more than His voice; neither is a husband when his wife obeys other men more than him. Dear wife, submit to your own husband; let him know he's the best in your world. Put no other man above him; make him feel he's the only one for you, the ultimate earthly king over your family.

According to the Bible, a wife must submit to her husband in everything. Some wives submit to their husbands only when it is convenient for them. Others set the standards to which they are willing to submit. But that's not what the Bible teaches. Everything means everything. As a wife, God is more interested in your attitude than He is in putting your husband above you. He only wants to build your character so that you can model to the world how their attitude towards Christ should be. Jesus will not always give you the instructions you are fond of carrying out, yet you must obey Him anyway. Same applies with your husband; he will sometimes make rulings you don't necessarily agree with, yet you need to submit to him in everything. This will ultimately benefit you more than it benefits him. It helps you exercise your character until it becomes like that of Christ; who, even when He wanted His own way, still chose to submit to God's way and proclaimed "*...not My will, but Yours, be done*" (Luke 22:42).

It is easy for the wife to submit to her husband when they see eye to eye; but the true test of submission is when you submit to him even when you disagree with him. Submitting to him when you agree is human; but submitting to him even when you disagree is divine. As a wife, can you boldly stand before the throne of God and tell Him you are submitting to your husband in *everything* as the church submits to Christ? What excuse will you give to Him? Maybe your response would be "well, if he... then I will..." But in this way you will be attaching a condition to God's instruction. You need to submit to your husband; not because of his deeds, but because of your character and out of obedience to Christ.

It is very important to notice that God is fully aware that men are not as perfect and flawless as Christ is; yet He commands wives to submit to their imperfect husbands as the church submits to the perfect Christ. If men were perfect like Christ, it would have been easier to submit to them because you could be sure he would never let you down or lead you astray. But wives are instructed to submit to their husbands weak as they may be. The implication here is that as a wife you should subject yourself to your imperfect husband as if he were perfect. See the image of Christ in Him. Even though he sometimes fails to keep his end of the bargain, see him not as he is, but as he will be when the character of Christ is perfected in him.

The reason why God instructs you as a wife to submit yourself to your imperfect husband as the church submits to the Perfect Christ is because He wants to challenge him to strive for perfection and become more like Christ. When you treat him the way the church treats Christ, you provoke him to treat you as Christ treats the church. In other words, you provoke the character of Christ in him. It may not happen instantly, but you can rest assured that at the right time the seed you are planting in his heart will finally bear the expected fruit. Do your part and never give up, and God will do His part and touch his life for your sake. Remember, marriage requires commitment, and commitment is displayed through consistence. *And let us not be weary of doing good, for in due season we shall reap if we do not lose heart* (Galatians 6:9).

A man grows more on one word of praise than with a thousand criticisms. Instead of bombarding him with endless criticisms for the wrong he does, compliment him for the good he is doing. This will provoke him to do everything in his power to keep the compliments coming; and to avoid doing anything that would break the heart of the only woman who adores him. I'm not saying a man should not be confronted or corrected for the wrongs he does; I am simply saying let it not be all about the mistakes he makes as if he never does anything good. Some wives speak when their husbands do wrong and keep quiet when they do right. This can have a very discouraging effect on a man. Every woman needs to treat her husband as the church treats Christ; this will help your husband rise to His likeness and be the better husband for you. Jesus responds well to praise, and so does a man. Just as Christ delights in hearing His church tell Him "You are the Christ", so your husband loves it when he hears you tell him "you're the man!"

As I journey through life, I observe numerous women who yell at their husbands thinking that it is a good way to gain control over them and get them to do what they want. Yet they still don't get what they want, instead all they get are plenty of hours alone at home after their husbands banged the door and stormed out of the house just to be away from that noisy environment. Soon after that they wonder how come their husbands left their mansion to stay in the shack with someone of a lower social class (I am in no way advocating for men who cheat on their wives here, neither do I condone that behaviour; I am simply stating that yelling or shouting at your husband only causes more harm to your marriage. This must never be used as an excuse for unfaithfulness). The truth of the matter is that to a man it doesn't matter where he stays as long as there is peace and quietness. *Better to dwell in the wilderness, than with contentious and angry wife* (Proverbs 21:19). Acting out of anger has never helped anyone achieve a happy marriage. In fact, anger is to a marriage what cancer is to the body. The angrier the wife, the more stubborn the husband, and this can never work for any marriage.

Wives, likewise, be submissive to your own husbands, that even if some do not obey the word, they, without a word, may be won by the conduct of their wives, when they observe your chaste conduct accompanied by fear. Do not let your adornment be merely outward – arranging the hair, wearing gold, or putting on fine apparel – rather let it be the hidden person of the heart, with the incorruptible beauty of a gentle and quiet spirit, which is very precious in the sight of God. For in this manner, in former times, the holy women who trusted in God also adorned themselves, being submissive to their own husbands, as Sarah obeyed Abraham, calling him lord, whose daughters you are if you do good and are not afraid with any terror (1Peter 3:1-6).

As a wife, the most effective way in which you can win your husband's heart is by submitting to him. This is also the perfect way to win your husband over to Christ without saying a word. Your influence over your husband is not in your words; it is in your conduct. Your submission to your husband is more than just a conduct; it is a ministry. It is the perfect tool for the preaching of the Gospel. Not only do you win your husband's heart when you submit to him; you also win the very heart of God. In fact, when you submit to your husband, you submit to the very God who gave you the instruction to submit to your husband. You cannot claim you submit to God if you do not submit to your husband. Actually, by failing to submit to your husband, you are disobeying the God who instructed you.

The beauty of the wife is not in the makeup she puts on or in the hair she wears; it is in her conduct towards her husband. Almost all women spend much time adorning themselves with clothes, jewelleries, makeup, manicures, pedicures and many other means, and that is very good, but the true beauty of a wife lies in her heart. All this physical beauty is temporary, but there is an incorruptible beauty that all wives can put on. The incorruptible beauty of a wife is characterised by a *gentle* and *quiet* spirit, and this is the kind of beauty that is very precious in the sight of God. No matter how many people see you as beautiful, if you do not have a gentle and quiet spirit, your beauty is worthless before God. According to the Bible, Sarah submitted to Abraham her husband and obeyed him, calling him lord, and you are the daughter of Abraham if you do the same to your husband.

You can't say you keep God's commandments if you do not submit to your husband, and you can't say you love God if you do not keep His commandments. Jesus said it: *"If you keep My commandments, you will abide in My love, just as I have kept My Father's commandments and abide in His love"* (John 15: 10); and: *"You are My friends if you do whatever I command you"* (John 15:14). You can't claim you have a friendship with Christ if you do not have one with your husband. As a wife, you submit to your husband not because he deserves it; but because you are the friend of Christ and the daughter of Abraham. You do so to carry out the commandment of Christ so that you may abide in His love. The true test of the wife's obedience to God is if she can submit to her own husband as the church submits to Christ.

A man can do anything for a woman who makes him feel he matters; he can go to great extremes to act in the favour of a wife who willingly seeks his approval for significant decisions to be taken in their family. This submissive attitude builds up a man's character and makes him feel obliged to decide in the favour of his family. A man who gets the praises and compliments from his wife is always very careful to never let her down. As a matter of fact, you are more likely to get your way in marriage as a wife when you put your husband at his position as your head than when you forcefully insist on having your way. Believe it or not, praising your husband for putting his shoes in their place works so much better than criticising him for leaving them on the floor. You win the love and approval of your husband by submitting to him, and that is the truth from the living Word of God.

Husbands also have a role to play. *Husbands, love your wives, just as Christ also loved the church and gave Himself for her, that He might sanctify and cleanse her with the washing of water by the word, and He might present her to Himself a glorious church, not having spot or wrinkle or any such thing, but that she should be holy and without blemish. So husbands ought to love their own wives as their own bodies; he who loves his wife loves himself. For no one ever hated his own flesh, but nourishes and cherishes it, just as the Lord does the church* (Ephesians 5:25-29). This is a glorious instruction, and obedience to this instruction produces a glorious marriage. As a husband you are instructed to love your own wife as Christ loves the church. If you are a man and you have not experienced the love of Christ in your own life, you won't be able to love your wife that much because you have no idea how that kind of love can impact a life.

Before I elaborate any further on this subject, I want to clarify that in this portion of Scripture God is not instructing men to love women; He is instructing husbands to love their wives. As a husband, no one should love your wife more than you do, and you should not love anyone else more than you love your own wife. Marriage suffers a great deal of damage when a man celebrates other women and disapproves his own wife. As a husband, what do you think it does to your marriage when you open the door of the car for your female colleague at work while at home you let your own wife see herself out? It is extremely detrimental to your marriage when you see other women as ladies and your own wife as the mere caretaker of your house. Marriage is most likely to fail when a husband becomes gentle on other women and rough on his own wife. If you want your wife to treat you like a king, then treat her like a queen and let her know she's the only queen in your world.

You may have a spiritual leader who is a woman, but to love her more than you love your wife or celebrate her more than you celebrate your wife is unbiblical; in fact, it is a recipe for marital disaster. I know a lot of men who regard everything their female pastors say and nothing their wives say. They spend more on them than they spend on their wives. What do you think will happen to your marriage if you give your female pastor R1500,00 for her hairstyle and then give your own wife R500,00 or nothing for hers? The deception around this is that you will be blessed abundantly; but the truth around it is that you are gradually removing building blocks from your marriage. This can also be offensive to the pastor's husband. There is no scripture in the Bible that requires a husband to love or celebrate his female pastor more than his own wife, and there is none that requires a wife to submit more to her male pastor than to her own husband.

I am not suggesting that our spiritual leaders should not be honoured or appreciated; in fact, I strongly believe in honouring servants of God. I am simply suggesting a more maritally healthy approach to honouring or appreciating them. If the spiritual leader is a man, he should most often be taken care of by the husband; and if she is a woman, let the wife take care of her the most. This can prevent unnecessary tensions whereby the husband feels like he is the pastor's runner-up to his own wife or the wife feels like the pastor is stealing her husband's attention away from her. Pastors should also play a helpful role to married couples. A male pastor should try by all means to avoid being closer to her female congregant than to her husband, and the female pastor should try not to overlook or disregard the wife of her male congregant. If the husband should take care of his female pastor or the wife has to take care of her male pastor, let it happen occasionally and by mutual consent of both the husband and the wife.

If you are the pastor and you are married, none of your congregants should enjoy your love and attention more than your wife. Some pastors often make the mistake of leaving their wives desperate for their attention and then attend to a female congregant who is complaining about her husband not paying attention to her. The truth of the matter is that if you do that, you are actually leaving your wife with the very problem you are trying to solve for another man's wife. In fact, you and your congregant's husband are equally guilty of the same offense. Eventually, both of you may lose your wives.

As the pastor, your wife should always feel that she is the first lady in your life. She is also human, and she needs to know without a doubt that she always takes the first place in your heart. She needs to be hundred percent confident in your love for her; but she cannot be that confident if you keep on making her feel like she comes second to every other woman in your church. Put her first at all times, and let others know through your consistent display of love for her that none of them can ever come between the two of you. It is dreadfully unwise to focus all your attention on your ministry and none of it on your marriage. Building your ministry at the expense of your marriage is a sure recipe for marital catastrophe.

As a husband, you have no justifiable reason to believe more in other women or other men's wives than in your own wife. If you smile at other women and frown at your wife, you are practically digging the grave for your own marriage. Love your own wife, celebrate her and let her know she means the world to you. It will be extremely difficult for your wife to submit to you if she does not trust you, and it is very hard for her to trust you if she does not feel loved by you. A woman who gets a lot of love from her husband finds it easy to trust him completely and submit to him because she knows he would never do anything deliberately to hurt her. A woman responds very well to love, and she would do whatever it takes to keep it coming. Therefore, the more you show love to your wife, the more she will open her heart to you and do everything in her power to keep that love alive. Love provokes a woman to give herself over to the one who loves her, especially if that one is her husband.

You get the most of your wife's devotion by magnifying praise and compliment over complaint and criticism. Men are not the only ones who respond well to praise and compliment; women do too. As a husband, always find something good to say about your wife. Do not keep on criticising her as if she never does anything right. Rather than giving her reasons why you might leave her, give her reasons why you will love and cherish her for as long as you live. Make her feel secure in your undying love for her, not because she is perfect, but because of your total commitment to her. As a man, it is very essential that you learn to see beyond where you are. Not only that, you should also learn to see your wife beyond where she is. Continue to believe in her even when she has lost faith in herself. That's what Christ does for you.

"Husbands, love your own wives..." This seems like an easy instruction to carry out. But the Apostle Paul takes it further by saying "...as Christ also loved the church and gave Himself for her". Let us pause for a moment and think about this. First and foremost there's nothing to love about the church, yet Christ loved her anyway. The church is a combination of thieves, liars, backbiters, murderers, fornicators, adulterers, idolaters, betrayers, drunkards and all categories of sinners, yet Jesus loved them so much that He gave Himself for them. Even so, the church keeps on disappointing Him, yet He never gives up on them. He loves them even when they keep on hurting Him and failing to obey His commandments. He keeps on restoring them each time they fall. He treats them not as they are, but as they will be. He is constantly loving and gracious to His own, and even though they are full of sins, He covers them with His blood and presents them blameless before God.

This material cannot contain Christ's countless thoughts and acts of love for His church. He lays down His life for the ones He loves no matter how often or how much they disappoint Him. *But God demonstrates His own love towards us, in that while we were still sinners, Christ died for us* (Romans 5:8). This is the highest degree of love, and this is how much we husbands must love our wives. Your wife may be completely out of control and show no respect for you, but you must continue to love her, forgive her, cover her and protect her. You must love her not for how she is behaving, but for who she is and who she will be. In fact, Christ loves you not for what you do, but for who He is. In the same way, your love for your wife should depend not on her behaviour, but on your character. It is your unconditional love that will win her commitment to you. It may not happen instantly, but in the fullness of time she will finally come around and be the wife you've always dreamt of. Just keep on loving her and never give up on her.

True love depends not on the *behaviour of the beloved*; it depends on the *nature of the loving*. Therefore, you should not base your love for your wife on *her performance*; you need to base it on *your own personality*. Which means that as a husband, you should love your wife; not because of what she has done, but because of who you are. That is how Christ loves you, and so should you love your wife. It is human to love her if she performs well; but it is godly to love her when she least deserves it. The Lord Jesus Christ wants you to reflect His love for you on your wife by loving her the way He loves you. As a husband, you need to assume the role of Christ over your wife by treating her with grace and loving her as if she never does anything wrong.

Jesus never exposes your weaknesses to anyone, neither should you expose the weaknesses of your wife, rather cover her and present her pure and blameless before the world. There are men who talk about the weaknesses of their wives to other people, even to other women. Others even allow other people to talk against their wives in their presence, and they have a nerve to participate in the conversation. This cannot solve any marital problem; it can only make it worse. Your wife may not be as strong as you are, but let her find her strength in you. Can you imagine how you would feel if Christ would keep on reminding you of the wrongs you have done? Thank God He doesn't! Neither should you keep on reminding your wife of her mistakes. Do not hold her wrongs against her; rather hold her hand and help her rise again, and again, and again... Dear husband, this instruction was not for your detriment, but to build the character of Christ in you so that you can enjoy the marriage that you've always wished for.

Christ loved the church and gave himself for her. Some men express their love to their wives by giving them money; flowers, jewellery, cars, cell phones, and many other material things money can buy. But true love is expressed when a man gives himself. To a woman, everything means nothing if she does not have you. She wants you more than your money. To her, love is not so much about your *presents* as it is about your *presence*. The gifts you buy for her cannot substitute you. You can't always be absent from your wife and think she is okay just because you do everything for her. The truth is that she does not want you to do things for her; she wants you to do things together. Gifts are good, but they are not as important as the giver. Give her gifts, but be there to see the smile on her face as she unwraps them, and while she's at it, let her hear you tell her that you love her, and that she is your 'Miss Universe' of all time.

One other significant aspect of this instruction is that husbands should love their own wives as they love themselves. Your wife is not the separate being from you; she is the female version of you. If you love her, you love yourself; and if you hate her, you hate yourself. Men who hate themselves abuse their wives, but men who love themselves protect their wives. Whatever you do to your wife, you are actually doing it to yourself. Men who hurt their wives always admit that they also get hurt in the process or immediately afterwards. There's no way you can hurt your wife and be happy. In fact, you are only as happy or as sad as you make her. When her heart breaks, part of you breaks as well.

The Apostle Peter also raises an important point that I believe every husband should consider: *Husbands, likewise, dwell with them with understanding, giving honour to the wife, as to the weaker vessel, and as being heirs together of the grace of life, that your prayers may not be hindered* (1Peter 3:7). As a husband, your love for God is demonstrated by the way you treat your wife. You cannot claim you love God if you fail to love your wife. You honour your wife not because she earned it; but because you are an heir of the grace of life. Your wellbeing as a husband strongly depends on your treatment to your wife. If you hurt your wife or disrespect her in any way or for any reason, you are hindering your own prayers. You are denying yourself access into the throne of God, and you are disturbing your own peace. Eventually you are the one who suffers more. So, do yourself a favour, love your wife.

Whatever God commands, He gives grace to carry out. Therefore, when you are under His command, you are under His grace. He is the One who commanded the husband to love His wife; and He is the One who commanded the wife to submit to her husband. Therefore, the husband is graced to love his wife, and the wife is graced to submit to her husband. The husband's love for his wife is more deliberate than spontaneous; and so is the wife's submission to her husband. This means that for the husband to love his wife and the wife to submit to her husband, it takes *human's will* and *God's grace.*

You may ask: "What then do I do if I keep on reaching out to my wife and she keeps on ignoring me?" The answer is very simple: do what God does when He keeps on reaching out to you and you keep on ignoring Him. He never gives up on you. He keeps on reaching out to you with love even if you fail to respond to Him. He does not fail to love you when you fail to submit to Him. You are sometimes unfaithful to Him, but He is always faithful to you. Even if you don't have time for Him, He always has time for you. He does not force you to stay with Him, but He always welcomes you whenever you come back to Him. He continues to express His love to you even if you give Him nothing in return. Even if you do nothing for Him, He will always do everything for you. The same attitude God has towards you, you should have towards your wife.

When you stop reaching out to your wife because she is not responsive you, you are no different from Adam, who decided to eat the fruit his wife offered him even though God commanded him not to eat it (the story is in Genesis 3). If you treat your wife the way she treats you, you become more like her; but if you continue to reach out to her with love even when she breaks your heart, you become more like Christ. Marriage was not designed to make you like your spouse; it was designed to make both of you become more like God. If you retreat because your wife ill-treats you, you are applying manly principles; but if you continue to love her even if she shows no signs of love to you, you are applying godly principles. By this I am not giving wives a licence to disrespect their husbands. This does not exempt wives from carrying out their part. The wife's responsibility of submitting to her husband still stands. All I am saying is that husbands should learn to treat their wives with grace just as God treats them.

Marriage is not of man; it is of God. Yes, it was designed for man, but not by man. Everything is operated not according to the user's interest; but according to the manufacturer's instructions. So is marriage. It was designed by God for man to enjoy; but man cannot enjoy it if he operates it according his own interests and neglects God instructions. It cannot be governed successfully by manly principles; it requires godly principles. Manly principles bring separation and destruction, but godly principles bring harmony and life.

The issue of *love* and *submission* is not about how you feel; it is about what God has commanded you and given you grace to carry out. But even though God gives us such orders, He will not force us to carry them out. He only instructs us and gives us permission to choose whether or not to obey Him. It pleases Him when we obey Him by *choice* and not by *force.* For humans, love and submission are matters of will, not coercion. Therefore, the wife cannot compel her husband to love her, and the husband cannot bully his wife into submitting to him; but each of them should play their own part and leave others to play theirs.

God did not instruct a wife to *make her husband love her*; He instructed her to *submit to him.* And He did not command the husband the *make his wife submit to him*; He commanded him to *love her.* Some marriages fail because of people who think they are responsible for making their partners love them or submit to them. Their main attitude towards their marriage is "I will not submit to you if you do not love me" or "I will not love you if you do not submit to me." This is not God's instruction; it is man's invention. Godly love is unconditional; it expects nothing in return. It is not your part to make your wife submit to you; your part is to love her, whether she submits to you or not. Submission is not what you make her do; it is what she chooses to do.

Let me quickly draw your attention into the animal kingdom. In this kingdom, males are *dominant*, and females are *submissive*. Think about the pride of lions for an example. The lion spends most of its day lying under the shades of the trees, while the lioness takes care of her cups and does all the hunting to fend for her family. Yet she submits to the male completely. But this kind of submission is different from human submission. In the animal kingdom, males *dominate* and females *submit*; but in the human race, men *love* and women *submit*. Generally, males are built to be physically stronger and more aggressive than females; so if the two were to fight, the female would not stand a chance. Therefore, female animals would not take chances to stand up to males in a fight because they could be killed. So, instead of trying to fight, they submit. They submit in order to survive; otherwise they will be put to death. In order other words, in the animal kingdom, submission is forced.

Not so with humans. As human beings, there are things we have that animals do not have. We have the power of choice, an independent will and intelligence. God did not create us to be forced or controlled; He created us to act out of our own will. We were created in God's image and likeness (See Genesis 1:26-27); and if He cannot be forced or controlled, neither can we. Even God Himself does not force us to submit to Him; He wants it to be out of our own will. In other words, as a human being, you can choose whether or not to submit to God. It pleases Him more when we choose to submit to Him than when He forces us to submit. Instead of trying to force us to submit to Him, He continually invents ways to win our hearts over to Him so that as we respond to His love for us, we may submit to Him as God. To win our hearts, He uses *affection*; not *aggression*.

The same approach should be followed by husbands towards their wives. As a husband, you cannot control your wife or force her to submit to you; it has to be something she does out of her own will and in obedience to God's instruction. If you use physical force to command submission from your wife, instead of submitting, she will lay charges against you, and you will go to jail. The submission that is imposed through aggression comes as a result of fear; but one that is earned through affection comes as a result of respect. Your wife should *respect* you and not *fear* you. In respect there is loyalty; but in fear there is betrayal. In other words, if you command submission from your wife trough *intimidation*, you provoke her to betray and sabotage you; but if you earn her submission through *intimacy*, you win her loyalty.

The matter of love and submission is often regarded by people as influenced by the law of *cause* and *effect.* "The husband cannot love his wife if she does not submit to him, and the wife cannot submit to her husband if he does not love her"; so do many people think. Well, this is partly true because it is the human interpretation of how love and submission work. But from godly interpretation, the subject of love and submission is more than the law of cause and effect. You don't wait for your wife to submit to you before you love her; instead, you provoke her to submit to you by loving her whether she submits to you or not. In other words, your love for your wife should not be the *effect* of her submission to you; it should rather be the *cause* of it.

Marriage is a reflection of God's relationship with his people. God's love for us is not *caused* by our submission to Him. He loves us whether we submit to Him or not. Godly marriage is actually a human expression of God's unfailing and unconditional love for His people. So, the idea of "If you... then I will..." is not a true reflection of a godly marriage. As God loves you, so should you love your spouse. People should observe your unfailing love for each other and ask you: "How do you manage to love each other so much when so many marriages are falling apart?" Then your answer should be: "That's how much God loves you and me." Your unconditional love for each other as husband and wife could then save many breaking marriages and win many souls to Christ for their salvation.

Sometimes marriage is like running on a treadmill, and God is a personal trainer who uses the Bible as His medium of instruction. Running on a treadmill is not getting you anywhere in terms of spatial position. No matter how fast you may run on it, you will still be at the same place when you stop running. The purpose of a treadmill is not to move you from one point to another; it is to make you fitter and stronger. Sometimes for a wife to submit to her husband and for a husband to love his wife is like running on a treadmill; it seems to be taking you nowhere. It sometimes feels like your efforts are futile, but the purpose of the exercise is not so much to get *things* better as it is to make *you* better; and as you get better, things begin to turn around in your favour.

Take a simple example of the Chinese Bamboo tree. You plant the seed of the Bamboo tree and water it consistently for some time. After about six months you check its progress and find that there is no sign of a tree. You keep on watering and nurturing it. After about a year you check and still see no sign of a tree. This goes on for two years, three years, four years; and still no sign. You continue to water and nurture that seemingly empty soil and, after five years you see a little shoot breaking out from the ground. About three months afterwards the tree has grown above hundred feet tall and become the tallest tree in the forest. During the process you may be discouraged and think your efforts are in vain. If you don't understand the nature of the Bamboo tree you might give up during the first six month.

The truth about the Chinese Bamboo tree is that during the five year period when you do not see any progress, something is happening below the soil where your eyes cannot see. The seed germinates and develops into roots. The roots of the Bamboo tree take about five years growing deep so that they may be strong enough to anchor the height of the tree. When the roots are fully developed and ready, the tree starts to break the ground and begins to grow tallest in the shortest period of time compared to other trees.

The Bamboo tree requires much patience and strong faith. You need to nurture it tirelessly and keep on believing that your efforts will pay off. The same principle applies in marriage. It takes time to develop a trusting and loving marital relationship. Both partners need to nurture their relationship by playing their part as God instructs in the Bible, no matter how long it takes. They need to believe that even if there is no sign, something great is taking place beyond the horizons that will take their relationship to greater experiences of ecstasy, love and harmony.

As a wife you may submit yourself to your husband for a long time and see no results in your marriage. As a matter of fact it may seem to be getting worse each time you submit yourself to your husband. You may find that the more you submit to him, the more he decides against you. Keep on playing your role and nurturing your relationship in the best possible ways. Be patient and have faith; trust and never give up, there are significant developments taking place beyond the surface. Fundamental elements of marital relationship such as love, trust, honesty, respect, loyalty and faithfulness are gradually developing beyond the curtains. Even as a husband you may find that the more you play your role and love your wife, the more she takes you for granted and breaks your heart. Keep on loving her. Never give up on her. God is working something out behind the scenes. It's only a matter of time, and all your tireless efforts will be rewarded. People will wonder how you managed to get it right so fast after such a long time of struggle.

The main problem among married couples is that we give up too easily and too soon. We don't give our marriages enough time to develop. We tend to let go each time we don't get our way. We may start well by nurturing our marriages for some time, but when it seems like we are not getting the expected results we stop trying and start adopting bitter and revengeful attitudes. We sow the seed, but we do not stay long enough to see it break the ground. In marriage there are times when you need to stop walking by sight and start relying on your faith (see 2 Corinthians 5:7). You never know how close you are to your breakthrough until you quit. Too many couples divorced on the verge of their marital breakthrough; do not be one of them. Stay in the course for a while. Delay is not denial. As a matter of fact, durable structures take a long time to build. Do good and never give up; it's only a matter of time, and God will give you double for your trouble.

Marriage was meant to strengthen your character just as fire refines gold. The fire experience is never a pleasant one, but its product is always precious and valuable. Genuine gold responds well to fire; the more the heat, the better the gold. Same applies in marriage. Marriage is to our character as fire is to gold. The more challenging the marriage, the stronger the character will be. Painful experiences in marriage were meant to build you as a person. The more you endure painful marital experiences and continue to do right and maintain a positive attitude, the stronger your character will be, and very soon your marriage will follow suit. The sad thing is that people abandon their marriages when they experience pain; but that pain is necessary for your growth. As the motto of bodybuilders suggests, "*No pain, no gain*". You gain nothing by running away from your marriage each time you experience pain; but if you stay long enough, you will learn valuable lessons that will make you a better person; and as you grow, so will your marriage.

Many people resist this order of marriage because they think God promotes gender inequality and oppression of women by men. This is as far from the truth as the east is from the west. Men and women are equally valuable before God; they are just positioned differently according to God's perfect order. The reason why parents give instructions to their children and set boundaries for them is solely for their protection. Children on the other hand perceive their parents' instructions and boundaries as a way of penalizing them unfairly; but the truth of the matter is that parents see what children cannot see from where they stand, and they are only trying to protect them from the unpleasant consequences that may occur.

Same applies with God. When He instructs us, we may think that He is treating us unfairly. We may even label Him as the God of injustice. But the truth of the matter is that God sees what we cannot see, and He is protecting us from the unpleasant consequences that may occur. We may not understand the instructions God is giving us regarding marriage, but we need to trust Him as the Author and Perfector of life that He sees what we cannot see, and He is protecting us from possible consequences such as infidelity, domestic violence and divorce. His desire is for us to enjoy marriage in the best possible ways.

Every device you buy comes with an instruction manual. If you adhere to the instructions written in that manual, you can be sure to enjoy the best performance of your device. In the same way, God created marriage and gave us the Bible as an instruction manual. If we adhere to that manual, we can rest assured that we shall enjoy the extremely pleasant marital relationships until the end of time. One thing is for sure: God's instruction is never for your destruction; it is always for your construction.

3

Marriage Implications

Marriage is a lifelong commitment, and it involves two people who live together under all circumstances. It is a transition that requires some degree of adjustment in order to accommodate the new person in your space. It is almost if not impossible to get married and succeed while you continue living the way you used to live before you got married. Many a times as I do marital counselling I come across cases with severe tensions because of people who feel their partners want to 'change' them. As I dig deeper into the problem, I very often discover that in most cases it is not necessarily their partners who want to change them; it is actually the nature of the new marital environment influencing the need for adjustment.

Not only marriage requires behavioural adjustment; in fact, every significant transition requires adjustment. For example, when you get a job after some time you have not been working, you need to adjust your lifestyle to accommodate the new job. You wake up earlier than you used to; you stop doing some of the things you used to do during the day so that you can be at work. You decrease the frequency of having some good times with your friends, and you begin to sleep earlier than you used to before you started working. Usually the adjustments you need to make are determined by the nature of work you are doing. For example, if you work night shift, you start a new habit of sleeping during the day so that you can be awake when you are at work during the night. It is not your boss or employer trying to change you; it is the nature of your work. It would therefore be unfair to personalise that change and attribute it to your employer when in actual fact it is the new working arrangement that propels the need for change.

Very often the changes in the marital environment are attributed to our partners trying to change us. The wife accuses her husband for trying to change her, and the husband accuses his wife for trying to change him. The question then comes: who is trying to change who? To which the answer is: no one is trying to change anyone; but the truth of the matter is that you cannot be married and expect your life not to change. If you want to embark on a bodybuilding programme, there are some habits you must kill and some you must adopt. You must kill the habit of sitting all day long in front of the television with junk food in your hands and start the new habit of going to the gym regularly and eating healthy food. If you fail to make these adjustments, you might as well forget about that good looking body you are dreaming of.

Same applies in marriage. If you want to enjoy a happy marriage, do not let things remain as they are. Be ready for change, and be prepared to make adjustments. As a husband, you cannot continue to spend most of your time with your buddies in the sports fields like you used to when you were still single and expect to enjoy a romantic relationship with your wife, who remains at home taking care of your house while you are away. You need to minimise the time you spend with your pals and maximise the time you spend with your wife. In the same way, as a wife you cannot spend most of your time in front of the television watching every soap opera that appears on the screen and expect to have a deeper connection with your husband. You need to invest more time in your relationship with your husband. Many people continue to insist on living their own lives as if they were still single; yet they have entered into a relationship that requires drastic change of habits. You can't be married and act single and expect your marriage to succeed.

You hear people defending themselves against their spouses and telling them: "I was already doing this when you met me, and now you are trying to change me!" The truth of the matter is that some habits can be healthy when you are single and poisonous when you are married. What succeeded when you were single may fail when you are married. Getting married is more like changing citizenship into another country. The laws in the new country may be different from where you come from. What was legal in your previous country may be illegal in your current. The laws of the previous country no longer apply in the new country. Failure to adjust to these changes may cost you your valuable freedom or your dear life. Some of the habits or behaviours of single people do not apply in marriage. Failure to make necessary adjustments may cost you your marriage.

On the other hand it is so true that some people do want to change their partners after the wedding. This also can cause too much strain on the marriage. While it is true that your partner needs to make adjustments in the marital union, it is also vital that you do not try to change them just because they are different from you. You don't have to be alike to get along, you only need to find power in your diversity and harness it towards strengthening your marital relationship. The main reason why you fell in love was not your similarities; it was your differences. You saw something in them that complements you. If you try to change them to be more like you, you may lose the magnet that keeps you attracted to each other. Opposites attract each other, and similarities often repel each other. To be successful in marriage you must learn to celebrate each other without trying to change each other.

Marriage has *social implications* upon the people involved. It affects how you relate with people around you – differently from the way you did when you were still single. Some of your friends cannot cross over with you to your marriage. That they have been good for you when you were single does not guarantee that they will be good for you when you are married. It is therefore essential that you pause and evaluate your relationships to check if they are still as valuable for your marital relationship as they were for you when you were single. Marriages suffer a great deal of harm when people drag into their marriage people they were supposed to have left behind. How would you know if a person is not good for your marital relationship? When that person continually puts pressure on you to continue living the way you used to live before you got married, even if that means you have to disregard your marital relationship. If your marriage suffers harm because of their influence, they are not fit to remain in your circle of friends.

He who walks with wise men will be wise, but the companion of fools will be destroyed (Proverbs 13:20). You ultimately become like people you associate with. If you associate with people who disregard their marriages or their spouses, it might rub off on you in the long run, and you might find yourself disregarding your own. To achieve a successful marital relationship, you must associate with people who respect their marriages; who make efforts to strengthen their marital relationships. If you want to be wise, spend your time with wise people. One of your criteria in the selection of friends should be to observe their attitude towards their own marriages. Every friend who advises you to disrespect your husband for whatever reason is not fit to be your friend.

Neither is a friend who influences you to abuse your wife or be unfaithful to her. Do not believe anyone who claims they love you and yet they encourage you to hurt your partner.

Very often in marriage you may find yourself in a one-must-die situation, where you have to either save your marriage by letting some of your friends go or save your friendships and let your marriage fall away. I tell you the truth; no friendship is worth the loss of your marriage. I met men who would do anything to impress their peers. They go as far as hurting their partners to prove their worth to people who pretend to care about them when in actual fact they don't. People lose their marriages in pursuit of worthless friendships. Any friendship that causes harm to your marriage is not worth keeping. *Do not be misled: "Bad company corrupts good character"* (1 Corinthians 15: 33 – NIV). In the same way, bad associations corrupt good marriages. For your marriage to be successful, let go of people who cause harm to your marriage and hold on to those who contribute positively to it.

If you happen to belong in the church where your spiritual leader puts pressure on you to neglect your partner or disregard your marriage so that you can "serve the Lord", that relationship is not good for your marriage. Serving the Lord does not have to exclude your partner. Which God are you serving when in your house you left a lonely and hurting soul wondering if you would ever pay attention to your family? Before you lead the church, get your own house in order. Do not be the kind of a person who would do anything for your fellow church members and nothing for your own family. If there be anyone trying to make you feel guilty for paying attention to your family, rather walk away than lose your marriage. It is not honourable to be celebrated at church and resented in your own home.

The reason why I make mention of this is because some marriages are enduring too much strain, and some are ending, because of people who are always at church and never at home. Some church leaders go so far as to praise their congregants for sacrificing their families for their local churches. This is not a good influence; it is harmful to marriage. A good spiritual leader will always regard your partner as much as he regards you or your ministry. He will take special interest in the success of your marriage and develop you maritally just as he develops you spiritually. He will respect your marriage as much as he respects your ministry. Maybe you take offense in the things I say, yet marriages continue to fail because of these very things. Day by day people are being made to feel guilty for paying attention to their partners and applauded for serving the church at the expense of their marriages. This often results in bitter marital relationships for them, and then they begin to blame the devil for what they have brought upon themselves.

The main cause of this problem is that there are people who think that to love God is to indulge in church activities. Much as it is good to be involved in church activities, it is more important that you be involved in your own family as well. It is true that you are not supposed to love your partner more than God, but you also need to understand that God and church are not synonyms. God is God, and church is church. Church is not God, and God is not church. Your love for God is more evident in your love for your partner than it is in your commitment to church activities. Yet marriages continue to suffer because of people who are committed more to the church of God than the God of the church. In the eyes of God, you and your spouse are one flesh. He expects you to serve Him together, or to at least be in agreement when one is to carry out a certain task without the other. From God's perspective, the wife is the female version of her husband; and the husband is the male version of his wife. The two of you are inseparable, and no one must come between you; not even your church or your spiritual leader.

Much as it is important to choose your friends carefully, always make sure that you are never without a friend. Marriage is not an island of two people in solitary confinement. It requires good associations in order to be successful. As a married couple, you need other people around you who will encourage you to grow in your relationship. You need good advices to help you sustain your marriage. *Where there is no counsel, the people fall; but in the multitude of counsellors there is safety* (Proverbs 11:14). *Without counsel, plans [fail], but in the multitude of counsellors they are established* (Proverbs 15:22). Without good advices you will fall, and your marriage might fail, but with many good advisors your marriage will dwell in safety and be established. Be careful who you allow to advise you in your marriage because not every advice is good for marriage. Test every advice against the Word of God to see if it is Biblical. Also test it to see if it can work for your marriage because what is helpful in one marriage may be harmful in the other.

Asking for advice from a trusted person does not mean you are weak; it only means you are strong enough to know your limits. It also means you are smart enough to know the person who is strong enough to help you where you are weak. Consulting other people becomes a weakness if you do it to expose your partner's weaknesses to them. The aim of consulting other people for advices should be to build your marriage; not to break your partner. After all, if you break your partner, you break your marriage. Asking for advices is different from opening a case. It's not about who is right and who is wrong; it's about learning from trusted people how to improve yourself for the sake of your marriage. When seeking advices, make sure that you seek it for yourself; not for your partner or on your partner's behalf. You are not responsible for your partner's behaviour; you are responsible for your own.

While it is important to seek advices for your marriage, it is also important to be careful to not adopt every habit or practice into your marriage. People have different likes and interests. Some people may impose their own likes and interests on your marriage, and the things they like may be the things you or your partner dislikes. Always evaluate your actions carefully before you conclude whether or not they work in your marriage. Two people react differently to the same stimulus. The very thing that turns your friend's wife on may turn your wife off. That is why you should not be hasty to adopt every suggestion from other people, but test it to see if it can work in your marriage. Some suggestions may come from people who are known to be the experts of marriage and relationships, but even so, the positive results are still not guaranteed. You still need to test them before you trust them.

It is also possible for one person to give you an advice that is good for marriage one moment and give you one that is bad for your marriage the next moment. What makes an advice good or bad is its application in a particular situation. Therefore, even if you get a good advice, ask yourself if it is good for your marriage in particular. Different habits and behaviours are applicable to different marriages, but the principles remain the same. An advice should therefore be based more on principles than on habits, likes, interests or behavioural patterns.

Habits and behavioural patterns *may* work, but principles *will* work. If I advise you to kiss your wife on the neck because it definitely turns women on, this may raise your expectations. You may apply the advice and kiss your wife on the neck, and if she does not give the expected response, you may get frustrated. How to turn your husband or wife on is not engraved on stone. It depends particularly on him or her. Stereotypes and generalisations do not necessarily apply in marriage. There's plenty of room for creativity and exploration. What I am trying to share with you in this material is not mere habits and behaviour patterns; it is the *principles* that will help you achieve marital success.

Marriage also has *legal* and *economic implications*, and these two are often interlinked. People have different preferences in their approach towards marriage. Most people prefer to marry in community of property, where they have joint estate and have equal shares of everything any of them acquires; and some prefer to marry out of community of property, accrual expressly excluded. Due to high prevalence of divorce, more and more people begin to show interest in marrying out of community of property for fear that they might lose their belongings should their marriage end in divorce. Yet people continue to marry in community of property as an expression of their trust, loyalty and total commitment to their partners. No one marries with an intention to divorce, but the fear of divorce continues to permeate people's minds and cripple their comfort in their marriages.

To some people, being married out of community of property threatens their sense of security in marriage because they consciously or subconsciously think "if he cannot share his possessions with me, will he really spend the rest of his life with me?" This may affect them psychologically and cause them to hold back their marital commitment in case the marriage falls apart, especially if the decision of marrying out of community of property is not theirs. It may cause them to spend their marital life on their toes, afraid that any time it might come to an end and leave them with nothing but a wasted time and commitment. It might make them sceptical about their marriage, perpetually questioning the motives of their partner about the relationship.

If you are rich and marry in community of property, the implication is that your riches are no longer yours alone; they now belong to the two of you equally. This often leads to rich people avoiding to marry in community of property. They opt for antenuptial contract instead, whereby they and their partners sign the contract before marriage that they will have separate estate. This is marriage out of community of property. They do not share any of their properties with each other. Therefore, if the marriage falls apart, they get to retain their riches instead of sharing them with their partners. This option is often preferred by people who have inherited the riches that are regarded as the legacy of the family. They do so to try and protect that legacy lest it gets to be shared if the marriage fails. This arrangement gives married couples a legal right to spend their money as they wish; but if not managed carefully, it can cause strain upon a marriage.

Marriage is a unifying institution, and it recognises married couples not as separate beings but as one flesh. This kind of relationship requires much cooperation if it is to survive. It is therefore wise for people married under antenuptial contract to be considerate to each other in the way they spend their money. It can be very unsettling for a person to stay with her husband in the house that she knows does not belong to her. If the husband is working and the wife is taking care of the house, it may put her at an unfair disadvantage because the husband will be accumulating more properties and the wife will only be looking after them.

It would therefore be unfair to expect a woman who is married under antenuptial contract to be the housewife and take care of the children while the husband continues to acquire more properties. Both of them should be at liberty to embark on economic activities of their own interests. The critical question is: what will happen in the event that each partner wants their own house? In whose house are they going to stay? And whose house should be left unoccupied? Such questions should be considered carefully before entering into marriage.

There is something about acquiring things together that enhances a strong sense of connectedness and teamwork between married couples. But it can be a major turn off to acquire things together when you know that those things do not belong to you. If this relationship is not managed appropriately, it can lead to unhealthy competitions and unnecessary power struggles. Ultimately divorce will be so much easier because both of you know that you have nothing to lose by ending your marriage. The sad part is that no amount of riches can protect you from the scars that will remain upon you even long after you divorced. No money can buy your heart out of misery due to the pain of separation or stop the pain you may be experiencing deep within after filing for divorce. Marriage was meant to last for a lifetime; but if it breaks, there is too much emotional bleeding which no money can stop. The excruciation of having to spend the rest of your life without the one you used to share your life with becomes too much to bear.

On the other hand, marrying out of community of property may give an indication that the motive of marrying is purely about love and commitment between the two, rather than possible obsession for someone else's possessions. It may show that the commitment is based on love for one another and not on each other's assets. People who are married in community of property may get carried away and start behaving more like business partners instead of lovers. They may even fall into the trap of putting little or no effort into the growth of their marital relationship, hoping that the fact that they share everything will make it hard for their partner to divorce them for fear of losing half of their possessions.

Whether you marry in community of property or under antenuptial contract (out of community of property, accrual expressly excluded), it is highly imperative that you nurture your love for each other more than your obsession for each other's possessions. Acquisition of property should not be the reason to tie the knot. People should get married because they love each other and are willing to share their lives regardless of who owns what. Marriage is not a business partnership; it is a love relationship.

One other legal system people can opt for is marriage out of community of property with accrual system. Under this arrangement, people retain everything they acquired before marriage as their own, but everything they acquire in their marriage belongs equally to both of them. For example, if you get married under this arrangement with properties to the value of R500 000 and acquire more properties to the value of R500 000 in your marriage, should the marriage fall apart you will retain the properties to the value of R500 000 as your own and share another R500 000, which you have accrued during marriage, equally with your partner.

Even though this is also marriage out of community of property, it still allows the couple to acquire things together. This is more reassuring than antenuptial contract because whatever you achieve or help your partner to achieve, you know it belongs to both of you. This can reduce unhealthy competition and promote some degree of unity in a marriage. It also allows people to protect their family legacy without making the other person feel totally excluded.

People who are married in community of property or out of community of property with accrual system should always be careful not to make major purchases or enter into major financial contracts without the expressed consent of their partners. It is very important that you come to an agreement with your partner in terms of major financial decisions you may want to make. *Can two walk together, unless they are agreed?* (Amos 3:3). The answer to this question is no. People cannot walk together if they do not agree; they will pull to different directions and go separate ways. Even in marriage, if you cannot negotiate until you reach an agreement, you can be sure to go separate ways should you insist on getting your way, and that is not healthy for marriage.

The same principle also applies to people who are married under antenuptial contract. That they have a legal right to buy whatever they want whenever they want it cannot make them pull towards the same direction with their partners. Whatever the type of contract they may be married under, they cannot walk together if they do not agree.

Religious implications also apply to marriage. Whether or not you marry the person of the same religion as you is not carved in stone. But the Bible does advise Christians to *not be equally be unequally yoked together with unbelievers* (2 Corinthians 6:14-15). The Apostle Paul in the above-quoted Scripture continues to ask: *For what fellowship has righteousness with lawlessness? And what communion has light with darkness? And what accord has Christ with Belial? Or what part has a believer with an unbeliever?* Even though religion is not the only criterion in the choice of a life partner, it is very important that you carefully consider the religious affiliation of the person you are intending to marry. The impact of religion upon the psychological, spiritual, social and emotional well-being of individuals should not be underestimated. Religion is where most people derive their sense of meaning and purpose.

Violation of religious principles can result into people perceiving themselves as worthless and not fit to live. It causes an overwhelming feeling of guilt, shame and defeat. It is therefore very important that you choose to marry a person who will not temper with your religiosity. The best way of achieving this is by marrying the person who shares the same religion with you. If you are a Christian and you marry a non-Christian, you may very often find yourself having to compromise your Christian values trying to maintain peace in your marriage, and this is usually accompanied by overwhelming feelings of guilt. Avoid therefore marrying a person who might ultimately make you choose between him and your God. If there is a clash of religions in marriage, the couple may be forced to either disregard their religious principles and live peacefully together, or insist on maintaining their religious principles and put their marriages in harm's way. It is therefore advisable that you marry the person with whom you share the same faith.

What if you are already married to the person who does not share the same religion with you? Should you divorce them? Not at all! All you need to do is find ways to live harmoniously without having to compromise your religious beliefs. "*...If any brother has a wife who does not believe, and she is willing to live with him, let him not divorce her. And a woman who has a husband who does not believe, if he is willing to live with her, let her not divorce him. For the unbelieving husband is sanctified by the wife, and the unbelieving wife is sanctified by the husband; otherwise your children would be unclean, but now they are holy. But if the unbeliever departs, let him depart; a brother or a sister is not under bondage in such cases. But God has called us to peace. For how do you know, O wife, whether you will save your husband? Or how do you know, O husband, whether you will save your wife?*" (1 Corinthians 7:12-16). It is not necessary for you to divorce your spouse if he or she does not share the same religion with you; neither can you be defiled by him or her. But if they decide to leave you because of your faith, you may let them go.

The number one principle here is: *Never impose your religious beliefs on the other person!* Practice your own religion without dragging your partner into it. Make peace with the fact that you will differ every now and then with your partner in as far as religion is concerned. While you are at it, make sure you find common beliefs among yourselves. Also make efforts to search for those things in which you agree and capitalise on them rather than focusing on your differing religious beliefs. If you feel that it is against your religious requirements to support your partner's religious activities, at least don't try to block them. If you do, you might block their perceived sense of purpose and cause them to be depressed in your marriage, and if one person is depressed in a marriage, the other person will be affected.

Another important principle to help you manage this situation is that you try by all means to *avoid judging your partner based on their religion*. This can cause rivalry in a marital relationship and put pressure on both of you to put more effort on defending your religions rather than building your marriage. The marriage then continues to suffer harm as the couple fights over whose religion is better than whose. As a married couple, nothing in this world must come between you; but you must also make sure that you don't try to stand between your partner and the God they worship.

If it happens that you do not approve of your partner's religion, always remember that religion is a matter of influence, not coercion. You cannot force your partner into your religion; you can only influence them by the way you conduct yourself. Religious practices are not healthy if they offend the other person in a marital relationship. It is therefore essential that you practice your religious activities without causing unnecessary offense to your partner. The golden rule here is to *treat the other person the way you want them to treat you* (See Luke 6:31).

Marriage is like working a garden. It requires perpetual cultivation and nurturing. If a garden is not consistently taken care of, it might grow weeds and ultimately die out. Marriage requires the same kind of attention. It must always be cultivated, nurtured and protected from any internal or external forces that may choke the life out of it. Change of habits and lifestyle is very often required in a marital relationship. Much as this is the case, it is equally important that you do not lose yourself trying fit in to the personal demands of somebody else's life. You need to learn the art of adjusting your behaviour without losing yourself in the process. Remember, you are not adjusting your behaviour to be more like your partner; you are adjusting to meet the demands of your marital relationship, different as you are from your partner. Marital adjustment is not healthy if it feels like you are losing and your partner is gaining. Whatever adjustment is made, it must benefit both of you, and the primary aim should be to build a stronger and more fulfilling marital relationship for both of you.

4

Preparation for Marriage

Preparation is very essential in the approach to marriage. Generally, what is received with no prior preparation is difficult to sustain. No wonder God gave mothers nine months of pregnancy before the child is born. The primary purpose could be to give parents enough time to prepare for the life that is about to be brought into the world. At the same time God could be using that time to prepare the baby for the outside world. Can you imagine how life would be if you would have to sleep tonight and wake up with a child tomorrow without prior knowledge that you would have a child? It would definitely be a great inconvenience and an overwhelming burden instead of the blessing it was meant to be, for the simple reason that you never got enough time to prepare for the child's arrival. Every significant change requires thorough preparation. Without necessary preparations almost every plan will fail.

Marriages fail for many reasons, and one of the main reasons is lack of preparation. If you don't take the time to prepare yourself for marriage, too many things will catch you by surprise, and you wouldn't know how to handle them. A successful boxer does not just wake up and go into the ring to compete for championship; he spends much time preparing for the fight. He exercises very hard in order to get fit for the fight ahead. He adjusts his diet so that he can be lighter and more flexible. He also spends much time studying the strengths and weaknesses of his opponent. He watches very closely to observe his opponent's most dangerous attacks so that he can come up with strategies to defend himself against them, and he also studies the most fragile areas in his opponent's body so that he can capitalise on them. He wins half of his battle in the preparation phase, and he only enters the ring to claim his victory.

In the preparation phase, the boxer works very hard to put himself in a position where he can handle every challenge and embrace every opportunity that may present itself in the fight. He also makes room for surprises and prepares for new strategies that his opponent might have come up with. Therefore, even surprises don't catch him by surprise because he has already prepared for them. The time he spends in effective preparation determines his level of confidence when he enters the ring. Preparation minimizes unnecessary fears and insecurities. It makes the boxer enter the ring with the anticipation of victory rather than the anxiety of defeat. It makes him rise to the level of whatever challenge he may be facing. Proper preparation often prevents possible perplexities. It provides power to prosper in every plan or endeavour.

Marriage should also be approached with the same attitude. Before you tie the knot, you need to learn as much as you can about marriage. Read relevant books, ask marriage-related questions and attend marriage seminars and workshops so that you may get as much information as possible on the subject. Familiarize yourself with necessary requirements for marriage; as well as the best possible moments in marriage and the worst possible ones. Check yourself against the possible extremes of marriage; the joys and the pains, the benefits and responsibilities. Learn about possible disappointments and prepare yourself beforehand to deal with them. Think about your strengths and weaknesses and how they may impact on your marriage. Start beforehand to deal with the weaknesses you think will impact negatively on your marriage. Begin to work on yourself until you become the person that the woman or man of your dreams is also dreaming of.

One other helpful thing you can do before you say "I do" is attend pre-marital counselling sessions. The purpose of these sessions is to prepare you for marriage by exposing you to the realities of a marital life. When you are warned beforehand about the possible challenges you may face, you will be least likely to get frustrated or discouraged by the time you encounter them and most likely to remain calm and handle them more effectively. Information is ammunition. More informed people often make better choices. Pre-marital counselling not only provides you with information, it also gives you an opportunity to reflect on yourself and see if you are ready for a lifelong commitment. It also gives you a platform to ask questions where you need clarity. Pre-marital counselling can also help you clear unrealistic expectations about your prospective marriage;

thus it prevents unnecessary frustrations that may occur in marriage. When you know better, you do better, and you get better results.

The most reliable source from which you can get information on marriage is the Bible. The Bible contains the Word of God from Genesis to Revelation. The Bible on its own is not the Word of God; the Word of God is the content therein. In other words, the Bible cannot help you if you do not give yourself time to read what is written in it. Just as the medicine cannot help you unless you get it into your system by swallowing it, neither can the Bible help you unless you get its contents into your system by studying it. People's opinions may vary from time to time, but the Word of God remains true all the time. *"Heaven and earth will pass away, but My words will by no means pass away* (Matthew 24:35). Everything else may fail, but the Word of God will never fail.

In the Bible you will get the information that will not only open your eyes but also change your life forever. You may make one decision when you are happy and make a completely different one when you are sad, but the Bible says the same thing whether you are happy or sad. It is more reliable than our feelings, judgments and opinions. It is therefore important to apply the Word of God as the basis of your marriage. This Word has the supernatural power to establish and sustain marriage under all circumstances. Remember, marriage was created by God, and He has given us the Bible to help us manage His creation. Without following the precepts of the Bible you will mismanage your marriage, and mismanagement most often leads to forfeiture.

Preparation precedes prosperity. It increases the possibility of success and decreases the possibility of failure. Preparation not only makes the things you want ready for you; it also makes you ready for the things you want. It does not fix your potential spouse; it fixes you. It not only betters your chances to find your dream partner; it also betters your dream partner's chances to find you. In other words, preparation not only helps you to get the partner you want; it also makes the partner you want to also want you. Preparation helps you become the success you desire to see in your marriage. It strengthens your retention muscles so that your marriage may last for a lifetime. Prepare yourself, and your marriage will be successful.

4.1 Why People Get Married

Why people get married can make or break a relationship. It is therefore significant to clarify your intentions before you finalise your decisions; especially in as far as marriage is concerned. People get married for various reasons. It could be for social status, or economic stability, or convenience, or legal reasons, or love, or emotional reasons, or sexual gratification, or physical attraction, or for spiritual or religious reasons, or for reproduction.

Marriage for Social Status

Everybody wants to be accepted, respected and celebrated in the society. We go to great extremes to gain a good standing among the people who share the environment with us. We often buy the things we don't need, with the money we don't have, to impress the people we don't know, simply because we want to be accepted and celebrated. Generally, people like to act like they don't care how others feel about them. They even say it with their mouths, but the truth of the matter is: they do care. To them it matters a lot how people feel about them. If you take a deeper look at why they are verbalising their carefree attitude instead of keeping it to themselves, you will find that they want to make an impression so that people may regard them as people who have a strong self-worth or self-esteem. The truth of the matter is that they know that there are kinds of people who respect people with that attitude. So, they do care how people feel about them.

Those who marry for social status are often concerned about what people will say or think concerning their decision. Their choice of marriage partners and the timing of their marriage are often determined by popular expectations. They marry to satisfy their parents, their friends, their colleagues, their church members, or their leaders. It is not completely wrong to marry the person you are expected to marry because it can guide your decision. Some people have better judgment than you; some see things better than you because they are observing you from a better view. Therefore, it can be helpful to let your decision be guided by popular expectation. But it is not always helpful; it can also be very harmful because it is possible that you can fulfil popular expectations and neglect your authentic self, the real you. Always bear in mind that no matter who influences your choice of a life partner, that partner is going to spend the rest of their life with you; not with them. It is therefore essential that you marry for you and not for other people. Welcome the advices, but make your own decision.

It does not help to have the whole world praise you for your choice of a life partner while you are hurting inside and nobody knows it but you. The success of your marriage depends not on what people think about it, but on the happiness of the two of you. It is better to make a decision that will disappoint people and make you happy than to make one that impresses people and depresses you. I know some people who would stroll in the park holding hands as public display, yet deep down they know that they are both unhappy in their marriage. Behind their smiling faces are deep regrets of marrying to impress people while they themselves are depressed. They married people's choice and later found that there's nothing in that choice for them. They sacrificed their own happiness to make other people happy. In this status-conscious world you find people giving the love they do not have, to marry the people they don't want, just to impress the people who don't care.

Before you decide to get married, it is very important to ask yourself: "Who am I trying to impress by this decision and why? Who is going to benefit from this decision? Is this decision good for me? What or who influences my decision? Why do I want to get married? Why do I choose to marry this person?" The answer to these questions should address your needs more than it addresses the expectations or needs of other people. Marrying to satisfy other people will most often earn you a good reputation and a bad marriage. People often attach stereotypes to other people. There are also myths that influence people's judgment. These very often make their judgments inaccurate. Therefore, it is not enough to rely only on people for important decisions such as marriage; you must also trust your own judgment. Do not marry for *them*; marry for *you*.

Marriage for Economic Stability

Everybody wants to be economically stable. It is essential for our survival. Without economic stability, life can be extremely stressful. People do different things in pursuit of financial security; some of which are good, some bad; some honourable, some disgraceful; some acceptable, some unacceptable; some legal, and some illegal. Some people open businesses, others seek employment. Some rob and steal, others prostitute themselves. Very often you find people lowering their standards and forsaking their values and principles so that they can get money into their hands. People always want money, and if they get it, they want more; no one is ever satisfied. Money is often associated with power and influence, and every human being wants both of these. Some people go to the extent that they marry to gain economic stability.

It is not wrong to consider the economic status of your potential life partner. After all, you don't want to be married and economically frustrated. This could have a negative effect on your marital relationship. Marriage can be financially demanding; food, bills, rent, basic services, furniture, transport, etc. The demand increases even more when children are born. Therefore, the last thing you want in marriage is to be broke.

In the not too distant past in some parts of Africa, men used to marry women who were not working so that they may focus on child rearing and homemaking while they were away. Women were socialized not to look for work but marry men who will be able to take care of them financially. But in the modern society things have changed. Husbands' income alone is often insufficient to sustain the family. Men thus prefer to marry women who are earning income so that they can share the cost of running the family. To completely ignore the economic potential of your prospective partner could be considered unwise by many people; but it would be more reckless to marry only for economic stability and ignore everything else that marriage requires.

While the economic status of the person you are intending to marry cannot be overlooked, it is also vital to not allow your choice of a life partner to be determined entirely by their economic status. You should consider other aspects as well. I know of couples who are rich in finances and poor in love; and you don't want to be one of them. There are things that money cannot buy, and love is one of them. Marriage is not a business partnership; it is the love relationship. The purpose to marry should therefore be not so much to find economic stability as it is to find a mutually fulfilling love relationship. Financial stability is something that can be achieved by the two of you in marriage; but the mutually fulfilling love relationship we are talking about cannot be achieved with money.

Marriage for Convenience

Life can be much easier for two people than it can be for one person. If you are alone, you are bound to do everything on your own, and this can be a burdensome experience. But if two people are involved, the load can be lightened by half because you can share responsibilities. Another advantage of two people is the diversity of interests and abilities. What one person is unable to do, the other one may do it with ease; and what one hates to do, the other one may do it with passion. Therefore, you don't have to feel like you are on your own because someone else is there to help you where you are struggling. Even when you go through difficulties, you still take comfort in knowing that you are not alone. If you do things alone, you are using one brain and two hands, but if you do things together, you get to enjoy the advantage of two brains and four hands.

Two are better than one, because they have a good reward for their labour. For if they fall, one will lift up his companion. But woe to him who is alone when he falls, for he has no one to help him up. Again, if two lie together, they will keep warm; but how can one be warm alone? Though one may be overpowered by another, two can withstand him. And a threefold cord is not easily broken (Ecclesiastes 4:9-12). Two people can achieve twice as much as one person can. Therefore, doing things together can be more convenient than doing them alone. This suggests that marriage promotes some degree of convenience for two people living together. A couple can keep each other warm during cold nights. They keep each other company. They help each other, love each other, take care of each other and protect each other.

Though convenience is part of a marital relationship, it should not be the only deciding factor if one considers marriage. Very often you may hear people uttering statements like: "My mother is sick and there's no one to take care of her when I'm not around; maybe I should get married"; or "Being a single parent is not easy; maybe I should get married so that I can have something to help me with my kids"; or "This house is too dirty, and I don't have time to clean it; I need to get married so that I can have someone to help me clean my house" (You can think of many other examples). If these are the things you are after, you might miss the very essence of marriage – the two of you living together under a loving and mutually fulfilling relationship. If you want someone to take care of your sick mother, find a caregiver. If you want someone to help you raise your kids, why not try your relatives or a nanny? To keep your house clean you can employ a domestic worker. If you want a lifetime companion to share your love with under all circumstances, then you may consider marriage.

Marriage for Legal Reasons

Marriage also has legal benefits for the people involved. A husband automatically gets the custody of his children, and he gets to register them in his surname (some cases may differ depending on the legal agreements between the two involved). If married in community of property, one gets the legal right to have equal share of the partner's belongings. Marriage can also help the immigrant gain citizenship in his foreign country. These are just a few I can mention; but there are more legal benefits in marriage. People can be tempted and decide to get married in order to be eligible to these benefits; but these benefits are not enough to sustain a marriage. You need more than citizenship to be successful in marriage. Citizenship can only help you enjoy the privileges within the country and not within the marriage. You cannot be a happy citizen if you are not happy in your marriage. There are alternative processes you can follow in order to gain permanent citizenship, and marriage should not be one of them.

Owning half of your partner's possessions does not automatically make you successful in marriage. As a matter of fact, there are people who have great possessions and yet are miserable in their marriages, and there are people who have almost nothing, but they are happy in their marriages. Therefore, there's more to marriage than owning half of your partner's properties, or gaining permanent citizenship, or registering your children under your surname. All these can be achieved without having to make a lifetime commitment to a person you are not even sure if you want to spend the rest of your life with. All these things come and go, but marriage is for a lifetime. Therefore, if you marry for the purpose of acquiring these things; you might acquire them, but even after acquiring them, you will still be married. Now the question would be: Now that you finally got what you wanted, do you still find it necessary to continue your life with this person? If all you want is a legal benefit, it would be unwise for you to get married because all those benefits cannot sustain a marriage.

Marriage for Love

Love is the most important factor you should consider if you are to decide to get married. It is in fact the most common reason why people get married. But still, love alone cannot ensure the success of a marriage. In the recent African history, marriages used to be arranged by parents. Parents would decide who their children would marry; and whether their children loved their arranged partner or not was not important. Even so, marriages were still established, and families were still managed successfully. From this we can learn that even though love is such an important aspect of relationship, it is still not the only requirement for marriage. Love is the most powerful force in the universe, yet marriage is bigger than human love. Love is essential for the success of a marriage; but the 'absence' thereof does not necessarily mean the end of marriage. The absence or deficiency of love should therefore not be used as a reason to end marriage.

People fall in love, get married and 'fall out of love' soon after the wedding. Does 'falling out of love' then mean the marriage should end? Certainly not! Like I explained earlier, marriage is bigger than human love. This means marriage will continue to exist even when the people involved fall out of love. In fact, love is not a feeling or an experience; it is a decision. But love is incomplete if the decision is not acted upon. Love does not grow on its own; it requires to be nurtured. The couple should make conscious efforts to make it grow. If love is not nurtured, people lose interest in each other, and they often refer to that loss of interest as "falling out of love". The reason why we 'fall out of love' is that we are not making enough effort to stay in love. Love does not mean things are always going well; it means that the two can remain committed to each other even when things go wrong.

It is possible for people who are not in love to get married and grow in love thereafter. Therefore, to wait until you find someone you are already 'in love' with can cost you a chance to be in a marital relationship with a person who could be a great partner to you. True love is unconditional, and waiting until you 'fall in love' is itself a condition. To sustain an existent marriage, unconditional love is required; but to start a new marriage, terms and conditions should apply. After all, you don't want to marry a person you are aware that has the potential to mess up your life and call that unconditional love. You need to have conditions that will help you make a sound decision.

Applying terms and conditions will help you gain insight into the actual reason why you intend to get married.

Love should not be viewed as the sole reason for marriage; it should rather be regarded as one of the primary requirements when deciding to get married. Love attaches no reason to the feeling. It has no conditions. It speaks not from the head, but from the heart. Thus, it is possible to fall in love with the person who may not be committed to you as a life partner; or to fall in love with the person who may abuse you for the rest of your life. You can love everybody, but you cannot marry everybody. So, if love were your only reason for marriage, your choice of a life partner would be extremely inaccurate. Although love is not the only reason for marriage, it remains the essential element that can help married couples hold their marriage together till the end.

Marriage for Emotional Reasons

Emotions are an integral part of human life. No human being is without them, and we experience them all the time. The other word for emotions is feelings. Feelings can be positive or negative; but whatever the case may be, they influence our behaviour to a large degree. In fact, most of our actions are influenced by our feelings. When we feel happy, we laugh; when we feel sad, we cry. When we feel excited, we may jump or dance joyously; and when we feel angry, we may scream or fight. Feelings can also be dependent on our behaviour. As human beings we often do the things that make us feel good and avoid ones that might make us feel sad. The argument of *feelings* versus *behaviour* is similar to the debate of chicken and egg. An egg comes from a chicken, and a chicken comes from an egg. Similarly, behaviour produces feelings, and feelings trigger behaviour. Whichever comes first is not really important; what is important is to know that one influences the other.

We make certain decisions because we want to feel a certain way, and very often we feel a certain way because we made certain decisions. This enables us to predict how we are likely to feel should we make certain decisions or undergo certain experiences. This puts us in a position to choose how we want to feel by deciding what we do. It also helps us avoid the behaviour that might make us experience negative emotions and practise the behaviour that will make us feel better. One can avoid disappointment by refraining from love relationships; the other may decide to engage in love relationships to avoid loneliness or boredom. One can do the acts of kindness because they want to feel appreciated. The bottom line is: People behave in certain ways in order to feel or avoid feeling a certain way.

Emotions can very strongly influence one's decision to get married. One can decide to get married because of their perceived potential to be happy; the other may make the same decision because they want to avoid feeling lonely. People may also decide to get married so that they can satisfy their inherent need to love and be loved. Marriage involves a lot of emotions; some positive, and some negative. But we all hope for positive ones. Therefore, people decide to marry because they want to feel good. Once they perceive marriage as a painful experience, they may be less likely to marry. Some people decide to marry because they already feel good in their love relationships, and they want to feel that way for the rest of their lives.

Truly speaking, you cannot rely on feelings when deciding to get married. Feelings change from time to time. One moment you are excited; a few minutes later you are sad; after some time you are frustrated; and soon after that you are happy again. Can you imagine deciding on such a stable thing as marriage being guided by such a fluctuating thing as feelings? That is a good recipe for marital disaster. Feelings cannot be trusted when it comes to marriage. It is not marriage that will make you feel good; it is the decisions you make and the things you do that will, whether you are married or not. Do not, therefore, rely on marriage to make you feel good. There are many other things you can do to make yourself feel good. To human beings, marriage should be seen as more important than the need to feel good.

Marriage for Sexual Gratification

Human beings are also sexual beings. They find intense pleasure in sex. Yet sex is considered a taboo in many cultures. People tend to freeze each time the word sex is mentioned. In fact, in many African cultures, the mention of sexual act or sexual organs in some African languages is considered an insult. The general attitude towards sex portrays it as an abomination. Yet children continue to born everyday in and out of wedlock, and this could only mean one thing: *People are having sex.* That is the fact that cannot be denied. But sex was not designed to be a causal act; it was meant to be enjoyed within the parameters of marital commitment.

Although sex is such a pleasurable experience, its harmful consequences are well-known throughout the world. Deaths that are caused by sexually transmitted infections are being reported on daily basis all over the world. People use condoms to protect themselves against such infections, but those condoms fail to protect their hearts. Pleasurable experiences of sexual activities are often followed by feelings of guilt, insecurity, disappointment, etc. Not long after the pleasure comes the break-up, and people begin to experience severe heartbreaks; especially when they remember that they once gave their bodies to people who pretended to love them so that they could easily navigate towards their genitals. These are heartbreaks no condom can protect anyone from.

To avoid disappointment, some people decide not engage in sexual activities before they get married. They view marriage as a pledge for lifelong commitment, and thus they find sex therein safer than sex within casual relationships. Some people abstain from premarital sex because of their religious belief that fornication is an abomination. So they keep themselves chaste until they get married. However, their decision to remain chaste until marriage does not by any means do away with their sexual desires. They keep on battling with sexual cravings and temptations. This can influence an individual's decision to get married so that they can satisfy their sexual urge within the safe environment of marital commitment. In this way they know they will not battle with feelings of guilt and insecurity after they gratify their sexual urge.

But marriage is not all about sex. The decision to get married only for sexual gratification is like using all the water in the reservoirs just to quench the flame of a candle. What about all other things that depend on that water – plants, animals, humans, etc? If it is lust that you want to address, then it is not marriage that you should be considering. Marriage does not address the problem of lust; because lust is never satisfied by one partner. Even if it is not lust but just a normal sexual desire, it is still not sufficient to become the basis for your decision to marry. What if a few months after your wedding you or your partner become sexually dysfunctional? Will the marriage end just because you no longer get what you came in for? Unfortunately that is not how marriage works. If it worked that way, we would marry different people at the same time; each person fulfilling the very thing we married them for.

We would marry one for sex, the other for citizenship, and another one for economic stability, etc. But marriage is a lifetime commitment not to multiple partners, but to one partner.

Marriage is bigger than sex; it cannot end when sex dies out. In fact, marriage is not only part of life; it is also similar to life. Whether you have everything or nothing, it goes on. There are lots of things you expect out of life, and many of them you have not yet achieved, and some you may never achieve; yet life still goes on. Same applies in marriage; whether there is sex, legal benefit, love, feelings, convenience or not, it still goes on. Before you decide to quench your sexual thirst by getting married, remember that sex takes only a few minutes; but marriage is for a lifetime. It would be extremely unwise to make a permanent decision based on the pursuit for five-minute pleasure. I'm not suggesting that you engage in premarital sex. I'm only advising you to rather wait until you know for sure that you really want to get married.

Marriage for Physical Attraction

Truth be told, some people are very attractive. You take one glance at them, and their image echoes in your heart for quite some time. When they look at you, their eyes seem to pierce through your eyes and proceed right into your heart. You look at their body structure and marvel "God is the Great Artist!" Their face makes lasting impression in the heart of the one who beholds. Overcome by the tremendous beauty you have observed, you find yourself constantly thinking about them. Their lips are shaped like Cupid's bow, and their voice like her arrow that shoots through their lips and pierces through your ears right into your fragile heart. Their beauty comes out so strong that you forget to assess their heart. After all, who cares about the heart you do not even see, while the treasure of beauty is laid so bare on the surface? You then convince yourself that the outward appearance will very well compensate for the heart in case the heart is not as pretty as the face.

Then you decide that you want to enjoy the view of this super-gorgeous physical structure for the rest of your life. Out of physical attraction you decide to get married. But physical attraction and successful marriage are two different stories. A beautiful face does not guarantee a loving heart, and attractive physical structure does not certify cooking abilities. You don't use beautiful eyes to pay the bills. The Bible puts it very well: *Charm is deceitful and beauty is passing, but the woman who fears the Lord, she shall be praised* (Proverbs 31:30). When it comes to marriage, you need to look through the container and see the content. It is not the physical appearance that builds a strong marriage; it is the character. The beauty that sustains a marriage is one that comes from the heart.

Always bear in mind that you do not marry to decorate your house; you marry to establish a permanent love relationship. Charm is deceitful. Do not go by what your eyes can see. True beauty requires a person with an x-ray vision; who can look through the face and see the heart. It is not wrong to marry a physically attractive person because there are many attractive people who have beautiful hearts as well. But you must be careful to not let your eyes decide for you. Beauty is passing. You may never know how true this is until your wife bears children and starts to gain weight. Will the marriage still be what you want when all you see are stretch marks and cellulite? What about the wrinkles that may appear in her beautiful face and hide all her beauty spots? See? Beauty is passing, but the fear of the Lord remains, and so does marriage. Marriage does not fade away with beauty. So, when you decide to marry, look through the physique and observe character.

Marriage for Spiritual or Religious Reasons

The significance of human spirituality cannot be emphasised enough. People value their spirituality more than almost everything else. For many people, spirituality is the main influence of the decisions they make. They decide to please not themselves but the One they worship. They submit their own will under the will of their Creator. The expectations of their religious community also play a big role in their decision-making processes. People who are highly spiritual are often perceived as "flawless", not necessarily because of their character, but because of their performance at church. They gain respect in their places of worship because of how well they preach, pray or worship.

Therefore, being close to that kind of a person can be perceived as an opportunity for spiritual growth or 'transference of the anointing'. Everybody wants to share their life with such a person. Even parents dream for their children to be married to such people. These people are often associated with every good thing and estranged from anything bad. Anyone who gets the opportunity to get married to such a person considers themselves the luckiest to find such a treasure. It is only when they are married that they discover that this 'angel' is human after all. Now that you are married, you can now realize that this saint can lie, cheat, hurl insults and be abusive. Worse yet, he gets fired at work because he was caught in the act having sex with the colleague he was supposed to be praying for, and this happened during office hours. You decided to marry the person who displayed angelic character at church not knowing that at home he was a 'demon'.

Now that you have learnt that he is not the angel he appeared to be, what then happens to your marriage? It goes on. But it becomes a miserable experience rather than the joyful union it was meant to be. It is therefore wise to develop a holistic approach towards marriage. You need to clarify to yourself why you are considering to get married. The question is not what you are looking for in a marriage; what you should be looking for is the marriage itself, and only then will you assess what it comes with before you decide. Impressions of spirituality do not guarantee marital sustainability.

Marriage for Reproduction

Reproduction is an essential part of existence for all creation; human beings included. Without it there would be no continuity. God created everything with an inherent ability to reproduce after its own kind. Therefore, the desire to reproduce is natural for everyone. Almost every human being wants to have children, and every child needs both his mother and father to grow well. The genes of the parent are always transferred to the child, and they very often influence the characteristics of that child. Thus parents become careful who becomes the mother or father of their children. One other thing they are careful about is whether the mother or father of their children will still be around to take care of those children. Child bearing thus requires commitment on the part of both parents not only to their children; but to each other as well.

No environment is safer or more convenient for reproduction among humans than marriage. Child bearing within a marital relationship is not only every parent's desire; it is also every child's dream. For this reason it is possible for people to marry for reproduction; it creates a safe and conducive environment for the children to be brought up. But much as reproduction often takes place safely within marriage, it should not be the only basis for marriage. I know many people who have no children but are happily married. I also know ones who have children, but their marriages are miserable. Therefore, having children does not guarantee a happy marriage; and the absence of children is not a sentence into marital disaster. You can be unhappy in your marriage with children, and you can be happily married without them. There's more to marriage than having children, and if it is children you want, don't marry just yet. Wait until you are ready for marriage; when you are ready, you may marry, and then children may come as a *privilege*.

Marriage fails or succeeds on the reason why it was established. If you get married because you want someone who can bail you out from your sufferings, what then happens to that marriage after you get what you wanted? Do you still find it necessary? What if you don't get what you wanted? Would you still stay? These are the questions you should be asking yourself before you decide to take the big step of making a lifetime commitment. If you marry because you want children, what then happens to your marriage when you have the children you wanted? What if it happens that the person you married is barren or impotent? Would you stay in your marriage, or would you walk away? Will the marriage stop for lack of children? Certainly not! It will surely continue because marriage is not about children. Marriage is far greater than reproduction; it cannot be nullified by anyone's inability to conceive or reproduce.

From what I know, people stay in the restaurant for as long as they await the food. When the food comes, they eat. When they're done, they go away. There's nothing that keeps them in the restaurant anymore because they already got what they wanted. If they happen to not find what they are looking for, they immediately walk away to find the restaurant that has what they want. Why should you stay in the restaurant that cannot give you what you are looking for? But marriage is not a restaurant because you don't enter into a covenant with the restaurant before you eat. Therefore, you cannot walk away from your marriage just like that because you have a lifetime covenant with your partner.

Marriage should not be seen as the *container*; it should rather be seen as the *content* itself. In simpler terms, you should not see marriage as the vessel that contains the things you want; but rather perceive it as the actual thing you want. Once you get the content you wanted, it becomes easy to regard the container as useless. In the same way, if you perceive marriage as the container for the things you want, it might be easy for you to regard it as useless once you get what you wanted out of it. But if you regard marriage as the actual *content* rather than the *container*, you will not forsake it whether you get the benefits or not. If marriage is what you want, everything else is just a *fringe benefit*.

If you want one loaf of bread, you don't have to drive to town and buy the whole supermarket. You can rather walk to the nearest store and buy a loaf of bread. This may sound ridiculous, but if you get married only to gain social status or any of the above, you are no different from the person who buys the whole supermarket so that he can get one loaf of bread. The responsibility of managing the supermarket when all you wanted was bread could be too overwhelming for you. Therefore, if you decide to get married, make sure that it is marriage you want; not only one or two of the things mentioned above, because to manage the marriage could be overwhelming for you if all you wanted was citizenship in a country or sexual gratification. Marriage is a permanent union, and the decision to get married should never be based on the pursuit of temporary gratifications.

Everything you expect in a marriage, you should rather be the one who brings it into the marriage than expect it to be brought to you by someone else. If you expect happiness, bring it along into the marriage. If you want money, bring it! Whatever you expect in marriage can only be there if you bring it in. If your partner happens to bring it as well, that would also be a fringe benefit. Refrain from using marriage as a tool to get all these things; rather use these things to strengthen your marriage.

If it happens that you are already in a marriage that was established over temporary things, and you feel like your marriage won't survive, do not give up just yet. There's so much hope for you. God does not create what He cannot preserve. If it can break, He can repair it. If it can suffer vicious ills, He can heal it; and if it can suffer destruction, He can restore it. Your marriage is never too dead for the resurrection power of the Most High God to restore it. Do not despair! Just stay with me until the end. While you are at it, reach out and get some help. Go for professional counselling so that you can be assisted to find new meaning for your marriage so that you can enjoy the brand new start towards a successful marriage.

4.2 Choosing a Life Partner

Who you chose to marry is just as important as why you decide to marry. Actually, your choice of a life partner can also make or break your marriage. It is therefore significant to be wise, sober and diligent in your choice of a life partner. It is not as simple as choosing the car you want to buy because if the car happens to not perform as you expected, you can change it and find another one. But you can't change your life partner just like that (take note that marital commitment is characterised mainly by our commitment to *one* person for a lifetime. Therefore, you can't change partners as you please in marriage). However, how you decide on a car you want to buy can hint you a little bit on how you can go about deciding on a person you want to marry.

A good car buyer does not go to the car dealer to look for the car that will catch his interest. Rather, he ensures that he already knows the car that he wants before he goes to the dealer, and when he sees it, it becomes easy for him to realize that it is just the car he wants. Not only does he know the car he wants; he has also learnt as much as possible about it – all its features, speed, comfort, fuel consumption, service history (if the car is not new), and every other important information he needs to know. He makes thorough research about the vehicle of his choice before he goes looking for it. This helps him know what to look for and where to look for it.

Same applies in the corporate world when a company decides to employ a person to fill a vacant post. Before they even start advertising the post, they already know who they want, for what position, the qualifications he should possess, his job experience and where to find him. This will help them develop specifications that will guide their decision in terms of who to employ out of all the candidates who may apply. Only the most likely candidates will be called for an interview, and only the candidate who meets most of their requirements will be employed. Many other similar examples could be made, but these two should suffice to give an indication of where I am heading with this conversation.

We can learn a thing or two from this approach. It can be helpful to start by determining beforehand your requirements or specifications about the person you might consider marrying. Be holistic but specific about the characteristics you expect from them – physical, intellectual, emotional, psychological, socio-economic, spiritual and social. Once you determine what you want, it can guide your decision and save you from the danger of deciding impulsively. It can also guide you in terms of where to look for your potential partner. For example, if you want to marry a Christian, you will know that you are most likely to find them at church. But your requirements should be as realistic and complementary to you as possible. You can't expect to marry a Christian if you yourself would not go to church. It would be like trying to catch a fish outside water.

If you know what you want, you will not only know how or where to find it; you will also be able to recognise it when you find it. It is possible to find what you want and still be looking around for it because you don't know that what you are looking for is right in front of you. Consider the Samaritan woman at the well (See John 4 in the Bible). She was patiently waiting for the Messiah to come; but the Messiah she was waiting for was right in front of her, and He was even having a long conversation with her, and yet she did not recognise Him. It would therefore make sense for me to mention that there are people who once found their life partners, but then looked away to continue the search because they failed to recognise them. This often happens when you do not determine beforehand what you want.

The other cataract that blinds us from recognising what we are looking for is the expectations we developed overtime because of our past experiences. We often reject the prospects of a bright future because we associate them with painful experiences of the past. The main thing that blinded the Samaritan woman from recognising the Messiah was that she associated Him with all other men from her past who brought nothing but pain and disappointment into her life. The pain of the past propelled her to reject what she was supposed to embrace. Sometimes we reject our 'soul mates' because of our association of them with our past disappointments. Before you even consider making your choice of a life partner, you need to always keep in mind and determine in your heart that not everyone is coming into your life to hurt you.

You should not penalize your potential life partner for the mistakes of the people in your past. The men in the Samaritan woman's past came to take her life away from her, but Jesus came to give back to her the life they took from her. But this woman started to treat the One who came to restore her life the same way as she treated the ones who took it away because she could not distinguish pleasure from pain. We cannot blame her, though; because all the men from her past brought her pain and disguised it as pleasure. If someone brings something bad to you and disguises it as something good, and this keeps on happening again and again, it may condition you to associate every good thing with pain because of the heartbreaking experiences of your past. This may cause you to reject every good thing you see for fear of being hurt again.

In the modern society, where people get into romantic relationships in their early teen years, the possibilities of hurt and disappointments are ever-increasing because most of those relationships do not last. This is most often the case because they enter into relationship in anticipation for pleasure and ecstasy; but they do not apply their minds to calculating the cost and anticipating possible consequences. At this point in time many teenagers become the casualties of 'love' over and over again until they begin to associate love with pain.

When the right time comes for them to be in romantic relationships, they have already become too sceptical because they have learnt to perceive the prospects of love as the risk of another heartbreak. Even if they do enter into romantic relationships, they enter with their guards up high to protect themselves from pain. The focus for them would be more on self-protection than on relationship building. This state of being has caused many people forfeiture of their 'soul mates' because they wanted to embrace their bright future with arms that were still holding on to their excruciating past.

Before you deal with the pain of your past and let go of the grudges it has caused you; you will not be able to embrace the happiness that lies ahead of you. Before you consider any love relationship, make sure that you become aware of every heartbreak you have sustained from your past. Once you become aware of it, acknowledge it and start working yourself out of it. However, it is not enough to work yourself out of it; you should also work it out of you. Do not be like the Israelites who moved out of Egypt but kept Egypt in their minds wherever they went (See the Book of Exodus in the Bible). Much as they were excited to finally be free, they kept on referring to Egypt whenever they went through challenging experiences. It is therefore important to not only get yourself out of the past, but also to get the past out of you. Do not allow your past to always determine your future.

The choice of a life partner should not be based only on feelings and attractions. You need to apply your mind as well. The heart wants whatever the heart wants, just like a child; but the mind, just like a parent, is always there to guide the decisions of the heart. Inasmuch as it is good to follow your heart, it is much better to let your *heart* follow your *head*. Remember, the heart cannot reason; it can only want what feels good to it. But the mind can go further and interrogate other aspects of the thing that the heart has fallen in love with. Simply put, the heart *recommends*, but the head *approves*.

The reason why there are so many casualties in love relationships is because many people decide on relationships based on the *feeling* and disregard the *reason*. Feeling is from the heart, and the heart cannot reason; only the head can. Deciding to marry a person merely because of attraction is like deciding to amputate your arm because of the cut on your finger. The heart can fall in love with a man not knowing that he is abusive; but the mind detects that abusive behaviour in a man and warns the one who possesses it about the danger. People who follow their hearts more than their heads in their choice of a life partner often find themselves in the relationships they always regret having entered into. The head will warn you that he is a cheat, but the heart will insist that you love him anyway. The heart wants pleasure, but the mind can see the danger behind the pleasure. What you need to do in this situation is give your head the power and authority to guide the decisions of your heart.

If it is infatuation you want, you may follow your heart, but if you want permanent commitment, follow your head. I am not suggesting that you ignore your heart completely; all I'm saying is that you use your head to guide your heart in your decisions. As I have illustrated earlier, the heart is like a child; it wants whatever feels good to it without calculating the cost or thinking about the possible consequences. The child may want to play with a knife because he finds it fascinating, but the parent knows that the knife can injure or kill him. Therefore, the parent will withhold the knife from the child. But the child will not just be okay with it and walk away to find something else to play with; he will scream on top of his voice and throw all the tantrums he can gather in his aggressive attempt to get the knife back. Will the parent then give the knife back to the child because he is throwing tantrums? Certainly not! At this stage the safety of the child is more important than his desire.

The role of the parent to the child should be played by the head to the heart. The heart may be attracted to someone else's husband and suggest to you that you should go and get him. The heart knows nothing about the consequences, but the head knows. The heart may do all the talking, but you should let your head decide; and you should not be afraid to let your head decide against your heart. When the head decides against the heart, the heart will not take it lying down. It will begin to throw tantrums and cost you sleepless nights and stressful days. It may scream to you: "I WANT HIM!!!" but your head should scream louder and say: "I WILL NOT LET YOU HAVE HIM!!!" Let your reason be firmer than your cravings. The safety of your heart is more important than the gratification of its ignorant desires.

Not everything that feels good to you is good for you. In fact, most of the things that are good for us do not feel that good. To the child, candies taste better than cereals, but cereals are better for his health than candies. Yet the child loves candies more than cereals, and that doesn't mean the parent should withhold the cereals and generously give candies. Rather, the parent should withhold candies and give cereals, even if she has to force-feed him. Sometimes the head should force-feed the heart with decisions that are healthier than they feel.

You should not always let your heart have its way; but you should let your head put your heart under control. The person who jumps at every attraction or craving that the heart suggests is like an accident waiting for an incident. A child left without supervision may set the house on fire and burn with it. So is the heart; without the supervision of the head, it can throw your whole life into the furnace of affliction, pain and misery. Therefore, do not let your heart decide on anything that your head disapproves.

The choice of a life partner should be based on reason, not infatuation. Before you decide on the one you choose as your potential partner, think about how they fit into your destiny. Your selection should go beyond how you feel and focus on how the future might be for the two of you. Feelings vary from time to time, but the decision made out of good judgment will remain. Most important to remember is that whoever you choose as a life partner will remain with you for the rest of your life, even when your feelings about them have changed or subsided. It is therefore wise to choose a person who will still be relevant to you many years from your first day of marriage. If you marry for physical attraction or how you feel about the person, those two may change, but true love attaches no merits to the beloved. Love is not a feeling or attraction, it is a decision. It is not only a decision; it is also the ability and willingness to adhere to that decision under all circumstances.

Marry the person you love, not the one you lust after. *Lust* never lasts, but *love* does. Marriage is a matter of commitment, not attraction. Attraction works like ignition to the vehicle. Ignition starts the engine, but it does not keep it running. Attraction ignites the relationship, but commitment keeps it running. Simply put, it takes attraction to fall in love, but it takes commitment to stay in love. The communication of attraction should therefore be regarded as an expression of feelings, not a declaration of intend. It should let the person you are attracted to know that you have feelings for them; but what you intend to do with those feelings is another story altogether. Much as it is true that attraction influences intention, it is also vital that you carefully study the person you are attracted to in the light of your set requirements before you decide on your intentions about them. *Attraction* is a suggestion from the heart, but *intend* must be assessed and approved by the head. It is therefore significant to draw a clear line between *attraction* and *intention.*

There are people who prefer to take a leap of faith and risk it all to be with the ones they love and leave to everything to fate. Some get lucky as fate decides in their favour, and that could be a very romantic love story. Even so, I would suggest that you should not take a leap of faith into the fire hoping that it would turn into water. Don't try to leap into a lifelong relationship with a cheat and hope that she will turn into this one-man-woman you are imagining. The reality is that she may change, and she may not. Even in this situation you should let your head decide where your heart leaps into. Better safe than sorry; on the other hand, the over-emphasis of safety can prevent us from taking the risks that could lead us straight to our destiny. However, the risks we take should not disregard our judgment. Good judgment will always help a person take only the risks worth taking, the ones that could most probably succeed.

Most important to do, even before you set your requirements, is to involve God in your plan and let Him know your intentions. Let Him guide your decisions and give you wisdom and discernment. *In all your ways know, recognize and acknowledge Him, and He will direct and make straight and plain your paths* (Proverbs 3:6 – AMP). Acknowledge God in your plans, and He will guide your decisions. *Roll your works upon the Lord [commit and trust them wholly to Him; He will cause your thoughts to be agreeable to His will, and] so shall your plans be established and succeed* (Proverbs 16:3 – AMP). There's no going wrong when you go with God. Align your thoughts completely to His will. Make His Word the pattern for your decisions, and He will guide you to make the right choice and help you find the love of your life.

4.3 Courtship

In the corporate world, no successful company employs the person they do not know. They want to know as much as possible about you before they decide about your future in their company. They require that you send them your personal profile so that they may get an idea of who you are and whether or not you meet their requirements. If they get *attracted* to you, they then call you in for an interview to know more about you – how you interact, respond to job-related questions and demonstrate your knowledge on the job you have applied for. They are also interested in how you present yourself because it gives them an indication of how you might present their company's image to the outside world in future. When they are fully satisfied with the potential you have demonstrated to them and all or most of their requirements are met, it is only then that they will call you with an employment offer.

The same principle applies in marriage. It is too much of a risk to marry the person you hardly know. It is always wise to learn as much as you possibly can about your potential partner before you decide on your future with them. You may not use the same approach as the companies because a day of discourse is not sufficient to know the person enough to decide whether to marry them or not. A relationship should be established that allows both of you to interact frequently over a period of time so that you may know more about each other. That period in a relationship is referred to as *courtship*. This period precedes the couple's engagement and marriage; and it often determines whether or not the couple will ultimately get married. If the two of you are convinced that you know each other enough to take the relationship further, it is only then that you may decide to enter into a lifelong commitment called marriage.

In the recent history, courtship was forbidden in some religions; especially those religions that did not permit sexual relations between people who were not yet married. People who intended to get married were thus expected to keep their distance and spend their time apart to avoid the temptation of premarital sex. Couples who violated these rules had to suffer rejection and stigma from their religious groups. The general belief was that you should trust God to show you the potential partner who is suitable for you and also trust that whoever God chose for you is good for you. Therefore, if you trusted God enough for your potential partner, there wouldn't be a need to try to learn more about each other. Thus courtship was strictly prohibited. People married each other without any prior love relationship or any effort to know each other. As a result many of those couples stayed in their marriages only because they knew that divorce was also forbidden in the same religion. Ultimately they had to spend the rest of their lives enduring their marriages rather than enjoying them.

At least those religions managed to lower the rate of premarital sex and the birth of children out of wedlock (with few exceptions of course). But they have practically underrated the significance of knowing more about each other before making a lifelong commitment. Now the pendulum has swung to the opposite direction. People have started to embrace the idea of courtship and reject the significance of virginity and chastity before marriage. They now confuse courtship for marriage. But these two are not the same. Courtship is the preparatory period towards marriage, but marriage is a lifelong commitment. The couple in the courtship period should therefore be careful to not prematurely enjoy the privileges of marriage. No company ever pays a salary to a candidate who comes to the interview because they understand that they are not employed yet. Neither should you start behaving like a married couple during the courtship period because you are not married yet.

People date and court all the time, but few get married. Why? People refrain from getting married for various reasons. Some people do not marry because they fear possible divorce or heartbreak; some do not want to find themselves in a binding commitment for a lifetime. Some do not marry because of their observation of people who are not happy in their marriages, and they avoid the possibility of going through similar experiences. Some associate marriage with loss of freedom, others associate it with a lifetime of pain and abuse. Some are afraid of losing touch with their families of origin; others fear that they might lose their belongings to someone else. Some simply avoid marriage because of their past experiences.

If you find yourself afraid or reluctant to get married even when you are in a stable relationship and are mature enough to take that step, you need to look into yourself and ask yourself why you are reluctant to marry. If you have fears, find ways to address them. You may discuss them with your partner if you feel comfortable. Sharing your fears with your partner may give them a platform to help you deal with them, to give you an assurance of their good intentions and commitment to you. Proper communication is highly essential at this stage of relationship. As a matter of fact, this is a good time to start learning how to communicate with your partner. You may also discuss such fears with a professional.

While you are dealing with your fears or insecurities, always bear in mind that marriage was designed by God for your enjoyment. Your observation of other people's failures does not necessarily mean that you will fail as well. On the contrary, it may help you to learn from their mistakes and use those lessons to make your marriage a success. The problem starts when you make the same mistakes they made. If you do what they did, you may end up where they are. It is also important to look around for the couple that inspires you by their love and commitment to each other. While you're at it, always keep it in mind that successful couples are not people who agree in everything; they are people who have learnt the healthy ways of handling their disagreements.

Some people do not get married, even if they are in long term relationships, simply because they find it unnecessary. Imagine this with me: If you have a company and I promise to work for you. Immediately after the promise, even before the signing of employment contract or the assumption of duty, you start giving me all the benefits you give to your employees. You pay my salary; you give me car allowance, housing allowance, medical aid subsidy, pension fund and unemployment insurance fund, even though I have not started working for you. This goes on for six months, a year, two years, five years, ten years, etc. Yet and still we have not signed an employment contract, and I have not started reporting for duty. Then, observing that I am not keeping my promise, you increase my benefits hoping that they will motivate me to start working. Still I don't. You ask me when I will start working, and I answer: soon. You then increase my benefits even more, and still I don't report for duty.

Do you think very soon I will decide to wake up and report for duty under this arrangement? The answer to this would be: Maybe, maybe not. The main reason why I wanted to work is to get the benefits; but if I get those benefits consistently before I sign an employment contract, I may find signing the contract or reporting for duty unnecessary. Unless you stop the benefits until I sign the contract, I may never report for duty. Why would I go to work while I get full benefits of employees in the comfort of my home? You may regard this example as a very stupid one, yet people use the same approach when it comes to marriage and relationships. A woman is in a love relationship with a man. The man promises her that he will marry her. All of a sudden the woman begins to behave like his wife. She sleeps with him, does his laundry, cleans his house, pays his accounts, cooks for him, moves in with him as if they were already married, gives him access to her accounts, her house, her cars, her body and her heart.

This goes on and on, but the man says nothing about marriage. She asks him when, he answers: soon. She increases the benefits hoping that it will speed up his decision to marry her. The more she increases, the less he talks about marriage. She irons some more, cleans some more, gives more sex, more money, more trust, and the more she gives, the more he delays. The significant question here is: Why would he marry her when he can get all the benefits of marriage from outside? To him marriage would seem unnecessary; unless all the benefits are stopped until he fulfils his promise of marrying her. But at this stage this woman is vulnerable to manipulation because if she stops the benefits, the man might threaten to leave, but the woman has already lost too much to let him go. If you give too much too soon, you may find yourself occupied but single for a long time. The best thing to do is withhold the benefits right from the beginning until the promise is fulfilled. You may talk about them to him, but this is not the time to let him enjoy them.

A job interview is not a guarantee for employment; neither is courtship a guarantee for marriage. The courtship period allows for the couple to change their minds about each other and end the relationship, but marriage requires that you continue with the relationship even if you change your minds about each other. Courtship is temporary, but marriage is permanent. It is therefore significant to understand that you should not be afraid to end a relationship in the courtship period if you perceive the possibility of malfunction in the prospective marriage. A broken engagement is better than a broken marriage. It would therefore be wise to be extra careful if you are in courtship with a person who treats you like you are already married to them.

You should also be careful of the person who acts like they own you; whereby you cannot go anywhere they prohibit nor do anything they disapprove. There is a difference between *passion* and *possession*; or should I say, there is a difference between a *partner* and a *property*. That they possess you does not mean they love you. Marriage is not about dictatorship; it is about mutual consent and joint decision-making. In marriage, no one is superior to another, and no one is inferior to another; both of them are equally important.

Anyone who treats you as if you were inferior in the courtship period would most probably treat you the same way (or worse) even in marriage. If he attacks you physically during the courtship period, then be assured that he would most probably continue to assault you in marriage. If he cheats on you during courtship, it might be impossible for him to be faithful to you in marriage. Yes, people change, but some don't; not because they can't, but because they won't. Avoid building your marriage on false hopes that someone may change from being a lion to being a lamb. If you have doubts about it, do not carry on with it. If you have a slight suspicion, take it as a warning. You can't afford to lose your mind in exchange for marriage.

Courtship is a good period in a relationship where the couple gets to build memories, and those memories had better be good because you may have to refer back to them when you come to a stage in your marriage where you start doubting your compatibility to each other. If you build great memories during the courtship period, you are making a great investment into your future marital relationship. When you are married and start feeling like you cannot have a great future together, you can always remember how great things used to be between the two of you. This will help you commit yourselves to restoring the harmony you used to share before you got married. Courtship is the best episode in a love relationship where you can take note of all the things you love about your partner; and when you do, make sure that you write down everything you love about them in a journal and put it safely where you can find it for later reference.

To tell you the honest truth, in marriage things are not always as blissful as we may anticipate. There are times in marriage when things seem to get completely out of hand. These are the times when couples are most likely to forget the traits that attracted them to each other to the point of deciding to share the rest of their lives together. This may be the time when you need to reach out for your journal and remind yourself about those things that you loved so much about your partner. You may also set aside some time to take each other down memory lane and remind each other why you got married in the first place. Reflect on everything that used to make both of you happy, and start considering the necessity of making deliberate efforts to recover what you seem to have lost along the journey of your marriage.

The truth of the matter is that nothing about your partner has changed since then; the only thing that has changed is that in marriage you got to discover some other aspects of your partner's personality that you did not know about during the courtship period. But your discovery of their weaknesses in marriage does not delete or nullify the strengths you once perceived in them during courtship. What actually happened is that both of you concentrated too much on each other's weaknesses that you forgot each other's strengths. But the truth remains: everybody has strengths and weaknesses. What needs to happen is for married couples to celebrate each other's strengths and complement each other's weaknesses. Whatever you focus on gets magnified. So, make a commitment from today to focus more on your partner's positives and less on their negatives. Do not let their weaknesses cloud your perception of their strengths.

4.4 Marital Expectations

Everybody enters marriage with expectations. Some enter with good expectations; others enter with bad ones. But what matters the most is that expectations should be realistic. Expectation is very important because it helps us make necessary preparations for whatever we hope to experience. You can't prepare for what you do not expect because what you do not expect will always catch you by surprise. What catches you by surprise may shock you, and people who are in the state of shock are less likely to make sound decisions. If you make wrong decisions, you make wrong moves, and if you make wrong moves, you get wrong outcomes. We can therefore conclude that expectation can determine experience. You are most likely to experience what you expect, especially if your expectation is realistic.

The reality of the expectation is strongly dependent on the ability of the object to produce the expected results. For example, if you marry an unemployed man, it would be unrealistic to expect him to take care of the financial needs of the family. The poor man has no income and therefore cannot afford to carry the family's financial burden. That this man cannot meet the financial demands of the family does not mean he is good for nothing. There are many other things he can be resourceful at. He can take care of the family while you are at work; do the chores in the house during the day; advise you on crucial decisions, support you and protect you. To expect him to do what he cannot do will discourage him and frustrate you; and this can have a detrimental effect on your marriage.

There are many factors that subconsciously influence people to develop unrealistic expectations about their spouses. One of those factors is gender stereotypes. Stereotypes can give an indication of what is generally expected from a certain category of individuals in terms of their roles, personalities and thought or behavioural patterns; but they are inaccurate because they do not consider the possibility of exceptions among individuals. They fail to acknowledge the unique qualities of humanity. Generally in societies, men are expected to provide for the family, and women are expected to do household chores and take care of the children. But the truth is that there are men who can do household chores better than women and women who can provide for the family more than men.

Stereotypes may suggest that all men are quiet, but the truth is that there are men who a very talkative, even more than women. Can you imagine what this can do to the woman who married a talkative man out of the expectation she derived from gender stereotypes in her society? This woman could be frustrated because she would expect her husband to keep quiet and listen to her speak; but contrary to her expectation the husband happens to be the one who does all the talking. This can also be discouraging to the husband because he might end up thinking that he is not man enough to shut his mouth.

Not all men are liars and cheaters, and not all women are nagging and quarrelsome. To conclude that all men are the same or all women are the same is inaccurate, and it very often creates unrealistic expectations about them. You cannot judge a person based on what the other person is likely to do. Not all men are the same, and not all women are the same. There are women who are talkative, and there are ones that are quiet. There are men who cheat, and there are men who are faithful. You should be careful not to reprimand your faithful husband because of the men who cheat on their wives. Each case has its own merits because people are not exactly the same. What excites one person may frustrate the other one. Therefore, expectations should be based more on specifics than generalizations.

The media is also contributing towards the formation of unrealistic expectations in marriage. Some people enter into marital covenant expecting that their marriages would be exactly what they see in the movies. Movies and soap operas often explore the trends they observe in relationships; trends such as love, passion, sex, betrayal, unfaithfulness, disappointments, backbiting, hatred, etc. Most often these trends are exaggerated and blatantly highlighted such that they catch the viewers' attention and keep them interested. When they show a love scene, they display unrealistic intensities of pleasure which could be misleading to married viewers. Those love scenes can generate the expectation in the viewers' minds to experience the same intensity of pleasure in their own marriages. When they fail to experience such, they get frustrated and start resenting their partners out of the opinion that they are not great lovers like the ones they saw in the movies. The other party may also feel discouraged for failing to please the lover who is trying to bring movies into their marriage.

Movies are most often imaginary and delusional, but marriage is real. In fact, some of the actors of those scenes, in their real lives, are struggling with their own marriages as well. Therefore, you can't bring fantasies into reality and expect reality to absorb them without a problem. The illusions of movies do not apply in the realities of marriage. To build your marital expectation around ideas from the movies would therefore be detrimental to your marriage. Those expectations are unrealistic, and they cannot navigate in the realities of marriage. Although some movies are educational, it is still unwise to base your expectations around them because they often display in those movies what they seldom practice in their real lives. Rather base your expectations within the parameters of your partner's ability to meet them.

The other factor is *wishful thinking*. Many people think about marriage as something that works only in their favour. Their idea of marriage is that all their problems will come to an end the minute they say "I do". They think they will have someone who will keep them warm whenever they feel cold; give them a sensual massage whenever they feel tired; watch them day and night when they are ill, etc. They think that by getting married they will find someone who will gladly give them whatever they want, whenever they want it, and however they want it. What they seem not to realize is that there is more to marriage than massages and being kept warm. There are also bills to pay, children to raise, weaknesses to tolerate, mistakes to forgive, etc. Very often people enter into marriages expecting to get the privileges, but they are not prepared to pay the price. They expect to get more than they are willing to give. Eventually they get frustrated because what they experience is not what they expected.

One other factor that influences unrealistic expectations in marriages is *fear*. You have been hurt many times before, and now you are afraid you might get hurt again. Your fear of being hurt again can influence your expectation negatively. You may find yourself not recognizing the best your partner is doing because you are expecting the worst. There are people who are so used to losing that they don't even realize when they have won. Out of the fear of being cheated they expect to be cheated, and they frequently sneak into their partners' phones to check if they are not being cheated on. Every "I miss you" or "I will call you" is quickly interpreted as "I love you" and reprimanded as an act of marital unfaithfulness. It is almost if not impossible to recognize the best that is happening to you when all you are expecting is the possibility of pain and misery.

FEAR is often regarded as an acronym for False Evidence Appearing Real. This is what false expectation can do to a person. It can make you see the pot plant in your house as a person coming to attack you. Fear causes you to gather false evidences to try and validate your false expectations as 'true'. The fear of divorce can make you feel, think and act like you are already divorced even if there is no sign or threat of divorce in your marriage. Fear can make you sit on the couch as if you are sitting on spikes. It can make you act like a victim of abuse even when you are in a safe and loving marital relationship in which not even a finger was ever lifted against you. You may even find yourself having joined victim support groups and having filed for protection order against the person who would never do anything to hurt you.

What you fear, you attract. If you fear divorce, you might find yourself doing the things that may attract the very divorce you are afraid of. One often meets his fears on the road he takes to escape from them. You might run straight into the thing you fear while trying to run away from it. Our expectations in marriage should therefore be based on the prospects of the bright future and not on the excruciating experiences of the past. To be successful in your marriage, you need to overcome your fears. But how do you overcome fear? You can overcome fear the same way you put out the fire. To put out the fire, you need to use the opposite of fire, and the opposite of fire is water. In the same way, if you want to overcome fear, you need to use the opposite of fear, and the opposite of *fear* is *faith.*

Faith is an antidote for fear. It does to fear what antivenom does to venom. For this reason faith can also be referred to as *anti-fear* or *fear-extinguisher.* Therefore, when fear strikes, always apply your faith to put it out. Faith and fear cannot co-exist; but the one you feed the most is the one that grows the most. If you entertain your fear more than you develop your faith, your fear will be bigger than your faith. The opposite is also true when you develop your faith more than you entertain your fear. Fear cannot abide where faith is applied. So, each time you experience fear for anything, quickly inject yourself with anti-fear, and that anti-fear is your faith. Always believe that things will be better than they are. Learn to look beyond where you are and see the prospects of success; because what you see is what you get in the end.

According to the Bible, *faith is the substance of things hoped for; the evidence of things not seen* (Hebrews 11:1). The New International Version says: *Now faith is being sure of what we hope for and certain of what we do not see.* What distinguishes *faith* from *fear* is the word *hope.* Hope is a positive word. You can't hope for the things you fear; you can only hope for the things you long for. Fear expects the worst no matter how best the situation is; but faith expects the best no matter how worse the situation may be. Fear attracts what you are afraid of, but faith attracts what you hope for. Fear is to believe that what you are afraid of has already happened to you even though it hasn't, but faith is to believe that you already have what you hope for before it happens. Faith is the expectation of the best, and fear is the expectation of the worst. But one thing is common between faith and fear: *They both attract what they expect.*

Fear believes *deception*, but faith believes the *truth.* Deception is what appears like the truth, but it's not the truth. It appeals to our senses as the truth, but it's a lie. It looks like the truth, smells like the truth, tastes like the truth, sounds like the truth and feels like the truth; but it is not the truth. A number of years back I had an incident with an automobile I was driving. I was driving on a gravel road, and I accidentally drove into thick gravel on that road. The car lost touch with the ground and floated on gravel, and it slipped out of the road into the open field. I was so afraid that the car was going to overturn and maybe kill me. But by God's grace it didn't; and I came out still intact. That was the truth: the car lost control and drove into the open field because it slipped on gravel.

A couple of weeks after the incident I started to experience panic attacks each time I drove a vehicle. It always felt like the car was slipping out of the road, even when I was driving on a tarred road. I almost developed the fear of driving even though my job depended on it. But that was no longer the truth; it was deception. I had to convince myself that the car does not slide on a tarred road under normal circumstances; unlike on the gravel road. I then overcame the fear that was based on deception by believing the truth. The deception was that the car was slipping out of the road because that was how it felt; but the truth was that the tarred road was constructed with the material that allowed the tyres of the vehicle to stay on it without slipping. I therefore drove on even when it felt like was sliding out of the road; but the car remained steady on the road because the feeling of the vehicle slipping was just a deception.

Believing the truth in the face of deception requires courage; and courage is the offspring of faith. Courage has no room for fear. It enables you to expect safety even in the face of perceived danger. It takes courage to expect the best in your marriage, especially in this world where people break each others' hearts day after day. You need to believe that your marriage will succeed and dismiss every thought that makes you feel that it will fail. Whatever you accept as the truth has a direct influence on your expectations. If you accept the possible failure of your marriage as your truth, it will make you expect the worst out of your spouse and your marriage; but if you accept the possible success of your marriage as the truth, you will expect the best out of your spouse and your marriage. Eventually, whatever you expect, you will experience.

Fear makes you act as if you were defeated even if it is evident that you are winning, and this makes defeat certain for you. But faith makes you act as if you were victorious even if it looks like you are losing, and this guarantees victory for you. Whether you act out of faith or out of fear, whatever you expect is surely coming your way. If you expect the worst in your marriage, then the worst is coming your way; but if you expect the best, the best is what you will get. This is what I call the *law of expectation*: 'What you *expect*, you *attract*'. The best thing to do is let your faith overcome your fear and expel the expectations of the worst with the expectations of the best.

5

Fusion of Two Different Entities

Marriage is the *fusion* of two *different* entities. Before we discuss the differences between these entities, let us look closely into the word *fusion.* Fusion is the *process* or *result* of joining two or more things together to form one. When two elements are fused together, they form one new product altogether. For example, if you fuse copper and zinc together, you get brass. Brass is therefore the *result* of copper and zinc joined together. But before these two elements are brought together, they are exposed to excessive heat until they melt. This is where they lose their original shape. Only after they melted can they be joined together to form brass, and that does not happen instantly; it is a *process.*

Before these elements are joined together, they are two completely different objects. But once they are joined together, they become inseparable. They are no longer *two* but *one.* Therefore, brass is one piece of metal with the characteristics of two different pieces of metal put together. This makes brass superior in value and quality to each of the two metals before the fusion. Take note that it is highly significant that the elements that are fused together be *different.* Otherwise the fusion will be meaningless. If you fuse *same* elements together, you only increase their quantity; but if you fuse *different* elements together, you increase quality. The fusion of copper with copper produces more copper; but the fusion of copper with zinc produces brass. Therefore, for more superior results, the fusion should take place between two *different* elements.

When a man and a woman get married, they are fused together to form one entity; and this is the *process* that requires intense heat. *Therefore a man shall leave his father and mother and be joined to his wife, and they shall become one flesh* (Genesis 2:24). The word *joined* in this text is the same one that is used in the fusion process – the *process* or *result* of *joining* two elements together until they become one. After the fusion process, a man and his wife become one flesh. The *result* of this union is strong sense of cohesion, healthy communication, mutual understanding and unity in diversity. Take note from the above text that a man *leaves* his father and mother before he *fuses* together with his wife. This is simply teaching us that we should be prepared to give up some of the things we hold dear in our hearts so that we can become one with our partners. This is indeed a painful process, and this is the pain that is often experienced when the two are fused into one.

The problem with many couples is that they want to involve their parents, children, siblings and friends in the fusion process that was supposed to take place between only the two of them. They drag their significant others into every disagreement or argument they have. As a result too many people get hurt in the process because the fusion process entails too much heat. This is where you find the parents hating their daughter-in-law because of the disagreement she had with their son. The siblings may also join in with hatred against their sister-in-law for 'putting their brother through pain'. Now they are being affected by the heat that was not meant for them because somehow their son dragged them into the fusion process that was meant exclusively for him and his wife. Remember, fusion can also occur between more than two elements; therefore, if you drag others into the process, they will also become part of the excruciating process and get hurt unnecessarily.

Once the two become one flesh, they become inseparable. If they decide to divorce, it would be as if they are undergoing the amputation process because they are trying to rip one flesh apart into two separate pieces of meat. There would be too much bleeding and excruciation because they are trying to put asunder what God Himself has fused together. Eventually the husband leaves a part of him in his wife and retains a part of his wife in him for the rest of his life. The same applies on the part of the wife. For that reason, if your marriage dies, part of you dies with it, and you become incomplete. If you hurt your partner, you yourself will also get hurt because the two of you are one flesh. Therefore, by hurting your partner, you are actually hurting yourself.

Notice that fusion does not make two people think alike, act alike or be alike; it makes them one even though they are different. Fusion does not change copper into zinc or zinc into copper; it only merges two different elements to form a completely different piece of metal. In other words, copper does not fuse with zinc to form copper or zinc; they fuse to form brass. But in marriage you will most often find couples who want their partners to be like them. Their general attitude in marriage is: "If you can't be *like* me, you can't be *with* me".

Marriage does not make two people alike; it makes them one. If you take flour, eggs, sugar, baking powder, margarine, milk and vanilla; mix them together and put them in the oven, they do not become sugar or milk or flour or any of those ingredients; they become a cake. Even one body is formed by different parts. The nose never blames or resents the other body parts for letting it be the only one that does all the breathing for them. The understanding is that the other body parts are also performing different but equally significant functions. Therefore, you can't marry a person and expect them to be like you. Both of you should put your differences together to form one thing that is bigger and better than each of you. Simply put, marriage helps *both* of you to be better than *each* of you.

The fusion process is a painful experience. It requires a particular measure of heat to happen successfully. From this we can learn that marriage thrives on adversity. Every difficulty in marriage works like heat in the fusion process of two metals. It melts your egotistic proclivities until you are ready to fuse together. No heat, no fusion; and without pain, there will be no union. The problem with many couples is that each time they experience pain, they walk away. They would rather be separated than be amalgamated through affliction. They ascribe the pain they feel to their partners and blame them for being the 'cause' of their calamity. Then instead of fusing together, they melt away from each other.

Such people always take the easy way out, but the easy way out often leads to harsh experiences of perpetual marital failure. This could explain why people who divorced and remarried usually divorce again. It could be that each time they experience the problems that were meant to fuse them together, they melt away from their spouses and start looking for alternative partners. But the truth of the matter is: There is no fusion without pain. The pain you ran away from in your previous marriage will surely catch up with you in your current or prospective marriage. Pain is a growth hormone for marriage, and without it your marriage could suffer dwarfism or retardation. Marriage requires that you give up "I" for "We" and "Me" for "Us", and this is usually a painful process; but it is essential for marital growth and success.

Marriage means you are better together than you are apart. This does not mean you are better alike than you are different. *Together* and *alike* are two different words. You don't have to be alike to get along. In fact, the power of a relationship is in the differences between the people involved. Diversity not only makes marriage successful; it also makes it possible. Two roosters cannot produce an egg; it takes a rooster and a hen. Neither can a mixture of sperm and sperm produce a baby; it takes fusion of the sperm and the ovum. This is the power of diversity. Our differences from each other are our main sources of attraction to each other. The main reason why you married a person who is different from you is because the one like you didn't like you. You were repellent to them. This is what I call the *law of attraction*: 'Opposites attract, but likes repel'. This means we usually attract people who are different from us and repel ones like us.

In marriage, it is very essential that we learn to find harmony in variety. You don't have to be like me to like me. Many couples get upset when their partners act, think or tackle problems or responsibilities differently from them. They tend to think that their way is the only way. But the truth of the matter is: There are many other approaches that are totally different from yours but can still yield same results as yours or better. In fact, it might not work for them if they do it exactly like you. If it always takes aggression and intimidation for you to get what you want, the other person may choose to approach the same situation gently and peacefully, and this may yield the same results as yours or even better. One may squeeze the toothpaste tube at the bottom, and the other may squeeze it in the middle; but whether they squeeze it at the bottom or in the middle, toothpaste will come out exactly the same way. It would thus be irrational to fight over whether to squeeze it at the bottom or in the middle.

5.1 Gender Differences

Men and women have more differences than similarities. If I didn't know better, I would strongly argue that men and women came from two different planets and happened to share the same environment on planet earth. In fact, the only thing I know that is common between men and women is that they are both humans, and they share the same human characteristics. But to make comparison between them as human beings, I struggle to find anything they have in common. You say the same thing to both of them at the same time, and they hear two different things. If you open the door of an automobile for a woman, she regards it as you being considerate. But if you do the same for a man, he regards it as a disgusting act that undermines his masculinity. When you give a woman flowers, she finds it romantic; but if you give a man the same, he finds it ridiculous.

All this war that is taking place between husbands and their wives can be summed up in one statement: Wives are mad at their husbands because their husbands cannot be women enough to relate with them, and husbands are frustrated because their wives cannot be men enough to understand them. It would make a huge difference if these two could learn to accept and appreciate each other just as they are. Men can never be women, and women can never be men; they will forever remain two entities that are different from each other so that they can complement each other in their marriages. They must learn to get along; otherwise their relationships will fall apart.

The differences between men and women in their entirety cannot be contained in just one chapter of the book. They are more than the book itself can contain. For this reason, we will not discuss all the differences between men and women in this section; we will concentrate only on a common few that can be helpful in marital relationships. Take note that this is just a general indication of different characteristics between men and women; therefore, they may not be accurate for all individuals. Not all men or women are as explained below; there are few exceptions to these rules. For example, there are women who are physically stronger than men, but most men are physically stronger than women. Thus, the differences mentioned below are observations from the majority, and they can give indication in terms of how men generally differ from women. The following are the 15 most common differences between men and women.

1. Women have weaker vessel and stronger content; men have stronger vessel and weaker content.

In the first epistle of the Apostle Peter, he instructs husbands to dwell with their wives with understanding, giving honour to them as *weaker vessels* (See

1 Peter 3:7). This instruction, though it was given in favour of women, seems to be very disturbing to them; precisely because it refers to them as *weaker vessels.* I want to assure you that what the Apostle Peter said is perfectly true and correct – women are weaker vessels, most especially as compared to men. Oh, wait! Before you close this book and walk away, let us look together at the word *vessel.* A vessel is a container, and a container in this illustration refers to the physical structure. I am sure you will agree with me that generally, men's physical build-up is taller and stronger than that of women. This is exactly what the Apostle Peter meant. Women are physically more fragile. But I want to assure you that even though women have weaker containers, they possess a stronger content. They are weaker on the outside but stronger on the inside.

The society expects men to be as tough emotionally as they are physically. When a man cries, they say that he is not man enough. But this is not how a man was created. Generally, men are physically stronger but more fragile emotionally, and women are more fragile physically but emotionally stronger. The problem begins when they start using these differences against each other. If the husband uses his physical strength to abuse his wife physically or the wife uses her emotional strength to abuse her husband emotionally, the marriage will be a great disaster. The husband must use his physical strength to protect his wife's body, and the wife must use her emotional strength to protect her husband's heart. Marriage will be an awful experience if the husband is physically absent and the wife is emotionally absent. As husband and wife, you must be there for each other and have each other's backs at all times. Successful couples never hit on their spouses' weaknesses; they always build on their strengths instead.

Your differences do not necessarily distinguish the better from the worse; they only indicate your strong need for each other. Whatever the wife lacks in herself as a woman, she has it in her husband. So, your physical strength as a woman is in your husband; and your emotional strength as a man is in your wife. There's no need to compete or envy each other, because whatever your partner has, you also have. That is the power of marriage. Instead of fighting over who is better than whom, rather take time to celebrate that you are better together than you are apart.

Men and women are *equally* but *differently* powerful. Competition between them is impossible because one's strength is another's weakness. They can only complement each other. Figuratively speaking, a man is like a lion, and a woman is like a shark. Both these animals are powerful, but each within the parameters of its own territory. The lion is not as powerful in the ocean as it is on land, and the shark is not as powerful on land as it is in the ocean. So, if these two were to fight, one would have to give up its territory and go into the territory of the other. If the lion provokes the shark in the water, the shark will destroy it; and if the shark gets out of the water to start a fight with the lion, the lion will wipe it out.

The shark cannot complain against the lion for not swimming with it because the lion cannot swim in the ocean; neither can the lion blame the shark for not walking with it because the shark cannot walk. The lion has no fins, and the shark has no legs. So, the lion is powerful where the shark is weak, and the shark is strong where the lion is feeble. But they are equally powerful. None is better than the other; they are just good at different things. Therefore, it would be unfair for the lion to oblige the shark to run with it, or for the shark to compel the lion to swim with it.

There are things men do with ease that women struggle with, and there are things women do excellently while men fail dismally with the same. There are areas where men are stronger than women, and there are areas where women are more powerful than men. If an average woman tries to engage in a physical fight against an average man, she will get hurt; and if an average man tries to engage in an emotional or verbal war against an average woman, he will be defeated. So, if these two are at war, they find themselves using their strengths against each other's weaknesses. The woman may lodge an emotional attack, and the man may react by attacking physically. This can never be a fair fight. Both of them will lose. The husband and his wife should therefore not try to compete with each other in any way; they should rather use their strengths to complement each other and make up for each other's weaknesses.

2. Men get attracted through their eyes; women get attracted through their ears.

Generally, what attracts men to women is how they *look*; but what attracts women to men is how they *sound*. This is one of the main reasons why men are usually the ones who initiate love relationships. Men get attracted to women even before they hear their voices or their words because they have already seen what attracts them – their bodies. But for a woman to be attracted to a man, she has to hear what he says and how he says it. She can only respond to him after several conversations. The physical structure of a woman is more attractive to a man than her speech or the sound of her voice, and the man's eloquence or the sound of his voice is more attractive to the woman than his physique.

This is not true all the time; but it is true in most cases. If an average man walks past the woman with a well-built physical structure, he would either turn his head to stare or steal a glance at her or desperately wrestle the temptation to look back at her. Few men would not even think about it. This happens because God created a woman's body to catch a man's eye. In the same way, God created the woman's ears to respond to the man's voice and his words. God also gave women the inherent urge to titivate their bodies to make them more attractive to men. Men on the other hand are given the eloquence of speech to enable them to say the things women love to hear. Ultimately, women consciously or subconsciously employ their beauty as the force of attraction to men; and men deliberately or involuntarily exploit their eloquence as a magnet to pull women towards them.

These unique media of attraction make women better with words than men, and men better with views than women. These also make men better drivers and architects than women, and women better listeners and readers than men. For example, most women struggle to reverse an automobile even though they know how to drive; but for most men it's never a hassle. Women are able to grasp the first time what they are required to do, but men need to be reminded over and over again. Ask a woman to pay your account, she pays it first thing after you ask her. But ask the same to a man, it might be paid after two weeks, if ever. The more you ask him, the more he hears you. If you want a woman to remember, tell her; but if you want a man to remember, show him.

For men to be better readers or listeners and for women to be better drivers or architects, they need extra practice. But for men to be good drivers or architects and for women to be good listeners or readers, it is almost natural. Therefore, the husband should go easy on his wife when she drives, and the wife should be patient with her husband when she requested him to carry out a particular task. Most often what the woman tells is not exactly what the man hears, and what the man shows is not exactly what the woman sees. This can be the major source of conflict between the husband and his wife if not handled with patience, tolerance and understanding. Such differences should work for the couple; not against them. The couple should create an environment where the husband hears through his wife, and the wife sees through her husband.

3. Men focus on the bigger picture; women pay attention to details.

If a man were to describe the person he saw, he would say something like, "I saw a tall and slender African man with a suit on". But if it were a woman who described that person, she would say something like, "I saw a tall, slender, dark and handsome man with a black striped suit, a white shirt, a black waist coat, a red tie and black shoes walk past the ice cream shop towards the bank (she may even mention the names of the ice cream shop and the bank). He put on a golden watch on his wrist, and he was walking as if he were tired..." And she can go on and on. A man would describe the bigger picture, but a woman would pay attention to finer details. This is how their brains were programmed. If both of them watch a television programme, a man would focus more on the main picture on the screen, but a woman would also pay attention to the pot plants, colours, decorations and lights in the background.

One of the major courses of conflict in marriages is that couples get frustrated because they always see things differently. On one hand the wife would be frustrated by her husband's inability to see things that are right in front of his face. On the other hand, the husband would be annoyed by the wife who pays attention to unnecessary details. From a man's perspectives, if the whole picture is right, everything is right; but from a woman's viewpoint, if one minute detail is wrong, the whole picture is wrong. It is for this reason that husbands often feel that their wives expect too much from them, and that wives feel that their husbands ignore important things. But couples should learn to understand things from each other's perspective and avoid forcing their own perceptions down each other's throats. They should learn to give each other permission to see things differently and still be at peace.

4. Men are governors; women are administrators.

Generally, men love to *plan*; and women love to *implement*. This makes it easier for a wife to submit herself to the husband who has a clear sense of direction. If the husband cannot communicate his vision clearly to his wife, she may develop her own vision; and this may cause division in marriage. Naturally, a man loves to establish, but managing what he established does not come naturally to him. This is where he needs a woman to help him manage it. As it is rightfully said, a man builds a house, and a woman makes it a home. A man provides money, and a woman stretches it to meet all the needs within the household. Whatever a man starts, a woman sustains. This is one of the complementarities that make them a great team as husband and wife.

5. Men are rationally illustrative; women are emotionally expressive.

From what we have learnt from the Bible, the husband is the head of his wife. That makes the wife the body of her husband. In the head you find the brain, and in the body you find the heart. The brain is associated with *thinking*, and the heart is associated with *feeling*. So, the husband is the *cognitive* part of his wife, and the wife is the *emotional* version of her husband. This is one of the many ways in which these two complement each other. As a married couple, you and your spouse are members of one body. You are fused together to form one flesh. Therefore, you cannot hurt your spouse without you yourself experiencing the pain. If as a wife you hurt your husband, you are practically afflicting yourself with a headache; and if as husband you hurt your wife, you are literally setting yourself up for a heartache.

If as a husband you think your wife is crazy, you are actually implying that she has a head problem. In short, what you are implying is that you are the problem; because you are the head. If on the other hand as a wife you feel that your husband is heartless, the finger points back at you; because you are the heart of your husband. So, if you say he is heartless, you are actually implying that your role as a wife is invisible in his life. Whatever measure of judgment you use against your spouse, the same is measured right back to you; because what you see lacking in them could be an indication of you not really doing your part to complement them.

When communicating, women verbalize their feelings, and men speak their mind. This is one of the things that make it so difficult for them to understand each other. The husband speaks his mind, and the wife listens with her heart. Then she interprets his opinion as a feeling and responds from her heart; and the husband would try to rationalize her feelings so that they may appeal to his mind. To improve communication between husband and wife, the husband should learn to listen to his wife's feelings and not try to rationalize them; and the wife should try to listen to her husband's reasons and avoid trying to emotionalize them. In short, when the couple communicates, the wife should learn to listen with her head, and the husband should learn to listen with his heart. This will not only improve mutual understanding; it will also promote empathy between the husband and his wife.

6. Men can do only one thing at a time; women can multitask.

For we have many members in one body, but the members do not have the same function, so we, being many, are one body in Christ, and individually members of one another (Romans 12:4-5). A woman, being her husband's *body*, has this special ability given to her by God to do more than one thing at a time. Just like the body, she has many members that enable her to perform various functions at the same time without losing her mind; and those members are all linked together. She can attend to four pots on the stove at the same time; at the same time washing the dishes, sweeping the floor, bathing the children, helping others with homework, going through letters from creditors and working out a payment plan, making tea for herself, her husband and her children, preparing clothes to be worn the following day, and going through the magazine to shop around for curtains and bedding sets. This makes her a good manager of time. It also makes her a great achiever because she can get a lot of things done at the same time, thus achieving more in less time.

She can take a good rest while peeling vegetables and watching her favourite programme on television. At the same time chatting with a friend on trivial matters or even serious issues of life. She can be talking on the phone and writing an important report at the same time, even if that report has nothing to do with that phone conversation. She is also capable of managing many different things, even her many accounts, at the same time. If I didn't know better, I would swear that she has more than two hands and two feet. But who needs more than two hands and feet when you can do more with only two? In a nutshell, a woman is a genius at multi-tasking.

Not so with men. A man, unlike a woman, can only handle his tasks one at a time. If you give him one more task on top of the one he is busy with, he gets distracted. The best thing to do is leave him to complete the task at hand before you can talk to him about another task. When he's watching his favourite programme on television, there's nothing else he can focus on. He naturally finds it hard to work and clean up at the same time. His brain is not built to focus on many things at the same time. Trying to do it all at once can be totally frustrating for him. If I didn't know better, I would vow that he has only one hand. However, this 'shortfall' gives him a strong sense of direction because he can focus on one worthwhile project until it is completed.

When you communicate something to your husband while he is busy with something else, he would either leave what he is doing and focus on what you are asking him to do, or he will continue with what he is doing and forget what you asked him to do. That does not mean he is ignoring you or disregarding your requests; he was not built to grasp a request to carry out a task when his focus is already on something else. It is not easy for women to understand this because they fail to understand why their husbands fail to do just one more thing when they themselves can carry out so many tasks at once. To expect a man to multi-task is like expecting a fish to walk. It is just not in him. The best thing you can do is give him permission to carry out his tasks one at a time. But when it comes to marital intimacy, the husband should rather leave everything else to focus on his wife in totality.

Husbands should also be considerate to their wives when they 'try to build Rome in one day'. It is not in a woman's nature to sit on the couch and enjoy television when the sink is full of dirty dishes. Try not to be too demanding of her attention when she's trying to carry out her tasks. Rather than trying to stop her, join her. After all, she can multi-task; which means she can fit you into her busy schedule and pay attention to you while she's getting her work done. However, this does not suggest that wives should ignore their husbands in the name of work. Remember, your partner is your number one priority. Husbands, knowing that they themselves cannot focus on more than one thing at a time, tend to be frustrated when their wives attend to them concurrently with other duties. It is not easy for them to understand that their wives are able to attend to them while they are dealing with something else.

Much as women are capable of attending to their husbands while they are working on something else, they should try to avoid making their husbands feel like they are part of their daily routine. After all, marriage is more than just work; it is an intimate relationship. Whatever the case may be in marriage, nothing should rob the husband and wife off a quality time spent together on each other. When it comes to intimacy, the wife should learn to shut down from everything else so that she can focus only on her husband. Likewise, the husband should learn to tune out from the previous activity and tune in to his wife completely. One of the most important things in marriage is for the couple to take pleasure in each other's company.

7. Men need to feel respected; women need to feel loved.

Men naturally have a strong need to feel admired and celebrated for their good qualities and achievements. It encourages them to know that their contribution is appreciated. Men have a godlike sense of achievement. They celebrate in milestones, even before the entire project is accomplished. We notice this trait in God when He created the universe (See Genesis 1). Whatever God created, He always paused to celebrate it; and He saw that it was good, even though He still had a lot more to do. No wonder God assigned a man to play his role in marriage. God loves to be praised, and so do men. From a man's point of view, little is much. Whatever he achieves, and whatever good quality he demonstrates, no matter how small, calls for celebration. Failure to recognize his efforts can be very discouraging to him.

Unfortunately for a man, his female counterpart was wired differently. A woman can hardly celebrate small steps when there are so many miles in front of her. This contributes a lot in her proclivity to perceive men as lazy; because she cannot understand why she should appreciate a man's little effort when he still has so much to do. For example, a man may want to be appreciated for washing the dishes; but to his wife, washing the dishes is the smallest piece of work in the house. Therefore, she finds it extremely difficult to appreciate her husband's effort to wash the dishes when she knows that she still has to sweep the floor, cook, bath the children, water the pot plants, etc. To a man, washing the dishes is great achievement; but his wife does not feel the same, and she would very often make her husband feel he is not good enough, which is very discouraging to a man. That is why you would most often hear men say, "I wonder if I will ever be good enough for this woman."

The best way to get a man to carry out the next task is by acknowledging his effort on the preceding one. On the other hand, a woman thinks a compliment is too much for such a small effort. What she needs to understand is that appreciation is not only a man's rewards; it is also his driving force. Men are more motivated to complete the journey if they are celebrated for the small steps they take. Women often make the mistake of criticising them for the larger portion of work they have not yet do; and they fail to appreciate them for the little efforts they are making. They keep on reminding their husbands how bad they are instead of showing them how good they are. Showing a man a thousand things he is not doing can cause him to stop even the few that he was doing; but appreciating him for one thing he is doing right can motivate him to do even a thousand that he is not doing.

Whether a man is hands on or laid back can always be traced back to the feedback he gets from his wife. A man is inspired more by the wife who believes in him than the one who doubts him. In fact, nothing can stop the man whose wife believes in him. If his wife reminds him how much he has failed, he may get discouraged and continue to 'fail'; but if she can show him that she believes he will succeed, he will most probably be motivated not only to do more, but also to correct his own mistakes. You can never get a man to do much if you keep on telling him that he is not doing enough. The best thing you can do is make him feel that the little he has done goes a long way in your heart; this is the best way to bring out the best in him.

Women on the other hand have a strong need to feel loved. Because of her reproductive cycle, a woman's emotions are generally unstable. Sometimes she feels good about herself, other times she feels bad. At times she feels beautiful, the other times she feels ugly. Her perception of herself changes from time to time. This being the case, she has a need for a more consistent love, which she cannot always find from other women because their feelings also oscillate every now and then. The love that she really needs can only come from a more emotionally stable person, and that would be her husband. There is no colder marriage than one in which the wife feels unloved. It makes her feel inadequate as a wife. It also impinges negatively on her confidence as a person.

Love is as important to a woman as respect is to a man. It serves not only as a reward to her; but also as a driving force for improved behaviour. A woman would do anything for a man who makes her feel loved. No love is ever too much for her. The more love she gets from her husband, the more confident she feels about herself; and the more confident she feels, the better she performs as a wife. There is no better way to win the woman's heart than to love and adore her; especially when she feels like she does not deserve it. Every man needs to understand that love not only rewards good performance in a woman; it also provokes better performance. So, you don't have to wait for her to do well before you can show her love; but you can motivate her to do well by consistently demonstrating love to her. A woman's actions are closely related to her feelings; so, however she feels, that is how she is likely to behave. If she feels loved, she will be more likely to behave lovingly.

As the adage suggests, what goes around comes around. So, whatever you do to your spouse will in time come right back to you. It may not come back the way you gave it, but it will come back the way you need it. How much you get out strongly depends on how much you put in. If you gave nothing, don't expect anything. Finally, to get the best of your husband, give him the best of your respect; and to get the best out of your wife, give her the best of your love. You don't have to wait for your spouse to make the first move; but you can sow the seed for whatever you desire by being the one to make the first move.

8. Men are initiators; women are responders.

A woman is like a mirror; whatever you put in front of her will be reflected back to you. She is also like a bank; you cannot withdraw from her anything you have not deposited in her. She was created to be responsive, and most often her actions towards her husband are reactions to his actions. We husbands often make the mistake of expecting out of our wives what we have not inserted in them. Then we get frustrated and complain about them not giving us the love and respect we deserve. I have met men who have become the victims of the pain they put their wives through. They are simply making withdrawal from the deposit they themselves have made. If you show your wife no love, she will have no love to reflect; and you will get no love in return. If you inflict pain in her, she will reflect it back to you in one way or another. If you take no initiative, you will get no response.

On the other hand, men are natural initiators. But even so, they are less likely to make the first move if they know they will get nothing in return. What makes them initiators is not the initiation itself; it is the response they get for initiating. For example, when a man is attracted to a woman; what gives him either the courage or fear to make the first move is the response he anticipates from her. If he anticipates rejection, he may not make the first move; but if he anticipates a positive response, he will be more confident to make the first move. In short, his actions are inspired or expired by her reactions.

This works just like the scenario of chicken and egg. A chicken produces an egg, and an egg produces a chicken; but if a chicken fails to produce an egg, there will be no egg to produce a chicken. This can lead to extinction of the chicken species. God did not create an egg first; He created a chicken, and He gave it the ability to produce and incubate an egg until it produces a chicken. Similarly, God did not make a woman first; he made a man, and out of him He made a woman. This is also the case with marital love. God pours His love into a man; a man passes it onto his wife, and his wife reflects it back to him, so that he can also reflect it back to God. The joy of the chicken is not to produce or incubate eggs; but to see the eggs produce other chickens. In the same way, what motivates a man to love a woman is not the love he gives, but the love and respect he gets in return.

In a nut shell, the wife will not perpetuate anything her husband does not initiate, and the husband will not initiate anything his wife will not perpetuate. Women respond to *results*, and men are motivated by *rewards*. A woman who gets no results gives no rewards, and a man who gets no rewards produces no results. Results come by man's initiative, and rewards come from a woman's response. At the end of it all, a woman's failure to respond to a man's action can block his future attempts; and a man's failure to initiate gives a woman nothing to respond to. These two characteristics build on each other; the more the husband initiates, the more responsive the wife will be; and the more responsive she is, the more motivated he will be to make the first move.

9. Men focus more on usefulness; women focus more on splendour.

When a man buys a set of curtains, his idea is to hang them on the windows so that people cannot see him from outside the house. But when the woman buys a set of curtains, her primary goal is to decorate the house. A man buys the pillows so that he can rest his head while he is asleep, but the woman buys them to make the bed look beautiful. A man would buy the couch to sit on; but the woman would buy cushions to make it look more elegant. When a man buys groceries, he buys food so that they can eat; but a woman would add the chocolates, snacks, fruits, and other household accessories to add more taste and magnificence. This can also cause conflict if marriage if not managed properly.

If the husband does not understand this trait in his wife as a woman, he may conclude that she is a wasteful spender; because he would not understand why she buys so many pillows when they need only two. The wife could also conclude that her husband is stingy if she does not understand the thought behind his actions. A man has no problem spending his money on the things he considers useful. To him, everything that does not serve a specific function is useless. For example, a table can be used for putting food when eating; but a vase on the table has no function in his opinion. But to a woman, it is equally important that the table looks attractive when people are using it. In short, a man focuses on the use, but a woman pays particular attention to the looks; and these two are equally important for the couple to be able to make their house a home.

10. Men are more protective of their egos; women are more expressive of their beauty.

A man's ego is very important to him. He prides himself dearly in his masculinity. There's no greater compliment to him than to tell him he's the man; and nothing hurts him more than to be told that he's not man enough. He can do anything (good or bad) to earn his respect as a man. The problem facing the world today is a false description of what constitutes a real man. As a result, they think you are the real man if you do not cry; and you are not man enough if you do. They also think a real man is qualified by smoking, drinking, physical strength, money, women, etc. The world calls you 'the man' if you can have a love relationship with more than one woman at the same time. In fact, they seriously question your manhood if you commit yourself fully to only one woman. Some go so far as to tell each other that you are not man enough if you have never killed anyone.

Because of these false ideas, men continue to populate the prisons all over the world, and some even lose their lives, trying to prove to the world, and to themselves, that they are men enough. Some have lost their marriages while trying to earn their respect as men. Sadly, all these things that cost us so much trouble are just fallacies in as far as real masculinity is concerned. The true characteristics of a real man include love, care, responsibility, honesty, loyalty, integrity, faithfulness, protection, provision, gentleness, self-control, etc. When a real man is around, people feel safe. Real men do not demand respect by terrorizing other people; they earn it through their loving and caring personalities. So, whatever honourable act your husband demonstrates, it will be very encouraging for him to hear you tell him he's the man.

On the other hand, women love not only to feel beautiful; but also to be told that they are beautiful. If you go to beauty salons, you will see how much pain they endure for their beauty. You will also observe how patiently they wait long hours awaiting their turn to be beautified. One of the greatest compliments you can ever give to a woman is to tell her that she's beautiful. It would crush her spirit if she could hear her husband tell her how ugly or fat she is. Her confidence lies in her beauty. Watch them at any social gathering, and you will notice that all women have put on their best dresses, hairdos and makeups. Meanwhile, their male counterparts would be very comfortable in their jeans and T-shirts; yet they want to be seen driving the best cars and hanging out with the most beautiful girls and wealthiest people around, because those things give them a sense that they are earning their respect as men.

Every woman wants to spend her life with the husband who makes her feel beautiful, and every man desires to spend his life with the wife who make him feel he's the man. The opposite is also true. A typical man would rather stay in the shack with the woman who respects his masculinity than reside in a mansion with a woman who makes him feel like he's less of a man. Similarly, a typical woman would rather be alone than be with a man who makes her feel ugly. For marriages to enjoy many years of success, husbands should learn to celebrate their wives' beauty; and wives should learn to honour their husbands as men.

11. Men are laid back; women are hands on.

One day I was attending a lecture at one of South African universities. During the time of questions and discussions, men were more participative than women. As an attempt to get women involved, one of the facilitators stood in front of the group and said: "My father, whom I believe is a very wise man, used to say, 'If you want to get things said, get a man; but if you want to get things done; get a woman'". This statement greatly excited every woman who was in the room. Then I thought to myself, 'If only they had known what that statement really means, they would not get so excited...' The statement excited them because they took it as a compliment; and they could not really perceive the reality behind it. The reality of this statement applies in their own homes with their husbands; who seem to be so much in love with idleness.

Men love to communicate their intentions, but very seldom do they implement them; the reason being that they would spend a few seconds talking about what they intend to do and then spend almost forever thinking about how they are going to implement it. They are always waiting for the 'right time', which almost never comes. One of their favourite phrases is "I will do it"; and when asked when, they would say "soon"; but "soon" to them can be three weeks to three month later, if ever. The most common scenario is when he says to a woman, "I will marry you"; then she asks "when?" to which he replies "Soon", and that soon sometimes takes forever. This is often very frustrating to women; even though they sounded so excited to hear it in the lecture room.

On the other hand, women communicate as they implement. By the time they say it, they have already started doing it. If she says "I want the curtains", you may ask "when?" and she would most probably reply "I have already placed an order". While men fold their arms to think about how it can be done, women think with their hands in it. As much as we men love to communicate our intentions, there is one thing that we love more than that. In fact, we love it more than anything else. Even though we sometimes hate how much we love it, we still can't help loving it. This thing that we love so much is to just sit back and do *nothing*. We love controlling from the couch; and our favourite device when we are reclining on the couch is the remote control. The remote control seems to fulfil our deepest fantasy – to control everything while we sit back and do nothing.

If men really loved to do anything apart from nothing, God would not have told Adam that his penalty for disobeying Him in the Garden of Eden would be to eat bread in the sweat of his face for as long as he lives (See Genesis 3:18-19). What makes this a punishment to Adam is not the work; it is a man's love to do nothing. If men really loved doing something, then this would be more of a privilege than punishment. On the other hand, women thrive on activity. Their brain hardly ever allows them to just sit back and do nothing. A woman's brain is always working, and whatever her brain thinks, her hands are quick to do. Her activity is closely linked to her emotion, and she feels satisfied when she knows she is doing something; even if that thing is more than one thing. Her femininity does not allow her to sit down when there is so much to do, and this makes her feel extremely furious each time she sees her husband just sitting. She fails to understand how he manages to sit so comfortably when there are so many things to be done.

If God were to give a woman the penalty that is similar to her husband's, it would also be more of a privilege than punishment. But God made it entirely different. He first declared that her body, which is the weaker aspect of her being, will bear the most excruciating pain of childbirth (See Genesis 3:16). As much as this penalty is painful, it is not as frustrating to a woman as the second one, in which God declared: *"Your desire shall be for your husband, and he shall rule over you"* (Genesis 3:16). Two things about this statement are very disturbing for a woman. Firstly, God gives you the brain that would not allow you to do nothing, but He gives you a desire for your husband. In other words, you have a desire to just sit and do nothing just like your husband does; but you cannot, because it is not in you to do so. Secondly, He makes the person who gets 'nothing' done a ruler over you; and this person expects you to do everything while he does nothing.

In marriage, the husband gets to sit and watch his wife do everything, and the wife gets to observe her husband enjoy all the ease while she carries the whole burden. This can lead to serious marital conflicts if left the way it is. The husband may feel neglected, and the wife may feel overburdened. For a man, it takes extra effort to get up from the couch and do something; but for a woman, it also takes extra effort to leave everything she needs to do and sit on the couch. If a man does get up and do something, no matter how small, he would perceive his lazy proclivity as a 'well-deserved' rest. Meanwhile, the woman on the other hand would feel guilty for having 'neglected' her responsibilities. Couples should find ways to manage this situation, and it begins with mutual understanding and mutual acceptance. This will help strengthen your tolerance for each other as a couple. It will also help you give each other enough room to grow.

This information should be used not as an excuse for the husband's laziness or the wife's workaholic tendencies; but rather as an indication for the need to grow. The couple will grow if the husband can make conscious efforts to get out of the couch and help his wife do whatever needs to be done. Only thereafter can he take his well-deserved rest. The wife can also make a conscious effort to plan her activities such that she may have enough time to just relax with her husband. As a husband, you need to know that you do not have the luxury of resting all the time. Very often you will have to defeat your craving for the couch and do what you don't want to do so that you can achieve the results you desire. Same applies for the wife. It is good to work, but working is not good if you do it all the time. There's a time to work, and there's a time to rest. As much as it is good to produce, it is also important that you take time to enjoy the product.

12. Women focus on the process; men focus on the product.

Generally, women want to enjoy the trip, but men want to arrive at their destination. When they are on a journey together, the wife would be looking around and enjoying the beauty of nature; but the husband would be looking for signs that show him how many kilometres or miles are left before they arrive. This is because women focus more on the process, and men focus more on the product. Women find satisfaction in doing; but men get satisfied when they are done. Even when they take a shower together, the wife would be enjoying the water, the touches and the relaxation; but the husband would be looking forward to finish.

Couples can manage this variance by learning to see things from each other's perspective. The wives should learn to understand that the product is as important to their husbands as the process is to them, and husband should learn to appreciate that the process is as important to their wives as the product is to them; and they should both learn to make deliberate efforts to help fulfil each other's needs. If you do not love it, learn to love the feeling it produces to your spouse; because it's not only about your pleasure, it's about your spouse's pleasure as well.

13. Women are quick to act; men tend to procrastinate.

Women have a strong sense of urgency. It is very unlikely for a woman to leave until later what can be done now. She cannot rest knowing that there is an outstanding work that does not have to wait until later. When there are dishes in the sink, she wants to wash them now, and when the house is untidy, she wants to clean it now. When there is an issue to be addressed, she wants to address it now. She has a strong here and now attitude, and she would rather do things now than regret later. Not so with a man. A man finds it unnecessary to do now what he can leave until later. He seldom sees the need to do things urgently; especially the things he feels he can live without, or things that pose no threat to him or his family. He would not fix the leak on the roof until water floods into the house on a rainy day. This makes him a procrastinator; another trait that a woman finds terribly frustrating.

14. Women are more affectionate; men are more sexual.

It is said that men give love to get sex, and women give sex to get love. This statement carries so much truth, and it can help us understand each other better as men and women. Men have more testosterone than women; and testosterone is the principal hormone for sex and aggression in a man. In men, testosterone plays a vital function in the development of male reproductive tissues such as the testis and prostate as well as promoting secondary sexual characteristics such as augmented muscle, bone mass, and the growth of body hair. In short, testosterone is a sex hormone, and it is this hormone that makes sex a necessity for men.

To a large extent, men are driven by their sexuality. Their sexuality has a great influence on their spiritual, emotional and marital well-being. A man's sexuality is also linked closely with his ego. Sex is a legitimate physical need for every man. Men physically feel the need for sex as much as they feel the need to eat. Men are aroused sexually not only by their environment; but it is also a biological experience. They don't have to see the naked woman to be aroused; it happens naturally, even if they are not thinking about anything sexual. You don't get hungry only when you see food; you get hungry whether or not you see or smell food. The sight or smell of food only increases your appetite. Similarly, seeing a naked woman can only increase a man's appetite for sex, but the need thereof is already prevalent in his system.

After having a meal, you feel satisfied. Then the body starts digesting the food, and soon you are hungry again. Same applies with men in relation to sex. Instantly after a sexual release, a man feels satisfied physically. Thereafter the sperms begin to build in his testicles; and very soon he will fill the need for another release. This is a continual process for every man. Science has it that an average man needs sexual release every seventy two hours. If he does not get that release, he may feel stressed or frustrated. He may even get aggressive. There is nothing else I know that has such a calming effect on a man as the emission of semen.

Sex is very important to a man. In fact, I believe men value sex more than anything else. You don't have to look very far to see men who risk their jobs, reputation, dignity, faith and marriage just to get sex. We see men leaving their wives at home and going out to get sexual release outside; thus risking their marriages and families. We also see others making sexual moves at women in the workplaces; thus risking their jobs. If you lose your job, you lose your money, and you can't buy food or shelter. So, some men risk food and shelter for just one sexual encounter. Others compromise their faith by indulging in sexual immorality. This shows how valuable sex is for men. They can do whatever it takes for sex.

God deliberately created men this way; not so that they can be adulterous or sexually immoral, but that they can be motivated to fulfil the needs of their wives hoping to get sex in return. On the other hand, women experience the need for sex differently. They do not have the build up that commands sexual release. Two factors determine sexual hormones in women; namely, the female reproductive cycle, and *hypothalamus* – a portion of the brain that is responsible for, among other things, important aspects of parenting and *attachment* behaviours. A woman's sexual drive is linked more to her emotions. This is different from a man's sexuality. A man does not have to love a woman to lust for her; he just has to see her naked. In other words, a man can have a sexual desire for a woman even if he has no feelings of love for her. But for a woman, there has to be a loving relationship for sex to be fulfilling.

A man can very well differentiate sex from a love relationship; and he can get sexual satisfaction with a woman even if there is no love relationship between them. But to a typical woman, sex and love go together. She cannot separate sex from love relationship and emotional attachment. Sex is more meaningful to a woman when there is a connection of love and commitment. While a man can initiate sex with a woman even if there is no affection, a typical woman cannot enjoy sex if there is no affection. So, for a woman, great sex begins with affection and ends with attachment. She is not easily aroused sexually if she does not feel loved. In short, a man's sexual satisfaction is physical; but a woman's sexual gratification is emotional.

There is mutual benefit in the relationship between husband and wife. The husband needs sex, and his wife can give it to him; and the wife needs love, and her husband can give it to her. Simply put, the way to a man's heart is through his body; and the way to a woman's body is through her heart. So, for a marital relationship to be mutually fulfilling, sex should be done *wholeheartedly* – the wife should give her whole body, and the husband should give his whole heart. It is not natural for the husband to give his heart to his wife, but it is natural for him to hunger for sex; so, he has to give his heart if he is to get a sexual release. Similarly, it is not natural for a woman to just give sex to her husband; but she has a natural hunger for love, and she has to give sex if she is to get love.

A husband's love for his wife is motivated by his desire for sex; and the wife's sexual attraction to her husband is driven by her need for love. Therefore, it is the husband's primary responsibility to take care of his wife's emotional needs, and it is the wife's core duty to take care of her husband's sexual needs. If these two needs are not met, things could go terribly wrong in marriage. Both the husband and the wife could be vulnerable to temptations, and Satan could use that to destroy the marriage. Sex and love should be treasured only in marital relationships, and both the husband and the wife should play their role in totality. Sex to the husband provokes his love for his wife, and love to the wife provokes her sexual desire for her husband.

The biggest question in every man's mind might be: "How can I show love to my wife?" Well, the answer to this question can be found in John 3:16, which says: *"For God so loved they world that He gave His only begotten Son..."* God's love was made clearly visible when He gave what He valued the most for our sake. Love remains invisible if nothing is given; and words mean nothing if no action accompanies them. What makes us responsive to God's love is not the sacrifices we made for Him, but the One He made for us. Similarly, a husband can show love to his wife by generously giving her what he values. One thing most men value the most is money; and money happens to be one of the most meaningful tokens of love to many women. You don't have to live very long to observe that women generally find men who spend their money on them attractive.

As much as it is true that money cannot by love; it is also true that *money answers everything* (See Ecclesiastes 10:19). It can give you access to places you've never even dreamt of. It can also earn you a special place in your wife's heart; and if you can touch her heart, you can have her body in totality. We know you love your wife when you give her what you value the most; or when you give up what you value the most for her sake. There's nothing a woman finds sexier than a man who spends his money on her. In fact, from a woman's perspective, the beauty of a man is in his bank account. Sadly, many husbands expect their wives to give more of their bodies than they themselves are willing to give their hearts and, needless to mention, their money. Money is not love; but it can serve as an expression of your love to your wife when you spend it on her. In short, money does not buy love; it communicates it. However, it's not only your money that she needs; she also needs your time and your undivided attention.

The law of *sowing and reaping* also applies in love and sex within marriage. The husband should not wait for sex before he gives love; he should instead sow love tirelessly so that he can reap a fulfilling sexual experience. In the same way, the wife should not wait for love before she gives sex; instead, she should make the first move and sow sex as a seed that will produce love as her harvest. However, each one of the couple should be a fertile soil. They should learn to be responsive to each other. It can be extremely discouraging for a person to keep on sowing and yet get nothing in return. As a wife, for every act of love your husband does for you, make sure you give him a good return. The husband should do the same for his wife after every sexual act. If the couple can commit to this arrangement, their marriage will go only two directions, upward and forward; and marital fulfilment will be their daily bread.

15. Women are caring; men are daring.

While women are more careful in their general behaviour, men are more audacious. This is what makes women more fearful and men braver when it comes to dangerous adventures. When women's adrenaline holds them back, men's adrenaline pushes them forward. The caring attitude of women makes them better parents than men; and the daring nature of men makes them better athletes than women. Thinking about every gangster you know, you will see that more than ninety percent of its members are men. Then take a moment to think also about every hospital and clinic you know, you will observe that the vast majority of nurses are women. This shows that men are more daring, and women are more caring.

The daring nature of a man makes him a good protector of his family; and the caring nature of a woman makes her a great homemaker. The husband makes the home feel safe, and the wife makes it feel warm. However, this daring nature of the husband can be threatening to his wife because some of the risks he takes could harm the whole family. On the other hand the caring nature of the wife can be very frustrating for the husband because it makes him feel restricted. This calls for the husband to be more careful for his wife's sake and perform his stunts when she is not around. He should also try to understand that his wife's restrictive behaviour emanates from her caring nature, and that her caring nature of a vital part of her femininity. As a woman, she would not stand to watch her husband put his own life in 'danger'. What he sees as an adventure, his wife sees as danger; a danger she feels obliged to keep him away from, and he should learn to respect that.

On the other hand, the wife should be careful not to be too restrictive of her husband, because his daring nature is part of his masculinity. It is in his nature to experiment with danger. There is something about flirting with danger that affirms that his manhood. He would even put his own life in harm's way trying to impress the woman in his life; and he loves it when that woman responds out of her caring heart. Both these characteristics should be acknowledged and respected. What matters the most is for both husband and wife to ensure that nobody gets hurt or frustrated unnecessarily.

5.2 Differing Family Backgrounds

Husband and wife are not siblings; which means they did not grow up together. Each grew up in their own families. Different families raise their children differently, and failure to acknowledge this truth in marriage may cause unnecessary conflict between husband and wife. In one family, children are taught to greet other family members everytime when they wake up, when they go out of the house, when they come back and before they go to sleep. Children in this family will most probably grow up believing that it is good to greed and rude not to. They may feel guilty when they don't greet and offended when they are not greeted. The other family may not require that members greet each other at any given time. The children therein may grow up seeing nothing wrong if they don't greet other people. Whether you greet them or not makes no difference. In fact, they may be annoyed if you greet them every now and then.

Destiny may decide for two people from these different family backgrounds to be joined together as husband and wife. On their first night together, they kiss each other good night and fall asleep in each other's arms. Early in the morning the wife wakes up to prepare breakfast for her beloved husband. A couple of minutes later the husband wakes up and walks past his dear wife to look for two cups so he can help her make some tea for both of them. To the husband, there is nothing wrong with this. But the wife on the other hand may take serious offense against her husband for not saying good morning to her. The husband then discerns that the wife is not happy, but he knows it has nothing to do with him because he has done nothing to offend her.

Before the tension subsides, the husband is out for a couple of hours to rent some movies and organise some snacks for them to have a good time together in their new home. While he is away the wife is left wondering "what kind of a monster is this who can't even greet?" Back from a worthwhile activity he comes home and proceeds straight to the remote controls. Then he walks past his wife to the kitchen to get some trays to put in snacks for both of them. After setting the mood he gladly reaches out for his wife to come and join him. But by that time his wife is totally off. Finally the husband realizes that his wife's resentful attitude is actually against him. But he gets confused because he cannot understand why his wife is so unappreciative of the efforts he takes to makes her happy and comfortable. Out of discouragement he storms out of the house and leaves the wife more furious.

Back from where only he knows, the husband comes home to unbearable tension. He asks himself "what is wrong with this woman who gets angry for no reason?" At the same time the wife is wondering "what is wrong with this man who storms in and out of the house as he pleases without saying 'hello' or 'goodbye'?" Time then comes for them to sleep. The wife lies in the far end of bed facing east, and the husband lies in the other end facing west. Both of them are wondering "what have I gotten myself into?" By this time they are not talking to each other; let alone touch each other.

Out of intense frustration the husband reaches out for his phone and initiates a chat with his sister back at home. But the wife in her upbringing was taught to never play with a phone while she's in bed; especially at this time of the day. This infuriates her even more. "Maybe he's having an affair, and he is chatting with his girlfriend" is all she can think of at this moment. Then she storms out of bed in pain and makes her way to the lounge to shed a few tears before she falls asleep on the couch.

Out of deep concern the husband makes his way out of bed to his wife and asks her "what's wrong?" To which the wife replies "nothing" as she gazes at him with tearful eyes. In her heart she is having a conversation with herself wondering "here is a man who cannot greet his wife and plays flirting games with a phone while his wife is asleep asking me what's wrong as if he has no clue what he has done! He does not even show remorse for what he is doing." All the while the husband is overwhelmed with confusion. He then decides to take a walk outside for a few minutes just to clear his head. Back in the house the wife is thinking "he was chatting with his girlfriend on the phone; now he has gone out to meet her." Before they know it, things are completely out of control. The wife concludes that her husband is a rude cheat, and the husband is drowning in the pool of confusion as he wonders "what do women really want?" At the same time the tension is sinking deeper and deeper.

A few weeks down the line they are already considering divorce. When the case is followed closely to examine their grounds of divorce; it all comes down to "my wife neither loves nor respects me" and "my husband is a rude cheat". The husband blames his wife for their marital problems, and the wife blames the husband for the same. Whose fault is it that they now have such a serious problem? To answer this question: If one of them is innocent, they are equally innocent; but if one is guilty, they are both guilty. No one is guiltier or more innocent than the other. The problem lies in their perception of each other's behaviour based on their own upbringing. Even if the wife confronted her husband frequently for not greeting her, it would still make no sense to him because he was never brought up that way. He could rather have concluded that she is unreasonable because she takes offense over 'nothing'.

I know that this sounds like a far-fetched story; but this is what usually happens when couples fail to apply their minds to understanding their differences according to their family backgrounds. Because of her family background, the poor woman could never have imagined that there could be a person who fails to greet and still be so perfectly fine with it. This is not how she was conditioned from her childhood. On the other hand, it would be extremely unfair to expect the poor man to all of sudden start saying all these hellos and goodbyes when he has spent all his life knowing nothing about them.

These two know no other life than what was conditioned to them throughout their lives until they met. It is extremely difficult to convince someone who has been practicing certain behaviour since childhood that what they were doing all along was actually wrong. In fact, this may sound like an insult to them. Even if they happen to admit that it was wrong and they want to change it, they cannot change it overnight. They need plenty of time, patience, encouragement and support to adjust. This is already in their blood, and to get it out of their system would be enormously complicated.

This is where the fusion process begins. The pain of letting go of what worked for "me" so that I may obtain what works for "us" can be too overwhelming; but it is necessary for marital success. This is where you learn to let go of the things that work *against* your marriage and find ones that work *for* it. You give up what works for *one* of you and adopt what works for *both* of you. Letting go is never easy; especially when you are not sure if it's worth it. You run the risk of losing yourself into your marriage without getting anything in return. What can help you overcome this is to know that you are not the only one making adjustments in this relationship; both of you are. The *result* of this [fusion] *process* could be the establishment of a new culture that accommodates and benefits both of you; and this is the culture you can transfer to your offspring.

I have made only one example as an illustration of my discussion on differing family backgrounds. I hope with this one example I have made my point to your full comprehension. I could use more examples, but all other examples cannot be contained in one book. The rest I leave for you to ponder on. Think of any particular differences in the backgrounds of your partner's family against yours; then start thinking about ways to deal with those differences together without breaking out into unnecessary disputes. Marriage requires high level of tolerance because you will very often have to train yourself to accept what you were conditioned to reject for the sake of your relationship.

You cannot get to where you want to be in your marriage without acknowledging where you have been in your families of origin. Where you were determines who you are. Therefore, you cannot understand your partner's current behaviour in marriage without considering their previous experiences back at home. Being raised differently does not mean one is better or worse than the other; it only means you are different. Judging each other based on your upbringing would only make you win the argument and lose the relationship. Much as you don't want your family background to be undermined, neither should you undermine your partner's. Just as you would like to be understood for your family background, be understanding of your partner's family background as well. Whatever the situation may be in your marriage, always remember the Golden Rule: *Do to others as you would have them do to you* (Luke 6:31).

5.3 Different Personalities

The difference between a husband and his wife lies not only in their gender or family backgrounds; it also lies in their personalities. People may be raised in the same family and be of the same gender and still be different because they have different personalities. One person may be outgoing, and the other may be reserved. One may be more liberal and the other more conservative. Whatever the personality differences may be between two people, most important to bear in mind is that no personality is better than or superior to the other. All personalities are diverse but equally significant. For this reason, you cannot judge the other person on the basis of your personality differences.

In most if not all cases, married couples have different personalities. One can be introverted and the other extroverted; or one can be trusting and the other sceptical. In this discussion we shall be exploring some (but not all) aspects that mark the differences between personalities and how they can make or break the marriage.

Introverted v/s Extroverted

Very often in relationships you will find an extroverted person married to an introvert. Very seldom will you find a relationship wherein an introvert married another introvert or an extrovert another extrovert. Extroverted people are outgoing, and they draw their energies from the crowds. They love social gatherings where they get to meet other people. The more the people, the merrier it is for them. An extrovert would rather be among people than alone. This does not mean they never want to be alone. Actually, there are times when even the most extroverted person wants to be alone. No one is totally extroverted. Every extrovert has an introvert in them, and every introvert has a bit of extrovert in them as well. There are also people who switch between the two. The more extroverted you are, the less introverted you will be, and the more introverted you are, the less extroverted you will be.

Even extroverts are different. No two extroverts are the same. Some people are more extroverted than others. In fact, there are people who think they are extroverts whereas they are actually introverts, and there are those who think they are introverted, only to find that they are in fact extroverts. Some extroverts can spend more time alone than others, but others cannot be alone for long. One of the common things about extroverts is that where there are social occasions, you will most probably find an extrovert mingling with almost every person that comes across. They like not only to be in a social gathering; but in those gatherings they also want themselves in the cliques where most people are. They take delight in meeting new people and making new friends wherever they go. An extrovert would very seldom leave a party without a few new friends.

Not only do extroverts derive their energy from the group; they discharge their energy into the group as well. Not only do they draw life from the group; they are in fact the life of the group. They have the natural ability to light up the environment wherever they go. Extroverts are very expressive of themselves; thus it is not difficult to get to know them. They most often portray positive attitude when they are with people, and this makes them likeable. However, what they display publicly is not always who they really are privately. Their main concern is to ensure that they always make good impressions; thus they may display a smiling face to hide the pain in their hearts. How people feel about them tends to be more important to them than how they feel about themselves. As a matter of fact, how they feel about themselves tends to be influenced largely by how others feel about them. However, extroverts with healthy self-esteem do not base their feelings about themselves on how others feel about them.

Introverts on the other hand are more into themselves than to crowds. They draw their energies from being alone. The fewer the people, the merrier they are. They often appear like shy people, but this may not always be the case. There are extroverts who are shy and introverts who are not. Yes, shy people tend to withdraw from people; but being shy is not the only reason why people withdraw from crowds. People may withdraw from others simply because they want peace of mind. Extroverts may derive their peace of mind from among other people; but introverts often draw theirs from being alone. Introverts, though, are generally shyer than extroverts. While extroverts draw energy from crowds, being in the crowds for introverts can take too much energy away from them.

Introverts are not as likeable as extrovert because they are not as expressive of themselves as extroverts are. They are often misjudged as hateful or full of pride or selfish. But that is not always the case. What you portray is not always who you are. That introverts are reserved people does not mean they dislike people. They just want their own space, and there's nothing wrong with that. There are hateful extroverts who pretend to be loving, and there are loving introverts who appear like they are hateful. As a matter of fact, introverts tend to be more intimate than extroverts. Generally, an extrovert establishes many but more superficial friendships, but the introvert establishes few but more intimate ones. Therefore, it takes more than just an external observation to understand the true character of people despite what they display.

Introverts can also be found in social gatherings, but their staying power therein is not as much as the extroverts'. They may enjoy themselves tremendously at the beginning, but before long they want to go home. If they are to stay longer, they would find a quiet spot to be alone or look for a person or two to interact with. They are most probably found in the smallest cliques in the gatherings.

They are most likely to be the first ones to leave the gathering as soon as they spot the opportunity. In contrast, extroverts are most probably the last ones to leave. They wait until everybody else is gone before they make their way home.

Generally, introverts attract extroverts, and extroverts attract introverts. In instances where introvert attracts another introvert or extrovert attracts another extrovert, you would most probably find that their levels differ. One is often more introverted or extroverted than the other in a relationship. Have you ever observed a marital relationship wherein one partner is more talkative whereas the other is quieter? Most probably you have, and this happens most often. You may even have overheard people marvelling at the tendency of the 'righteous' people to marry 'evil' ones. This is because extroverts, who are often perceive as the 'righteous' ones, tend to be attracted to introverts, who are often regarded as the 'evil' ones.

Remember, opposites attract. But much as opposite may attract you to each other, they do not keep you attracted to each other. As a matter of fact, your main source of attraction before marriage may become your main source of repulsion in marriage. A quiet person may be attracted to a talkative one because the talkative will be his mouthpiece to the external world. The talkative one may also be attracted to the quiet one because she gets to do all the talking. A couple of months after marriage, the quiet one may start to get irritated by the one who cannot shut her mouth and leave him in peace not even for a second. On the other hand, the talkative one may be frustrated by this 'robot' who seems uninterested in anything she says. However, if these differences are managed properly, they can serve to their advantage.

The quiet one should not judge the talkative one; neither should the talkative one condemn the quiet one. They should rather use their differences to complement each other. One talks more but listens less, and the other listens more but talks less. But these two traits are essential for proper communication. If these two partners can fuse these traits together, they will become one flesh that can talk and listen very well. Then *both* of them will be able to communicate more effectively than *each* of them. Alike you will achieve a little, but different you will achieve so much more. Otherwise, if both of you are talkative, just imagine how chaotic the relationship would be. All may want to talk, but none may want to listen. Or else, imagine how your relationship would be if both of you are quiet all or most of the time. I would rather not imagine what this would put your children through. Instead of fighting over how different you are, rather join your differences together and use them to take your relationship to greater heights.

Trusting v/s Sceptical

Some people are naturally trusting, and others are more sceptical. Trusting people do not find it difficult open their hearts to others. They find it easy to take people at their word. They often continue to trust even after they have been disappointed. Their trust is based more on their own ability to handle disappointments than on whether other people will be faithful or not. This attitude makes them highly tolerant of pain or disappointment. They seldom distrust a person based on the unfaithfulness of the other. They tend treat each case according to its merit. Their strong sense of resilience makes it easy for them to take risks. They find it easy to believe that people will do what they said they will do, and this often makes them reluctant to monitor if people are really doing what they promised to do.

Trusting people are not afraid to leave their gates open when they go to town because they trust that no one will break into their house. They most often give people a benefit of a doubt because they believe that every person has the potential to be faithful. They are the kind of people who would leave valuable things lying around, seldom anticipating that they might get stolen. They walk around with purses in their hands, tread where others dare not go, and confront the things that others are afraid to deal with. Their trust happens to minimize their fears. They always find reasons to trust and dismiss every thought of doubt or mistrust. They have a tendency to trust more and doubt less.

Such people are most likely to be preyed upon and taken advantage of. Unfortunately for them, their trusting attitude does not make the world around them faithful. In this world it is never safe to trust too much because you could suffer too much loss. It might be helpful to always *test* before you *trust.* But even the tested cannot always be trusted. It is good to trust, but sometimes trusting too much is a risk not worth taking; especially in situations where you have everything to lose and nothing to gain. You can't easily trust the person who is reputable for lying and cheating; this could also be the risk not worth taking, and it happens to be the weakness of many trusting people.

On the other hand we have these sceptical ones. Trusting for them is never easy. They continue to doubt even when they have every reason to trust. Before they leave the house they make sure that they have locked every door a shut the gate as well. Even after they locked, they double check to see if they have locked properly. Then they would ask the neighbours to keep watch over the house while they are away. But they won't leave them with the keys. While they are away, they would frequently make a call to the neighbours to check if everything is still okay in the house. If they can, they would stop whatever they are doing in town for a while to go and check the house for themselves. I have no doubt in my mind that these are the chief users of phrases like "Better safe than sorry."

Sceptics would never leave their valuables lying around regardless of how safe the surroundings appear to be. Should they trust you enough to carry out any project for them, they will be forever on your case to monitor if you are doing what you are supposed to do the way you are supposed to do it. If they leave you with their children, they would probably call you after every minute to check if their children are still safe. They usually have low tolerance for disappointment; so, they would not take chances. They happen to be suspicious about almost everything. They generally operate on a rule: *Guilty until proven innocent.* But even if you are proven innocent, they would still find it difficult to trust you.

To sceptics, *prevention is better than cure.* It is better for them to suspect now than regret later. Because of this attitude, they tend to scare great contracts away because people often get irritated of being perpetually checked on like criminals in jail. You make a promise to them today, and by sunset they have already called you several times trying to find out why you have not fulfilled your promise yet. They follow up on almost everything on short intervals. Many people get annoyed by this and start ignoring their calls. And this only makes them more suspicious. They would even go so far as to call from different phones or call the police before they even know what is going on. This is how they take things out of hand and scare good deals away.

Different as they are, sceptics and trusting people are also likely to attract each other. Doubting too much is as much a weakness as trusting too much is. But they can also be strengths if they are not exaggerated or blown out of proportion. We normally get attracted to people when we perceive in them something that could complement us; that is, something they have that we don't. So, the sceptic may be attracted to the trusting person because of the trusting person's ability to trust people enough to secure the best deals with them; and a person who trusts too much may be attracted to the sceptic because of the sceptic's tendency to not be preyed upon or taken advantage of. A marital relationship between a sceptic and a trusting person can help them bring balance between trust and doubt.

Much as these differences can be their main source of attraction, they can also be their main source of frustration when they are married. A trusting wife may infuriate her sceptical husband by leaving the gate unlocked. At the same time the sceptical husband could frustrate his trusting wife by 'always' throwing tantrums at her because of his 'insecurities'. The sceptical husband may ask "what if they break in and steal?" and his trusting wife may reply "what if they don't? After all, they didn't!" The husband may perceive his wife as careless, and the wife may conclude that her husband is timid. But judging each other will not solve their problem. What will help them is if they can first acknowledge their differences, then join them together so that they can celebrate each other's strengths and complement each other's weaknesses.

Liberal v/s Conservative

Attraction can also take place between liberal people and conservative ones. Liberal people are usually open-minded and flexible. They find it easier to adapt to change. They are the type of people who would 'go with the flow' and venture into new experiences. They are more interested in what will be than what used to be. Generally, liberal people are willing to understand other people's opinions, beliefs and behaviours, even if they differ from their own. They are of the opinion that people should be able to choose how they behave. They are less judgmental in their approach to people around them because they seldom judge what *is* based on what *was*.

Liberal people are usually free-spirited. They are extremely independent from other people's opinion about them, and they often do what they want rather than what other people do or think should be done. Instead of following the crowds, they would find their own way. They can be very controversial because of their tendency to think, speak or behave contrary to popular belief. Doing things 'by the book' is just not for them. They can break the rules and not feel guilty because of their independent thinking from the general belief system of their society. They never settle for mediocrity; they challenge the status quo and seek better ways of doing things so that they can attain excellence.

Liberal people usually suffer rejection in their societies because they do not conform to their generally accepted rules. They are usually perceived as 'perverts' who disregard their culture. This seems not to bother them that much. They continue to hold on to their beliefs despite the rejection they may endure from their community members. They would rather side with the minority for what they believe in than go with the crowds for what they do not understand. They would rather be rejected for who they are than be respected for who they pretend to be.

Conservative people are the direct opposite of liberal ones. They are conformists who think, speak and behave like the rest of their community members. They hold no belief of their own. In whatever they do, they make sure to follow every rule that makes them acceptable in the society. They are opposed to sudden social changes and prefer to do things the way they have always been done. They would do anything in their power to preserve their culture and protect their social traditions. What *used to be* is more important to them than what *could be*. They would rather hold on to the past they know than venture into the future they are not certain of.

Conservative people love to do things 'by the book'. Their conformity to their social beliefs makes them the darlings of their societies. They love what their communities love and detest what they detest. They usually give no other reason for doing what they are doing except that "it has always been done this way". This can choke their creativity and make them average achievers because they take comfort in maintaining the status quo. They find it safer to follow the crowds than to stand out and risk the possibility of rejection.

Liberal people are great inventors with poor reputation; and conservative ones have good reputation but can hardly achieve above average. This can be their source of attraction to each other because their differences are complementary to each of them. One has what the other needs. The fusion of these two personalities can result into one socially acceptable entity with high levels of achievement. But this can also be the main source of conflict between the two. A liberal wife may request her conservative husband to help her wash the dishes as she prepares food; but the conservative husband is of the opinion that the kitchen is a woman's place. He could rather go outside and wash the car than do dishes. He may interpret his wife's request as an act of disrespect to him. But the wife may find nothing wrong about her husband helping her out with the dishes. This could lead to the husband judging her wife to be disrespectful and the wife perceiving him to be lazy.

The wife may try to introduce new things in the relationship; but the husband may insist on holding on to what he has learnt from his society. What the husband regards as 'safe', the wife can perceive as 'tedious'. Eventually they begin to speculate that the 'wicked' is married to a 'bore'; and this becomes an ongoing battle between *rigidity* and *flexibility*. Pointing fingers is not what these two need; what they need is the art of combining their differences and making them work for them and not against them. They need to focus less on the things that push them apart and more on the ones that bring them closer together. The conservative should allow the liberal to add more elasticity to his rigidity, and the liberal should allow the conservative to add more firmness to her flexibility.

Emotional v/s Rational

Emotional people are inclined to decide more with their heart than with their head. They usually follow their feeling more than their reason. They settle more for what feels right, seldom considering the logic behind it. They would rather spend their money now out of compassion to feed the hungry than invest it for future use. They often do things 'for the love of it' and not so much for the outcome thereof. In fact, the outcome of whatever they do is the impact it will have on their emotions. If it will make them feel better, then it's worth doing. Such people enjoy the journey more than the destination. The heart-warming views of nature and the tranquillity it brings into their soul make every trip worthwhile no matter where the destination may be.

While it is good to follow your heart, some things require more logic than feeling. Emotional people need to apply their minds as well so that they may be able to anticipate the possible outcomes of their decisions. Feelings cannot be trusted; they fluctuate from time to time. You may feel excited one moment and miserable the next moment; but the decision you took when you were excited remains the same even when you feel sad. Therefore, making decisions based on how you feel can be misleading. People whose behaviour is influenced more by feelings than reason are usually unstable. They are most likely to retreat from their own decisions from time to time.

On the other hand, rational people follow their head more than their heart. Their decisions are based more on reason than feeling. They would invest money for future use rather than to use it now to gratify their cravings. Such people usually focus more on the destination than the pleasures or pressures they may experience throughout the journey. They look beyond how they feel and see what they want to achieve. They do things not for what they feel, but for what they're worth. Their general behaviour is usually more stable because they most often stick to their decisions. But they are not as compassionate as emotional people because compassion comes from the heart; and they decide from the head.

Emotional people are usually attracted to rational ones because of their firmness and stability; and rational people are often attracted to emotional ones for their sensitivity and compassion. But if these two can focus on each other's weaknesses, they may judge their marriage as a combination the 'insensitive' and the 'unreliable'. For their marriage to grow and be successful, they need to focus more on each other's strengths than weaknesses. The fusion of these two entities can result into one flesh possessing both sensitivity and stability. The mixture of the feeling and reason will help the couple to strike balance between firmness and compassion. Instead of judging each other for your *weaknesses,* rather appreciate each other for your *strengths.*

5.4 Diverse Abilities

We were all born with different talents and abilities. None is born without these. All of us are equally gifted to fulfil our purpose on earth. Each gift is linked to a particular purpose, and each person has a different purpose. Therefore, we are differently gifted. That I can do what you cannot do does not mean I am better than or superior to you because you can also do something else that I cannot do. No one can do everything better than everybody else. We are different but equally important; no one is better than the other.

I have very often observed chaotic tendencies in the workplaces where one employee performs better than the other; and the other feels discouraged as the better performer enjoys his superiority. The general belief is that the better performing employee is better than the one who performs less. But the truth is that performing better does not necessarily mean you are better or superior; it simply means that you are gifted in that area, and the other person is gifted in something else. There is definitely something that person can do better than you. That is why competition is not always healthy; especially if you are gifted differently. The best marathon runner in the world may be the worst boxer in town.

You can only be the best in your area of gifting. The cheetah is known as the fastest mammal on earth; but even so, it can never win a swimming contest against a dolphin. Neither can a dolphin win a race against the cheetah on land. In fact, the cheetah cannot make it alive to the end of the race in water; neither can a dolphin make it to the finish line on land. That a cheetah runs faster where the dolphin cannot even move does not make it a superior being to dolphin. Similarly, the dolphin's ability to swim where the cheetah drowns does not make it a better animal than a cheetah. Each of them is differently gifted, and they are both the best in their areas of gifting.

Gifts and talents are territorial. You can't be the best at everything. You could rather be the best at one and the worst at the other. The best basket ball player in the world could be the worst golfer in town. That is why it is best to identify your gifts and operate in them. The rest you can leave to people who are better at them than you. 'Jack of all trades' is the master of none. Rather find that one thing and master it. Very often you will meet people who chose certain careers based on their observation of other people's success in those fields. That does not necessarily mean you would also succeed in that career. If a person succeeds in a singing career, you can't succeed in the same career if you can't sing. Maybe you could be successful as a medical doctor instead. Where others swim with ease, you can sink if you don't possess the abilities they have.

People are easily attracted to people who possess abilities that are different from theirs. Most men cannot cook and wash the dishes and sweep the floor and bath the kids at the same time; but most women can. This special ability in women is one of men's greatest forces of attraction to them. On the other hand, most women cannot do physically challenging jobs like lifting heavy objects or plumbing; but most men can. This can also be one of women's great forces of attraction to men. This is how beauty and the beast fell in love. The beast protected beauty, and beauty decorated the beast. Couples usually experience marital problems when they force each other to do what they cannot do. If the wife expects her husband to cook like her or the husband expects his wife to tighten the screws like him, their marriage could be chaotic; especially if the husband cannot cook and the wife cannot tighten the screws.

Instead of complaining that her husband cannot cook, the wife should rather celebrate that he can fix the leaking pipes. The husband should also learn to rejoice that his wife can sweep the floor rather than grieving over her inability the change the electric bulb. There is no need to argue about who is better than who. The truth is: no one is better than the other. You are differently gifted but equally important in this relationship. None can make it without the other. As a wife you need to understand that whatever your husband has and you do not have, you have it in him. Same applies to you as a husband. You need to develop appreciation for your wife for being able to do the things you cannot do because whatever she can do and you cannot do, you can do it because she can. *Both* of you are better than *each* of you because in your differences you complement each other, and the two of you can achieve better results in your marriage.

Power Struggles

The differences between husbands and wives often lead to power struggles and unnecessary competitions within marriages. Your differences were designed to make you complementary to each other, not competitive against each other. They do not make one better than the other; instead, they make the two better together as one. Judging each other does nothing good for your marriage; what can help it grow is if you stop judging each other and starting celebrating each other. Do not lose sight to the value your partner adds to your marriage. You need your partner just as much as your partner needs you. The dispute of who is better than who is highly detrimental to your marriage. Marital relationship is not about power and competition; it is about love and commitment.

Instead of perceiving your partner as better than you, rather see him or her as the better part of you. If you are right handed, your right hand is not stronger than you; it is the stronger side of you. Similarly, if your husband can do some things better than you, it does not mean he is better than you; it simply means he is the better part of you in those areas. Remember, both of you are no longer two but one. The eye is not better than the ear; they are different organs performing different but equally significant functions. Neither are you better than your partner; you are just two different organs of one body who are gifted differently to contribute equally to one purpose – a successful marriage.

Differences are Necessary for Marriage

Identical pieces of the puzzle cannot fit together; only different ones can. Their difference is the only quality that allows for them to fit together. The picture can never be complete if the pieces cannot fit together; neither can marriage be successful or complete if couples cannot put their differences not aside, but together. Differences put aside are not as effective in marriage as differences put together. Putting difference aside only postpones catastrophe in marriage; but putting them together exterminates it.

In marriage, differences should not work against you; they should work for you. It is therefore advisable to stop judging each other over your differences and starting harnessing those differences towards building your marriage. Allow yourselves to fuse together until you are one flesh and endure whatever pain it entails in the process; then you will see your marriage grow as you enjoy the benefits of unity in variety and power in diversity.

6

"Forsaking All Others" – Get Your Priorities Right

Humans are multi-dimensional beings. They are physical, social, psychological, emotional, intellectual and spiritual in nature. These dimensions have a variety of demands; and such demands require much of our time. The physical demands require one to set aside time to eat, exercise, bath, sleep, go for medical check-ups, adhere to the doctor's prescription, etc. The social demands require that we take time to love, communicate, pay a visit to a friend, make phone calls to loved ones, attend social gatherings, spend time with family, etc. Intellectual demands require that you give yourself time to read, reason, learn, listen, etc. Spiritual demands require that you take time to pray, go to church and reflect on your life – it's meaning and purpose.

All these demands cannot be met all at once because human beings are limited entities. However, it is highly essential to strike a balance in life by ensuring that all the demands receive some kind of attention. Time should be allocated for each of the demands in order of significance. This necessitates the essential skill of prioritization. To prioritize simply means to put responsibilities in order of importance so that you can deal with the most important first. Therefore, for you to prioritize all life's demands, you need to clearly define which one is the most important, and which one is the least. Starting with the least important tasks can hinder you from fulfilling the most important ones; but prioritization helps you to focus most of your attention on what matters the most.

For married people, the significance of prioritization cannot be adequately emphasised. Couples usually experience serious marital problems because of failure to set their priorities right. They focus more on the least important and less on the most important. They put too many things before their marriages. The priorities of married people are different from those of unmarried ones. Therefore, if you are married and insist on setting your priorities like unmarried people do, you are practically inflicting fatal wounds into your marriage. To a large degree, priorities that work for single people work against married people. For this reason, when you get married, your priorities must change; and if they don't, your marriage will suffer.

When you set your priorities as a married person, it is very important that you do so according to guidelines from the Bible. I want to take this time to share with you the *top five* godly priorities that should always be on your list as a married person in order of significance. The number one on your priority list should be *God*. First and foremost, God is the One who created you (See Genesis 1:26-28); and He is the One who gave you every good and perfect thing you have today (See James 1:17). This includes your spouse. God is the One would joined you together in matrimony (See Matthew 19:4-5), and He is the only One who can keep you together. God is your *Giver*, and your spouse is your *gift*. What caused Adam to fall was that he focused more on the *gift* than the *Giver* (See Genesis 3). God was the Giver, and Eve was the gift. Adam's *gift* offered him what his *Giver* had forbidden for him to eat, but he rejected the Giver's order and settled for the gift's offer.

God is the One who began the good work in your marriage, and he is the only One who can carry it to completion (See Philippians 1:6). It is Him who sustains all things by the word of His power (See Hebrews 1:3). *He is before all things, and in Him all things consist* (Colossians 1:17). Your marriage is one of *all things* that God is holding together. Without Him you do not have what it takes to hold your marriage together. Therefore, if you forsake the Giver and embrace the gift, you stand a good chance of losing both of them. God is not only the Source, He is also the Sustainer. So, whatever He began in you, let Him sustain it until He completes it.

"If anyone comes to Me and does not hate his father and mother, wife and children, brothers and sisters, yes, and his own life also, he cannot be My disciple" (Luke 14:26). In this portion of Scripture, Jesus is teaching us that we should put nothing before Him; not even our own lives (including our spouses). Well, you may say: "My spouse is my life, and we are one flesh." But Jesus emphasises His

point more clearly by saying *"even his own life"*. Nothing is more important than God; not even your spouse. In fact, your spouse is God's creation; therefore, make sure that for all the days of your life you honour the *Creator* more than His *creation* by putting God first in your marriage. If you stick to your Giver, He will give you wisdom to handle your gift; but if you forsake Him and stick to the gift, you will not be able to sustain it. God gave it to you, and He will keep it for you if you put Him at the top of your priority list.

Marriage does not begin with your love for your spouse or your spouse's love for you; it begins with your love for God and His love for you, and then it overflows to your spouse. The depth of your love for your spouse depends on the depth of your love for God. You can't understand how much you should love your partner if you don't understand how much God loves you. It is in Him that we draw the very love that we share with our partners. As we respond to God's love, we learn to love others. Therefore, God's love for us and our love for Him are the foundation of our love for our partners.

Second to God on your priority list should be *your marriage*. Apart from your relationship with God, nothing should be more important to you than your relationship with your spouse. Remember, your spouse is your flesh, your life. Both of you are one. You are fused together. You are inseparable. You hold the keys to each other's hearts, and you fulfil each other's deepest needs. You both share so much more than you share with anybody else. To neglect such relationship is to leave the door open for temptations to come in. Satan usually takes advantage of people who leave their marital relationships unattended and then frustrates their lives through them. As a married person, you have a responsibility to shut him out of your marriage by putting your spouse at the top of your priority list.

Many marriages suffer a great deal of harm because of couples who neglect their marriages and pursue less important things. The husband would rather be at the soccer match with his friends than at home with his wife, and the wife would rather spend more time taking care of the house than nurturing her marital relationship. Now more than ever, we observe highly successful actors, politicians, business people, sport stars, academics, entertainers and ministers failing at a high rate in their marriages; mainly because they put their spouses at the bottom of their priority lists. They spend most of their time building their fortune and none of their time working on their marriages. Then they end up conquering the world at the expense of their marriages.

God is serious about marriage. No human relationship is more honourable to Him than this. He takes deep interest in the husband and his wife finding complete pleasure in each other. Nothing reminds Him more about His relationship with His people than a relationship between a husband and his wife. To Him, nothing is more important than this. If God our Creator honours marriage this way, so should we as His creation. To dishonour your marriage is to dishonour the God who instituted it; but if we honour our marriages, we honour Him.

What should be third on your priority list should be *your children.* Your children are your main responsibility. They are here because of you; and they totally rely on you for their survival, protection, growth and development. They are a perpetuation of your name; the fruit of your seed, and they represent you in the next generation. They are a gift to you from above. No one can take better care of them than you. They require most of your attention; and they need you not only as their provider and protector, but as their role model as well. It is therefore essential that you invest in them not only your finances, but your time as well.

If anyone does not provide for his own, and especially for those of his household, he has denied faith and is worse than an unbeliever (1Timothy 5:8). Ungodly parents neglect their children and pursue less important things. Some of those parents are nation-builders; they are respected by the world, but resented by their children, their own flesh and blood. They make the world prosper while their own children continue to suffer. They are everybody's friends but their children's enemies. Their goal is to reach the top and be the best; but they seldom stop to tell their children how much they love them. They are usually too busy for their children. They seldom show up at their children's important activities. Even if the children fall ill, they would leave them with the other parent and pursue their dreams as if nothing wrong happened. But godly parents take deep interest in their children and always have their best interest at heart. They take time to play with them, talk with them, learn their personalities and teach them life skills.

Much as it is important to always be there for your children, you should guard against the mistake of putting them above your spouse. Remember, your marriage is their family. Married couples should not neglect each other because of their children. They should raise their children together, but they should not forget to be lovers. Children were not there when you met; neither were they the reason why you married each other. They are the product of your union; not the source of your disconnection. You did not unite because they were born, but they were born because you united. In other words, your relationship came before them, and it should not suffer because of them. Remember, your children will not stay with you forever; they will grow up and leave you to start their own families, but you will still be married by then. Do not allow their presence to make you absent from your partner.

Your relationship with your children does not substitute you relationship with your spouse; it builds on it; much as your relationship with your spouse does not substitute your relationship with God. These relationships are hierarchically arranged; you can't have a good relationship with your children if you don't have one with your partner, and you can't have a good relationship with your partner if you don't have one with God. Your relationship with God empowers you to have a good relationship with your partner, and your relationship with your partner enables you to have a good relationship with your children. This order of priority in terms of relationships is most fundamental to your general well-being as an individual.

One of the best gifts a mother can give to her children is to take care of their father, and one of the greatest gifts a father can give to his children is to love their mother. But if you neglect each other because of the children, you are depriving them the joy of seeing their parents happy together; which is every child's dream concerning their parents. If it ever happens that your children find out that you are neglecting each other because of them, they may spend their lives feeling guilty for 'causing separation' between their parents. Whether couples love each other or hate each other, the ones who get affected the most are children. When you fight against each other, they get more upset; and when you are at peace with each other, they get happier. Whatever you do to each other as a couple affects them. Therefore, to neglect each other as a couple, even for the sake of the children, makes them suffer more. So, as part of taking care of the children, focus more on each other.

The fourth on your priority list can be *your work or business*. This is how you make a living for yourself and your family. *If anyone will not work, neither shall he eat* (2 Thessalonians 3:10). Your work or business is you source of income; and it is God who gave it to you. Without work, you get no money, and without money, you cannot take care of your family. Yet it is amazing how people neglect their jobs and pursue things of lesser value. They give too many excuses for not being at work, and they fail to honour their business appointments. They show no appreciation for their work, and despite them getting regular income from their jobs, all they do is complain about everything – the demanding boss, the heavy workload, the unfavourable workplace conditions, the rude colleagues, etc. They fail to realize how blessed they are to be employed while many people are wandering jobless in the streets.

Some people believe that *church* should be placed above work or business on the believers' priority list. But honestly, I find it disgraceful to the Kingdom of God that Christians abscond from their workplaces in the name of the Lord to be at the church activities. There is nothing honourable about dishonouring your job. I believe that the ministry of the Christian is needed more in the workplace than in the worship house. You can't win people in the workplace over to the worship house if you keep on leaving them with the burden of your work while you are away to 'worship'. True worship is to bring glory to God by excelling in our workplaces. People are more likely to believe in your God when they see you excelling at work than when they see you 'sacrificing' your job to be at the church service.

Remember, your time at work is being paid for. Therefore, if you use your work time for church fellowship, you are stealing from your employer, and you are serving your God with stolen time. But God is not pleased with the person who dishonours their employer. It is very disturbing to see Christians brag about their God at their workplaces, yet when reports are required, they have nothing to produce. You don't show your love for God by praying when you should be working; you show it by obeying His Word, and His Word says: *Bondservants, be obedient to those who are your masters according to the flesh, with fear and trembling, in sincerity of heart, as to Christ* (Ephesians 6:5). You can't say you obey God when you disobey your master in the flesh, whom God commanded you to obey as to Christ. The modern term for *master* is *employer*. Therefore, you show love for Christ by your attitude towards your employer.

The Great Commission (See Mark 16:15-18 and Matthew 28:18-20) does not send us into the church, it sends us into the world. The world we are sent to is not in the church buildings, it is in the streets and in the marketplaces; it is also in our workplaces. *You are the light of the world. A city that is set on the hill cannot be hidden. Nor do they light a lamp and put it under a basket, but on a lampstand, and it gives light to all who are in the house. Let your light so shine before men, that they may see your good works and glorify your father in heaven* (Matthew 5:4-16). As believers, we are sent into the world to give them light. In other words, it is the world that is in darkness; not the church. Our light makes no difference in the church because the church is already in light. For our light to make a difference, we need to shine it in our workplaces by doing our jobs with diligence and excellence; then our colleagues will see our good works and glorify our God.

If you can just take time to study the lives of people who made significant history in the Bible, you will notice that they brought glory to God by excelling in their workplaces. When Jacob was working for his uncle Laban, he excelled so much that his uncle had to beg him to stay, requesting him to determine his own wages. It was in Jacob's work that Laban saw that the Lord blessed him for Jacob's sake (See Genesis 30). Joseph excelled in executing his duties as a slave in Egypt, then as a prisoner, and he ultimately became the governor of Egypt (See Genesis 39-41). Even as the governor of Egypt he continued to be a good steward of God by excelling in his work. Daniel also excelled more than all officials in the government of Babylon (See the Book of Daniel in the Bible); and the king himself had to declare as a decree that no one in Babylon must worship any other god except the God of Daniel. You can't win your employer over to Christ by being at church when you should be at work.

As a Christian, the fifth on your top five priority list should be *your local church*. Your local church is your spiritual home. It is where you get all the teachings, encouragement and edification. It is the place where your spiritual gifts are identified, nurtured and perfected so that you may be better equipped to fulfil your purpose in life. In your local church you can get all the spiritual support you need to grow in your knowledge of God.

And they continued steadfastly in the apostles' doctrine and fellowship, in the breaking of bread, and in prayers (Acts 2:42). It is not enough to be a Christian; you need to spend your time with people who will nourish you spiritually. *Let the word of the Lord dwell in you richly in all wisdom, teaching and admonishing one another in psalms and hymns and spiritual songs, singing with grace in your hearts to the Lord* (Colossians 3:16). These can only happen in the fellowship of believers. You can't make it on your own as a Christian; you need other Christians to survive and grow spiritually. It is therefore highly essential that you take time to go to church, and to contribute towards the growth and development of your local church.

And let us consider one another in order to stir up love and good works, not forsaking the assembly of ourselves together, as is the manner of some, but exhorting one another, and so much the more as you see the Day approaching (Hebrew 10:24-25). In these last days Christians no longer treat church as a necessity; they take it as a hobby, something they do when they have nothing else to do. They substitute their local churches with television programmes. But television programmes cannot replace the warmth that you can only get in fellowship with the saints. It is good to watch Christian television programmes, but it is not good to make them your spiritual home. The preacher on the screen cannot visit you at your house even when you need him the most; but the pastor in your local church can take time to come over to your house and offer you prayer and words of encouragement. He can even be there to listen to you when you need someone to talk to.

These should be your top five priorities; the rest can come after them. Failure to prioritize can lead to failure in your marriage. The thing that you allocate most of your time to is the one that will most probably succeed the most. If you spend most of your time on the least important, you will make the least important succeed at the expense of the most important. The skill of prioritization is like building a house. You don't start with the roof or the furniture; you start with the foundation, then the walls, the roof, plumbing, painting and furniture. In the same way, if you want to build a successful marriage, let God be the foundation; then your marriage, your children, your work or business, your church, and then you can focus on other commitments such as social groups, recreation and entertainment. Proper prioritization produces power to prosper. When you prioritize your marriage, you are actually making a sure investment in its success.

7

"For Better or Worse" – Stages of Marriage

Marriage was established by God, and everything the He established grows. Growth involves various stages, and it is mainly characterised by perpetual transformation. This process is usually referred to as *metamorphosis* – the process in which an organism changes completely into something different as it progresses through developmental stages. Let us take a butterfly as an example. The butterfly's life begins not as a butterfly, but as an *egg*; which hatches into a *caterpillar*. After some time the caterpillar turns into a *cocoon*. While it is in the cocoon, it transforms into a *butterfly*.

Where there is life, there is growth; and where there is no growth, there is no life. In other words, when we stop growing, we start dying. Marriage is a living organism; and therefore, it is a progressive relationship. It develops through the stages from time to time, and each stage has unique characteristics. Some stages are warm and exciting, and others are boring and cold; but what is important is that couples should be aware of such stages and find ways to cope and stick together throughout the processes. If couples fail to understand the normality of such stages, their marriage may not survive. In this part of the discussion I will share information on the seven stages of marriage. These stages are explained from various approaches by various experts; but I want to share with you the stages of marriage as outlined below.

Stage One: The Infatuation Stage

This stage is best known as the *Honeymoon Stage*. This stage is characterised mainly by romance and great passion between couples; and this can take six months or less to two years or more, depending on the uniqueness of marital relationships. The excitement of finally being together becomes their main obsession. This is where they leave the world behind them and focus exclusively on each other. The excitement within the infatuation stage is more like one a person experiences after buying a new automobile. After buying a new car, it becomes the main thing in your mind. It makes you want to spend most of your time on the road so that you can enjoy the drive. Even when you are asleep, your mind remains awake because you can hardly wait for the next day so that you can get your hands on your new-found love. A mere look at your new car makes you feel so good inside; it makes you feel that you are the 'man of great taste'.

When you drive your new car, you become extra careful; and you pay careful attention to anything that sounds or feels strange in it. You wash it twice a week, and you spend most of your time thinking about ways to enhance its elegance. Throughout this process you develop a strong attachment to it. This is what newlyweds experience in their marriages. During the first few months of their marriage, couples cannot take each other out of their minds; and likewise, they cannot keep their hands off each other. They spend most of their time together, and they enjoy each other's company. While they are asleep, they cuddle; thinking about the better days that lie ahead of them. This is the period in marriage where couples develop strong bonds with each other and build memories that will sustain them throughout the rest of the stages.

The infatuation stage is actually God's way of saying *"be fruitful and multiply..."* (Genesis 1:28). At this stage, lovemaking is not only frequent, but also ecstatic. This is where couples allocate plenty of time to explore each others' bodies; and in this they experience great pleasure. At this stage they are very polite to each other, and they are overly cautious in each other's presence; as if to make great first impressions not only to each other as a couple, but also to the outside world. Couples do not really know what to expect from each other at this stage, and they will naturally try to understand their roles as partners in marriage. While they're at it, they are always extra careful to keep their marriage stainless; and to prove to the world that true love in marriage is possible. This is very important in marriage because it creates a bond that couples need in order to navigate successfully throughout the rest of the stages.

Stage Two: The 'Rude Awakening' Stage

As time goes by you get used to your car, and it no longer excites you like it used to. It's getting older and slower; and the pleasure you used to find in it begins to subside. It is only then that you realized that this car is actually more of a liability to you than it is an asset. Suddenly the money you lose every month on fuel, instalments and insurance becomes more important than the car you are spending it on. The pressure of maintaining it becomes more overwhelming than the pleasure of driving it. While you are still caught up in your frustration, you learn that the car is due for service, and the licence disc has expired. By this time you have already received a few traffic fines in your mailbox; and this means more money out of your coffers. As you calculate the costs, you conclude that travelling with a public transport is five times cheaper than using your car. You start regretting why you got yourself into this 'mess'; but you're already in too deep to pull out, and still, the convenience that this car has brought into your life is one thing you can no longer live without.

Same applies in marriage during the second stage, which I call the *'Rude Awakening' Stage*. At this stage, couples get used to each other; and the euphoria that kept them intensely attracted to each other begins to fade away. This stage marks the end of the 'honeymoon'. This is where reality strikes. Couples are now more comfortable and less careful around each other. This is where they realize that the ones they married are not really the 'angels' they appeared to be. The strengths they used to see in their partners are now clouded by the weaknesses that are beginning to surface. At this stage, the wife realizes that this man who appears neat on the street actually leaves a mess in the house; and now she always has to clean up after him. Meanwhile, the husband finds it hard to believe how such a sweet melodious voice of his wife can make such 'toxic' utterances.

This is where couples wonder "What have I gotten myself into?" At this stage they begin to have doubts about their marriage, but they are already in too deep to pull out. After all, they can't just let go of the wonderful times they used to have together; because who knows, things might get back to the way they used to be. Moreover, the convenience this marriage has brought into their lives has become nothing to live without. They are drifted apart by their differences, but they are kept together by the bond they developed in the infatuation stage. Even though they may experience the feelings of regret, they still cannot deny their love for each other. This stage is a rude introduction of reality. It reveals the couple's imperfections and awakens them to the significance of tolerance in their marital relationship. This is where couples either try to change each other or learn to accept each other just the way they are.

This stage is characterized by acute episodes of conflict; which are often followed by passionate love experiences. This often produces mixed feelings whereby couples frequently 'fall in and out of love' with each other. This is one of the difficult stages in marriage, and unfortunately some marriages do not survive through it. This stage, like all other stages, can be handled better if couples can first accept it as a normal process which is experienced in all marriages. Couples who gave up at this stage probably thought it is abnormal to have such experiences. They gave up their marriage to search for the 'match-made-in-heaven'; and this search will never end because unless they learn to acknowledge this stage as normal, none of their marriages will make it through it. Even if God Himself were to bring your spouse to you on a silver platter, you would still go through this stage in your marriage. Successful marriage is not always blissful; but it can always be peaceful, and such peace begins with the acceptance of this stage as a normal and inevitable part of marriage.

Stage Three: The Uprising Stage

During the *Uprising Stage*, both partners are starting to miss their premarital life. The wife is starting to miss her friends and family; and at the same time, the husband is beginning to miss his buddies and leisure activities. This is where they begin to feel like their marriage is holding them back or wasting their time. They begin to put the interests of their marriage second to their individual interests. At this stage the couple diverts their attention from each other and focus more on their personal dreams. This involves intense competitions and power struggles between the couple; and their main obsession is for one to appear to be better than the other. This stage also involves sharp disagreements and severe conflicts between the couple. Most of the activities at this stage are selfish; and most couples use an 'every man for himself' approach, forgetting that they have become one flesh.

This is the most difficult stage for married couples to weather, but it is also necessary for healthy marital growth. It is the fusion process that heats the couple until they melt so that when joined together, they may become one permanently. This is where couples air their differences and point fingers. The great impressions they used to make to each other are no longer important to them. This is where they begin to show their 'true colours'. By this time, the love they used to share during their infatuation stage is gradually fading out of their memories. This is where most marriages fail. People give up on each other and blame each other for their separation. Couples can learn to navigate through this stage by learning to surface their conflicts and finding healthy ways to address them. They should also agree on peaceful ways to address their disagreements. This is the most relevant time to keep the words of Jesus in mind when He said: *"...the love of many will grow cold. But he who endures to the end shall be saved."* (Matthew 24:12-13).

Stage Four: The Collaboration Stage

During the *Collaboration Stage*, what was once a love affair becomes a business affiliation. The children must be raised, and the bills must be paid. This is where the couple realizes that even though they 'no longer' feel for each other, they still need each other. They learn to put their differences aside and cooperate for the sake of their family. At this stage they begin to communicate more peacefully, but their communication is more task-oriented than love-based. They focus less on their relationship and more on their responsibilities. This is where many couples forget to be lovers and start experiencing feelings of loneliness. Even though they spend much time together, they still miss each other; but they cannot get through to each other at an emotional level. Their conversation is mostly about what needs to be done; and they seldom reflect their feelings for each other as a couple.

This stage, like all others, is normal, and every marriage that has survived past the first three stages experiences it. Yes, there is that time in marriage wherein couples feel like they have lost their spark; and yet they feel that they are getting along very well. This is the time when they feel that their need for each other is stronger than their love for each other. During this time, even the intimate acts such as lovemaking become more of a chore than it is a love experience. This is where some people start looking outside for relationships that would make up for the love experiences they are not getting at home; and as a result, things get worse in their marriages. Then they would consider divorce so that they enter into another marriage covenant and begin at stage one; then history keeps on repeating itself.

This stage, like all other stages, is temporary; but divorce is permanent, and so are the consequences of infidelity. I consider it very unwise to make permanent decisions based on temporary situations. The collaboration stage is not the time to look for love outside; it is the time to make deliberate efforts to celebrate your love for each other as you work together to achieve your common goals. As much as it is important to pay the bills and raise the children together, always remember that there is one thing that is more important than all these things, and that is, your marriage. So, as you work together to achieve your material goals, never forget to be lovers.

Stage Five: The Reconciliation or Settlement Stage

The children have grown, and the mortgage is almost paid up. The pressures of life have subsided; and interruptions are diminished. Careers are fully established; and much has been achieved through the couple's collaboration. The couple has now learnt to accept each other as they are, and also to deal with their differences more peacefully. This is the time to reconcile and settle down. During the reconciliation or settlement stage, couples find their way back to each other's hearts; and this time not as parents or business partners trying to run a family as an enterprise, but as friends and lovers. They learn to appreciate each other again as husband and wife. This is the stage where the marriage regains its romantic appetite, and the couple starts focusing more on mutual fulfilment. They spend more time together and rediscover the pleasure of being in each other's company.

The reconciliation stage is a comeback from a setback caused by all other stages. The couple has now become aware of their individual needs, and they have learnt healthy ways to communicate them to each other such that they help each other in fulfilling them. However, as much as this stage is natural, the extent to which the couple is happy therein is strongly dependent on how they handled the previous stages. If they engaged themselves in violent or adulterous behaviour during the previous stages, they may struggle to rebuild their trust and affection for each other; but if they maintained their loyalty and remained committed to each other throughout the previous stages, it may be easier for them to regain mutual trust and affection and enjoy the benefits of the settlement stage.

Stage Six: The Explosion Stage

Midlife has its own challenges. Midlife crisis involving andropause for the husband, menopause for the wife, chronic illnesses, death of parents, career frustrations, children leaving home, and many other experiences, often rub off on the marriage. This often leads to sudden outbursts and changes in behaviour as the couple tries to adjust to their aging selves. During this stage of marriage, couples feel more insecure because of diminished physical activity. Depression is one of the common experiences when one is experiencing midlife crisis, and depression can have a negative impact on marriage; especially if the couple leaves it unattended. The best way to handle this stage is that the couple should each try by all means to deal with the changes they experience and the challenges they pose. They should also try to give each other all the support they need to make it through.

Stage Seven: The Fulfilment Stage

The children are all grown up, and the mortgage is fully paid. The working days are over, and the couple has much time to spend together without worrying much about the future. They have known each other for a while, and now they not only know each very well; they have also learnt to adjust their behaviours to accommodate each other, and they have also learnt to accept each other just as they are. This is the fulfilment of their dream to grow old together, and they have a strong feeling a satisfaction for their achievements. They feel deep connection to each other, and they take pleasure in the simple things in life; like watching their grandchildren run around and play; or take pride in their children's achievements. They celebrate their lifetime successes together, and they regain their childhood passion for life; which they gladly enjoy together.

Summary

Marriage begins with the couple having strong infatuation for each other. This is usually called the Honeymoon Stage. It is during this stage that the couple establish a strong bond between them. The marriage then progresses to the Rude Awakening Stage, wherein the couple discover the things they never knew about each other. While they are still wondering in their hearts 'who is this that I married?" they progress to the Uprising Stage. This is the stage wherein the couple starts rebelling against each other and pursuing their selfish ambitions. After this stage the marriage progresses to the Collaboration Stage, wherein they learn to put their differences aside and work together to establish their family. This is not a romantic stage; it is rather is cooperative one. Then it develops into Reconciliation or Settlement Stage. This is where they experience emotional reunion after all the toils and conflicts. During this stage they shift their attention from what needs to be done and focus more on each other.

While the couple is enjoying the reconciliation, they then grow into the Explosion Stage. This is mainly characterized by the physical and psychological changes that occur as they age, the loss of parents to death, career frustrations, and all other problems that form part of midlife crisis. It is during this stage that they start feeling inadequate and insecure in their marriages. Then they progress into the Fulfilment Stage; where they start relating more closely to each other. They have reached the stage where they celebrate their lifetime achievement and enjoy their lives together till the end of time.

Most important to bear in mind concerning these stages is that they are natural; and just like human developmental stages, they are inevitable. But the good thing about these stages is that each one is temporary. Every couple will go through these stages one way or the other; even if they are in their second or third marriage. Some stages are wonderful, and others are awful; but all of them are necessary for marital growth. These stages will be extremely difficult to navigate if couples can just 'go with the flow'. Couples should learn to acknowledge the reality of these stages and find ways to cope as they progress through them. If you do not acknowledge its reality, you cannot handle its adversity; and the very thing that was meant to build you might end up breaking you. As you navigate through the stages of marriage, it would be very important that you learn to perceive them not as *problems*, but as *progress*; because they were not meant to make you drown, but to help you grow.

While the earth remains, seedtime and harvest, cold and heat, winter and summer, and day and night shall not cease (Genesis 8:22). These stages of marriages are as sure as the times and seasons; they will continue to exist for as long as there is marriage. We cannot change nor block the seasons; but we can adjust our practices so that we may cope throughout the seasons. For example, when it's winter, we cannot change the weather and make it hot; but we can put on warmer clothes so that we are not affected by the cold. We cannot stop the rain; but we can use umbrellas and rain suits or just stay indoors. Similarly, we cannot avoid nor block the different stages in our marriages; but we can find healthy ways to cope throughout all of them. For example, if you're going through the Rude Awakening Stage, instead of filing for divorce, learn to give each other room to communicate your frustrations without attacking each other. Also learn to develop tolerance and mutual understanding. This will be easier if you both acknowledge the reality, the inevitability and temporality of these stages.

And we know that all things work together for good to those who love God, to those who are the called according to His purpose (Romans 8:28). Not all these stages are good, but they all work together for your good. They strengthen your retention muscles so that you are strong enough to hold your marriage together till the end. They also help us grow not only in our marriages, but also in our personal lives, our ministries, our businesses, our workplaces, as well as our relationships with other people. They put us through the fire so that our characters can be refined until they are as pure as gold. Even though some of them are painful, just like all the cake ingredients put together to produce a cake, they all work together to bring out the best in us.

8

"For Richer or Poorer" – Financial Matters

The general belief is that money is not important in marriage as long as you love each other. Yes, it is important for couples to love each other; but quite frankly, love does not pay the bills or buy the essentials in the house. "But there are things that money cannot buy", you may say; but there are lots of important things money can buy for your family. No matter how much in love you are with your spouse, you still need to eat, drink, put on clothes and sleep in safety. Even the best lovers in the world need shelter; and love cannot give it to them, but money can. Marriages suffer much harm when couples underestimate the importance of money in their marriages. Much as it is true that marriage is not about money, it is also true that money is one of the most important factors in marriage.

A feast is made for laughter, and wine makes merry; but money answers everything (Ecclesiastes 10:19). Money is the most powerful medium of exchange there is. It puts you in a position to be able to get almost everything you want in life. Without it, life can be extremely difficult. Valuable as money is, people still have negative attitude towards it. They associate it with evil because of people who do evil in order to get it and those who use it to do evil. They are even afraid to admit that they would be glad to have some of it in their banks accounts because they think people will think they are evil. But money cannot be evil; it can only fall into evil hands. But it can also fall into good hands and serve good purposes. Therefore, we cannot develop negative attitude towards money because of people who kill to have it or people who use it to kill. Actually, it is not wrong to want money, as long as you want it in the right way, and for the right purpose.

I have already mentioned that it is unhealthy to get married for money. In other words, money should not be the reason to either start or end marriage. This chapter is about finances; but we cannot talk about finances without talking about money. In fact, when you talk about finances, you are actually talking about money. It is not necessarily money that can make or break the marital relationship; it is how money is handled within the relationship. Good financial management by couples can make the marriage, but poor financial management can break it. Marriages suffer not because couples have no money; but because they cannot handle the money they have. Similarly, having a lot of money does not guarantee a successful marriage. It's not so much about how much you have as it is about whether or not you can manage it. Whether you have a million or a thousand does not really matter; what matters is whether or not you can handle it.

For the love of money is the root of all kinds of evil, for which some have strayed from the faith in their greediness, and pierced themselves through with many sorrows (1 Timothy 6:10). Money is not evil; the love of money is. Marriages are falling apart because of greed, and couples are sustaining serious injuries trying to get more money at the expense of their marriages. They love money more than their spouses, and they value it more than their marriages. Some even use their spouses for their own financial gain. No marriage can succeed if one or both of the married couple can go after money even if it means they have to trample on each other to get there. Money is important for marriage, but marriage is more important than money. In other words, as much as money is important, it is not worth losing your marriage for.

A successful marriage entails good financial management by the couple. The couple should learn to be responsible and considerate as they try to acquire or spend money. You cannot manage your finances when you are married the same way you did when you were still single and expect your marriage to succeed. When you were still single, you made your financial decisions alone; but when you are married, you make them together. When you were still single, your financial decisions suited only you; but when you are married, they should suit both of you. In other words, financial management in marriage is no longer a one man play; it is a team effort.

Couples usually experience serious finance-related conflicts because people manage finances differently. The husband may want to save money before buying some things in the house; but the wife may feel those things should be purchased on credit. Or the husband may want to buy an automobile while on the other hand the wife wants a house. Conflicting situations like these require good communication and conflict handling skills. Moreover, they require that couples think more about themselves as a couple than as individuals. In marriage it's not about what you or I want; it's about what we both want. Therefore, we should think more about what's good for us than what's good for me or you. The main question should be "How is this going to benefit our marriage?" instead of "What's in it for me?"

Generally, men and women differ in the way they handle their finances. Women are generally more liberal with their finances; but men tend to be more conservative. Men want to have money; but women want to spend it. Women love beautiful things, and they don't mind spending for them; but men prefer to spend their money only on what they consider as meaningful. For an example, a man can spend his money to buy a house (because it will be their shelter), chairs (because they will sit on them), tables (because they can put food on them or use them for writing) beds (because they will sleep on them), curtains (because they will prevent other people from outside from seeing them), pots (because they can use them to cook), cars (because they can use them for travelling), clothes (because they can use them to cover their bodies), etc. But a woman can spend her money on vases, flowers, bedding sets, cushions, table cloths, curtains, pots, dishes, necklaces, earrings, hair dryers, bracelets, etc, all because they fill their lives with beauty.

So, a man spends for usefulness, but a woman spends her money to decorate what a man spends his money on. A man buys a table to put food on when eating or pen and books when writing, but a woman buys a cloth and flowers to decorate the table. This is how they were built, so that they can complement each other. To a man, the things a woman buys seem unnecessary or useless; and he may try to accuse his wife for 'wasting' money. Well, this is true from his perspective. But a woman has a different perspective. She may see a man as unreasonable or stingy for not allowing her or finding it difficult to allow her to buy the things that will beautify his own house. This can cause serious conflicts if the couple does not learn to see things from each other's perspective.

What does it mean to see things from each other's perspective? It means what your spouse perceives does not have to make sense to you; you just have to understand that it makes sense to them. You don't have to love it; you just have to understand that they love it. And if you are not selfish, you will respect what they love and let them have it. Let me make a simple example, if you love a fish, you will not prevent it from going into the water just because the water is not good for you to live in. Just because you cannot survive under water does not mean even the fish can't. In fact, even if you cannot survive in the water, you need to understand that the fish cannot survive out of the water. How a fish survives under water does not have to make sense to you; you just have to know that it can only survive under water; even if you yourself cannot survive there. So, if you take it out of the water, you will kill it; even if you did it out of love. In the same way, if you really love your partner, you will let them have what they love, even if you don't understand why they love it.

Instead of fighting each other for having different spending preferences, couples need to embrace each other's differences and spend to complement each other. However, they should always be careful not to buy more than they can afford to pay. That will be financial mismanagement; and it can kill a marriage. If you spend more than you have, you will end up having nothing and living in debt. One other habit that can kill a marriage is the habit of spending secretly. Couples should be careful not to spend money without their spouses' knowledge. It may seem to work for you in the beginning, but it will surely work against you in the end. It will break your partner's trust for you and can cause serious tension that can lead to a breakup. Transparency is as important in marriage as water is to a car. Lack of transparency can cause serious overheating in marriage, and things might fall apart when the truth comes out.

If you do not tell your spouse about your financial decisions, the sheriff will; and it will be a dreadful experience. A secret always has a way of coming out; especially a financial secret. If you have a bank account that your partner does not know, you will always have a burden of having to hide every withdraw slip or bank statement. But even so, the truth has a way of coming out, and trust will be broken, and the marriage will suffer. The best thing to do as a married couple is to get in the habit of making financial decisions together. Make sure you always reach an agreement before you make a decision. If you insist on having your way over your partner; your decision may backfire, and your partner may hate you. But if you decide in agreement, there will be no pointing of fingers because you will know that you are in it together.

You cannot walk together unless you agree (See Amos 3:3). Always remember that whatever financial decision you make in your marriage, you need to decide with the best interest of your marriage at heart. Even if you make sure that you make every financial decision in agreement, there might still be times when your wells run dry; times in which you might find yourself in financial difficulties. This is the time when your vows will be tested: *"...to love and to cherish...for richer or poorer..."* Will you love and cherish each other the same way when you have no money as you did when you had money? Money comes and goes, but marriage is for a lifetime.

9

Sex in Marriage

In the world today, the love for sex is growing day by day. From time to time people think about it, talk about it and practice it. When you watch television, billboards, magazines, news papers and internet, you will observe words or pictures that are sexually appealing. The rate of prostitution, pornography and casual sex is increasing at an alarming rate. Almost every movie you watch features at least a 'love scene' of two. You listen to songs, and you hear words that communicate sexual messages. Even when non-sexual objects such as cars are advertised, you can still observe sexually appealing images of half-naked women with seductive expressions on their faces. In this way, sex has become so much popular that almost every business entity uses it as part of their brand.

Sex is one of the most essential aspects of life. It is through sex that souls are brought into the world. The pleasure that is derived from sexual activities is far more than words can explain. People go so far as to sacrifice their own health, wealth, jobs, relationships, families and reputation just to have what they regard as a sexually fulfilling experience. It seems like they can't get enough of it; the more sex they get, the more sex they want. Even though they are fully aware of the damages that can be suffered as a result of sex, they still continue to indulge in it. Before they think about their future or health or safety, they have already had sex; and afterwards they experience the feelings of guilt, fear and anxiety as they wonder whether or not they have fallen pregnant out of wedlock or acquired sexually transmitted infections. Severe heartbreaks are sustained by many people in pursuit of sexual pleasure; then they resort to more sex hoping it will ease their sexually inflicted pain, only to fall into more heartbreak.

Human beings are sexual beings. In fact, many people, especially men, derive their egos from their sexuality. They connect with their masculinity (or femininity) through their sexuality. Even their emotions are strongly connected to their sexuality. It is in their sexuality that they get the highest intensity of pleasure and self-worth. Sexuality also means continuity for humanity. Therefore, the significance of sexuality in humanity cannot be underrated.

Sex was created by God to be enjoyed by a husband and his wife within the parameters of their marital commitment. God created it not only for procreation, but also for pleasure. Sex is not a mere penetration of the man's organ into the woman's body; it is the transfusion of one's blood into the other's system. It is the fusion process between two souls. It is a solid combination of two spirits until they become one. It is the mixture of a sperm cell with an ovum to bring life into the world. This kind of a bond was not meant to be experienced within casual relationships; it requires a lifelong commitment – marriage. Sex was created not for casual lust, but for permanent love; the love that can be found only in marriage between the husband and his wife.

Sex outside the confines of marriage is referred to either as *fornication* or *adultery*. The sexual intercourse that is practiced by two unmarried people is fornication; but if one or both of the pair participating in a sexual intercourse with each other are married but not to each other, they are committing adultery. Both these practices are unacceptable before God. *Marriage is honourable among all, and the bed undefiled; but fornicators and adulterers God will judge* (Hebrews 13:4). Godly marriage, as God designed it, is between the two and not more. Therefore, threesome, foursome and group sex are also unacceptable before God (See Galatians 5:17-21); and He will ultimately judge people who indulge in such practices. All such practices are referred to as *sexual immorality*. The only sexual practice that God accepts is one that is performed between a *man* and a *woman* who are *married to each other*. This kind of sex is holy and pleasing to Him.

Now and then I hear 'relationship experts' say that a great marriage starts with great sex. Well, at face value I agree with them; but as I take a deeper look into this, I get a different view. In my opinion, this is true the other way round: Great sex begins with a great marriage. Marriage was not created for sex, but sex was created for marriage. So, marriage is bigger than sex, and good sex begins with good marriage. Sex is just a room in mansion called marriage; so, you can't improve the whole mansion by decorating just one room. But it is one room that can make a huge difference in this mansion. Sex alone cannot make the marriage great; but it can play the most vital role in improving a marital relationship. It can form strong bonds between husbands and wives. It is the most intimate act that can ever happen in marriage. Therefore, it is highly essential for couples to take time to perfect their sexual lives in their marriages. However, sex within marriage is fuelled by mutual affection.

Let the husband render to his wife the affection due her, and likewise also the wife to her husband. The wife does not have authority over her own body, but the husband does. And likewise the husband does not have authority over his own body, but the wife does (1Corinthians 7:3-4). Within the limits of marital commitment, sex has no limits. It is therefore very important for married couples to lay aside all their inhibitions and go all the way when it comes to sex. When the couple gets married, the husband loses authority over his body to his wife, and the wife loses authority over her body to her husband. In other words, your body belongs no more to you, but to your partner; and your partner's body now belongs to you. Your body is for your partner to enjoy, and your partner's body is for you to take pleasure in.

In marriage, it is highly essential that you render to each other due affection. Make each other feel loved and celebrated. Take pleasure in each other's bodies. Hold nothing back, and allow no external force to interrupt your sexual connection with each other. *Let your fountain be blessed, and rejoice with the wife of your youth. As a loving deer and a graceful doe, let her breasts satisfy you at all times; and always be enraptured with her love. For why should you, my son, be enraptured by an immoral woman, and be embraced in the arms of a seductress?* (Proverbs 5:18-20). It is not necessary to find affection outside with someone else when you can find it inside with your spouse. According to the Bible, the affection you render to your spouse within your marriage can reduce their vulnerability to outward seduction. Enjoy your partner to the fullest, and let your partner enjoy you likewise. Find mutual fulfilment in each other. Make it your goal to make your sexual life a memorable experience.

Do not deprive one another except with consent for a time, that you may give yourselves to fasting and prayer; and come together again so that Satan does not tempt you because of your lack of self-control (1Corinthians 7:5). In marriage, it is very important to ensure that you do not deprive your partner an access to your body. Remember, your body is no longer yours but your partner's. Therefore, your partner deserves full access into your body; and if you deny them access to that body except by mutual consent for the purpose of prayer and fasting, you are opening the door for temptation to sneak into your marriage. If it ever happens that your partner considers having sex with someone else, let it not be because you deprived them sex in your marriage. The more you enjoy each other sexually within your marriage, the less you will be tempted to look for sexual gratification outside, unless you have a serious problem of lust.

The hungrier you are, the more tempting food will be to you. Similarly, extramarital sex can be more tempting if you're not getting sex in your marriage. Remember that your partner cannot have sex if they do not have it with you; and if you deprive them, they cannot be sexually satisfied within their marriage. Depriving your partner full access to your body does not make them asexual; it only makes them vulnerable. Sexual deprivation causes *sexual starvation*, and sexual starvation leads to sexual immorality. Close the door to temptations against your marriage by opening your body to your partner in totality. Never be too busy to enjoy your partner's body or let your partner enjoy yours. As you enjoy each other's bodies, you enjoy each other's attention as well. Sex is one of the most effective ways to enjoy each other's affection. If sex is poor, the marriage suffers harm.

It is possible to have sex everyday and still feel deprived. If you keep on eating the same food that is prepared the same way over and over again; you will end up suffering from malnutrition even if you are eating sufficient food everyday. Malnutrition is a condition that is closely linked to starvation. Unless you vary your diet, you will always be full but still suffer from malnourishment. The same applies with sex. Even if you can have sex three times a day, if you keep on doing it the same way over and over again, it becomes boring, and you begin to feel deprived. Sex should be an adventure; not a chore. It should be enjoyed and not endured. It should be fun; not dull. It should be memorable; not miserable.

The human body was designed such that couples can enjoy each other in many different ways for as long as they live. There is no need to change partners to enjoy sex; what needs to be done is vary sexual techniques with one partner from time to time. Always try new things together and never allow yourselves to get stuck in a sexual rut. A fulfilling sexual experience is one in which couples explore each other's bodies searching for new ways to please each other sexually. Every couple has the potential to enjoy sex to the highest degree; but many couples find it boring because it always takes them where they have already been to a million times before. It gives them nothing to look forward to. Eventually they suffer severe sexual starvation despite them having sex every single day.

The couple should get in the habit of exploring each other's bodies in the most pleasurable ways possible. Their bodies should be each other's greatest delight. They should always find creative and interesting ways to take their sex life to higher dimensions. If you still feel that you are not fully satisfied immediately after sex, it could be that there is something that you wanted but did not get. For example, if the husband ejaculates as soon as he enters his wife and then falls asleep immediately afterwards, the wife may toss and turn for the better part of the night feeling totally deprived. The husband may also feel deprived if his wife lies dormant on her back and let's him do all the moves and thrusts. This is what I call *inactive sex*; and inactive sex is partial sex deprivation. Such experiences do happen, but they should be seldom; not regular. The better part of your sex life should be pleasurable and fulfilling to both of you. This is your Biblical right as a married couple.

Great sex is not so much about the penetration or size of the sexual organs as it is about connection, performance and creativity. Although sex experts agree on common erogenous zones in the human body, humans are unique, and they respond differently to different stimuli. What works perfectly for one person may be a complete turn-off for the other. It is therefore important to explore such areas as clues, not truths. Clues only point you towards the truth, and they can sometimes be misleading. God has deliberately hidden sexual treasures in our bodies, and He has given us the privilege of spending our entire lives exploring our partners' bodies in search of those treasures. If all the erogenous zones of individuals were so obvious, then sex would not be so interesting. The fun of sex is the search for what really turns our partners on.

Humans are some of the few beings I know whose sexual organs were designed to enable them to penetrate each other from different angles. This allows humans to enjoy sex from different positions and in different ways. Some sex positions are obvious, but some are yet to be discovered. Every sex position is worth trying. No sex position or sexual act is wrong as long as it is practiced within the perimeters of marriage. Marriage creates the best environment where the couples are totally free to explore all their sexual fantasies. Married people should hold nothing back when it comes to pleasing each other sexually. When it comes to sex, whatever works for you is perfect for you. Forget about taboos and enjoy each other. Nowhere in the Bible are married couples restricted in their sexual behaviour within their marital relationships.

To enjoy your sex life to your full satisfaction, be flexible and open-minded. Do not base your sexual expectations on social stereotypes. Remember, stereotypes are socially constructed, not God created. Generalizations are highly restrictive when it comes to sex; and this can be very frustrating. Stereotypes often lead to myths or fallacies. One of the most common stereotypes, especially in ancient African cultures, is that only men enjoy sex, and women don't. This leads to female enjoyment of sex being judged as a taboo. But the truth of the matter is: women are capable of enjoying sex even more than men; and they can experience sexual satisfaction in more ways than men can. Therefore, it is not wrong for women to enjoy sex.

The other false idea is that wives should always wait for their husbands to make the first sexual move. It therefore becomes a culture shock when a woman initiates sex. This could lead to women feeling guilty for initiating sex and rather wait for their husbands to always make the first move. But the truth is that most men find it sexually fulfilling when their wives initiate sex. At the same time, it becomes easier for women to achieve sexual gratification when they have taken the first move because they get to be in control. However, it doesn't really matter who initiates sex; what matters is that it becomes an enjoyable experience for both of you no matter who initiated it. Married couples should therefore unlearn the restrictive norms of their societies and develop their own flexible approach towards sex.

Another myth is that men love to be always on top of women in a missionary position and be in total control when having sex. As a result, women end up being afraid or reluctant to come on top and take control. Even though they know they want it, they would rather not do it because they are afraid to suffer rejection from their husbands. But the opposite is true in most cases. The majority of men actually love to have sex with their wives on top. They love it when women take control in sexual activities. Being always on top and in control during sex can be extremely frustrating to men. This can make them feel sexually deprived; and they may end up losing interest in sex with their wives. On the other hand, studies continue to reveal that women are most likely to reach orgasm when they are on top and in control. Being on top and in control puts women on the right platform to control the depth and direction of the penetration. It also gives them power to control the movements and pace such that they can enjoy sex to the fullest while they provide maximum pleasure to their husbands.

Sex is a beautiful thing; it is one of the best gifts God ever gave to married couples. God loves it when you get intense pleasure from your spouse. Orgasms are not demonic; they are godly. You and your spouse deserve the ecstatic life filled with sexual fulfilment. It is your divine right to receive sexual pleasure from your spouse, and it is your responsibility to render to your spouse the pleasure due to them. There is no excuse for not enjoying sex in your marriage, except when one or both of you are suffering from the condition that affects your sexual performance; which is also nothing the doctor and good medication can't handle. Sex is the warmth of the marriage, and marriages with poor sex can be very cold.

More and more couples are beginning to admit that their sex life was so much better when they were still dating than when they are married. Even though they do not admit it to each other, they do complain when their partners are not around. On the other hand, more couples in casual relationships testify that they are enjoying their sexual experiences, but fewer couples in marital relationships share the same testimony. This makes marriage appear like an extinguisher for sexual ecstasy in love relationships. It makes married people seem like they are doomed to excessive boredom and sexual starvation.

Couples who should be enjoying sex the most seem to be the ones enjoying it the least. This can be true for various reasons: 1) People in casual relationships value the time they spend together because they know they do not have much time; but married couples do not have the sense of urgency when it comes to enjoying each other's attention because they think they have 'forever' together, yet they seldom, if at all, use a minute in that 'forever' to spend together. 2) Couples in casual relationships put each other first all the time; but married people put their careers, children, hobbies and household responsibilities first most of the time. 3) Couples in casual relationships celebrate each other as lovers; but married couples tend to behave like business partners trying to run a family. To them, having sex is like "mixing business with pleasure". 4) Casual couples are using *affection* stay together; but married couples seem to be using *affiliation* more than affection. 5) Casual couples maintain *companionship*; but married couples are mainly after *convenience*. However, marriage creates the safest and most convenient environment for sexual ecstasy.

Marriage should not be used as a replacement for sexual pleasure; it should rather be used as a safe and loving environment in which sex can be practiced without fear or limitations. Sex is exclusive to marriage; it is the only factor that cuts a clear distinction between people who are married and those who are not. Anybody else can cook for you, clean your house, drive you around, do your laundry, iron your clothes, wash your car, work your garden, pay your bills, take care of your children, etc. without your spouse feeling cheated. So, if you feel you don't want to do any of the above for your spouse, you can request anyone else to do it for you. But only your spouse can have sex with you; and only you can have sex with your spouse. If you fail to please your partner sexually, no one can do it for you without you feeling cheated. Therefore, sex in marriage is not only about whether you feel like it or not; it is also about you giving pleasure in totality to your partner, even if you don't really feel like it. If you don't, no one will, and Satan might sneak in and prey on your partner's vulnerability by 'providing' the one who might do it for you. This can put your marriage under serious attack.

Sex should be one of the top priorities in marriage. Other things can wait. After all, great sex is not always about penetration in the bedroom during the night. In fact, great sex often happens in awkward times and places. Sometimes you need to steal the moment wherever you are and just go for it. This can be not only pleasurable; it can also be a bonding experience for the couple. Amidst your busy schedules, you need to learn to put each other first. Remember, it is your relationship with your spouse that constitutes a marriage, and without this relationship, there will be no marriage. The better the relationship; the greater the sex, and the more successful the marriage will be. Sex is one of the greatest relationship builders in marriage. It is therefore worth spending your time on.

Sex is not only about genital penetration. It is much deeper than foreplay or orgasm. It is a lot more than kissing and caressing. Sex is not a mere physical act; it involves every dimension of humanity – the spirit, the mind, the body and the soul. It is about people sharing their humanity in totality. It is true that sex provides maximum physical pleasure to those who practice it; but physical pleasure alone cannot be the sole reason why people have sex. Sex should provide gratification in all dimensions of humanity; not only to the flesh. It should be spiritually fulfilling, physically pleasurable, mentally enchanting and emotionally delightful. Sex is not a mere act of the flesh; it is a divine experience involving the whole being.

You cannot enjoy sex if your mind is not in it. No matter how sexually gifted your partner may be, you cannot have a fulfilling sexual experience if you are not physically, mental, spiritually and emotionally involved. To get the most out of sex, you need to give it your all. Great sex requires the full commitment of both partners. It cannot be one-sided and mutually fulfilling at the same time. It is your partner's responsibility to please you sexually, but it is your role to enjoy the pleasure. If you do not participate, you cannot enjoy the totality of sexual delight. Sexually fulfilled couples are passionate, not passive. They do not wait for the perfect mood, they create it. Your body is for your spouse to cherish, and your spouse's body is yours to enjoy. So, both of you should regularly take the uninterrupted time to celebrate each other's most valuable sexual assets.

Delightful sex is not always spontaneous; it also requires deliberate efforts most of the time. It also requires cooperation and communication. Unfortunately, many people wish their partners could read their minds and give them just what they wish for without being advised or guided. But this only happens in movies and fairy tales, not in real life. Successful sex requires proper guidance, adventure and feedback. You need to know your body so that you can guide your partner through; and as your partner navigates through it, you need to provide clues and feedback. This will increase your partner's sexual confidence. It can be very discouraging to explore your partner's body and not have a clue how far or how close you are to blowing them away with ecstasy. Even if you do find the right spot to touch, you still need to know how much pressure and speed you should apply. The secret is to touch the right part, at the right time, with the right organ, and in the right way; but you will never know if you do not get honest feedback from the person you are touching.

One other reason why a fulfilling sex cannot always be spontaneous is because men and women differ in their sexual responses. It takes longer for women to go through the *sexual response cycle* than it does for men. The sexual response cycle has four stages. The first stage is the *arousal* or *excitement* stage. This is the stage that prepares the couple's bodies for sexual intercourse. It involves much kissing, touching, caressing and fondling of genitals. This battery of activities is commonly known as *foreplay*. This is where the man's penis and the woman's nipples erect; and the woman's clitoris begins to engorge, her breasts begin to enlarge, and her vagina gets lubricated. There are several other changes that occur in their bodies, until the couple is ready for intercourse. For an average man, full arousal can be achieved in a minute or less; but for an average woman, it can take up to ten minutes and more; depending on her mood.

When the coupe's bodies are fully aroused, they are then ready for the second stage, which is known as the *plateau* stage. Plateau is the stage of actual intercourse. This stage is characterized by an augmented blood circulation and heart rate in both the man and the woman. The couple also experience increased sexual pleasure with increased sexual stimulation; which further increases muscle tension in both of them. The breathing gets deeper and heavier as the pleasure intensifies. This stage also takes longer for an average woman than it does for an average man. As the tension builds up and the pleasure continues to heap on, the couple then progresses to the third stage.

The third stage in the sexual response cycle is known as *orgasm* or orgasmic stage. This is the climax of the intercourse. It involves quick cycles of involuntary muscle contractions in the lower pelvic muscles surrounding the anus and the primary genitals. This is where a man releases his semen in an intensely pleasurable experience called ejaculation. Ejaculation is characterized by repeated release of semen into the woman's vagina (semen can also be released outside the vagina). Usually the first release is the most powerful in pleasure because it releases the highest quantity of semen. Then it is followed by the second and starts diminishing with each release. Orgasm in women can differ extensively from woman to woman; but the common thing about it is that it is also characterized by the highest intensity of pleasure. This stage only takes seconds, but it produces the highest intensity of sexual pleasure of all the stages for both sexes.

After orgasm comes the *resolution* stage. This is the last stage in the cycle. It occurs immediately after orgasm and allows for muscles to relax and the blood pressure to drop. It also allows for the body to calm down from its state of extreme excitement. During this stage, the penis begins to shrink; and for women, the clitoris becomes hypersensitive. This stage also lasts longer for women than for men. However, how long it lasts also varies from person to person and from situation to situation. Sometimes it becomes so short that the couple could undergo the cycle again in a few minutes; and sometimes it can last so long that they take more than a day before they start another cycle.

On average, the sexual response cycle of a woman takes longer than that of a man. It is therefore possible for a man to complete his cycle while the woman is still in her first or second stage. This often makes women feel dissatisfied and frustrated. The resolution stage can also cause so much relaxation in a man that he may even fall asleep right before the eyes of his sexually famished wife. This calls for every man to ensure that they find ways to delay their cycles in order to accommodate their wives. This can be accomplished during the arousal stage through foreplay. The husband should take more time stimulating his wife before penetration; starting from non-sexual organs and moving slowly towards the genitals.

The most sensitive part of the woman's genitals is the *clitoris*; a button-like portion that is situated near the front junction of the inner lips of the vagina and just above the opening of the urethra. This organ is the primary source of the woman's sexual pleasure. In fact, experts agree that they know not of any other function of the clitoris except to provide sexual pleasure to women. The sensitivity of the clitoris requires that a man be extra careful not to put too much pressure on it. It can therefore be very helpful to the husband if the wife can guide his movements around her clitoris. The husband should also be extra-careful when performing direct stimulation to the clitoris as it can be very painful to the wife. Nonetheless, direct stimulation of the clitoris can also be extremely pleasurable to the woman if proper care is taken. The correct stimulation of the clitoris can lead to intense orgasm for the woman. The orgasmic explosion that is caused by clitoral stimulation is known as the *clitoral orgasm*.

The other way you can stimulate your wife sexually to the point of orgasm is by the use of your fingers to stimulate her *G-Spot*. The G-Spot is defined as the bean-shaped area of the vagina which, when stimulated, can lead to strong sexual arousal, powerful orgasms and female ejaculation. Although experts do not agree on the existence of the G-Spot, it has been reported on several cases that women experience intense orgasms through the stimulation of this area. The G-Spot is said to be located about one to three inches up the front vaginal wall between the vaginal opening and the urethra. The G-Spot can be stimulated directly during sexual intercourse with the penis or manually using fingers.

The G-Spot can be located when you insert your finger or two of them into the vagina with the palm of your hand facing upwards; pressing your fingertips against the center of the upper vaginal wall. However, it can be difficult to locate it when the woman is not sexually aroused. It is therefore vital that you first stimulate your wife to the point of arousal before you attempt to locate or stimulate the G-Spot; especially if you are trying to locate it for the first time. The G-Spot is known to swell up when the woman is aroused.

When the G-Spot is stimulated properly, the woman will experience the sensation that feels like she is about to urinate. Although this feels like urine, it is actually the female ejaculation about to gush out as the woman experiences *vaginal orgasm*. The reason why this liquid feels like urine is that it gushes out through the urethra; the very opening that is responsible for urinating. When the wife experiences such a sensation, she should not hold it back or stop to urinate because if she does, she will block the powerful orgasm that will make her 'squirt'.

A woman is also capable of experiencing a *blended orgasm*. This is a double-impact kind of orgasm. Blended orgasm is a combination of clitoral orgasm and G-spot orgasm. It usually occurs when the G-spot is stimulated simultaneously with the clitoris. Any woman can experience blended orgasm, but it requires much patience, time and practice. It also requires that the wife be willing and desiring to experience it – it is extremely difficult to have it if you don't really want it. But most importantly, it requires strong communication. Without proper feedback and guidance from the wife, it will be extremely difficult, if not impossible, for the husband to help her achieve a blended orgasm. This cannot be achieved in a rush; it requires plenty of time and full attention by the couple.

As you know by now, men, by nature, tend to focus more on the destination than the journey; and women on the other hand enjoy the journey more than the destination. The woman's enjoyment of the destination is strongly determined by the pleasure she experienced in the journey. The husband should thus try to take this into cognisance when it comes to sex. For a man, the greatest pleasure in sex is ejaculation; but the woman derives more pleasure from stimulation. It will be hard for her to experience orgasm when she is not stimulated properly. The husband should therefore learn to patiently take his wife through the journey, and the destination will take care of itself. Some husbands are failing in their sexual performance because rather than allowing their wives adequate time to enjoy the stimulation, they become impatiently preoccupied with getting them to reach orgasm. The plan should be to pleasure your wife sexually and let orgasm take care of itself.

In as much as it is true that the man should stimulate his wife into sexual pleasure, he cannot do it without her help and cooperation. The wife's body is like a tourist's attraction, her husband is like the tourist, and the wife herself is like a tour guide. The tourist cannot navigate in the area without a tour guide, and the tour guide cannot guide the tourist through the area if he does not know it. The tour guide will first have to spend much time in the area and learn as much as he can about it before he attempts to guide the tourist around. The more time the tour guide spends in the area, the more he learns about it. In short, the success of the tour depends strongly on the tour guide's knowledge of the area and his ability to guide the tourist around. Without such knowledge and ability by the tour guide, the tourist cannot do justice to the area he is touring around.

Similarly, the husband cannot navigate successfully around his wife's body without her guidance, and she cannot guide him around her body if she does not know it. She first has to spend time on her body and learn how it responds sexually. If she can't give herself sexual pleasure or bring herself to orgasm, how can she guide her husband to do so? The tourist cannot learn about the area if the tour guide does not guide him around; neither can the husband learn about his wife's body if she does not guide him. The more time the wife spends exploring her body, the more she will know about it, and the more she knows about it, the more she will be able to guide her husband successfully around it.

It is extremely difficult, if at all possible, for the wife to reach orgasm or achieve sexual satisfaction if she cannot participate in the process and guide her husband around her body. In fact, sex cannot be successful if the wife cannot guide her husband's movements on and around her body. The husband may also be discouraged when it comes to sex if he feels that his wife is not participating. It may make him feel like he cannot please his wife sexually, and this can make him feel like a complete failure in sex. Nothing makes the husband feel more sexually confident than to know that he is touching the right place at the right time and applying the right amount of pressure in the right way. Eventually, sex will become the experience none of you can wait to go home for. Instead of sex being a bore in your marriage, it will become a blast.

Without proper communication, female orgasm is extremely difficult to achieve. In fact, couples who talk to each other about their sexual needs, preferences and fantasies are more likely to experience amazing orgasms and intense sexual pleasure than those who do not communicate about their sexuality. Many couples experience problems when they are to talk about their sexuality; precisely because sex talk is considered a taboo in some societies. It is highly essential for the married couples to start creating an environment where they can freely talk about sex until it becomes their habit. Sex cannot be effective if it is not interactive. Every couple should make it their goal to experience powerful sexual encounters in their marriage, and the best way to start is to talk about it; then go for it.

In the modern society, couples have come to realize that sexual pleasure is not only about the penetration of the penis into the vagina; there are also other alternatives. The most popular alternative is *oral sex*. This is where couples stimulate each others' genitals using their mouths. Some couples still do not perform oral sex because it is regarded as a taboo in their cultures or religions. Some thinks it's weird, some find it 'sinful', and others think it's unhealthy. Even so, more and more couples are beginning to embrace oral sex as part of sexual activities in their marriages. The oral stimulation of the genitals can be extremely pleasurable for couples. This method can be used during the excitement stage to prepare each other for intercourse. It can also be used to bring each other to orgasm.

The oral stimulation of the penis is commonly known as *falletio*. When performing falletio, the wife takes her husband's penis into her mouth and then moves her mouth up and down the penis rhythmically as she mimics the thrusting movement of vaginal penetration. As she performs falletio, the wife uses her saliva as a lubricant; and she is always careful not to bite the penis with her teeth. Some men, though, are turned on by those little unpredictable bites that their sexual partners do occasionally as they perform falletio on them.

Falletio involves kissing, sucking and licking the penis and using the mouth to play with it. It also involves deep-throating – an act of inserting the penis deep inside the mouth until it enters in the throat. This act can bring powerful pleasure upon the husband. When deep-throating, the wife should be very careful because it can make her throw up. Falletio can be performed on the husband to prepare him for penetration or to bring him to orgasm.

Depending on the agreement between the couple, the husband, when he reaches orgasm, may ejaculate inside the wife's mouth or outside. The wife does not have to swallow her husband's semen if she feels uncomfortable. The husband will then have to alert his wife when he is about to ejaculate so that she may remove her mouth and stimulate him manually with her hand to the point of ejaculation. However, it is almost every man's fantasy to have his semen sucked and swallowed by his wife. It can be tremendously pleasurable for them, and it can lead them to powerful orgasms and the more intimate resolution phases. Almost every man would let go of anything else just to hold on to the woman who gives him this pleasurable oral experience.

When performing falletio, the oral stimulation may be varied with hand stimulation to increase the pleasure on the husband. The pace can also be varied randomly from slow to moderate to fast to add more pleasure to the husband. The wife can also increase her husband's pleasure by using her mouth to stimulate his testicles. However, she should be very gentle because testicles are very sensitive, and when squeezed too hard, they can be very painful. Variation of movements and techniques around the penis can also knock your husband down to his knees for you. It can blow him away with ecstasy and keep him hooked on you. After all, falletio is not called "blow job" for nothing.

Oral sex that is performed on a woman is referred to as *cunnilingus*. When the husband performs cunnilingus on his wife, he uses his lips and tongue to stimulate her clitoris and her entire vulva. He can also stimulate her with his tongue inside her vagina. The most pleasurable erogenous zone the husband can stimulate with his mouth is the clitoris. Cunnilingus can be used to arouse the wife and prepare her for penetration; or it can be used to bring her to orgasm. There are various positions that can be used when performing cunnilingus, and it doesn't matter which position you use; what matters is that you enjoy. The wife may guide her husband's movements around her vulva to ensure that she gets nothing but the best out of the cunnilingus experience.

Cunnilingus can be very helpful to the husband in terms of helping him delay penetration so that he can keep his wife on par with him in their sexual response cycle.

The partner performing oral sex on the other is referred to as the *giver*; and one on whom it is performed is called the *recipient*. The recipient enjoys the pleasure directly from the stimulation, and the giver gets satisfaction by observing the recipient's responses as he or she enjoys the stimulation. The couple can both become givers and recipients at the same time by performing oral sex simultaneously on each other. The name given to the position used during simultaneous stimulation is the 69 position. This is where the couple lie on top of each other facing each other; but their heads face opposite directions such that the husband can perform cunnilingus on his wife as the wife performs falletio on him. Whatever position or approach is used during oral sex is not really what matters; what really matters is for both partners involved to enjoy it to the maximum degree.

Sex should never be used as a means of punishment in marriage. It should also not be used for violence or manipulation. That's not what it was designed for. Sex was designed to strengthen the bond between the husband and his wife as they celebrate their love for each other; not to be used as a weapon against each other. Couples who threaten each other about sexual deprivation or harassment have their marriages treading on thin ice.

Remember, your partner has authority over your body; and you have authority over your partner's body. But that does not give you permission to force yourself on your partner or your partner to force himself (or herself) on you. Do not force your partner to do sexual acts that are not comfortable to them; neither should you allow yourself to be forced to do sexual acts you are not comfortable with. Sex is about cooperation, not coercion. However, as much as you feel comfortable, make sure you do not deprive your partner. Also try to deal with your sexual discomforts and be open-minded so that you may be able to rise to any occasion in your sexual adventures.

Your partner's body is full of treasure chests that are hidden in it for your sexual pleasure; all you have to do is search and keep searching, and while you're at it, enjoy. When it comes to sexual gratification in your marital relationship, you have absolutely nothing to lose and everything to gain. Your sex life as a married couple is always as good or as bad as you make it. No one will ever come from outside and spice up your sex life for you; it takes only the two of you. If you do not make it exciting, it will be boring; and if sex is boring, so will the marriage be. More often than not, when I interact with couples about their marital problems, sexual problems tend to be the greater part of those problems; not only problems that are related to sexual dysfunctions, but also sexual deprivation or boredom in the bedroom. Most of such problems can be solved if the couples can pay more attention to their sexual needs and be equally involved in fulfilling each other's sexual desires.

As I take a deeper look into sexual problems that couples are experiencing, I notice that the problem is not *lack of knowledge*; but *lack of application* to what they know. Many couples know what they should do to please each other sexually, but they just don't do it. They consider it a waste of time to focus their attention on sex; but I consider it a waste of marriage to neglect your partner's sexual needs. If you have no time for sex, you have no time for marriage. To neglect your partner's sexual desires is to put your marriage in harm's way. Some perceive sex as something that makes them appear foolish or too vulnerable to their partners. But the only thing that is foolish is to neglect your partner's sexual needs and expect your marriage to be successful and free from infidelity. If people who are in casual relationships can be so vulnerable to each other during sex, how much more vulnerable should married couples be to each other? Unlike people in casual relationships, you have the benefit of a lifelong commitment; use that advantage and sex your way to a better marriage.

Do not allow your fear and pessimism to steal your God-given privilege to enjoy sex to the fullest with your spouse. Do not block your current pleasure by worrying about what might happen in the future. Give it your all today and let tomorrow worry about itself. After all, most of the things you worry about today will never happen to you; so, you might as well forget about tomorrow and enjoy today with your life partner. Remember, today's events are tomorrow's memories. Therefore, you might as well stop worrying about what will happen tomorrow and start building great memories today that will help you look forward to tomorrow. If you allow yesterday's pressure to steal today's pleasure, you may lose tomorrow's treasure as well. So, forget about yesterday's pain and focus more on today's passion; then you will enjoy tomorrow's gain. If you want a better marriage, start with better sex and watch your marriage make progress towards success.

10

"To Love and to Cherish" – Romance in Marriage

On a hot summer afternoon you decide to take a walk in the park just to clear your head. As you walk relaxed in the park, a few yards away you notice two teenagers with school uniforms on hugging and kissing slowly and passionately under the tree. You try so hard to look away, but you find yourself staring. You start feeling guilty for watching with deep interest what you know you should detest and disapprove, but your deep desire to enjoy that experience seems to be stronger than your conviction. You know that those children should be at school studying rather than at the park kissing, but you can't help envying them for doing what you should be enjoying with your spouse. As an adult you want to reprimand them for what they are doing, but you find yourself admiring their act and wishing it were you under that tree.

You've been married for some time now, and all that's going on in your mind is: "I have never done this ever since I got married. The last time I enjoyed this experience with my partner was when we were still dating". In the process you find yourself asking yourself: "has our marriage extinguished our flame of love and romance? Is marriage a passion killer?" Then you find yourself longing for those days when you were still dating, when all you thought about was your partner, and all your partner thought about was you. You start feeling like the most important aspect of your relationship was lost when you said "I do". This then directs your concern from the children who are practicing in acts that could damage their future to your marriage that seems to have lost its flame. Instead of seeing the children who are misbehaving, you see the marriage that is boring. Have you ever found yourself in a similar situation? If you have, you are not alone. Most people have, and they still do.

People who are dating seem to enjoy the love and the romance more than married couples. This may be true for various reasons. When you are still dating, the only thing that brings you together is love and deep affection, and after you fulfil your passions, you go back each to your own homes. As soon as you depart, you start thinking about your lover; and you text them a message telling them that you are missing them already. At this stage nothing else matters, only that you be together and take each other to the world you've never before been to. Holding hands, hugging and kissing become an integral part of every meeting you have. You find it hard to take your hands off each other. If it happens that you have a quarrel or argument, you walk away from each other out of anger and frustration. Before you fall asleep you make a one hour phone call of a make-up conversation. Soon after the conversation you can't wait until the next day so that you can be together and enjoy the love you have for each other.

At this stage you can't get enough of each other. The more you get, the more you want. The song: *"A thousand kisses from you is never too much... a million days in your arms is never too much..."* makes perfect sense to both of you. You just don't want to stop. The more time you spend together, the more time you want to spend together. The feeling is always mutual, as if you can always read each other's minds. You seem to agree in almost everything. Every love song you hear reminds you of the love of your life. Every time you interact, you talk about how much you love each other, and each time you hear those words, it feels like music to your ears. It melts you down and knocks you off your feet.

When you are together, you forget entirely about anything else that exists. The only thing that matters is that you are madly in love with each other. Every time you receive a text message from your loved one, you start smiling even before you know what the message is about. The heart beats faster, and the breath gets heavier as you open your inbox like a treasure chest to read the much treasured text message from your beloved. The message then becomes a self-fulfilling prophecy, telling exactly what you wanted to hear as if the writer wrote from within your head.

Before you meet, you make sure that you look your best for each other. Every detail of beauty never goes unnoticed. You stare in each other's eyes for hours, and the longer you stare, the heavier you breathe. If anyone warns you about your beloved, you quickly conclude that they are just jealous. You seem to be blinded from every blemish. When you are in the meeting at work, every now and then you catch yourself smiling at every thought of the one you love. You attend the meeting from the beginning to the end, and when the meeting adjourns, all you have picked up from that meeting is that it is so good to have somebody to love.

The anticipation of seeing each other increases the rate of your heartbeats. At this stage songs like: *"I don't know much, but I know I love you; and that may be all I need to know"* become your favourite songs. All these experiences generate a strong anticipation for an ecstatic future that you could spend together. The feeling of not having enough of each other becomes so strong until you decide to spend your lives together forever. Very often the expectation is that you will have all the time you need to fulfil all of each other's fantasies.

At the climax of the relationship, the man arranges a special romantic dinner and pops out the big question on bended knees with an elegant diamond ring in his right hand, and the lady does not hesitate to say "YES!!!" as the man gently slides the ring into her finger. The deal is then sealed with a passionate kiss, and soon they start making preparations for their big day. "I can't wait to spend the rest of my life with you" becomes the most common statement at this stage of relationship. The lady communicates her deepest desires about how the wedding should be, to which the man replies: "Your wish is my command" – whether he means it or not does not really matter; what matters is the radiant smile that statement puts on her face.

As time goes on the interactions become less and less pleasurable and more and more strategic as they both work on preparations for their big day. At this stage it might be their first time talking about anything else rather than their crazy love for each other. They start to kiss less and talk more. Some of their interactions may be full of tension and conflicts, but their consolation would be that this situation is temporary, and when it's all over they will be back in each other's arms forever.

Finally the day you have been waiting for dawns, and the wedding becomes more successful than you anticipated. The day is filled with beauty and ecstasy as the guests celebrate your special day with you. Time for matrimonial service comes, and the priest goes on with his divine assignment of joining you together as husband and wife. He skilfully leads you through the exchange of vows, and as you repeat those vows, you mean every word you say. The priest then concludes his work by publicly pronouncing you husband and wife. The witnesses start ululating with big shouts of joy as you and your spouse enjoy your first kiss as husband and wife. You finally got what you have long been waiting for, and the future looks blissful for both of you. The things you wanted to do but had to stop because of time, you finally have all the time to do them without interruption or any feelings of guilt. After the wedding you set out to honeymoon to enjoy the beginning of the rest of your lives together.

Back from the honeymoon you come home to disturbing realities. You need a place of your own, and if you are leasing, you have to pay the rent consistently. If you buy a house, you have to pay your mortgage consistently on monthly basis. You also have to pay for water and lights, groceries, policies, bills – the list goes on and on. In the morning you have to wake up on go to work. After work the husband comes home with great anticipation to meet the love of his life. He goes straight home after work to meet his wife. All the way he is completely restless because he can't wait to meet his one and only lady.

When he arrives he makes advances towards his beloved, but his beloved is too busy preparing dinner for her husband. At the same time she is tidying up the house so that they may reside in a clean environment. After cooking she dishes out to herself and her beloved husband. As they eat, she is busy going through mails from their creditors. Thereafter she washes the dishes, thinking about how the bills will be paid by the end of the month. Before they sleep, they engage in a short discourse strategising about the payment of bills. Thereafter they engage in an intimate act as husband and wife, and during that time the wife is thinking about new curtains, and the husband is thinking about his demanding boss at work.

This goes on and on until it becomes a habit. At this time they no longer smile when they see their partner's text message or phone call because they have come to know that it no longer says the same message it used to say before they said "I do". The message used to be something like: "I miss you too much"; "I can't wait to see you"; "I can't stop thinking about you"; "I love you more than anything in the world"; "You're all I think about all the time" – the list goes on and on. But now things have changed. If the message is from the husband, it would probably be saying: "I have a late meeting at work today, and I won't make it home on time"; and if it is from the wife it would probably say: "Please don't forget to buy the onion on your way home". What used to be the biggest turn on is now becoming a major turn off. The things that used to make them smile start to make them frown. Chores and routines seem to take the place of hugs and kisses.

They keep on hoping that the bliss will come back, but more responsibilities are piling up instead. In the midst of that turmoil the wife becomes pregnant, and the husband gets affected. He tries to be nice and supportive to his wife, but her perpetual demands and mood swings weigh him down and ware him out. The focus drifts more and more away from each other towards chores, routines, bills, as well as the new member of the family, who is still growing in the womb and causing too much discomfort for the potential mother. After nine months of pregnancy the baby is born and immediately steals all the attention. He becomes an addition of responsibilities in the house – food, diapers, clothes, toys, medication, toiletry, etc. Now the sleepless nights become part of their daily living. Romance becomes almost, if not, impossible to even think about under such circumstances. Acts of marital intimacy also become mission impossible as the focus now is totally on taking care of the baby.

As the baby grows, they start redirecting their focus to each other, but the baby keeps on interrupting almost everything they try to do together. They wait for the baby to fall asleep, but they fall asleep long before he does, and even that sleep is interrupted every now and then. After all, no parent wants to sleep and leave the child awake. The baby wouldn't let them sleep either. By the time they find ways to adjust to the situation, the wife is pregnant again, and history repeats itself. The relationship then becomes less about romance and more about parenting and managing the household. By this time two lovers have already started to behave more like business partners trying to run the family. They seem to have totally forgotten that they were once lovers who couldn't get enough of each other. Words like "I love you"; "I'm thinking of you..." have now begun to sound ridiculous. If one tells the other how much they love them, the other simply looks in disbelief as if to say "Yeah right!" The stares they used to enjoy seem to be more and more disgusting, and occasionally they ask themselves: "What was I thinking to marry this one?"

At this stage, looking your best for your beloved seems no longer necessary. A husband would wear a torn T-shirt, short pants and worn out sandals. On the other hand the wife would put on her old pyjamas throughout the day. It also seems like all the good things you used to see in each other have been replaced by all these flaws you see today. Anyone else seems to be better than your spouse, even though you once regarded them as the best there is. Even though you used to agree in almost everything, you now seem to disagree in almost everything. Differences appear to be more than similarities. You still love and miss each other, but you struggle to find your way to each other's hearts again. The prospects of the future seem to contradict the memories of the past, and it begins to feel like your best days are behind you.

The difference between people who are dating and people who are married is that people who are dating focus only on each other and their passionate love, but people who are married focus on many other responsibilities as well. However, married people should always be careful to not allow their roles and responsibilities to dissolve their love for each other. In a marital relationship, romance is no longer as spontaneous as it used to be in a dating relationship; but it is not impossible. The truth of the matter is that the roles and responsibilities of marriage do not erase the human's inherent need to love and be loved.

Couples who neglect romance in their marriage tend to behave more like enemies or colleagues than lovers. They also tend to enjoy the convenience of their marital relationship more than they enjoy each other's company. It should therefore be part of the couple's responsibilities to make deliberate efforts to keep the flame alive in their marriages. For married couples, romance is still possible, just not spontaneous, but deliberate. It's no longer so much about how you feel as it is about want you want. If you don't make time for it, you may never experience it, and your marriage may not be as emotionally and sexually fulfilling as it was meant to be.

When you were still dating, everything your partner said or did was 'valuable' and 'exciting'; but since you got married, everything they say or do seems 'boring' and 'worthless'; not because their utterances have changed, but because you value them less in your marriage than you did in your courtship. Your value for them in your dating relationship was impulsive, but in your marital relationship it is more intentional. Unless you make a deliberate decision to value your spouse more in your marriage than you did during your courtship, romance in your marriage will be just an illusion. It is not your spouse's value that has depreciated; it is your ability to recognise it that has diminished. So, if you fail to see the value of your spouse, it does not mean they have lost their value; it could be that you are losing your sight.

The main problem in marriages is that when couples go through these experiences, they tend to be too quick to divorce or have extramarital affairs trying to seek romance outside their marriages. This very often makes their lives bitter instead of better. Well, you may decide to find new love outside of your marriage to look for the romance you seem to have lost in your marriage. You will most probably succeed because that relationship may be more romantic for the simple reason that there are no other responsibilities to focus on except to pleasure each other.

Now that you found what you seemed not to be getting in your marriage, the extramarital affair may seem more appealing, and you may be tempted to leave your spouse to start a new life with your new found love. You then decide to divorce your spouse and marry your new found love with whom you managed to recover the seemingly lost ecstasy, and soon after your second wedding, history repeats itself, and this time it may become worse because the first partner is most probably the best one. Ultimately you might find yourself unnecessarily going through a series of unsuccessful marriages.

Many couples are suffering from what I call *The Martha Syndrome.* The Book of Luke (10:38-42) says: *Now it happened as they went that [Jesus] entered a certain village; and a certain woman named Martha welcomed Him into her house. And she had a sister called Mary, who also sat at Jesus' feet and heard His Word. But Martha was distracted with much serving, and she approached Him and said, "Lord, do you not care that my sister has left me to serve alone? Therefore tell her to help me." And Jesus answered and said to her, "Martha, Martha, you are worried and troubled about many things. But one thing is needed, and Mary has chosen that good part, which will not be taken away from her."*

Martha did well to welcome Jesus into her house, but she could not enjoy Jesus' company because she was busy trying to serve Him. What she did for Him distracted her from spending time with Him. She spent her time *for* Jesus but not *with* Him, and she focused more on serving than on the One she was serving. She missed Jesus while trying to [cook] for Him. But Jesus did not come to her house for her services; He came for her. Eventually, even though Martha was the one who welcomed Jesus in her own house, it was her sister Mary who enjoyed the teachings of Christ and His presence. Jesus wanted Martha's attention more than her services; but Martha gave Jesus her services and missed His presence. To Martha, it was all about her *presents*; but to Jesus, it was more about her *presence.*

Many couples have fallen into this trap. They focus on what matters the least at the expense of what matters the most. They spend more time *for* each other than they do *with* each other. They miss each other while trying to serve each other. The wife would be spending more time cooking for her husband, doing his laundry, cleaning his house, bathing his children, preparing his lunch box, etc. and then finds no time to spend with the very husband she was trying to serve. Much as those things are good, they are not as important as the time you spend focusing on your husband. All the things you do for your husband do not mean anything if they hinder you from spending time with him. You are busy spending your time *for* him; but all he really wants is for you to spend it *with* him and *on* him.

Same applies on the husband's part. He would spend most of his time trying to make a living for his family. He always works overtime to provide for his wife, but he seldom spends his time with the very wife she is trying to provide for. He spends his money on her, but he hardly ever spends his time with her. Much as your wife appreciates your money and your gifts, she would be much more contented to have you. She needs the warmth of your heart more than she does the works of your hands. Of all the presents you can give her, the best and most valuable is your presence in her life. Spending time with her does not mean staying in the house; it means being with her and focusing completely on her.

If you find yourself spending more time serving your partner than you do focusing on him (or her), you might be suffering from *The Martha Syndrome.* Romance is not about spending your time for partner; it is about spending it with them, focusing on nothing else but your partner. Couples need to learn to take time to disconnect totally from anything else so that they can connect totally to each other. This is what I call *The Mary Character.* Rather than getting distracted with much serving, Mary decided to sit at Jesus' feet, enjoy His presence and draw from His wisdom. While Martha worried and troubled herself about many things, Mary chose one thing that could not be taken from her; she chose Christ. Martha decided to spend her time *for* Christ, but Mary chose to spend hers *with* Him. Eventually, Martha was exhausted, but Mary was exhorted. To couples suffering from *The Martha Syndrome*, marriage is *demanding*; but to ones with *The Mary Character*, it is *rewarding*.

Romance is just as important to married couples as worship is to God. Romance and worship are both about *intimacy* and expressions of *affection*; romance expresses intimacy and affection between husband and wife, and worship expresses the same between God and humans. How, then, can you be intimate with God, whom you do not see, if you cannot be intimate with your spouse, whom you see everyday? It takes more faith to be intimate with God than it does to be intimate with your partner. To touch the heart of God or please Him, you first have to believe that He is (See Hebrews 11:6); but to please you partner, you just have to reach out and go for it. When we worship, we render our affection to God, and when we perform acts of romance, we render our affection to our spouses. Think about your attitude of worship towards God; the same should be your attitude towards your partner. Worship is not influenced by how we feel, and neither should romance be determined by our feelings.

If you wait for the right time, or place, or mood, or feeling, you may never be romantic in your marriage. You as a couple are the ones who should determine the time, place, mood or feeling for romance. In fact, you don't show affection to your spouse when you feel good; instead, you feel good when you show affection to your spouse. Romance is not produced by good feelings; it produces them. It also creates a strong bond between the husband and his wife. It provides a platform in which the couple can creatively express their love for each other. The more time you spend expressing your love to each other, the more you will grow in love with each other. Romantic people are not *victims* of circumstances; they are *pioneers* of circumstances. They do not wait for the mood; they create it. Victims leave things to chance, but pioneers change things by establishing what they want to experience. Victims wait for the wave, but pioneers stir up the waters to create the wave they want.

Successful couples have learnt to put a balance between their family responsibilities and their love lives. They do not allow the demands of family life to steal their attention from each other. Amidst their busy schedules, they often make time to spend quality time together. They have managed to make their love relationship their number one priority. Despite their ever-increasing workloads, they make time to go out together, buy gifts for each other, communicate the messages of love, hold hands, kiss and caress each other, and do everything else that may contribute positively to their love relationship. They make deliberate efforts to nurture their love and make it grow. They make the most of every opportunity they get to take each other to the world of ecstasy.

As a married couple, don't let things go their own direction. Take control and direct the currents towards your direction. Don't expect things to remain the same as they were before you got married, but that does not mean you should deprive yourselves the pleasures that you so rightfully deserve. In your busy schedule, you need to find time to just relax and play together. If you find yourselves stuck in too many chores and routines, why not try to creatively infuse romance therein? Try to make those chores fun and romantic by doing them together as you enjoy each other's company. Try to change your perceptions about them and see them no longer as burdens but as opportunities to enjoy your time together. It can be fun for a married couple to 'mix business with pleasure' as they carry out their household responsibilities. Make efforts to look your best for each other. Value and respect each other. Cherish your love above your achievements. Celebrate each other's strengths and tolerate each other's weaknesses.

Always bear in mind that when you discover your partner's weaknesses, it does not mean they have changed from who they used to be. What it really means is that they had those weaknesses when you met them; you just didn't know, but still you loved them. Your discovery of their weaknesses does not make them any less of who they really are. We all have weaknesses, but we choose to present our strengths instead. In fact, during the dating period, people show each other the edited version of who they are. But in marriage you get to see their uncensored and true selves. They no longer have chances to secretly edit their personalities before they show up to their partners. Nonetheless, your observation of their weaknesses does not erase the strengths they possess.

Of all the things you may acquire as a married couple, nothing is more important than your love for each other. Take time out to celebrate it. If need be, take leave from work so that you may enjoy each other when the children are at school. You can also make arrangements for your children with the people you trust and go out together for a couple of days. Not everything I am suggesting will work for you because different practices work for different couples. All I'm trying to do is help you think of creative ways to keep the flame of love alive in your marriage. You have nothing to lose and everything to gain. Just make time regularly for each other and let your hearts to the talking as you recline securely in each other's loving arms.

Let the husband render to his wife the affection due her, and likewise also the wife to her husband (1 Corinthians 7:3). Affection between the husband and his wife is the essence of every marriage. It is the distinguishing factor between marriage and any other relationship. Marriage without affection is like business with no profit. Lack of affection not only obstructs progress in marriage, it also increases insecurities in couples. People who are not rendering affection to their spouses are always afraid that their spouses might find it elsewhere. They are always afraid that they might lose their partners to more affectionate people, and as a result they become unreasonably jealous, always monitoring every move their partners make. On the other hand those who are not getting affection from their partners are fearful that maybe their partners are no longer in love with them. This is a chaotic situation for marriage, and it can be avoided if couples can fulfil their duties to each other.

As a married couple, you deserve each other's affection, and only you can render that affection to each other. You need to enjoy each other's love in totality. Hold nothing back when it comes to each other. Without affection, marriage becomes an extremely lonely and cold experience. In order for affection to be rendered effectively in marriage, the flame of romance should be kept alive at all times. It should be nurtured everyday; otherwise it will die out. There is no better gift you can ever give to your partner than to show them that you have strong feelings of love for them. It does not help to love your partner deeply and keep it to yourself; you need to find creative ways to express that love to the person to whom it is due. As the Bible rightfully puts it: *Better an open rebuke than hidden love* (Proverbs 27:5 – NIV).

Marriage should not lose its feeling of excitement and adventure; otherwise it will be a tedious hive of chores and routines. But excitement and adventure do not happen by chance; they require deliberate efforts from both partners. So, if the flame of romance dies out in your marriage, before you walk away from your spouse, ask yourself what deliberate efforts you took to keep it alive. Keeping the flame alive requires more than just a once off act; it takes regular and consistent nurturing. Buying your partner flowers only on Valentine's Day will not keep the flame alive in your marriage. There must be something you do on daily basis to keep your partner's heart won over to you. It is therefore important that you use every opportunity you get to contribute positively to your marriage in order to make it a more romantic relationship.

Marriage was designed for you to enjoy, not to endure. Therefore, it is important to try by all means to minimize pressure and maximize pleasure in your marriage. There is no law in the world that says you should be unhappy in your marriage. I say this because some couples often act like they are obliged to hurt each other or be unhappy in their marriages. It seems like they feel guilty if they are happily married in a maritally frustrated world, as if they owe somebody an explanation for their happiness. Other people tend to feel left out when their peers complain about their marriages. They feel they cannot make their contribution to the conversation because they may sound strange for being happily married while others are not.

Happiness in marriage is your right, the right only the two of you can exercise. No one can come from outside and make your marriage delightful for you; only the two of you can do that. Take responsibility for your own happiness. Communicate your desires to each other and have fun as you try to fulfil them. Do not hold back. This requires full commitment on the part of both of you. It cannot be a one-sided effort; it takes the two of you. Busy as the world can be, whatever you do, never forget to be lovers; and while you're at it, celebrate your love together.

11

Children in Marriage

Children are precious gifts from God – the gifts every couple would be so glad to have. They are the life and energy of every family, and without them, the family feels totally incomplete. Their presence lights up every home with splendour, and very often, we observe the pleasure of their presence more in the void of their absence. They fill every house with happiness, and they are such a joy to have around. They can be very demanding, but every demand comes with twice the reward. They are the dream of every couple, and only a handful of couples want to live without them in their marriages. Not only are they an indication of continuity for human race; but they are also treasures to be cherished in every family. In a nutshell, they are not called bundles of joy for nothing.

Children are the pride of their parents. They dignify their parents in the sight of their communities; and they save them from the reproach and rejection that comes with barrenness. Their presence eliminates the possible feelings of stagnation; and without them, couples become objects of scorn in their societies (See the story of Hannah and Peninnah in 1 Samuel 1:6-7). *Behold, children are a heritage from the Lord, the fruit of the womb is a reward. Like arrows in the hand of a warrior, so are the children of one's youth* (Psalm 127:3-4). Children are legacies to their parents. They are their parents' most wonderful reward, their ammunition against the heartbreaking feelings of loneliness and unfruitfulness.

Inability to bear children can make couples feel like they are failing their predecessors by failing to produce successors in their lineage. It can make them feel like they are stagnating. Unfortunately, there are couples who have been trying to have children for a long time, yet without success. They feel that time is running out for them because they are not getting younger. This can cause too much strain in marriages, especially if childless couples point fingers and blame each other. If you are married and without children, don't stand against each other; stand together. Continue to love and cherish each other. Find your joy in the Lord, and the joy of the Lord will be your strength (See Nehemiah 8:10).

The value of your marriage is determined not by the presence of children, but by the presence of the One who created it. Therefore, your marriage is still valuable before God even if you are without children. For as long as you don't have children to focus on, focus more on each other and let your love for each other grow stronger each day. Don't let childlessness work against you; let it work for you instead. There are couples I know who are childless, yet their marriages are still priceless. They have learnt the secret of being happy together no matter what they have or do not have. They have also learnt to overlook social stigma and find total fulfilment in each other. Marriage is not so much about children as it is about the husband and his wife. Though the presence of children is extremely vital in families, it does not validate marriages. What validates marriage is the solemn oath that was taken before God and men to be together till the end.

There are alternatives to become parents without bearing children. After all, real parenting is not about giving birth; it is about raising the children, whether you gave birth to them or not. The most common alternative to becoming parents without having to give birth is *adoption*. There are plenty of people who can give birth but cannot parent their children. You can be that parent by adopting such children and raising them as your own. There's no need to abort children when there are couples who can adopt them. Adoption gives you a legal right over the children you are parenting, even though you are not their biological parents. Who knows where the Israelites would have been had Moses not been adopted by Pharaoh's daughter in Egypt (See Exodus 2)? Rather than quarrelling over your inability to bear children, you can make a difference in this world by adopting as many children as you can afford to bring up; and who knows, one of them could become the president of your country.

Malcolm X, the man who became the "Black Power" leader and one of the most influential civil rights activists of the modern era, was not raised by his biological parents. His father was killed when he was a small boy, and his mother had a nervous breakdown and was admitted to a mental institution. As a result, Malcolm X spent his childhood in the orphanage, being raised by people who did not give birth to him. Even the co-founder of Apple Computers and the brain behind the iPod, Steven Paul, was adopted as an infant by the couple named Paul and Clara Jobs in February 1955. That was where he got his surname *Jobs*. Even today he is known as Steven Jobs, and he lived to become one of the greatest minds in the world.

There are many other internationally prominent people who were adopted and not aborted, and still they lived to make a huge difference on the planet. If these people were aborted or left to die as children, the world would not have benefitted this much from their talents and creativity. No couple should be childless and miserable when there are so many parentless in the world. Rather than spending the rest of your married lives grumbling about not having children, just reach out for those fatherless and motherless children and adopt them as your own.

The family in which the couple (mother and father) are staying together with their own children is called a *nuclear family*. There are also families that consist of two people and their children from their own relationships and from previous ones. Such families are called *blended families*. Now more than ever, people are giving birth to children out of wedlock; and most often their relationships with the fathers do not survive to the point of marriage. If the mother marries the man who is not the father of her child; and if the father marries the woman who is not the mother of his child, they become a blended family. Due to high rate of childbearing out of wedlock as well as divorce and remarriage, blended families are becoming more and more common in societies. It is in blended families where we get stepfathers, stepmothers, stepsons, stepdaughters, step-brothers and step-sisters. We also get 'half-brothers' and 'half-sisters' in blended families.

Being a stepfather or stepmother can be very challenging. It can be even more challenging when the biological parent is still connected to the biological father or mother because of the child. It can fill your mind with doubts and flood your heart with insecurities. It can even make you feel like you are the spectator in the relationship where your partner and his (or her) ex seem to be reliving the life they claim no longer exists. Every time you try to communicate your insecurities to your spouse, all you get in return is "it's only because of the child". Meanwhile you feel like you are being excluded as the other person seems to be enjoying all of your partner's attention. Time after time you catch yourself thinking "maybe they are still in love, and they are using their child as an excuse to see each other". Eventually, this can make you feel resentful towards the children because of what their parents are putting you through.

The relationship between the biological parent and the other biological parent of the child should be totally transparent and carefully regulated. There should never be secret interactions or private meetings between the two. The couple should always guard against the other biological parent using the child as an excuse to sneak back into the life of the biological parent; and the biological parent should play a leading role in this. The interaction between the two biological parents should take place within clearly defined boundaries. The ex partner of the biological parent should never be allowed to see the child or interact with the spouse who is the biological parent whenever and however he (or she) pleases. If need be, such interactions should be regulated with the help of the court of law. Otherwise the marital relationship could suffer a great deal of harm by the intrusion of your ex into your current relationship. Interference from an ex in the relationship is one of the main culprits in marital catastrophe.

It is normal to feel doubtful or insecure as a step-parent, especially during the initial stages of your marriage. But as time goes on, you will get used to the idea and start feeling better until you don't feel bad anymore. However, how soon you start feeling better depends strongly on how this situation is handled, especially by your step-child's biological parent. It is mainly up to the biological parent to carefully regulate their interactions with the other biological parent. As the biological parent of your partner's step-child, you are the main role player in aggravating or alleviating your partner's insecurities. Always be considerate in how you deal with your partner, your child and your ex; bearing in mind that your partner has insecurities that you need to help ease until they vanish. Be totally open and accommodating to your partner with patience and understanding. Let your partner know for sure that he (or she) takes the first place in your heart; not only in speech, but also in deeds.

As a step-parent, you need to love your partner enough to accept, love, protect and nurture his (or her) children. It will be extremely difficult, if not impossible, for your partner to accommodate you fully into the relationship if you keep on hurting or rejecting his (or her) children. To a large degree, your treatment towards your step-child determines the extent to which your partner interacts with the biological parent for the sake of the child. You win the heart of the parent through your kindness to their child. Learn to love your step-children as if they were your biological children, then they will love you as if you were their biological parent, and so will your spouse. Do not expect to be included into the family if you exclude your step-children from your life. No matter how hard you try, you cannot break the bond between the parent and the child; if you dare try to break it, what might be broken is your heart.

Learn to allow your spouse to be the parent he (or she) needs to be to his (or her) children. Do not try to get in between; otherwise you will get hurt. Every child deserves loving parents, even if one of those parents is a step-parent. Make deliberate efforts to get over your insecurities and start to embrace your family as a whole. If your spouse can trust you with his (or her) children, he (or she) can also trust you with his (or her) heart. No parent can be cheerful in marriage when his (or her) children are fearful in their own home. You can't say you love me when you hate my offspring. Therefore, if you really love your spouse, you need to take good care of his (or her) children. Love them as your own and cooperate with their biological parent in bringing them up to be the best they can be.

Some step-parents put pressure on their partners to send their biological children to their grandparents to be raised by them. That is not exactly a good idea, especially if you know how much your partner wants to raise his (or her) own children. Remember, your step-children are the siblings of your biological children, and therefore they deserve to be treated the way your biological children are treated. Do not send your step-children away if you know you won't send your biological children away. Your biological children need to be raised together with their brothers and sisters, and your partner deserves to raise all his (or her) children uniformly and in the same environment. This relationship is more than you and your self-absorption; it also involves the welfare of other members of the family. Therefore, the decisions taken in this relationship should benefit not only you; but the rest of the family – you included.

If you insist on compelling your partner to send his (or her) children to their grandparents, it will be extremely difficult, if at all possible, for you to enjoy your marital relationship. Your partner cannot focus fully on you when he (or she) does not know what is happening to his (or her) children on the other side of town. You will be stuck with your partner's body while his (or her) mind is back at home pondering deeply on the children. Humans are mammals, and mammals have parental care. No parent can enjoy marriage while his (or her) children are left 'unattended' somewhere away from their real home.

You can't have a pleasurable marriage with a miserable partner, and nothing makes the parent more miserable than not being part of his (or her) children's upbringing. By forcing your partner to send his (or her) children away, you are indirectly forcing him (or her) to choose between you and his (or her) children; and no normal parent can turn his (or her) back against his (or her) own flesh and blood. You can't build your marriage by ill-treating your step-children. If you hurt them, you break your partner's heart; and if your partner's heart breaks, so will yours. Therefore, as a step-parent, value your marriage enough to love and accept your step-children. If you nourish your step-children, your partner will be joyful and begin to cherish you; and you will also be joyful because whatever you do to your step-children, you do it to your partner; and ultimately to yourself.

Being a step-parent is highly significant from Biblical perspective. Let's take the story of Joseph and Jesus as an example (See Matthew 1-2). Take note that Joseph was technically the step-father of Jesus. Mary, the biological mother of Jesus, was impregnated not by Joseph, but by the Holy Spirit (See Matthew 1:18). Therefore, Joseph was not Jesus' biological father; he was His step-father, yet it is through Joseph that Jesus is linked to the lineage of King David. That's how much God honours marriage. He can take your stepson and link him to your lineage as if he were your own flesh and blood. It takes more than just a sperm cell to be a father; it is a divine responsibility from God the Father.

Joseph brought Jesus up as his own Son, transferring his skills and wisdom to Him as a man and a carpenter. He went with Jesus to the temple at His early age. Before anyone realized who Jesus was, God had already revealed Him to him and gave him full responsibility over His life. Joseph was raising Jesus not for himself, but for God. The purpose of Jesus was to save the people of God from sin; Mary's purpose was to conceive and give birth to Him, and Joseph's responsibility was to bring Him up and shape Him into the great Man that He was.

Jesus was regarded as the firstborn in Joseph's house. In other words, He was Joseph's firstborn, even though He was not his biological Son. The relationship between Joseph and Jesus was beyond one of stepfather and stepson. It was the relationship of father and Son. Being a stepfather means being a steward over the life that God has chosen before conception and ordained before birth to fulfil His divine purpose on earth. It means that God saw it fitting to use one man's seed to give birth to the child and use another man's wisdom and personality to bring him up. Joseph was the carpenter, which means he worked with wood; and Jesus' destiny was to save the world by dying on the wooden cross. Jesus, being the Son of the carpenter, grew up carrying wood; as if to prepare his shoulders for the weight of the cross. As God, Jesus had to be begotten by the Holy Spirit; but as a Man, He had to be raised by a man, and that man happened to be His stepfather.

Take note that God did not speak to the biological mother of Jesus concerning His name; He spoke to the stepfather instead (See Matthew 1:20-21). God went so far as to reveal the name and purpose of the Son to His stepfather. Joseph was the one who, by God's revelation, gave the Son the name *Jesus* (which means *God Saves*), linking Him to His purpose through His name. Joseph was not the biological father of Jesus, yet he was bringing up the Saviour of the world as his own Son.

Stepfathers have a significant role to play in their step-children's lives. They should assume their God-given role and take full responsibility over those innocent and gifted children that God has placed under their care. God has entrusted a huge responsibility upon stepfathers, and they owe it to themselves and to God to provide godly upbringing to their step-children. Being a stepfather does not happen to wicked people. In fact, Joseph was a righteous man (See Matthew 1:19). As a stepfather, do not lose heart in raising that precious gift; just rest assured that God has found you worthy to bring up the life that will change the world for His glory.

It was not to Mary, but to Joseph, that the angel of the Lord appeared and warned: *"Get up, take the child and His mother and escape to Egypt. Stay there until I tell you, for Herod is going to search for the child to kill Him"* (Matthew 2:13 – NIV). It was Joseph's sole responsibility to protect Jesus and find a safer place for Him to stay. The stepfather may feel excluded because he is not the biological father, but God regards him as the father who must see that the child is growing to be exactly as He has created him (or her) to be. Joseph did as the Lord commanded him concerning Jesus, and through it all, Mary never questioned him. She gave him full fatherly authority over Jesus.

Even after Herod had died, the angel of the Lord appeared again to Joseph saying: *"Get up, take the child and His mother and go to the land of Israel, for those who were trying to take the child's life are dead"* (Matthew 2:19-20). Again he obeyed the Lord, and still the biological mother did not question him or doubt his decisions concerning the child. He was responsible for finding the place of safety for the child, and his partner was comfortable allowing him to do so. Though Mary was the biological mother of Jesus, God did not speak to her concerning how He was to be brought up; He spoke to Joseph the stepfather instead. Mary had to cooperate with Joseph in bringing up the King of kings.

Jesus is called the Lion of Judah, the Root of Jesse and the Son of David because of His link to the lineage of His stepfather – Joseph. It is actually Jesus' connection with Joseph that earns Him His right to be the King of the Jews. Though Joseph was not Jesus' biological father, it was still Jesus' birthright to be called the Son of David because of His relationship with Joseph. Therefore, parenting is not so much about the release of semen as it is about the establishment of relationship between father and son. It takes a man to impregnate a woman, but take takes the father to raise the child. Impregnating a woman makes you a *biological* father, but raising the child makes you the *real* father.

Stepmothers also have a significant role to play over their step-children. Generally, mothers would not treat other women's children as their own; it is not in their instinct. It is easier and more natural for a mother to love and care for the children she has carried in her own womb than to accept the children that were conceived by other women. This is also true in the animal kingdom. A motherless calf or cub is always left vulnerable to fend for itself even when other mothers are around. Naturally, a mother is a mother only to the one she conceived. This makes it difficult for a woman to accept the other woman's children as her own, especially if their biological father is her husband. It's easier for them to accept their adopted children than it is to accept their step-children.

The wife's natural rejection of her step-children is probably linked to her awareness that her husband was once sexually involved with another woman. So, it could be that she subconsciously links her step-children to her husband's ex. Nonetheless, the stepmother, like the stepfather, should learn to love her step-children as her own. Though it might take some time, it will finally work out. Always remember that your step-children are siblings to your biological children. So, you need to love your biological children enough to take care of their siblings. Though it's not easy for them, wives are well able to love and accept their step-children as their own children. It all begins with a willing heart. If they are willing, they will make it; because as the saying goes, *where there's a will, there's a way.*

The husband also has a role to play in helping his wife accept his children completely as her own. He can ease his wife's discomforts and insecurities by carefully regulating his interactions with the biological mother. Secret meetings and private conversations between the husband and his ex can make it impossible for his wife to ever accept her step-children. At the same time, the wife's rejection of her step-children could lead to her husband resenting her and pursuing a friendship with the biological mother for the sake of his children. Ultimately, the marriage may not survive. The truth is, you can't ill-treat your husband's children and expect your marriage to be a paradise. Your marriage can be as good or as bad as you treat your step-children.

A blended family is not only about the husband and his wife; it is also about the children. Parents should make sure that when they start new relationships or consider establishing a blended family, they involve their children. It will be extremely hard for children to wake up to a man or woman walking around their house acting like their parent. This can make them feel like their comfort has been tampered with. It can shock their peace of mind and make them start feeling like strangers in their own home. Children should be properly introduced to the new person in their parent's life; and this should not happen until both lovers are completely sure about the future of their relationship.

Parents usually make a mistake of introducing the new person in their lives during their infatuation stage; before they even know that person. Before their children know that there is a new member in the family, that new member is already staying at their house, sleeping in their parent's bedroom, driving their car, eating their food and giving them household rules. All the while their parent is highly intoxicated by the chemistry he (or she) is experiencing with the newly found love. By the time infatuation stops and reality kicks in, the children are already getting used to the stranger in their home. Or maybe they have already suffered severe physical and emotional damages which were inflicted upon them by their parent's lover.

Parents should avoid rushing into introducing their children to the new love in their lives. The introduction of the lover to the children should be done when both lovers are settled in their relationship. Even so, the introduction should be done gradually. Children should be allocated adequate time to get used to the idea one step at a time. Without trying too hard or moving too fast, the potential step-parent should establish a friendship with the children. At the same time the parent should also be observant on how the children respond to the new person in their lives. The parent should also take it upon himself (or herself) to keep on assuring the children that this new situation is never going to make him (or her) love them less. The children should never feel like the new person is snatching all of their parent's attention away from them. They should find comfort in their parent's undying love for them as they struggle to adjust to the new situation.

It is easier for children to accept the new person in their parent's life when they are younger. Older children find it harder to accommodate the new person in their space who would play a parental role to them. The couple should therefore be more patient and understanding when it comes to older children. They are the ones who might throw more tantrums and become more difficult so to resist or reject the new person in their family. Those children should be given permission to feel that way until they come to realise that they must adjust to the new situation. However, the potential step-parent should be careful not to play along. He (or she) should be the hero of the situation by demonstrating love to the one who treats him (or her) hatefully. On the other hand, the biological parent should be always on guard lest the child manipulate the situation and use it as an opportunity to misbehave. At this stage, the biological parent, not the step-parent, should be the main disciplinarian to the child.

Meanwhile, be sure not to allow your love for each other as a couple to be diminished by the children's fits of temper. After all, this love affair is between the two of you; and the children will join you as you go along. Focus more on each other without forgetting about them. Let them know for sure that you love them, but you will not always keep your life on hold. Just as you accommodate them, they should accommodate you as well. Make efforts to help them accept your relationship, but whatever you do, use influence; not intimidation. If you use influence, you will get a buy-in from them; but if you use intimidation, they may give you passive resistance. Rather than coercing them to accept your relationship, convince them that this relationship can benefit them as well.

The new person can win the children's hearts not only on the way he (or she) treats them; but also on the way he (or she) treats their parent. By being friendly and loving to the children, the potential step-parent will also continue to win the parent's heart. Notice how parents go so far as to deprive themselves the things they really want for the sake of their children. Every parent puts his (or her) children first, and no matter how great a lover you are, you can never take the children's place in the heart of their parents. All you can do is earn your own place in their parent's heart by creating one for them in your heart. The more love you give to the children, the more love you will get from their parent. But if you keep on hurting them, their parent will be forced to focus all his (or her) attention on protecting his (or her) children – even against you; and the more he (or she) focuses on the children, the less he (or she) will focus on you.

Blended families are just as normal as nuclear families. In fact, with appropriate efforts, blended families can feel like nuclear families or even better. After all, both of them are families, and they both require good interpersonal skills to function properly. Marriage in a nuclear family is no better than one in a blended family. Same marital and parenting principles apply to both nuclear and blended families. The success of a blended family begins with the success of the step-parent in accepting and loving his (or her) step-children as his (or her) own. And the success of every family, whether nuclear or blended, is strongly dependent on the success of the marital relationship between the husband and his wife. How the issue of children is handled in marriage can also determine the success or failure of marriage.

Parenting is a team effort involving both parents. It is not a competition between two parents who battle for their children's affection. It requires equal efforts from both parents, and whatever decisions that are taken concerning the children, both parents must agree. In fact, it is wise to discuss the upbringing of the children even before they are born; so that there can be harmony between the parents as they bring them up. Parenting also requires cooperation between the parents. If only one parent is involved in the upbringing of the children, the marriage could suffer because that parent would have to focus more on the children and less on the partner. No parent would leave their children unattended and attend to the partner who is not involved in their upbringing. If you play an active role in the upbringing of your children, it will be easier for your partner to focus on you.

The husband should not have a problem bathing the child or changing his diapers when the wife is busy with something else. Even if the wife is not busy with anything, the husband still needs to take full responsibility over his child. As a father, it is not enough to spend your money on your children; you also need to spend your time with them. Even to your children, your presence is more important than your presents. You may give everything, but everything means nothing without you in it. Boys lack good role models because their fathers are missing in action. They are always around, but they are never there. Their absence is felt more when they are present because they think children are their mother's responsibility, and all they need to do is buy and pay. Children need more than your money; they also need your love, your wisdom and your shield. Whatever you buy for them, they cannot enjoy it without you.

Parenting also requires consistency and congruence on the part of both parents. When one parent says "No" to the child, the other parent should not say "Yes". Both parents should speak the same language at all times when it comes to children. If they happen to disagree, let it not be in front of the children. The parents in disagreement should always bear in mind that whatever they decide should be in the best interest of the child. If the other parent says "Yes" when you wanted to say "No", do not oppose each other in front of the child. If "Yes" will not yield harmful results for the child, let it remain a 'yes' for the sake of the child; then it can be discussed in his (or her) absence until agreement is reached. The best thing to do is to refrain from taking a decision if you are not sure whether or not your partner will agree; then you can discuss it and decide on it together.

If parenting is not handled appropriately by the couple, it could be the source of conflict and unnecessary disputes in marriage. Remember, marriage is the fusion of two different souls, and different people may want to raise children differently. Such differences must be acknowledged and managed properly.

None of the couple should impose their way of raising children upon the other. Sometimes you may agree to disagree, as long as the wellbeing of the child is not compromised. If you use intimidation to discipline your child, your partner may want to use influence to achieve the same results. If your partner uses different approach from you, it does not mean they are not doing it correctly. Your way is not the only way. Actually, the mother and the father cannot raise children the same way. As a matter of fact, the role of the father in raising children is typically different from that of a mother. Those differences are necessary to bring balance upon the children as they develop into adults.

Children first learn behaviour at home. They learn the culture of their society by observing their parents. It is therefore essential that parents behave in such a way that their children will regard them as best role models. Actually, effective discipline of the children begins with the proper modelling of behaviour by their parents. Children pay attention more to what they see than what they hear. So, as parents, make sure that you show them what you told them. Do not tell them one thing and then show them the other thing that contradicts what you told them. Eventually they might lose trust in you; and if they lose trust in you, you will lose influence over them. If they can't trust you, you can't instruct them.

Every boy has a desire to be like his father, and every girl wants to be like her mother. That is where they first discover their identity. If the father drinks liquor, smokes cigarettes and abuses his wife, the boy will observe it and try to imitate him, thinking those things will make him more like a man like his father is. On that breath, whatever the mother does, the daughter will imitate. If the mother spends half of her day basking in the sun and the rest of the day gossiping and sleeping, the daughter will also observe it and start imitating her. Same applies when parents behave positively. For example, if the parents spend their time loving each other, reading their Bibles, going to work, attending church and praying regularly; it will also rub off on the children. Children say nothing they did not hear, and they do nothing they did not see.

As a mother, would you be happy if your sons' wives treated them the way you treat your husband? And as a father, would you like it if your daughters' husbands treated them the way you treat your wife? If your answer is no, then you need to change the way you treat your spouse. Believe or not, however you treat your spouse, you are sowing a seed into your children's future, and they might have to reap what you have sown. If you are a great mother to your sons and poor wife to you husband, your sons may love you so much that they may want to marry someone like you when they're old so that they can be loved the way you love them, and once they do, their father's history may repeat itself on them. Even if you are a great father to your daughters and a poor husband to your wife, your daughters may adore you so much that they may get attracted to men like you when they are older; and then they might relive their mother's experiences in their own marriages. You can sow a good seed into your children's future by being nice to your partner today.

Train up a child in the way he should go, and when his is old he will not depart from it (Proverbs 22:6). Parenting is not only about feeding and bathing; it is also about training. Successful parents develop the skills of their children. Always keep in mind that whatever you teach your child in his early age will remain with him for the rest of his life. Even if he may ignore what you taught him, life will keep on throwing it back in his face, and he will not forget it. Parents often become lenient to their children when they are infants and toddlers, and they want to be harsh to them when they are teenagers. This is not a good recipe for parenting. Effective parenting is about training children when they are still infants and toddlers; then reminding them when they are teenager what you taught them when they were infants and toddlers. Whatever you do to your child, you plant a seed into his future; and whatever you teach him in his childhood, he will not depart from it in his adulthood.

Training is not only about telling and showing; it is also about allowing the child to make mistakes and learn from them. Parents who always do things for their children are failing in their parenting. They are actually creating an attitude of dependency in their children. If the task is safe and simple enough for the child, let him try it on his own and keep on encouraging him until he gets it right. That will give him a sense of worth and boost his confidence. It will also improve his leadership and innovative abilities. Couples should always be careful not to stand in each other's way when it comes to raising their children. For example, if one parent allows the child to carry out a task on his own, the other parent should not interfere by trying to carry out that task for the child. Divided parents produce confused children; and cooperative parents produce confident children.

Children have a way of diverting their parents' attention from each other. This is one thing couples should guard against at all times. Remember, these children are here because of you, and they are not here to stay; and before you became parents, you were already lovers. Therefore, as a couple, it will be helpful for you to live your married lives in such a way that you won't struggle to reconnect when your children have moved out to start their own lives. If one of the couple focuses more on the children, the other partner might feel excluded and then begin to withdraw gradually from the relationship, and he (or she) can go missing in action. So, even as you enjoy the presence of your children, never do it at the expense of your relationship as a married couple.

Be parents; but never forget to be lovers. Love your children; but never at the expense of your love for each other. Give them attention; but don't let it steal your affection for each other. Celebrate them, but never let them come between you. They can never be joyful when you are not happy as a couple. A rare gift that you can ever give to your children is to be joyful together as a couple. The merrier you are as a couple, the happier they become as your children. Therefore, if you want to bring joy into your children's hearts, you have to let them observe how much you love each other as husband and wife.

Whenever dispute breaks out between the two of you as a couple, always be careful never to use your children as weapons against each other. Don't even try to have them on your side against your partner. Do not let them get caught up in your quarrels. Always bear in mind that your children love both of you equally as their parents. If you try to turn them against their other parent, it hurts them more than it hurts your partner. Even if you can spend lots of money on your children, you can't buy them out of loving their other parent; you will only break their innocent hearts more and more as you try.

Getting along as a couple is vital for the children's wellbeing. It makes it easier for them to love both of you without being afraid that one of you might want to punish them for loving their 'enemies'. But please remember, that 'enemy' of yours is a parent to your children. Therefore, as you attempt to settle your disputes as a couple, leave the children out of it.

Much as children must be cared for by both parents, couples should always be sure not to allow their children to come between them. As much as you think about your children, think more about your partner. Your children should under no circumstances be used as an excuse for not spending quality time together as a couple. Couples should learn to take time out to be alone, with no children interrupting. As you bond with the children, bond more with each other. Be careful not to fall into the trap of behaving more like parents and less like lovers. There should be a balance between the two. Learn to take care of the children without neglecting your relationship as a married couple. This will help you achieve not only a happy marriage; but also a happy home for you and your children.

12

The In-Laws – *Part of the Package*

All of us, except Adam and Eve, have parents who gave birth to us; and most of us have siblings we grew up with. Those who were not privileged enough to be raised by their parents have at least had some people who raised them as their own children. Such people have played a vital role in our lives, and we continue to treasure them in our hearts for as long as we live. Our relationship with our parent figures and our siblings is one of the most important relationships in the human race. This kind of relationship is unbreakable because our parents' and siblings' blood runs in our system. Our bond with them is so strong because we have known them since we were born (or since they were born if they are younger siblings). It is in our relationship with them that we find love and acceptance. Not only that, they are also the ones who taught us most of the things we know. For this reason we always feel indebted to them for what they did for us since our childhood.

When we get married, these relationships do not die; they still exist, and they cannot be ignored. Therefore, by the time you get married, never lose sight to the significance of your partner's parents and siblings in his (or her) life. As soon as you are declared husband and wife; your partner's family becomes your family; they become your *In-Laws* (i.e. your father-in-law, mother-in-law, brother-in-law and sister-in-law). It is impossible to marry your partner in isolation; when you marry them, you automatically adopt their family. Your partner also adopts your family, and your family becomes your partner's in-laws. Your partner's family means a lot to them, just as must as yours means much to you. It is therefore important that you value your partner's family just as much as you value yours.

This may sound very easy, but it's not really that easy. Remember that your family is not the one that was attracted to your partner; you are. And your partner's family was not the one that decided to marry you; it was your partner who decided. This means your family needs to accept your choice whether they like it or not, and your partner's family will have to accept their child's choice whether they like it or not. On the same breath, you were attracted to your partner; not to their family, and your partner was attracted to you; not to your family. Therefore, your decision to marry your partner makes you part of their family, even if the only person you love in that family is your partner. However, no matter how you feel about your partner's family, your partner loves and values them tremendously; just as much as you love and value your family. This poses a challenge to both of you to learn to love each other's families as your own.

Imagine how you would feel if your partner disregarded your family and treated them with disrespect; how would you feel? How would you feel if your partner took you for a visit to their family most of the time while they hardly ever pay a visit to your family? The same way you would feel if your partner treated your family that way is most probably how your partner might feel if you treated their family likewise. It is therefore important that you learn to treat your partner's family the way you want your partner to treat yours. Learn to treat them not according to how you feel about them; but according to how your partner feels about them; because the truth of the matter is, that is the way you would like your partner to treat your family. Anything that is good for your family is also good for your partner's family. So, it will be wise to try by all means to avoid making your partner feel like your family is more important than theirs.

Much as you may play your part to learn to love your in-laws the way you love your own family, the feeling may not be mutual on their part. They may dislike you or even resent you for 'stealing their child from them'. As you try to love and respect them, they may hate and reject you in return. In most cases, families find it difficult to accept their child's partner. The husband's family is mostly the one that finds it difficult to accept their daughter-in-law. Generally, it is easier for the wife's family to accept their son-in-law than it is for the husband's family to accept their daughter-in-law. This is very puzzling because you would expect the wife's family to be the ones who are mean to their son-in-law since he is going to change their daughter's surname into his own. But the son-in-law would be treated with so much respect by his in-laws, whereas the wife on the other side is being abused in every possible way by her in-laws.

The rejection of wives by their in-laws usually happens in most African cultures where every boy is expected to grow up and work for his family so that he can take care of his parents and siblings. In most African cultures, males are seen as 'bread winners' in their families; and this causes those families to see their sons' wives as intruders who came to steal their 'source of income'. This is probably where the rejection of wives by their in-laws stems from. This is somehow unfair for the male child because he also has the life of his own, and he needs to establish his own family just as his parents once established their own. This rejection may also be caused by the stigma attached to women as 'witches' who are in this marriage to rip their son off his possessions and leave him for dead. If the wife dies, 'she was too weak to handle her family'; but if it is the husband that dies, 'his wife bewitched or killed him'.

Because of such rejection, many wives avoid any kind of contact with their in-laws. They seldom visit them nor participate in their activities. This usually leaves the husband in a dilemma as he gets caught up in a love triangle between his mother and his wife; who clearly don't get along. He wants to go and see his beloved mother, but he does not want to leave his beloved wife alone at home; yet he knows he can't take his wife along to his family. This is usually the time when the husband feels like he should not have made a marital commitment in the first place. He loves his wife, but he doesn't want to hurt his mother; and he loves his mother, but he doesn't want to hurt his wife. Humanly speaking, this problem is impossible to solve; but from God's perspective, there is a clear solution.

Therefore a man shall leave his father and mother and be joined to his wife, and they shall become one flesh (Genesis 2:24). Many a times you will hear the husband complaining that his wife is trying to separate him from his mother (or father, or siblings). Some husbands even decide to file for divorce as a result. However, to divorce your wife for 'trying to separate you from your mother' is the violation of God's principles. It's like trying to use human means to solve God's problem. Marriage is not a human thing; it is a God thing. It cannot be operated through human means; it requires God's principles. According to God's principle, a man shall *leave* his father and mother and be *joined* to his wife, and they shall become *one flesh.* Husbands who use human means to operate marriage leave their wives for their mothers; but husbands who apply godly principles leave their mothers for their wives.

According to godly principle, there can be no marriage if the man is not prepared to leave his mother and father. There is a need for every man to outgrow his overdependence on his parents and start living independently with his wife. If you are not ready to leave your mother and father (and siblings), you are not ready to get married. You can't *cleave* to your wife if you won't *leave* your mother. Yes, you may be popular in your family, even in your society, for refusing to leave your mother and father for your wife's sake; but you will surely be single very soon. In fact, I have learnt that man-pleasers cannot hold their marriages together; only God-pleasers can. It pleases men to leave your wife for your mother; but it pleases God to leave your mother for your wife; and *we ought to obey God rather than men* (Acts 5:29).

Not only should a husband leave his family for his wife; he should also protect her from them. Sometimes they will make unreasonable demands on her, and only her husband can protect her. If you leave your wife to see herself around your family, you are practically worsening the situation. If you leave her to stand up for herself against the unreasonable demands of your family, they are going to see her as rebellious and hate her even more. And the more they hate her, the less interaction she will have with them, and the more miserable you will be in your marriage. Whether or not your wife is accepted in your family strongly depends on you. It is your role to teach your family to love and accept your wife; and if you don't, they never will. One other thing to bear in mind is that how you speak about your wife to your parents and siblings will also determine their attitude towards her. If you keep on complaining to them about her, they may never come to a point of accepting her.

Your family might make you believe that they are only trying to protect you from 'that woman', and that they love you too much to let her 'bewitch' you. But this is not really about love. They can't say they love you if they hate your wife; because the two of you have become one flesh in a marriage covenant. If they love your wife, they love you; but if they hate her, they are actually being inconsiderate about what's important to you. If they really cared about you, they would respect your decision to marry your wife and love her for your sake. Trying to separate you from the woman you love is not an indication of love;

it is a sign of selfishness on their part. If it had anything to do with love, they would be happy to see you happy with the woman you love.

Much as it is true that a man should leave his family and be joined to his wife, it is also important to understand that *leaving* is not *forsaking*. Therefore, the Bible does not say "abandon your parents (and siblings)"; it says "leave" them. You still have a responsibility over your parents and siblings as their son and brother, but you should put your wife first and ensure that her wellbeing is not tampered with by them. You still need them, and they still need you; but your wife needs you more. Be sure not to allow your family to say anything harmful to or about your wife. Let them know you love her unconditionally; and that it hurts you just as much as it hurts her when they slander her. You should be the one to let them know that how they treat your wife affects you. As soon as they realize how serious you are about your wife, they will start to respect her and change their attitude for your sake; thus making it easier for your wife to reach out to them.

One other thing you may have to guard against as a husband is to allow your family to disregard your wife and communicate only with you over matters that require both of you to make decisions. Let them know that you are not the only decision maker in your family; your wife is the co-decision maker. No one should disregard your wife, and it is your responsibility as a husband to ensure that it does not happen. Trying to please your family by disregarding your wife will cost you your marriage. Eventually your family will be impressed; but you will be depressed and alone. You can move from one woman to another, but as long as you do not learn to let go of your mother and father, the result is always going to be same – unhappy marriages ending in divorce.

It may sound unfair for you as the husband to have to leave your mother and father and be joined to your wife, but that is exactly what the Lord Jesus Christ did when He came to save humanity. He left His Heavenly Father on His Heavenly Throne and came to earth so that He can be joined with us. He loved those who hated Him and prayed for those who persecuted Him. He also ministered healing and deliverance to those who had no place for Him in their hearts. He even died a brutal death on the cross to establish a church for Himself on earth. Remember, according to the Word of God, you as a husband are to your wife as Christ is to His church. If Christ left His Father to come for you, so should you leave your father and mother and cleave to your wife.

Marriage requires sacrifice on the part of the husband; which is exactly what Jesus did for us. If you cannot sacrifice your life or your family for your wife's sake, then you are not worthy to be her husband.

Your responsibility as a husband does not end with your family; it also extends to your in-laws. Think about how valuable your wife's family is to her and learn to also see it that way. To understand how much her family means to her, think about how valuable your family is to you. Learn to accept and love them for her sake as if they were your own. Remember, it could be that you have two families that love and respect you, but she only has one at the moment, the one she comes from. Therefore, as you think about your family, also remember hers. You can be as much a blessing to her family as you are to yours. Do not lose heart as you do so; always remembering that your love for your wife should reflect Christ's love for His church. Let the world know how much Christ loves them by observing how much you love your wife. Marriage is not about you getting what you want or deserve; it is about you becoming more and more like Christ as you reflect His love to your wife.

Wives also have a role to play in as far as the in-laws are concerned. First and foremost, as a wife, the way you present your husband in your family strongly determines whether or not they respect him. You are the only one who can make him feel welcomed in your family. You are also the only one who can make your family understand that it is the voice of your husband that approves all major decisions that are taken in your marriage. Be sure not to humiliate him or belittle him in any way in front of your family. Let them know he is the king of the house in which you are the queen. Do not give your family an impression that you 'call the shots' in your marriage; by so doing, you will be degrading your husband before them, and they may start to disregard his authority as your head. The way you treat your husband when your family is around sets a standard for them in terms of how to treat him. In other words, they can only treat your husband the way you treat him.

If you want your husband to be involved in your family, you need to present him well to them. Men have fragile egos. They would not go where they are not respected; it may strain their egos. It may also tamper with their masculinity and make them feel like they are less than men. When it comes to the in-laws, the husband would be glad to go where he is celebrated; not where is merely tolerated, and whether he is celebrated or tolerated in your family depends on you as the wife. It is advisable for you to avoid bad-mouthing him to your parents or siblings, and try by all means to protect his image in your family. If you present him well in your family, he will be received well, and he will have no problem paying them a visit every now and then just to check if they are still doing fine.

You also have a responsibility towards your in-laws. How you react to their treatment can either alleviate or aggravate the tension. If you react humanly, you may aggravate the tension; but if respond in a godly manner, you will alleviate it. The human approach is *an eye for an eye* approach. You treat people as they treat you. If they don't greet you, you also don't greet them. If they do not go to your house, you also do not go to their house. Whatever they do to you, you 'return the favour'. Such reactions cannot solve the problem; in fact, they multiply it by two. Their actions become problem number one, and your reactions become two times problem number one.

You solve nothing by 'giving people a dose of their medicine'; rather than solving the problem, you become guilty of similar offense. Simple logic applies to this: if they assault you, they become guilty of assault; and if you return the favour and assault them back, you become guilty of the same offense. So, it becomes two times assault and problem made worse. Given this scenario, we can conclude that human approach of *an eye for an eye* cannot solve your problem; it can only aggravate it. *An eye for an eye* approach does not restore the damaged eye; it damages the second eye instead. It worsens whatever you are trying to better.

Godly approach is different from human approach. Human approach says "an eye for an eye and tooth for tooth"; but godly approach says: *Love your enemies, do good to those who hate you, bless those who curse you, and pray for those who spitefully use you* (Luke 6:27-28). A godly approach to problem solving in relationships empowers you to remain steadfast in your character. Godly people are loving people, and their nature or behaviour is not determined by other people's actions. We love even when we are hated; and we bless even when we are cursed. It is not in us to hate, and it is not in us to curse. When you use godly approach in dealing with your in-laws, your actions will be consistent because they will be based on your nature rather than on their treatment. For every hatred they demonstrate against you, you will respond with sincere expressions of love.

If you treat people the way they treat you, you will be inconsistent in your reactions because you will be basing your actions on how you are treated. Not only that; if you treat people the way they treat you, you are practically taking their problem and making it your own. If they curse you, that's their problem; but if you react by also cursing them, it then becomes your problem as well. Not only are you adopting their problems, you are also adopting their sins, and you might even miss heaven because of them. If they hate you or offend you, they are sinning; but if decide hate them for hating you and offend them for offending you, you are also sinning. Human reactions aggravate problems, but godly responses alleviate them.

When it comes to your in-laws, do not treat them as they treat you; rather treat them as God would treat you if it were you doing that to Him. Our God is loving, gracious and kind, and *as He is, so are we in this world* (See 1John 4:17). We have the nature of our Father. God is Love (See 1John 4:8), and so are we. Love cannot deny itself, and neither can we deny ourselves. Because of our resemblance of God, love is not what we do; it is who we are. We do not treat people based on what they do; we treat them based on who we are. When you do good to those who hate you, you give them no valid reasons to hate you. You cannot put out fire with fire; you need water instead. In the same way, as a godly wife, do not try to 'beat them at their own game'; rather operate from your position of strength and quench their hatred with love and their curses with blessings. *Do not be overcome by evil, but overcome evil with good* (Romans 12:21).

In your reactions to your in-laws' treatment, you will end up becoming either like them or like Christ, depending on the approach from which you choose to respond or react. If you follow human approach, you will become more like them; but if you follow godly approach, you will become more like Christ. Becoming more like Christ means victory on your part, but becoming like them means defeat for both you and them. Let your responses to them always be humble and gentle, that you may appease every rage in their 'hateful' hearts. Eventually you might win them over to Christ through your conduct and godly responses. Do not stop loving; keep on reaching out to them with passion even when it hurts. Ultimately they will see Christ in you and make a decision to follow Him. Your cross is your crown. Carry it with diligence, that you may wear your crown with contentment at the end of your struggle.

Wives should be committed to their in-laws no matter what the situation may be. There is no way God would not reward the wife who is committed to her in-laws. Let us have a brief look at the example of Ruth (See the Book of Ruth in the Bible). Ruth was fully committed to Naomi, her mother-in-law, even when there was nothing in that relationship for her. Having lost her husband, and knowing that her widowed mother-in-law had no other sons that could marry her, she decided to cling to her anyway. Ruth could have left her mother-in-law to look for another man, but she remained committed to her even after she insisted that she should go her way. Naomi made it clear that Ruth will gain nothing by remaining with her; yet Ruth insisted that she will stay with her. Eventually God rewarded her by joining her with Boaz as husband and wife; and within that marriage she became the great grandmother of David. Ruth's commitment to her mother-in-law ultimately earned her a place in the lineage of Christ.

If Ruth, knowing very well that there was nothing left for her in her mother-in-law, decided to stay committed to her, how much more should you, who still has your husband, be committed to your in-laws? And if God took it upon Himself to reward Ruth for her commitment to her mother-in-law by putting her in the lineage of the King of kings and the Lord of lords, will He not remember to reward you for your commitment to your in-laws? Your reward does not come from your in-laws; it comes from the Lord God Himself, and if your in-laws fail to recognize your unconditional commitment to them, God will never leave it unnoticed. Even if they may continue to reject you, continue to respect them, not for their sake, but for God's sake; knowing very well that your reward comes not from them, but from the Lord. The smaller they make you feel as you do good to them, the greater God will make you before them and the whole world. God will ultimately transform their rejection of you into their respect for you.

Godly approach applies not only to your in-laws; it also applies in every other relationship you may be involved in, including your relationship with your spouse. 'Returning the favour' or giving your partner 'the dose of his (or her) medicine' cannot improve your marital relationship; it can only damage it even more. You cannot repay pain with pain and expect things to get better; they will get bitter instead. If you really want to build your marriage, learn to treat your partner based on who you are and not on what they did. Do not react to what is happening; rather respond in such a manner that you will create what you want to see happening. Do not let the situation shape your reactions; rather shape your situation by your reactions. To build a better marriage, be the better person and do what is right no matter what the other person does.

Married couples usually make the mistake of confiding in their families when they have disagreements in their marriages. It is normal to have disagreements when you are married to each other, but it is harmful to your marriage if you keep on updating your family on your disagreements with your partner. When you confide in them about your partner's weaknesses, they will side with you against your partner and hate him (or her) more and more based on your information. Take note that when you confide in them against your partner, you will only tell them about the frustrations your partner is bringing you through, and you would not tell them about the pains you are also putting him (or her) through. This will only aggravate the tension between your partner and your family. If you feel you really want to ventilate your frustrations, rather talk to a neutral trustworthy person (preferably a professional counsellor). Confiding in your family may make you feel better, but it also makes your marriage bitter because it widens the gap between your partner and your family.

Marriages are also enduring high intensities of strain because of partners who have allowed their families to take over their marital lives. They spend more time with their parents or siblings than they do with their spouses. If they are not with them, they are on the phone chatting with them. Meanwhile their partners are hopelessly desperate for their attention. Some people even accept phone calls from their family members at night and converse with them for hours while their partners can do nothing but lie in their lonely bed and watch their marriages fall apart. The intimacy that was supposed to be shared with their partners is shared with their parents and siblings instead. For every decision that should be made in their marriages, they consult their families, as if their partners are incapable of deciding for themselves. They are in their marriages with their bodies, but their hearts are left far behind where they came from. This can cause their partners to resent their in-laws even more. It can also damage the marriage because their partners feel left out and lonely.

It is good to converse with your family, but not at the expense of your marital relationship. As soon as you get married, you priorities change, and your partner becomes number one on the list. You need to understand that your partner comes first, and your family should also understand that and stop interrupting the harmony of your marriage. But your family cannot give you space if you keep on taking all their calls at all times. You need to put your foot down and let them know that you can no longer give them the time you used to give them when you were still single. Your interactions with your family should be regulated such that they do not interfere with your marriage. Your marriage is not about you and your family; it is about you and your spouse, and this makes your spouse the most important person in your world.

Our families and in-laws can be a very good support system for us if we can learn healthy ways to manage our interactions with them. As a married couple, you are equal partners, and both your families are equally important. Numerous marriages are suffering a large degree of harm because of imbalances on how couples relate with their families and in-laws. If you focus more on your family and less on your in-laws; your partner will have to focus more on your in-laws and less on your family. Marriage is not only about you and your family; it's about your partner and your in-laws as well. Selfish partners will focus more on their families and neglect their in-laws; but godly partners will always remember that their in-laws are just as important to their partners as their families are to them, and they learn to love their in-laws like their own families.

Marriage is not about doing things because it feels good to do them; it is about doing things because it is the right thing to do. Everything we do should reflect who we are, not how we feel. You don't love because that's how you feel; you love because that's who you are. This is the true nature of love: *Love loves based not on the performance of the beloved, but on personality of the loving.* Marriage is all about love. If you cannot love, you cannot stay married. Love is not a *practice*; it is a *trait*; it is not something you do, it is who you are. Love is also not a *feeling*; it is a *feature*. Feelings are subject to change, but features are built to last. From this we can conclude that love is a *constant*, not a *variable*. A constant is not subject to change; it remains stable no matter what happens around it. But a variable is subject to change, and it takes the form of anything that happens around it. Loving your in-laws should not be subject to what they do; it should be fuelled by the love of Christ that comes from within you.

Marriage is for mature people, and the main quality of maturity is love. Immature people react based on what is happening; but mature people respond based on what they want to see happening. In other words, immature people are *reactive*, but mature people are *creative*. They respond to their surroundings with the aim to create desired results. Immature people justify their action by what happened, but mature people influence what should happen by their actions. Immature people treat people as they are treated, but mature people treat people as they themselves would like to be treated. Immature partners treat their in-laws the way they treat them, but mature people treat their in-laws the way they themselves want them to treat them. Only mature people can change the situation for better in their marriages, but immature people only change it for worse. As long as couples are reactive in their dealings with their in-laws, in-law rivalry will not end; but if couples can turn the tables and continue to love even when they feel abused, in-law rivalry will be reduced, and marriages will be improved.

13

Marriage and Technology

The rise of technology has simplified the lives of billions of people all over the world. It has turned the planet into one global village. Not only does it enable us to move from one place to another; it also enables us to communicate with people all over the world with just the tips of our fingers. Through technology we are able to know the people we never met and to interact with people we have never seen. We are also able make serious transactions and conduct important meetings from within our houses through technology. The job that could only be done by hundreds of people can now be done by just one person because of technology. Even the hardest jobs can be done easily by just pressing the button.

With the rise of technology, human interactions become easier. In the recent history, communication with people who lived far away was extremely difficult. It took several days for the message to reach the intended recipient; but things began to ease up when the telephone was introduced. People could then exchange words from a distance. Even so, people to whom the message was intended could only be reached when they were in the house with a telephone. Things got much better with the introduction of internet and cell phones. People could then interact wherever they were and as often as they pleased. Things kept on improving, and there was Skype and social networks. Today, because of technology, we can interact with our loved ones no matter how far they are from us; and we are well-informed about everything that happens worldwide.

Lately many people cannot live without their cell phones, and many can hardly keep their fingers off them. People tend to sink their eyes into their phones; and as their eyes sink in, so do their hearts and minds. Some bump their heads into walls while fixing their eyes into the screens of their cell phones, and others have gone so far as to lose their lives in terrible car accidents because they kept their eyes off the road and into their phone screens. Some people were hired into their dream jobs through cell phones, and others were fired because of the same. Some couples got married because of their phones, and others got divorced because of the same. Technology was meant to simplify our lives, but it can complicate them if we do not learn to use it wisely.

In the recent history, before the rise of social networks and the internet, families were strongly integrated. There were stronger bonds among family members because they spent most of their time focusing on each other. There were fewer external interruptions and more internal interactions within families. Children learnt more from their parents than they did from anywhere else. Married couples were able to connect at deeper levels because they could focus totally on each other when they were together. They didn't have to wait until a certain television programme ends before they got intimate with each other. There were no phone calls or messages that could interrupt their interactions. Life then was not as convenient as it is now; but it was more fulfilling because people could focus more on the things that really mattered.

Now things have changed. Televisions, social networks, play stations and cell phones have taken over in families. Family members can be together in one house and yet be far apart from each other. They interact more when they are apart than when they are together. When you enter into a typical technologically advanced family, you are very likely to find all family members together in the house, each one burying their heads into their phones. They often interact with people outside the house; but they seldom interact with each other as family members. In the process, children learn more from the outside world than they do from their parents; and this leads to rapid diffusion of culture and family disintegration in modern societies.

Marriages are also affected. Couples now tend to judge each other against the characters they see in the movies. They spend more time watching television, and very seldom do they take a moment just to look into each other's eyes. They touch their phones more than they touch each other; and they smile with their phones more than they do with each other. They wink to everybody else in the social networks but never to each other as couples. The prevalence of internet dating continues to tear marriages apart. Nowadays couples lie together on one bed and flirt; but not with each other. When they communicate, they don't speak from the heart anymore; they instead download love messages from the internet. They don't talk anymore about the things that bother them; they instead prefer to air their concerns out into social networks and get advices from people who don't really care about them.

Technology is a powerful tool couples can use to strengthen their marriages; but it can also become a lethal weapon against marriages. Technology can be as good or as bad as the manner in which you use it. How you use it can make or break your marriage. Some couples use social networks to express their love publicly to each other, while others use the same to publicise their partners' weaknesses. Some use them to chat with their partners; and others use the same to chat with their partners' rivals. Some use it to connect with their partners; and others use it to disconnect from theirs. In short, some people use technology to build their marriages, but others use it to destroy them.

Some husbands no longer find their wives attractive because they keep on comparing them with the women they flirt with in the net. Even wives would fantasise about men on television while spending time with their own husbands. What was meant to simplify life seems to be tearing relationships apart. People now substitute faces with screens; and they seem to be developing a strong liking for things that are not real. Now there is internet sex. You can have sex with as many people as you want without even touching them. Meanwhile your spouse is sitting in the same room, and they cannot even notice what you are doing because they are also swallowed up in their own net activities. Couples now risk their marriages and date people they have never met physically; and they neglect their own partners, whom they live with everyday.

As I browse through the status updates in social networks, I am sometimes disturbed by people posting status updates like "I'm having quality time with my wife [or husband]"; then they would respond to every comment that follows their update afterwards. When I check closely, I would observe that the time intervals between such comments are five to ten minutes apart. The truth is, by so doing you are not spending quality time with your spouse; you are actually spending it next to your spouse with the rest of the world. Sitting next to your partner does not make it quality time spent with him (or her); what makes it quality time is when you switch off from everything else and focus only on your partner. Some couples would sit next to each other and then focus all their attention on the television programme. That also is not quality time. It only becomes quality time when you both switch off the television and focus completely on each other. Sadly, couples nowadays would rather give up their marriages than switch off their cell phones.

Another tragedy that I have observed as I navigated through the social networks was that some people use social networks as a platform to ventilate their emotions. They use social networks as counselling rooms, and they air their marital frustrations out to strangers. They do so hoping that things will get better in their marriages; only to find that the opposite happens. Then they would go back to the same and try to make things better; only to make them even worse. Social networks were not meant for marriage counselling. Airing your marital problems therein can only cause more problems. If you need marital counselling, go and see a professional counsellor; and thus save your marriage from falling apart because of a wonderful resource such as technology.

Some of the serious disputes couples get caught up in involve their cell phones. The improper use of cell phones can disintegrate families to a very large extent. Some people spend too much time talking or chatting on the cell phone; and they neglect their partners in the process. Some would be chatting for hours with people of the opposite sex; thus making their partners feel unnecessarily insecure. This often leads to couples sneaking into each others' phones to check who their partners have been chatting with and what they were chatting about. Then they start keeping their cell phones away from each other; and with that evolves lack of trust in marriages. As much as a cell phone is vital in our lives, it is better to live without it than to lose your marriage because of it. Your marriage is far more important than the phone calls you receive and the status updates you make in the social networks.

Marriages do not have to fall apart because of the developments that are brought forth by technology. Couples should learn to use technology as a tool to strengthen their marital relationships. They should use it to stay connected even when they are miles apart; not to keep away from each other even when they are together. They should also learn to put their cell phones away when they are together. As a couple, instead of using the internet as an emotional exit point from your marital relationship, you should rather use it to search for holiday destinations where you can spend quality time together. Use it to benefit your marriage; not to break it.

If you can switch off your cell phone when you are in an important business meeting, what hinders you from doing the same when you are with your spouse? If I could ask you why you switch off your cell phone when you are in a business meeting, you would most probably tell me that you do so because you respect you work or your client. If you respect your marriage or your spouse, you will have no problem switching off your cell phone when you are with him (or her) just like you do when you are in an important meeting. Successful couples know how to monitor their phone calls. They are able to put everything else aside and direct all their focus on each other. You can also make your marriage a success by learning to use technology wisely. As you celebrate technological improvements in the world, make sure you always use such improvements to improve your marriage.

14

Baggage from the Past

Like it or not, people bring their baggage into their marriages, and that baggage is brought forward from their past. Consciously or subconsciously, all of us have a past that continues to affect us even today; and to a large extend, our past experiences influence our present decisions. Some aspects of our past are great, but others are horrible. There are things in our past that we wish could happen again, but there are also other things that we wish never happened. In our past we have the things we are proud of, and we also have those things that we are ashamed of. There are things that make us smile when we remember them, but other things only make us relive the pains we thought were gone. Extensively, our past has played a significant role in making us who we are today.

Behind every *glory* there is a *story*, and behind every *victory* there is *history*. There is also a *past* behind every *pain*. We often wish to be like other people when they succeed, but we seldom pause to ponder what they have been through before they succeeded. We see the *crown* on their heads today, but we fail to see the *cross* they carried on their shoulders yesterday. Some are where they are because they had strong support systems in their past, but others had to struggle through afflictions to pursue success against all odds. For every pride they have attained, there was a price they had to pay. Some had to become prisoners before they became presidents, but we think too much about the presidency that we fail to realise the prison that preceded the presidency.

Generally, our decisions to get married are influenced mainly by our knowledge of who our partners are, what they do and what they have; and we seldom, if ever, consider what they have been through or where they came from. Only after we got married do we realised that they have come in with baggage from their past. Then we end up living a life of torture wherein we are punished for what someone else has done to our partners in their past. We also bring our own baggage along into the marriage. Then we spend our marital lives interpreting every word, action or event according to our past experiences. We tend to get offended by the acts that were meant to delight us because of our association of such acts with our past. Eventually, our marriages may suffer severe damage if we do not learn to deal with our past.

There are many psychological theories that can help us understand the impact of our past experiences in our present lives; but in this chapter I will approach this discussion from the *Learning* perspective. According to the learning theory, there are various types of learning; but our focus in this chapter will be on *Associative Learning*. This is where we learn by associating the *experience* with the *response*; and we are conditioned by a stimulus to behave in a certain way. For example, when you see or smell food; your mouth begins to salivate, and your digestive system prepares for digestion. In this case, the food is the stimulus, and the secretion of saliva is the response. There are two types of associative learning, namely: Classical Conditioning and Operant Conditioning. For the purpose of this discussion, only classical condition will be explored.

Classical Conditioning is the type of learning that occurs when one is conditioned to respond to a stimulus that would not naturally lead to such response because one associates it with a stimulus that does lead to that response. An example of this is the experiment that was done by Ivan Pavlov, a Russian scientist who was studying digestion in dogs. Pavlov's experiment was motivated by his observation that dogs salivated not only when they saw or smelt food; but also when they heard sounds that they associated with food. In his experiment, Pavlov rang the bell just before he gave food to a dog. The dog then began to associate the ringing bell with food, and it salivated when the bell was rung even though there was no food present. So, even though the bell has nothing to do with food, it produced in a dog the similar response to that which is produced by food.

Such conditioning also occurs in humans. There are many horrible incidents where fathers, uncles or stepfather repeatedly abuse their daughters or nieces sexually; and each time this happens, the man would tell the girl that he does this because he 'loves' her. Each time the girl is abused sexually, she experiences severe pain and emotional damage; and each time she hears "I love you" during such act, she gets conditioned to associate "I love you" with sexual abuse. Because of this association, the girl would learn to respond to "I love you" the same way she responds to the act of sexual abuse.

If she gets married without having dealt with this pain, her husband would most probably have to suffer the consequences of what the father or uncle or stepfather has done in his wife's past. He would be puzzled to see his wife freak out everytime he tells her that he loves her because both of them would not know about her association with those words with sexual abuse. Everytime the husband says "I love you" to his wife, he triggers the pain she felt when she was sexually abused. "I love you" is in itself a good phrase; but in this instance, it has come to produce negative responses because it has become a conditioned stimulus of pain. Eventually, such experience could destroy the wife's concept of love and sex such that she may think that every person who says "I love you" to her actually hates her. Or she may conclude that love is a 'horrible' thing.

The wife who was sexually abused in her childhood may also freak out everytime she has sex with her husband because the act may trigger similar responses to those that were produced when she was sexually abused. She may perceive sex as a way of inflicting more pain and damage into her life, and she may resent her husband for trying to have it with her. Eventually, the act that was meant to unify them as a couple may tear them apart. This in itself can cause serious problems in marriage because sex is one of the fundamental aspects of marriage.

Not only "I love you" can stimulate such response; in fact, anything else that is associated with the pain of the past can trigger similar responses. Let's say there was a specific song that was playing each time the man molested the girl. That song would also be associated with the pain and produce similar responses to those that were produced during the abusive act. This can also follow the girl to her marriage. If that song can play when they are in the middle of a romantic activity, it could trigger the response of pain and anger and thus spoil the mood. It can be worse if it is the husband who is playing that song. If the man wore a specific perfume each time he molested the girl, the same perfume can trigger similar response in her even decades after the incidents.

I cannot touch on many other examples in this chapter; otherwise it will become a book on its own, and it will be a book of too many pages. Therefore, for the rest of the chapter I will be referring to the example stated above. The bottom line is: all of us were conditioned in one way or another from our childhood to respond in certain ways to certain stimuli because of our association of such stimuli with painful experiences. Some stimuli can still be associated with pleasure or gladness; but the stimuli that are detrimental to our marriages as well as our future are ones that are associated with pain. Therefore, in order for us to progress successfully in our marriages, we need to acknowledge the pains brought forward from our past and deal with them thoroughly.

The first thing you need to do in order to deal with the pain from your past is acknowledge it. You cannot deal with it if you do not acknowledge it, and you cannot solve it by denying it. One of the best ways to deal with the pains from our past is to change the meaning we attached to them. We should also learn to deal with each person or incident or series of incidents separately. In order to achieve this, the couple must cooperate with each other and deal with their past together. In classical conditioning, there is also an effect that is referred to as *extinction*. Extinction is the disappearance of previously learnt responses as a result of the stimulus not being reinforced. For example, in his experiment, Pavlov also discovered that dogs soon stop salivating when the bell keeps on ringing and food is not presented.

In the case of the wife who was told "I love you" everytime she was molested in her childhood, the husband should refrain from using the phrase while his is at the same time hurting her; instead, he should ensure that every "I love you" is immediately followed by a stimulus that will produce positive responses. The continuation of the infliction of pain together with verbal expressions of love will perpetuate the association of love with pain; but if the verbal expressions of love are accompanied by gestures that bring pleasure to the wife, her association of love with pain will ultimately be extinguished and replaced with the new association of love with pleasure. The couple should also try to change the wife's negative perception of sex by first creating a loving, warm, friendly and romantic environment before they make love. Much patience is required from the couple in the process because the changes will not happen overnight; it will take some time.

Naturally, the wife would learn to hate sex if she has a history of sexual abuse; but she should learn not to hate sex simply because of the person who used it to hurt her. Let us think about money for a moment. Money is a good thing. With it we are able to better our lives in many ways. However, there are also people who use the same money to make other people's lives miserable; but that does not make money a bad thing. So, you cannot hate money because of people who abuse it. Sex, like money, is not a bad thing; what is bad is the person who abused it on you. Therefore, instead of resenting sex itself, try to direct your resentment specifically to the person who molested you sexually. At the same time, you should purpose in your heart that you will not hate a good thing because of the person who used it badly on you.

Some marriages have come to a brutal end because people punished their partners for the pain that was caused by other people in their past. They could not let go of the pain; thus they brought it into their marriages and inflicted it upon their partners. Other marriages continue to suffer great harm because of people who have fallen in love more with their past than with their partners. There can be no future for your marriage if you won't let go of the pain and bitterness from your past. The arms that are holding on to the past cannot embrace the future. It is only if you let go of the pain that was inflicted on you in the past can you progress towards the future that God has in store for you.

Brethren, I do not count myself to have apprehended; but one thing I do, forgetting those things which are behind and reaching forward to those things which are ahead, I press toward the goal for the prize of the upward call of God in Christ Jesus (Philippians 3:13-14). One of the effective ways of dealing with pains from the past is by learning to separate the present from the past. We need to learn to forget what lies behind and press on to what lies ahead. God has a calling that is higher than our past; and we cannot fulfil His purpose if we keep holding on to what used to be. God operates in your future, and Satan operates on the past. Satan has always used people's past stories to stop them from attaining future glories. Your calling is linked to your future, and you cannot fulfil it by looking back. As long as you look behind, your marriage will have no progress.

God's plans for you are intended not to harm you, but to prosper you; they are meant to give you hope and a future (See Jeremiah 29:11). There is no hope in the past. But your future is secure in the ever-lasting arms of the Almighty God. Things will not be as they have been. If you remove your eyes from the past and set them on the future, your story will change for better. The fear that is produced by the pains of the past usually causes the past to repeat itself; but faith produces hope for the future and cancels the negative effects of the past.

You can hide your past, but you cannot hide from it. It always has a way of coming out when least expected. If you don't deal with it, it will deal with you. You don't have to deny it; you just need to acknowledge it, find ways to get over it, let it go and move on. If need be, get professional help. Whatever you do, do not let your past hold you back from advancing towards your future. You cannot afford to miss out on what will be simply because of what used to be. If you don't rub your past miseries off your heart, they may rub off on your marriage and cause severe damages to it. If there is anyone who hurt you in the past, learn to forgive and let go. If you don't let go of the person who hurt you, then the pain won't let go of you. Forgiveness does not start with healing; rather, healing starts with forgiveness. The moment you decide to forgive, your healing starts.

Hurting people tend to hurt people. As long as you are holding on to the pain, you may find yourself subconsciously hurting the people who love you. Your loved ones might have to suffer the consequences of someone else's behaviour. Forgiveness does not necessarily let the offender off the hook; it in fact lets you off the hook of pain. Unless you learn to forgive the person who hurt you, you will carry them with you wherever you go. Forgiveness benefits you more than it does your offender; but holding a grudge devours you instead of your offender. Lack of forgiveness is a self-defeating attribute. Your healing from the pain depends on your forgiveness for the person who inflicted it. When people hurt you, it's like a nail piercing into your flesh. By forgiving the person who hurt you, you are pulling the nail out of your flesh, and with time, it will heal. But if you don't forgive, you are leaving that nail in your flesh, and it will only get worse with time.

Joseph demonstrated the power of perception in helping us to forgive when he forgave his brothers for what they did to him in the past (See Genesis 45:5-8). The reason why it was not difficult for Joseph to forgive his brothers for the pain they caused in his life was because he perceived it differently. He saw it not as his brothers' way of hurting him, but as God's way of sending him ahead to prepare for their future as a family. What his brothers intended for his destruction, he perceived as an experience that was constructed by God for his construction. So, to Joseph, it was not about his brothers inflicting pain in his life; instead, it was about God preparing him for the glory that lied ahead of him.

Joseph counted his present gains and overlooked his past losses. Had he focused more on his losses, he would not have been able to forgive his brothers. He lost thirteen years of the time he should have spent with his family; and during that period he lost his freedom when he was sold as a slave to the Ishmaelites and the Egyptians. He also lost his reputation when he was framed by Potiphar's wife on the count a rape. Moreover, he lost his freedom when he spent about twelve years in prison with his wrists and ankles bruised with chains. But it was actually his losses that led him to his gains; because it was in prison when his gift was discovered and exposed to the Pharaoh who was to make him governor over Egypt.

Had Joseph held on to his past losses and pains, he would not have noticed the power that came with that pain. But he chose to let go of the pain and embrace the promotion that came as a result of it. He saw his brothers not as enemies, but as the instruments that were used by God to propel him to the next level. Not only did he forgive them, he also reaffirmed them and gladly accepted them back into his life. This would not be possible if he had not changed his perception and attached the new meaning to his painful experiences of the past. What they did to him out of hatred, he perceived as God's act of love for him and his family. His painful experiences could not kill him; instead, they made him stronger. This is another truth in life: *What does not kill you makes you stronger.*

We, like Joseph, should learn to change our perception about our past experiences if we are to get over the pain. We should learn to attach a positive meaning to our negative experiences. Only then shall we be able to forgive, let go and move on. You cannot embrace the gains of the future with the arms that are holding on to the pains of the past. If you live your life looking behind, even your marriage will be as good or as bad as your past experiences. Do not live your life based on past experiences; rather live it based on the future expectations. For you to succeed in your marriage and your life in general, you should learn to make your decisions based not on how things used to be; but on how things should be. Refuse to be the prisoner of your past; rather become the pioneer of your future.

The pain that is brought forward from the past is most likely to repeat itself in the future. God has always used pain to propel his people to their destiny; and He is still doing it even today. That painful past would not have happened to you if God had not let it happen, and He would not have let it happen if it were not going to propel you to greatness in your future. Maybe that obstruction was meant for your destruction, but God meant it for your construction. Gold is refined in the fire, and we are perfected through affliction. The enemy used your past to kill you, but God used the same to build you. The fact that you are reading this book confirms that you are an overcomer. You overcame the pain that was meant to destroy you. Others could not make it through it; but you made it, and you are still going strong. You are free from your past; but you need to set it free from your mind.

As much as it is true that your past has taken too much away from you, the other truth is that you still have so much to celebrate; but it will be extremely hard for you to realize how much you still have if you focus only on what you have lost. You might have lost your virginity through rape, but you still have the husband who loves you, the children who cherish you, and the God who sustains you. Most importantly, you still have the gift of life. What you have lost so far is nothing compared to what you still have, and what you still have is no match to the magnitude and significance of what lies ahead of you. But your focus on what you lost may cost you all that you have and all that God has laid in your future. Let go of anything that holds you back, because glorious days are not behind you; they are ahead of you.

15

Essential Values in Marriage

Every human relationship requires a solid value system in order to succeed. Values are the roots of every relationship; and without them, relationships will fall apart. In this chapter, our discussion will be about the essential values that should be present in every marital relationship. As we discuss these values, I advise that you look into yourself and check which values are present in you, and which ones are lacking. As you do so, I also want to challenge you to work on yourself to develop those values that are lacking in you. This exercise is what I call *Valuing Your Marriage.*

There are many essential values that can help you make your marriage a success, but in this chapter I will focus on twelve of them, namely; Love, Tolerance, Faithfulness and Trust, Mutual Fulfilment, Mutual Understanding, Mutual Empowerment, Intimacy, Respect, Devotion, Transparency, Companionship, and Forgiveness.

15.1 Love

Though I speak with the tongues of men and of angels, but have not love, I have become sounding brass or a clanging cymbal. And though I have the gift of prophecy, and understand all mysteries and all knowledge, and though I have all faith, so that I could remove mountains, but have not love, I am nothing. And though I bestow all my goods to feed the poor, and though I give my body to be burned, but have not love, it profits me nothing. Love suffers long and is kind; love does not envy; love does not parade itself, is not puffed up; does not behave rudely, does not seek its own, is not provoked, thinks no evil; does not rejoice in iniquity, but rejoices in the truth; bears all things, believes all things, hopes all things, endures all things. Love never fails... And now abide faith, hope, love, these three; but the greatest of these is love (1 Corinthians 13:1-13).

Love is the most important value in human relationships. It is the glue that holds our hearts together. Without love, everything we do means nothing. Marriages cannot succeed without love. Even if you can give your spouse the world on a silver platter; if that act is not inspired by love, it doesn't mean anything. From the above text we read about important characteristics of love. Firstly, we learn that love is *patient* (suffers long). We all make mistakes, especially in our marriages. We often make promises we cannot keep and commitments we cannot adhere to. We wrong each other every now and then as married couples, and it's not always deliberate. We are not perfect, and we all need a plenty of room to grow. While we strive for growth and perfection, we need to be patient with each other; but we cannot be patient with each other if we do not love each other. Thus, if you cannot be patient with each other as a couple, it could be that you lack love for each other.

Many couples claim to love each other; but they seldom speak kind words to each other. They treat each other harshly; and they expect the worst out of each other. They are usually rude to each other. In fact, they are kinder to other people than they are to each other. They are easily provoked by each other, and they think evil of each other. They suspect each other most of the time because they expect nothing good out of each other. They cannot tolerate each other as couples; and they can hardly endure the hardships they experience in their marriage. They quickly lose hope in their marriages because they do not believe in each other. They feel happy anywhere but in their own marriages. They measure their marital success on their partners having to 'change'. Yet they claim to love each other. However, this is not the reflection of true love.

True love bears all things, believes all things, hopes all things and endures all things. True love does not act out of suspicion or expectation of evil. It is not selfish, and it is not easily provoked. It never ceases to amaze me how married couples are so easily offended by each other. Spending their lives together is like a lifetime of walking on eggshells. They are too quick to retaliate, even before they understand what their partners are doing. They are too paranoid in their marriages because the bitterness and hatred in them make them perceive their loving partners as enemies who are out to destroy their lives. It is love that enables us to look beyond our partners' weakness and see their meekness. Without love, marriage becomes a place of heaviness; but with love, it becomes a place of happiness.

My little children, let us not love in word or in tongue, but in deed and in truth (1 John 3:18). True love is not only expressed in words; it is also demonstrated in action. You cannot say you love your spouse when you keep on hurting them. Love in action is more meaningful than love in word. In fact, if you love in words and fail to put action to those words, you are not loving in truth. True love is revealed when words and actions agree. Don't say you love your wife if you keep on leaving her lonely and vulnerable in your house while you go out to have a 'good time'. If you really loved her, you would either take her with you to 'good times', or give up the 'good times' and be with her even in bad times. Don't say you love your husband if you keep on criticising and suspecting him for everything he does. True love trusts and encourages good. If you truly loved him, you would believe in him and compliment him for a great man you believe he is.

Better is open rebuke than hidden love (Proverbs 27:5 – NIV). If you love your spouse, be the first to express it. "I love you too" is better than nothing; but "I love you" carries the most powerful meaning. When last have you taken the initiative to tell your spouse that you love him (or her)? What have you done deliberately to demonstrate that love? If you fail to express your love to your spouse in word and action, he (or she) might very easily interpret that as hatred. It would therefore be wise for married couples to express their love to each other on regular basis; fully understanding that the effective expression of true love is a deliberate combination of words and deeds. Even God Himself demonstrated His great love for us by giving His only begotten Son so that we may not perish but have eternal life (See John 3:16). It takes more than "I love you" to express love; you also have to show it. Love makes deliberate efforts to meet the physical, social, spiritual, physical and emotional needs of the beloved.

God is Love (See 1 John 4:8), and He is eternal (See Psalm 90:2). Therefore, love never dies. It is not affected by what people do of fail to do. It survives even beyond the most excruciating experiences. It continues to help even when it's been hurt. It is more solid than feelings. Feelings change from time to time, but love never changes. In reality, we do not fall in or out of love. Falling in or out of love refers to emotional experiences, which are very unstable. Love is not something we 'fall into' or 'fall out of'; it is who we are. We are made in God's image and likeness. God is Love; and so are we. So, we do not 'fall in love'; we instead release love as we give ourselves to our beloved. God never fails; so, love never fails. Therefore, a marriage that is full of love never fails.

15.2 Tolerance

As it has been mentioned in the earlier chapters, marriage takes place between two different people. It is our differences that attract us to each other before marriage, and it is the very differences that annoy us in marriage. Before marriage, we see more strengths than weaknesses in each other; but in marriage, we tend to see more weaknesses than strengths. So, the strengths that brought us together before marriage get to be replaced by the weaknesses that annoy us in marriage. It is in marriage that we begin to realise that our partners like some of the things we hate; and we like some of the things they hate. We are impressed by our partners' strengths; but we are also annoyed by their weaknesses. Sometimes instead of celebrating them for their strengths, we reject them for their weaknesses; and while we reject the good in our partners and focus on the bad, we forsake something better, our marriages.

We don't have to reject our partners because of their weakness; rather, we need to learn to celebrate them for their strengths and tolerate them for their weaknesses. No matter how hard you try, you can't have it all exactly the way you want it. All of us have strengths and weaknesses; but we can't afford to keep on missing on each other's strength simply because we cannot tolerate each other's weaknesses. Usually, couples who cannot celebrate each other's strengths cannot tolerate each other's weaknesses. Some end up getting a divorce because they are always looking for what they will never find – a 'perfect partner'.

If you want honey, you must be able to put up with the bees. You don't throw the honey because of the bees, but you tolerate the bees because the honey. Furthermore, if you want to enjoy swimming, you must be prepared to get wet. Similarly, if you love your partner's strengths, you must be able to tolerate their weaknesses. Do not divorce your partner because of their weaknesses; rather tolerate them because of their strengths. If you want to enjoy a successful marriage and stay together till the end, you should learn not only to celebrate each other; but also to tolerate each other.

15.3 Faithfulness and Trust

Faithfulness and trust go hand in hand. It is extremely difficult to trust the person who is not faithful, and it is very hard to be faithful to the person who does not trust you. If you are not faithful to your partner, it will be hard for your partner to trust you; and if you do not trust your partner, you will not be comfortable around him (or her). Couples who are not faithful to each other cannot trust each other, and thus, they cannot be intimate with each other. They cannot be vulnerable to each other, and they will do everything with their guards up and eyebrows raised. Without faithfulness and trust, there can be no full commitment in marriage; and without full commitment, marriage cannot be successful.

As an individual, you need to make a promise to yourself and to your partner that you will be faithful at all times; even under strong temptations. Be the man (or woman) of your words, the person that can be trusted. You should commit yourself to honour your marriage by always being faithful to your partner. Through your faithfulness, let your partner know that he (or she) can trust you. Continue to be faithful even if your partner does not trust you; it is your unwavering faithfulness that will ultimately win your partner's trust. After all, your faithfulness is not only to your partner; but also to yourself and to God. The true essence of faithfulness is that it pleases God. Therefore, whether you are faithful or not, your partner may not see it or acknowledge; but God sees it, and He acknowledges it. He is faithful, and He will not let the guilty go unpunished; nor will He ever let the faithful go unrewarded.

While you remain faithful to your partner; you should also learn to trust them. Nothing can discourage your partner more than to know that you don't trust them no matter how faithful they try so hard to be to you. Yes, it is true that trusting your partner does not guarantee their faithfulness; but neither does distrusting them. For you to trust effectively, you should learn to base your trust not on your partner's faithfulness; but on your ability to cope with their possible unfaithfulness. If you base your trust on your partner's faithfulness, you are actually handing your power and control over to them because then their actions will determine whether you trust them or not. But if you based your trust for your partner on your own ability to handle whatever possible disappointment on their part, you are taking control over your own life because your trust will not be subject to their actions.

If you trust your partner and they still become unfaithful to you, it does not mean you are a fool; it simply means you trusted them more than they deserve. A fool is not the one who trusts; it is the one who through unfaithfulness breaks in a minute the trust that took them years to build. Maybe you are reluctant to trust your partner because you feel that trusting them makes you vulnerable. It does make you vulnerable if you base you trust on what they do. The only way to trust without feeling vulnerable is if you can determine in your heart that you trust them not because of their possible actions, but because of your resilience; knowing that whatever they do, you are strong enough to handle. The only person you can control in this world is you. Therefore, if you base your trust for your partner on you, you take control; but if you base it on their past, present or possible actions, you give your control away to someone else. The question is: If you can't control them, why let them control you by letting their actions determine your trust?

The world we live in today is very dangerous; and with the risk of crime, corruption and sexually transmitted infections, there is a strong need to be faithful in our marriages. Little signs of unfaithfulness can shutter your partner's trust in a minute; if they cannot trust you, they cannot open up to you, and if they cannot open up to you, you cannot enjoy them. Eventually, if you cannot enjoy your partner, you cannot enjoy your marriage. So, for you to enjoy your marriage to the fullest, be faithful to your spouse.

15.4 Mutual Fulfilment

Marriage is not a one-sided relationship; it is a mutual benefit union. No marriage can succeed if one person carries all the burdens while the other enjoys all the benefits. The needs of one person should never be met at the expense of the other's happiness. Both partners should benefit equally from the relationship. *Parasitism* is a marriage killer; yet there are people who behave like parasites in their marriages and feast on their partners' blood and sweat. They gain everything while their partners lose everything. They enjoy all the *help* while their partners endure all the *hurt*. Such marriage cannot succeed.

What makes marriages successful is *mutualism*. Mutualism is a relationship where both partners benefit. The benefits may not be similar; but they are equally significant. Biologists usually use a cow and a tickbird for an example. While the tickbird enjoys the tick as food, the cow also benefits by losing the ticks that are feasting on its blood and sucking the very life out of it. For marriage to be successful, both partners must benefit. The needs that the wife meets in her husband may be different from the ones her husband meets in her. The wife needs love, and the husband needs sex; so, while the wife meets her husband's sexual needs, the husband should also meet his wife's emotional needs by showing love and affection to her. If the wife can enjoy her husband's love and fail to meet his sexual needs; or if the husband can enjoy his wife's body and fail to meet her emotional needs, one might perceive the other as a parasite, and the marriage might suffer serious damages.

In essence, marriage is about give and take. If you keep on taking and fail to give, you become a parasite; and you are causing harm not only to your spouse, but also to your marriage. As an individual within this marriage, you need to make sure that you play your role to fulfil your partner's needs to the best of your ability. While you're at it, make sure that you don't hand over your power and control to your spouse by failing to play your own role because of your partner's failure to play theirs. Couples need to grow so much that they learn to continue playing their role despite the other person's behaviour. You cannot let yourself become a bad husband (or wife) simply because your partner is a bad wife (or husband). In that way you will only double the trouble because now this marriage will be having two bad people making a couple. How can that marriage succeed?

Always do your best to be the initiator in your marriage. If your partner does not initiate it and you also decide not to initiate it, no one will initiate it, and both of you will be without it. If none of you plans a romantic dinner, then none of you will enjoy a romantic dinner; but if you initiate it, both of you will have it. If your partner keeps on initiating and you keep on enjoying, that makes you a parasite. You should also take initiatives so that both of you can be fulfilled. If your marriage benefits only you, it will fail; but if it benefits both of you, it will succeed.

15.5 Mutual Understanding

Generally, people want to be understood; but they don't want to understand others. They want things to be perceived from their perspective; but they hardly perceive things from other people's perspective. While they work so hard to get other people to understand them, they fail to realise that those people also want to be understood. This is true for every relationship, especially in marriage. Some people want their partners to understand them and accept them just as they are; but at the same time they are not willing to understand or accept their partners as they are. The husband wants his wife to understand that he cannot do more than one thing at a time; but he does not want to understand that his wife cannot remain silent when things are not done in the house. On the other hand, the wife wants her husband to understand that she needs to feel loved; but she does not want to understand that her husband needs to feel respected.

Very often in marriages you may find people ordering their partners not to try to change them; yet they themselves are also pressuring their partners to change. If they are the ones on the wrong and they get confronted, they most often respond with "This is how I am, I was born and raised this way". If it is the partner on the wrong, they would remark with "You need to work on this and change if we are to be happy in this relationship". This does not work in marriage. What works is for you to understand your partner just as much as you want them to understand you. If you think you cannot change because you were born and raise that way, you also need to understand that your partner could be in a similar situation as yours. Do not expect your partner to understand about you what you don't want to understand about them.

You are not the only one who 'had a bad day' in this marriage; your partner probably had a much worse day than you, and you need to understand that. Successful marriages are characterised by couples who have learnt to understand each other and accept each other just the way they are. Couples who lack mutual understanding often put pressure on their partners to do the things they themselves cannot do. This often leads to unnecessary conflicts and recurring disputes in marriages. If you want to live harmoniously in your marriage with no unnecessary disappointments, learn to understand each other mutually as a couple and accept each other just as each of you wants to be accepted.

15.6 Mutual Empowerment

Married couples should learn to empower each other. They should develop the tendency of helping each other become better individuals; and they should always be careful not to block each other's growth. They should learn to believe in each other and support each other as they work on improving their lives. They should be able to communicate their dreams with each other and motivate each other to pursue them. They should develop the habit of learning from each other and learning together so that they may also grow as individuals as they grow as couples.

As a married person, your partner should not remain the same after marrying you. There should be a notable difference in your partner's life as a result of your positive influence. This is not about changing your partner into the person he (or she) is not; it is about adding value to his (or her) life so that he (or she) can grow to become a better person. It is also about helping your partner discover his (or her) potential so that he (or she) can live to fulfil God's purpose for him (or her). If we can learn to empower each other as husband and wife, we will stand a better chance of growing up together in harmony.

15.7 Intimacy

Intimacy is one of the essential values that seem to be left on the altar on the wedding day. Couples tend to grow apart as they grow up; and they spend lesser time together as time goes on. The only time they get intimate is when they have sex; and that sex would be just a routine that is practiced to 'scare temptations away'. Numerous married couples seldom give themselves a *'we time'*; where they forget about anything else and focus only on each other. When they do spend their time together, they would be talking about how they will pay the bills at month end. They would be discussing their family chores and work stress. Very seldom would they be talking about how much they love and appreciate each other as husband and wife.

Married couples should work on their relationships and maintain close connections between themselves. They should develop a friendly and loving relationship that allows for them to share their deep feelings and aspirations. Intimacy provides a wonderful opportunity for couples to know each other very well. The more time you spend together as a couple, the more you grow in love with each other; and the more you grow in love with each other, the more successful your marriage will be. As a couple, make sure that every now and then you set aside a 'we time' so that you can develop deeper connection and affection with each other. The deeper the connection and the more the affection there is in your relationship as a couple, the greater your chances to enjoy a successful marriage and live happily together till the end.

15.8 Respect

Respect is one of the fundamental values in human relationships. To a large degree, respect acts as the glue that holds relationships together. We cannot talk about a successful marriage without talking about respect. Respect is not only a value for healthy relationships; it is also a need for every human being. Disrespect insults the dignity of humanity; but respect reinforces it. Everybody wants to be with the person who shows respect to them; and nobody wants to be around the person who disrespects them. As a married couple, you need to make sure that you show each other due respect on regular bases.

As a human being, you have a right to be respected by your spouse; but you also have the responsibility to respect your spouse. The measure of respect you expect from your spouse should be the same measure you use to him (or her). Not only should you respect each other as a couple; you also need to respect your marriage. Only if you respect your marriage will you be able to preserve it. If you don't respect your marriage, you will most probably indulge in practices that could cause severe damages to it. It is also easy to disrespect your spouse if you disrespect your marriage. Without respect, marriage falls apart. Respect involves being polite to each other as a couple; and this politeness emanates from you perceiving each other as important. The more important you think your partner is, the more you will respect them; and the more you respect them, the more they will feel that they are important to you.

If you respect each other as a couple, you will feel safe around each other; and if you feel safe around each other, you will be more trusting to each other. Where there is no respect, people get hurt; but respect makes people feel secure. Couples therefore need to learn to respect each other in every way. They should respect each other's feelings, opinions, religions, gender, needs, rights, careers, dreams and privacy. They should learn to never do anything that makes each other feel uncomfortable. They should also learn to never do anything that affects each other without each other's consent. In this way they will be treating each other with due respect, and thus promoting love and harmony in their marriages. If you want to enjoy happy days in your marriage, do yourself a favour; respect your spouse.

15.9 Devotion

As they say, a family that prays together stays together. A couple that is truly devoted to God will be devoted to each other. Married couples should learn to be fully devoted not only to God; but also to each other. This will help them create a strong bond between them as husband and wife. Marriage is not a partial relationship; it is a full commitment for a lifetime. It requires total devotion between the husband and his wife. As a married person, you need to make a conscious effort to give most of your time, energy, love and attention to your spouse. Your spouse should enjoy great support and care from you; and you should enjoy the same from your spouse. If you can learn to be devoted to each other as a couple just as you devote yourselves to God, you will see yourselves finding so much pleasure in each other's company.

So many people are holding back too much when it comes to their spouses. They give themselves sparingly to them; yet they expect their partners' full commitment in return. They give part of their love to their partners and yet expect all their partners' love in return. They want to give little in exchange for much. They want to enjoy full attention while they divide their attention to many other things. This is not a reflection of devotion. True devotion requires full commitment by both parties. If it is one-sided, it is not a true devotion. A one-sided devotion is very tiring to the devoted partner. It makes them feel like they are fighting a losing battle. It also makes them see their marriage more as a burden than a blessing. You don't want to be perceived by your partner as a burden; but if you are not fully devoted to them, that's how they will see you. You can change your partner's perception of you as a burden into a blessing by giving your whole being over to them.

Your relationship with your spouse cannot be effective if you give part of you into your marriage; you need to give all of you and hold nothing back. This is a lifetime covenant; it is not a temporary contract. It is not like a job or a business deal. You can resign from one job and immediately get the other, and you can walk out of one business deal and immediately walk into the other; but you cannot resign from your current marriage and enter into the other, and you cannot walk out of your current marriage and walk into another. You are here to stay; and you had better make that stay good by giving your all into your marriage. A lifetime is too long for you to spend with one foot in your marriage and the other foot elsewhere. You cannot afford to live the rest of your life with a divided heart. You have to give your whole heart to your spouse for as long as you both shall live. If you can be fully and equally devoted to each other, your marriage will be strengthened, and you will stand a better chance of staying together till the end.

15.10 Transparency

First and foremost, people who have nothing against them have nothing to hide. If what you are doing is good, then why are you hiding it? If your calls are truly innocent, why do you always have to act nervous and then rush to a solitary place before taking them? If you are spending money correctly, why are you doing it behind your partner's back? If you are doing it for the benefit of your marriage, why make it a secret? The truth always has a way of coming out when least expected; and when it does, the outcomes are usually so much worse than they would have been if you had disclosed it from the beginning. If you keep the truth from your partner, you gradually break his (or her) trust in you. It would therefore be very wise to be honest to your partner from the beginning. It is much worse to get caught while you are hiding than it is to voluntarily disclose yourself.

Marriage should be a transparent relationship. There should be no hidden friendships, expenditures, calls, decisions, intentions, commitments, etc. Even if you do it with good motives, it can still harm your marriage if your partner does not know about it. It can be very dangerous for your marriage to make vital decisions or take crucial steps and leave your spouse to find out. It can make your spouse feel betrayed, and it can crush his (or her) trust for you. This can also develop serious divisions in your marriage; unless if you are planning a surprise for your spouse, and that surprise should be carefully calculated before you begin to carry it out. Marriages are breaking because of hidden issues. Evil gains more life and power when it is kept as a secret; but when it is exposed, it loses its power and begins to die away.

Transparency promotes honesty and faithfulness in marriage. It also encourages openness between the husband and his wife. The less you hide from each other as a couple, the more trust will develop between you, and you will enjoy perfect peace in your marriage knowing that your consciences are clean. It takes more energy to keep a secret from your spouse than it does to open up to them. However, transparency in marriage does not mean your personal privacy should not be respected, and it does not mean you should disclose everything that is going on in your life; it simply means that nothing that involves your marriage should be hidden from the person you are married to. If you have nothing to hide now, you will have nothing to explain later.

15.11 Companionship

As soon as you and partner get married, you become *companions*. What makes you companions is that from the day you said "I do" until one or both of you is no more, you will be spending most of your time and journeying through life together. Sadly, many couples live their marriage lives as if they were not companions. The only time they spend together is when they talk about household issues and responsibilities; and immediately afterwards each one goes their own way. They are kind to everybody else; but they are mean to their own spouses. On several occasions you will find a person having many friends, and his (or her) spouse is not one of them. This happens because people tend to forget the important aspects of their companionship within a few months of their marriage.

Marriage is not only about family responsibilities and reproduction; it is also about friendship. More than everybody else, married couples should enjoy each other's company. They should be able to share in their personal joys and pains. They should learn to find total pleasure in each other's arms. Marriage should be the friendliest of all human relationships. How can you spend the rest of your lives happily as a couple if you don't enjoy each other's company? Your spouse is the only person you are bound to spend the rest of your life with, and if you cannot be happy together, you might have to spend the rest of your lives miserable. If lovers cannot become friends, it would be very easy for them to treat each other as enemies. Love involves deep feelings, and only close friends can be trusted for such feelings.

It is very painful to be married and still feel lonely; and painful as it is, many couples are experiencing this feeling. One of the main reasons why people still feel lonely even when they are married is lack of companionship in their marriages. When they are together in the house, they would rather be busy with everything else than to take time to enjoy each other's company. They have been together for years, yet they still miss each other because both of them are missing in action. Some go so far as to compromise their marriages and look for companionship within extramarital affairs. If your spouse were really your friend, you would not go out of your way to hurt your friend by establishing extramarital affairs. Friends are always careful never to betray each other or hurt each other in any way. You do not lie to your friend nor cheat on them, because you value not only him (or her); but also your friendship with him (or her).

Friends are kind to each other. They are also gentle and considerate. They believe in each other, complement each other and appreciate each other. If they happen to hurt each other, it is never deliberate. It is better to trust a friend who hurts you than it is to trust the enemy who kisses you. As it is stated in the Bible, *Wounds from a friend can be trusted, but an enemy multiplies kisses* (Proverbs 27:6 – NIV). Touching and kissing does not necessarily make you friends; what really makes you friends is the sincere hearts full of love and kindness. Friends enjoy being together. They see every time they spend together not as an obligation, but as a privilege. Successful couples are those couples who have learnt the secret of companionship in their marriages. So, if you want to build a successful marriage, always be lovers; but never forget to be friends.

15.12 Forgiveness

We all make mistakes; and none of us is perfect. Imperfect as we are, we marry imperfect people, who also make mistakes. We try hard to make things right, but very often we fail; and thus we disappoint the people we care about. The only way to avoid making a mistake is to do nothing; and that in itself is a mistake. We were not born to do nothing; we were born to do something, and whenever we do something, we risk making mistakes. It is human to make mistakes; that's one of the best ways in which we can learn valuable lessons of life. Conversely, it is very disturbing how we humans hate each other for the mistakes we make. We also go so far as to hate ourselves for our own mistakes. We expect too much out of ourselves and our loved ones; and we punish ourselves and our loved ones profusely for failing to be perfect as humans.

No human relationship is immune to mistakes. Even so, relationships do not have to end because of mistakes. We need a way to sustain our relationships despite the mistakes we make, and that way is *forgiveness*. No relationship can survive without forgiveness; especially marriage. To forgive means to stop behaving angrily against somebody who has done something to harm, annoy or upset you. It also means to stop acting angrily against yourself. Believe it or not, our partners will at some point do things that harm, annoy or upset us because they are human; and we will feel angry because we are also human. We also do things that make us feel angry with ourselves. But we still remain responsible for how we deal with our anger. We can use it to avenge ourselves, or we can let it go by deciding to forgive.

In your anger do not sin. Do not let the sun go down while you are still angry, and do not give the devil a foothold (Ephesians 4:26-27). If you do not forgive the person who offended you, the sun will go down, and you will still be angry; and if you go to bed angry, Satan will gain a foothold and suggest unhealthy ways of dealing with your anger. Do not let your anger cause you to sin. Learn to let go of the anger by learning to forgive. Holding a grudge is like swallowing acid; instead of harming your offender, it devours you from within. Failure to forgive does not hurt your offender; it hurts you. It actually gives your offender the power to control how you feel and when to feel that way. So, by forgiving, you are actually spitting out the acid and bringing healing upon yourself. Moreover, by forgiving, you are taking your power back and starting to take full control over your own happiness.

"He who is without sin among you, let him throw a stone at her first" (John 8:7). The only thing that qualifies you to condemn the person who offended you is for you to be without mistakes. But if you hold a grudge against the other person while you yourself make mistakes, you are basically implying that you must also not be forgiven. *"Judge not, and you shall not be judged. Condemn not, and you shall not be condemned. Forgive, and you will be forgiven. Give, and it*

will be given to you: good measure, pressed down, shaken together, and running over will be put into your bosom. For with the same measure that you use, it will be measured back to you (Luke 6:37-38). You are literally under the very judgement and condemnation that you use against your offender; because the measure that you use against them when they offend you is the same measure that will be use against you when you offend others.

Forgiveness does not mean the person who offended you is right; it simply means you acknowledge that you also make mistakes, and you need forgiveness. *...Forgive us our sins, for we also forgive everyone who is indebted to us* (Luke 11:4). If you cannot forgive, you cannot be forgiven. So, you forgive not for the sake of your offender, but for your own sake; that you may also be forgiven for your offenses. This is also the case in marriage. Forgiving your partner does not make him (or her) right; it makes you eligible to forgiveness when you are wrong. Before you remove the speck in your partner's eye, first remove the plank from your own eye, and then you will see clearly to remove the speck from your partner's eye (See Luke 6:41-42). If you attempt to deal with your partner's faults while you overlook your own, you may cause damage in your marriage because you will be blinded by your own faults. You may find yourself hurting the very person you are trying to help.

Many people can easily recognise mistakes when they are made by their partners; yet they themselves make the same mistakes, and they are not even aware. They only wonder why they get punished for their partners' mistakes; but they are not aware that they are actually being judged with the very same judgement they use against their partners. They keep on accusing their partners for the very things they themselves also do. This often leads to serious quarrels in marriages. Failure to forgive your spouse is one of the main barriers that are blocking the success of your marriage. So, if you want your marriage to be successful; learn to accept each other as human beings, and whenever you make mistakes, forgive each other.

16

Communication in Marriage

Human beings are social beings. They cannot survive on their own; they need one another. No human being can live on in solitude. We were created to belong, and we survive in communities. Our interdependence on one another as human beings compels us to live together. But for us to live peacefully together, we need to get along with one another; and for us to get along, we need to understand and respects one another's rights, needs, feelings and opinions. However, for us to respect other people's feelings, we need to know what those feelings are and what causes them, and we cannot know them if those people do not let us know. We are not communities of psychics; therefore, we cannot read minds or determine what other people want unless they let us know what's on their minds or what they want. The only way for us to understand one another is by means of *communication*.

Communication refers to the activity or process of expressing ideas, thoughts, feelings, information, needs, etc. in order to make them known and understood to other people. Theories on communication hold the thought that communication consists of three elements, namely: the *sender*, the *message* and the *receiver*. The *sender* is the person or group of persons expressing the idea. The *message* is the idea being expressed. The message includes the initial idea that is expressed as well as the *feedback* that is provided after the expressed idea is received. The *receiver* is the person or group of persons to whom the idea is expressed. Simply put, communication is the process of *sending* the *message* and *receiving* feedback. Without these three elements, communication is incomplete, and thus, ineffective.

Communication can be *verbal* or *non-verbal*. Verbal communication occurs when the message is conveyed in words. Non-verbal communication occurs when the message is communicated without words. Non-verbal communication involves facial expression, body posture, bodily gestures and voice tone. Non-verbal communication can either *confirm* or *contradict* verbal communication. You can verbally convey the message that you are sad, or it can simply show when you cry. Crying is a non-verbal communication that confirms the message of sadness that was conveyed verbally. When non-verbal communication and verbal communication agree, the communication is said to be *congruent.*

One the other hand, you can verbally convey the message that you are excited; whereas you are frowning and crying. In this communication, the verbal and the non-verbal do not agree. Frowning and crying is the non-verbal communication that contradicts the excitement you communicated verbally. This type of communication is said to be *incongruent.* This suggests that for effective communication, it is very important to pay attention to both the verbal and non-verbal communications. Usually, people communicate the truth non-verbally unaware that they are doing so. Even though the verbal communication can communicate only what the sender wants the receiver to hear, non-verbal communication can reveal what is really going on beyond the words being spoken.

There are a number of barriers to effective communication. The most common barrier is *language.* If the sender conveys the message in the language that the receiver does not understand, the message will not be received, and the communication will be ineffective. It is thus important to consider the language of the receiver before you send the message. Another known barrier to effective communication is *culture.* Different gestures mean different things to people in different cultures. For example, some cultures, especially African cultures, hold a belief that not looking an elder directly in the eyes is an expression of respect; but in other cultures, especially Western cultures, doing the same could mean dishonesty or criminal behaviour. The message can be received either the right way or the wrong way depending of the culture of the receiver.

One other barrier to effective communication is the *context* in which the message is conveyed. Even if the message can be conveyed correctly, it may be received out of context and lose its intended meaning. For example, if I say to you, "We were beaten"; you may think I could be injured if you receive the message within the context of a physical fight. But I could be talking within the context of a soccer match. You received the correct message within the wrong context; and as a result you heard what was not being said. Therefore, to receive the message correctly, make sure that you understand the context in which it is communicated.

Another barrier is *personal barrier*. People differ from person to person. Different personalities mean different styles of communicating. How individuals communicate is strongly influenced by their needs, feelings, experiences, personal beliefs, values and perceptions. People usually communicate their needs and feelings obliviously and unintentionally. This can affect the clarity or accuracy of the message being communicated. The sender may be the sarcastic type, and the receiver may be the hypersensitive one; and if care is not taken, the receiver may take offense over how the message was communicated and miss the message itself. To improve the effectiveness of communication, the sender should seek to understand the personality of the intended receiver.

Every human relationship requires good communication to grow. The closer the relationship, the more communication is needed. The closest of all human relationships is the marital relationship. Communication is a *must* for every marital relationship. If you fail to communicate today, you will definitely have to deal with harsh consequences later on. Lack of communication in marriage usually leads to terrible outbreaks. Remaining silent about the problem makes it worse; but talking about it addresses it before it gets out of hand. It is better to deal with the immediate consequences of communication than to experience the overwhelming explosion that may come as a result of not communicating. An uncommunicated problem is like a time bomb; it builds more and more pressure until it explodes, and when it explodes, it will be impossible to manage it.

No marriage can thrive without *healthy communication*. Healthy communication is the safest way to express oneself and settle individual differences without hurting each other unnecessarily. The reason why I mention *healthy* communication is that not all communication is healthy. Communication is not only about what you say; it is also about how you say it. Healthy communication entails conveying the right message, to the right person, at the right time and in the right way. Many couples argue that they can communicate. True! Everybody can communicate, but not everybody communicates the right way.

Communication is part of our daily lives, but to master it as a skill is easier said than done. Even experienced relationship experts, who train people daily on communication, also struggle to apply it in their own relationships. Couples always communicate, but the outcome of their communication is usually a bitter experience. Marriages suffer a great deal of harm not only because of *lack* of communication, but also because of *unhealthy* or *poor* communication. They communicate to address their own feelings and needs; not the problem at hand. Instead of solving the problem, they tackle each other. They point fingers and pass judgements against each other instead of focusing on the problem. They fail to distinguish between the person and the problem. In fact, they perceive the person as the problem and tackle them as such.

Healthy communication solves the problem more than it does the person. It addresses the situation; not the sender's feelings. The aim of healthy communication is to build the relationship; not to break the receiver. You don't communicate to 'feel good'; you communicate to improve the relationship, and you will feel better as the relationship improves. Healthy communication is the best way to solve any kind of marital conflict. It provides a safe environment wherein disagreements are settled peacefully. Healthy communication does not condemn; it corrects, and it reassures. It also helps couples address their own *blind spots*.

Very often we offend each other as couples, and we are not even aware that we do. We often think we are doing well when in actual fact we are messing up. We usually find ourselves doing the very things we think should not be done in marriage without being aware that we are doing them. This is all because we all have *blind spots* in our lives by which we are blinded from our own flaws even when we can notice them in our partners. This often happens when we criticize our partner for hurting us while we ourselves are doing the same things unaware. In this case, healthy communication can clear such blind spots and give couples insight into their own behaviour that is hidden from them. If communication is unhealthy, they may point fingers and blame each other for what they themselves are also doing, and it may become a battle over who is wrong and who is right.

The secret to healthy communication is to understand *what* you communicate, to *whom*, *why* you communicate it, *when* to communicate it and *how* to communicate it. Being clear and specific about what you are communicating can help you improve your communication. It is important to avoid communicating ambiguous and subliminal messages; which are not very clear to the receiver. It is also important to clarify to yourself why you are communicating. Is it to address the problem, or to make a request, or to compliment, or to start an argument, or to correct, or to commend? Asking yourself why you communicate can help you clarify your intentions. Even if the message you are communicating is clear and specific, it can still not serve the intended purpose if it is not communicated correctly. This comes to the question of how you should communicate.

Have you ever communicated the correct message to your spouse and ended up with more problems in your relationship? Well, this happens to many couples. It happens mainly because we communicate the right messages in the wrong way. For example, your husband wears the tie that does not match with the shirt; and you, trying to help him, yell at him, "Didn't your mother teach you how to dress? Take off that tie and put on another one!" Even though he gets the message, he will be exceedingly offended; and a simple correction of a tie may lead to a fight that could last for weeks. I am sure that some marriages that ended in divorce started with a quarrel over trivial issues such as a tie. It is not the tie that broke the marriage; it is the hostility that was ignited by bad communication over a tie. Yelling at your partner does not solve the problem; it magnifies it, and it strains the marriage.

A gentle answer turns away wrath, but a harsh word stirs up anger (Proverbs 15:1 – NIV). Healthy communication is characterized by gentleness and consideration. Many people think if they raise their voices and speak harshly they will be heard. Of course they will hear you, and instead of responding to your message, they will fight back; they will attack you. All of us have some degree of anger within us; and whether that anger is stirred up or turned away depends on how we communicate. If you communicate gently, the anger will be turned away; but if you speak harshly, it will be stirred up. The purpose of communication should be to turn anger away; not to stir it up. Therefore, rather than being harsh in your communication, be gentle.

If you communicate out of anger, the receiver will also react in anger, and things will be worse than they were before you communicated. Therefore, it is better not to communicate at all and leave things as they are than to communicate out of anger and make them worse. *A hot-tempered man stirs up dissension, but a patient man calms a quarrel* (Proverbs 15:18 – NIV). Hot-tempered people usually fail in their communication. They almost never get good returns out of the messages they convey. Couples who are not patient with each other cannot communicate healthily; instead, they provoke each other's anger. Married couples should always keep this in mind: You can never get what you want in your marriage as long as you communicate harsh words and speak out of anger. Start today to be patient with each other and learn to communicate considerately.

There is a way that seems right to a man, but in the end it leads to death (Proverbs 16:25 – NIV). To many couples, communicating harshly seems right. They believe when they speak or act out of anger or intimidation they will have their way. But that's not true at all! The outcome of such behaviour is domestic violence and broken marriage. It may even lead to one partner killing the other. If your partner gives you what you want even if you communicate harshly, it is not out of their respect for you; it is out of their respect for their marriage. So, don't even be deceived to think that it is because of your anger that they respond positively. Your anger only stirs up theirs, but they are mature enough to respond gently even when they feel like fighting back. Healthy communication requires maturity. Immature people speak to satisfy their emotions, but mature people communicate to address the problem and to improve the relationship.

If as a couple you keep on screaming at each other, you are practically providing an immediate solution by inflicting a permanent problem. When you communicate harshly with your spouse, their hand may immediately give you what you want; but that comes with a steady build-up of resentment in their heart for you. Meanwhile you may think you are having it right, but in reality, the words you say today and the manner in which you say them will be a snare for you in the future. With each harsh word you speak, you sow a seed of bitterness in your partner's heart; and very soon you will wonder how it all went so wrong when it looked like it was going on so right. It seems okay in the beginning, but it has a bitter ending.

Some people were left in their houses and later given divorce letters as a result of the seeds they were sowing in their spouses' hearts thinking they were doing just the right thing; and they were left wondering "what went wrong?" Words work like seeds. They do not always bring forth the required outcomes immediately. Therefore, communication requires patience, it may seem like your words are making no difference, but you need to have faith that the seed is planted, and it shall break the ground in its time. By forcing immediate changes through your harsh words, you are planting the tares that will soon choke your harvest. For every harsh word, a negative seed is planted; and for every polite word, a positive seed is planted; and either way, you will ultimately reap the harvest of the seeds you planted.

Starting a quarrel is like breaching a dam; so drop the matter before a dispute breaks out (Proverbs 17:14 – NIV). A good communicator knows not only what to communicate and how to communicate it; they also know when to communicate and when not to communicate. You know you should drop the matter when you notice that the quarrel is about to start or the dispute is about to break out. The aim of healthy communication is to win the relationship, not the argument. What profit does communication bring if you win the argument and lose your partner? Remember, healthy communication points fingers to the problem, not to the person. So, if communication begins to tackle the person rather than the problem, that becomes a good indication that you should retreat right away and move on.

A man of knowledge uses words with restraint, and a man of understanding is even-tempered (Proverbs 17:27 – NIV). Good communicators are even-tempered, and they choose their words carefully before they speak. They do not act out of impulse, and they do not react to every offense that comes their way. Healthy communication is not always about correction or criticism; it is also about commendation and compliment. In fact, compliment works better than criticism in a marital relationship. In marital relationships, there are people who never open their lips except to criticize. When their partners do well, they never say a word; they only speak when there's a mistake to correct. This can be discouraging to your partner; it makes them feel like they are fighting a losing battle.

If there is an issue that you feel needs to be addressed in your marriage, raise it not as a *complaint*, but as a *concern*. If you raise it as a complaint, it could appear like you are implying that your partner is 'the wrong one'. That is not a healthy approach if you are to address a problem in marriage. Who knows, you could be the main culprit in this situation without realising it. Complaining can blind you from your own flaws; but if you raise an issue as a concern, you create a room for discussion, and it would be easier for you to acknowledge your mistakes and work on your own shortcomings. A complaint points a finger way from you and towards the other person, but a concern points a finger away from both of you and towards the problem.

A complaint might sound more like an accusation, and it can provoke *retaliation*; but a concern incites *cooperation.* A complaint focuses more on the person, but a concern focuses more on the problem at hand. Remember, it is the *problem* you are trying to solve, not the *person.* Raising an issue as a concern detaches it from the person and singles it out as a problem to be solved together. A *complaint* most often leads to one person winning, but a *concern* creates a room for both parties to win. Within a marital context, if one person wins, both of them lose. The only victory in marriage is if both partners win. When you raise an issue as a concern, you open a discussion, and everybody wins; but if you raise it as a complaint, you open a case, and nobody wins.

Better to live on the corner of the roof than to share a house with a quarrelsome wife (Proverbs 21:9 – NIV). *Better to live in the desert than with a quarrelsome and ill-tempered wife* (Proverbs 21:19 – NIV). Nobody wants to live with the quarrelsome partner. It breaks the heart and crushes the spirit. An ill-tempered person pushes people away with anger. If all you do in your marriage is criticize and correct, you need to change your approach before it's too late. Start today to minimize the criticisms and maximize the compliments. From now on, make up your mind that you will correct less and commend more; this will help you improve not only your communication, but your relationship as well.

If only we could learn to communicate with our spouses at least the way we communicate with our friends and colleagues, our marriages would be so much better. The easiest way to tell if people are married to each other is by listening to how they address each other. They are either talking harshly, as if they are trampling over scorpions; or timidly, as if they are walking on eggshells. Otherwise they just keep quiet and say no word to each other because they are afraid they could start another argument. One moment you talk to your partner, and you sound extremely cold and tense; the next moment you talk to your friend or colleague, and you are a completely different person. You suddenly become a lively person because you are now talking to your friend or colleague.

When your spouse offends you, you say the first word that comes into your mind; but when the offense is from your friend or colleague, you choose words carefully before you speak. You communicate better with your friends and colleagues than you do with your spouse; even though all of them annoy you equally. Your friends are completely free when they talk to you, and you laugh at every joke they make even if it is not funny; but even the funniest joke your spouse makes does not even make the slightest move on your cheeks. You celebrate your friends no matter how much they offend you, but you can't even tolerate your spouse no matter how hard they try to be nice to you. When talking to your friend or colleagues, you always wear a smile; but when you talk to your spouse, you always wear a frown. Why is it that you don't speak to your spouse at least the way you speak to your friend?

If I were to ask you why you are being so nice to your friends and colleagues even though they keep on offending you, you would most probably tell me that it's because you value your friendship with them, and you also value your work or business. If, then, your friendly and polite communication with your friends and colleagues is based on your value for your friendships and work or business, why don't you at least value your marriage enough to be friendly and polite when you communicate with your spouse? The truth is, how much you value your marriage determines how well you communicate with your spouse. Maybe we as couples should make introspection and ask ourselves: "Do I really value my marriage? Do I value my spouse enough to communicate well with him (or her)?" If we really value our marriages, we won't have to tell; it will just show in the way we speak with our spouses.

Communication is not only about talking; it is also about *listening.* The skill of listening is not as easy as it sounds. We often listen to people and think we heard them; only to find that what we heard is not exactly what they said. The essence of listening is paying attention to what is being said, not what you think is being said. Married couples end up not communicating because they know that they will be saying something in one minute and then spend the next hour trying to explain that what their partners heard was not what they were saying.

Poor listening is poor communication, and poor communication leads to poor marriage. Some people want to be heard; but they don't want to hear. To them communication is always about what they have to say. They love to advise, but they hate to be advised. They like to correct, but they dislike being corrected. They teach but never learn. They already provide an answer before the question is finished. They love the sound of their own voices and find other voices inferior. Their approach to communication is one-sided; and one-sided communication cannot achieve mutual satisfaction in a relationship; especially in marriage. Marriage is not a teacher-student relationship; it is the union of two fully grown companions whose voices deserve to be heard.

So then, my beloved brethren, let every man be swift to hear, slow to speak, slow to wrath; for the wrath of man does not produce the righteousness of God (James 1:19). It is wiser and more honourable to listen than to speak. Speaking before you listen is like providing the prescription before making the diagnosis. You could be solving what is not the problem and worsening the actual problem. You could hurt the person you were supposed to help. There are people who burst out in anger before they hear what is being said; and by the time they hear that what was said was not meant to provoke their anger, it is already too late. Before their partners finish telling them how much they love and appreciate them, they have already ripped them into pieces. They act before they get the message because they are quick to wrath and slow to listen.

There are barriers that make listening ineffective in relationships. One of those barriers is *selective listening*. Selective listeners hear only what they want to hear. They twist the meaning of words to make them suit their expectations or suspicions. What they choose to hear has nothing to do with what they are told. They find fault in every fact. With such people on board, communication loses its meaning and eventually dies out. 'Which means...' is one of their favourite phrases. Their partner may say, "I feel bored today"; to which they may answer, "Which means I'm boring to you". But the partner never said they are boring. In fact, nowhere in this statement were they mentioned. They just had to craft that statement into a personal attack against them even though it has nothing to do with them. The partner was just communicating how they feel; but the selective listener decided to hear, "You are such a bore!"

Eventually, the selective listener will notice a frown on the partner's face and ask "What's wrong?" To which the response will be "Nothing". That is where the partner will bottle up their feelings until they cause an explosion; because there will come a time when they can take this no more. This could lead to a bitter ending for their marriage. Selective listening kills communication; but moreover, it kills the relationship. If you happen to be a selective listener, now it is the time to make a full turnaround and improve your listening skill. Do not listen for what you want; listen to what you are told.

The other barrier to effective listening is the *know-it-all listening*. The know-it-all listeners cannot be told anything they do not know. They know what you think, how you feel and what you are about to say before you tell them – so they think. No information is new to them; so, you can't teach them anything. You can only learn everything from them. Before you say a word, they know it. Whatever you tell them, their response would very often begin with "I know..." This is delusional behaviour. The truth is: you can never know what the other person wants to say until they say it. Such delusion only blocks their listening; and to be precise, it blocks their communication and harms their relationships.

One other barrier is *corrective listening*. Corrective listeners do not listen to the message; instead, they listen for mistakes to correct. They want to make sure that you are using the correct grammar and speaking etiquette. Before they hear what you are trying to say, they have already picked up some flaws in your communication; and rather than responding to your message, they respond to your mistakes. You ask them, "May I sit next to you?" they reply, "How about 'please' when you ask?" Then you correct yourself and add "please!" then they reply, "It would have been nice if you started with 'sorry'". Eventually, a simple request ends up as a series of 'do's and don'ts' instead of whether or not to sit next to them. Whatever you communicate to them, you get a lecture in return. This can have a negative impact on communication in a relationship.

There are also *interruptive listeners*. To this type of listeners you never get to finish your statement; and they either finish it for you or respond before you finish. As soon as you give them the introduction, they reach the conclusion and communicate it to you. Then you find yourself having to explain to them that what they added was not what you were saying. This is one of the major courses of disputes in marriages because it undermines the other person's intellect. If you respond to the person before they finish what they are saying, the impression it gives them is "I know better than you what you are about to tell me"; or "since you can't speak that well, I might as well do it for you". If you respond before your partner finishes, you are most likely to respond to what is not being communicated. This can be very offensive to the sender and harmful to the relationship.

When someone is talking to you, it is very important that they know you are listening. This is called *attentive listening*. You need to show interest in what they are telling you; otherwise they will shut down. To show that you are listening attentively, you need to apply the *SOLER* technique. SOLER is a famous five-letter abbreviation outlining five important things you need to do to non-verbally communicate your attention to the speaker. The letter S suggests that you "Face the person *Squarely*". It is very important that you face the person talking to you directly as you listen to them. Looking away or facing the other way communicates lack of interest or no involvement on your part as a listener.

The letter O stands for "*Open* Posture". An open body posture communicates a welcoming message to the speaker. It signals to the speaker that the listener is willing to engage in a conversation. Sitting with crossed legs or arms may signal discomfort and lack of interest on the part of the listener. The speaker can pick that up and retreat from speaking. Communication is thus blocked. The letter L stands for "*Lean* Forward". Tilting forward a little bit usually communicates deep interest on the part of the listener. It thus encourages the speaker to open up. Leaning backwards can also communicate lack of involvement and boredom on the part of the listener. It can also communicate that the listener is not interested.

The letter E stands for "*Eye Contact*". Directing your eyes towards to speaker indicates that you are paying attention. However, eye contact does not mean staring. Staring can be very uncomfortable to the speaker. It can create an impression that there could be something wrong with them that catches your attention. The idea is to remove your eyes from around and focus them towards the speaker without making them feel like they are being stared at. Last but not least, the letter R stands for "*Relax*". The speaker can easily pick it up when the listener is restless or uncomfortable or preoccupied; and this can limit or block their communication because it makes them think your discomfort has to do with them. It is thus important to relax as you pay attention to what is being said.

Effective listening is not only about listening and hearing; it is also about understanding the content of the message and the context in which it is communicated. It can be very helpful for the listener to ask open-ended questions to help the speaker expand or elaborate further. It can also be helpful to try and summarize the message to the speaker just to check if you understood. One-way communication is never effective. There should be a two-way discourse that allows for questions and feedback between the people communicating. People who are too quick to respond are likely to be inaccurate in their communication. It is better to remain silent than to provide an answer to the question that was never asked. So, before you respond, listen carefully and make sure you understand what is being communicated to you.

One other important form of listening is *empathic listening.* Attentive listening shows that you are paying attention to the person communicating, but empathic listening demonstrates an understanding of what the person is communicating. Empathic listeners do not respond until they are sure they understand what is being said. They put themselves in the communicator's shoes to ensure that they see what the communicator sees the way the communicator sees it. They make sure that they do not apply their own understanding on what is being communicated; rather, they make effort to see the message from the communicator's perspective. Having acquired that understanding, they communicate it back to the communicator to demonstrate that they understand. This type of listening can make the communicator feel comfortable opening up and exploring more on the message without the fear of being judged.

Empathic listening demonstrates an understanding of the communicator's feelings, thoughts, needs and actions. *Empathy* is different from *sympathy.* Sympathy says, "I feel your pain"; but empathy says, "I understand that you feel pain". In other words, sympathy feels what the communicator feels, but empathy demonstrates an understanding of the communicator's feelings. Sympathetic listeners cry with those who cry; but empathic listeners comfort those who cry. Sympathetic listeners are affected by what is being said; but empathic listeners are able to listen with understanding without being affected. For example, when a person falls into the pit, the sympathetic listener will throw himself in the hole with that person; but the empathic listener, out of the understanding that the person is hurting, will throw in a rope and try to pull that person out.

When the wife communicates her frustrations about work, the empathic husband will start by demonstrating his understanding that his wife is frustrated. For example, the husband may demonstrate his understanding of his wife's frustration by saying "you feel frustrated..." or "you must be feeling frustrated..." However, this should be communicated rather as a suggestion or assumption than a conclusion or diagnosis. This will help the communicator correct you by exploring further in case you did not pick up the correct feeling. If you make conclusion or diagnosis, you might appear more like an incompetent practitioner than a good listener. The purpose for listening at this stage it to understand and demonstrate your understanding, not to discover the problem and try to solve it. Before you even try to suggest the solution or speak your opinion, you first give an indication that you understand the effect the issue at hand has on the communicator.

Healthy marriages begin with healthy communication. It is thus essential for every married couple to start working on their communication skills. Start today to identify your communication problems and deal with them together. Make a commitment to communicate gently and considerately with each other. Also agree that you will *ring the bell* everytime your partner communicates harshly or inappropriately. Your partner should do the same when it happens to be you who communicates inappropriately. *Ringing the bell* means you will immediately make each other aware everytime you breach your commitment to improve your communication. Agree that you will interrupt each other everytime you communicate harshly or inconsiderately. This will not be as easy as it sounds; but the more you practice it, the easier it will become. Eventually it will become a habit.

Set targets in terms of timeframes and commit yourselves to a *quarrel-free relationship through healthy communication* for some time. Depending on the frequency of your quarrels, agree that you will not entertain quarrels for a particular period of time. It may be a week or a month or a quarter of a year. During this period you will be practicing gentle communication and compliments rather than harsh communication and criticisms. If that time passes without a quarrel; you may set aside some time to celebrate it as an achievement. Those little rewards will keep you motivated. Afterwards, you may set another timeframe; a longer period this time around. The plan is to start small and go big. There might be some relapses along the way where you find yourselves yelling at each other or putting each other down again, but you should not give up; you need to stay in the course. Remind each other frequently about your goal. This is not an overnight experience; it is a process, and it requires perseverance.

Once you master the skill of communication, you will stand a better chance of making your marriage a success. Poor communication or lack thereof chokes the life out of the marriage. In fact, without healthy communication, there can be no healthy marriage. Therefore, to improve your marriage, you need to improve your communication. Do not be discouraged, you are not alone. You have the Creator of the universe on your corner, and you can do all things through Him because He gives you strength (See Philippians 4:13). He will never fail to help you build your marriage by improving your communication with your spouse. He is the One who created both of you and brought you together, and He knows how to keep you together until the end of time. You *can* build a healthy communication in your marriage. On your own it may seem impossible, *but with God all things are possible* (Matthew 19:26).

17

Love Languages in Marriage

"*Cara mia, ti voglio bene*". Not everybody understands what I have just said. Only those who speak that language will understand; to the rest it is nothing but a strange writing. It means nothing at all to those who do not understand the language; it is just the same as not saying anything. For the benefit of those who do not understand, that phrase is Italian for *"My darling, I love you"*. It is a powerful massage, a message of love to the beloved; but it is meaningless if the hearer cannot understand the language. In other words, language gives meaning to the message. No matter how powerful the words you say, they mean nothing if the language cannot be understood. Suppose I told you these words everyday: *"Cara mia, ti voglio bene"*; and you do not even know what language that is, would it ever make sense to you? Certainly not; unless I communicate it in the language you understand.

People communicate in different languages, and whether they understand one another or not depends on whether or not they speak the same language. If they speak the same language, the message will be received and understood; but if they speak different languages, the message will not be received, and it will not serve the intended purpose. Couples communicate their messages of love daily to each other, but seldom is the message received; even if they speak the same language. They tell each other everyday that they love each other, yet each of them will complain that the partner does not love them. This is because love has its own language, and different people speak and understand different love languages. They may both speak English and yet speak different love languages.

If you do not understand each other's language of love as a couple, you will both experience the feelings of frustration and discouragement. If your partner complains that you do not love them even if you do your level best to show them everyday how much you love them, you feel discouraged. And if your partner keeps on telling you how much they love you even if you feel like they don't, you feel frustrated. This happens all the time in marriage. The messages of love that are communicated daily are not received by the other partner because the couple understand different languages. If the couple communicate their love to each other in the love languages they do not understand, their messages of love become meaningless; just as if they were never communicated.

There are five basic love languages, namely: Words of Affirmation, Gifts, Acts of Service, Quality Time, and Physical Touch. Whatever race or nationality, all people all over the world communicate with at least one of these five languages. Of all the five love languages, we all have our primary love languages. The primary love language speaks at the deepest level compared to all other love languages. People who receive the messages of love in their primary love languages feel truly loved. The key to communicating the messages of love effectively in marriage is to first learn each other's primary love language as a couple, and then communicate your love messages using each other's primary love languages. If you insist on communicating your love messages in any other language except your primary love languages, the messages will not be received, and you will start feeling like you do not love each other despite the efforts you take to show each other how much you love each other.

Words of Affirmation:

This language refers to verbal expressions of love, compliment and appreciation. It serves to affirm the person receiving the message on anything that will make them feel good. People with words of affirmation as their primary love languages have a strong need to be told that they are beautiful (or handsome), smart, valuable, kind, etc. Most importantly, they need to be told that they are loved. To them, it is not much about many words; it's just about those few words that are spoken from the heart. Every word of affirmation they receive goes straight to the heart and makes them feel loved. Negative words tend to put them down just as much as positive words lift them up. They feel loved when they are complimented and feel unloved when they are criticised time after time. Buying them flowers or touching them means nothing if you do not tell them verbally how much you love them and how bless you feel to be their partner.

If your partner's primary love language is words of affirmation, it will be wise for you to ensure that you never miss an opportunity tell them how much you love them. Never forget to tell them that they look beautiful (or handsome) before they leave the house, and when you are apart, make use of every opportunity to tell them you miss them. Whether you make a phone call or send a text message, make sure that you tell them words that make them feel special. Whatever you may do to show your love to them, nothing will touch their heart more than to hear you tell them how much you love, need, miss and appreciate them. Your praise arouses their passion for you, and words of affirmation arouse their affection towards you.

When it comes to communicating messages of love to your partner whose primary love language is words of affirmation, every word counts; and no word ever goes unnoticed. It may not makes sense to you, especially if your primary love language is different, but it means the world to your partner to hear you say something good about them and your relationship with them. Whatever will make them feel loved, say it to them even if you do not feel it; only make sure that you mean it. One thing to avoid is passing unnecessary criticisms to your partner whose primary love language is words of affirmation. This may make them feel unloved. Another thing to avoid is to pass more compliments to other people than you do to them. This may make them feel that there are other people whom you love more than them.

A wife whose primary love language is words of affirmation would be glad to hear her husband tell her she's a great cook, or a great mother, or a great wife. She feels loved when every detail of her beauty is noticed and communicated to her. Offensive words put her down and make her feel unloved and undesirable to her husband. The husband should therefore be careful not to make negative remarks on how they look, or cook, or sound, etc. Rather find something good to say, and if there is nothing good to say, rather say "I love you". These three words can never miss an entrance into the heart of the wife whose primary love language is words of affirmation.

Sometimes she may ask you: "I look fat, don't I?" That is not exactly a question; it is a plea, and the plea is: "Please tell me I look gorgeous!" When she makes negative remarks about herself and asks if you agree, the worst answer you could ever give is "yes". Instead of agreeing with such remarks, rather tell her why you disagree by making positive remarks about her. The reason why she feels ugly or fat or inadequate could be because you probably haven't communicated words of affirmation to her for some time, and she needs to hear you tell her words that will make her feel loved. If you tell her words that she loves to hear about herself or your relationship with her, she will most probably receive them as messages of love from you to her.

Husbands whose primary love language is words of affirmation also need to be told how much they are valued, respected and appreciated. They need to be affirmed for every good thing they do. They also feel more loved when they are praised than when they are criticised. Criticism shuts them down, but praise encourages them to do even more. They should not be left to assume that they are loved; they must be told. Let your husband know how safe he makes you feel when he is at home. If there's any good thing you think about him, tell him. You may iron his clothes and cook for him, but he will not get your message of love if you do not tell him. That is the language he is most likely to understand. There is no limit to what a husband can do for the wife who tells him he's the best, especially if his primary love language is words of affirmation.

Gifts:

People whose primary love language is gifts can receive messages of love mostly when they are wrapped up as gifts. You can spend quality time with them, tell them how blessed you are to have them, touch them in the most loving ways, or even open the door for them every time they enter or exit the automobile or wake them up with a cup of tea every morning, but none of those things touch their hearts more than the simple acts like buying them flowers or giving them presents. In fact, even if you can be consistent in doing all those things, they will still feel unloved if you do not give them gifts.

To these people, it is not so much about the size of the gift; it is the thought that counts. Even if you pick up a flower on your way home and give it to your wife whose primary love language is gifts, she would gladly receive it and appreciate the fact that you were actually thinking of her. Whether you buy them a car or a cup, they will still feel loved. This does not suggest that you keep your gifts cheap. To some people, the depth of your love can be measure by the size of your gifts. They may calculate how much you love them by how much you are willing to spend for them. This, though, should not cause pressure to you. Whatever you give them, just make sure you give them your best. When you give presents to your spouse, give them not only to show them you love them, but also to show them *how much* you love them. If you give the best you can, you reveal the best of your love.

If you think your spouse is the best, then you will give them only the best. If you give a coffee mug, give the best; and if you give a car, give top of the range. However, whatever you give to your spouse, let it be within your affordability range. After all, you don't want to give gifts to your spouse and have the sheriff come to repossess them later. The value you attach to your spouse determines the money you are willing to spend on them. However, you don't have to spend more than you have; you just have to make sure that whatever you give is the best. Even if you pick up a flower for your spouse; do not pick up just any flower, pick up the best in the garden. If you buy a screw driver for your husband, make sure you buy the best screw driver in the shop. Your gifts for your spouse reveal your love for them; but the quality of your gifts reveals the *depth* of your love.

Acts of Service:

Acts of Service is the expression of love to your spouse by doing some things for them. People whose primary love language is acts of service associate your love for them with the things you do for them. A wife whose primary love language is acts of service feels truly loved when you open the door for her. She feels very special when you pull out a seat for her at the restaurant. She also feels loved when she is assisted with some household chores. She will be very glad if you offer to help with the dishes while she is cooking, or bath the children while she cleans the house. When left to do everything on her own, she feels unloved; even if you buy her gifts, spend quality time with her, touch her lovingly, and tell her everyday that you love her. Your help to her is received as the expression of your love for her.

Wives who communicate with this love language love husbands who are hands on. Husbands who leave broken things unfixed in their houses turn them off. When you respond urgently to fix a leaking pipe in the sink, it makes her feel that you love her and care about her. She attributes everything you do in your house to your love for her and associates everything you leave unattended with your lack of love for her. She measures how much you love her by how much you do for her. If she goes to work and you remain at home, she will feel truly loved if she comes home to find dinner already prepared; especially if you are the one who prepared it. From her perspective, you don't really love her if you do not serve her.

There are also husbands whose primary love language is acts of service. Whatever you do to express your love for him, nothing will touch his heart more than the simple acts of service for him. He feels most loved when you make tea for him or prepare delicious food especially for him. The time you spend ironing his clothes means a lot to him. Nothing you do for him goes unnoticed; even the slightest acts like fixing the collar of his shirt go a long way. When he is about to leave for a couples of days, you can express your love for him by helping him pack his luggage. If you leave him to pack his luggage for himself, he will most probably feel like you don't love him. So, to show your love for him, do something for him, and he will understand and receive the message.

Quality Time:

Quality time is a love language that expresses love by spending time together. Quality time is not only about being together; it is also about focusing on each other. For example, if you are spending time together but each of you is chatting on a social network with other people, that is not quality time; it is more like sharing a space. Or you may sit side by side and watch a movie together; but if your attention is more on the movie than on each other, it is also not quality time. Quality time is not about sharing the space; it is about sharing your love, your thoughts, your feelings and everything else that really matters to both of you. Quality time is also not about being in your house; it is about being with your spouse and focusing on nothing else. To people whose love language is quality time, a true expression of love is not only about the duration of time spent together; it is also about the quality of time spent focusing on each other.

Quality time is not time spent talking about the bills; it is about focusing on each other. Even if you do not say a word, what really matters is that you enjoy each other's company. You may take a walk together, or sit together to watch the sunset, or just lie down together and feel each other's heartbeat. Quality time also involves going to the restaurant together and enjoying each other as you eat and drink. It is not about the food; it's about you having fun together. If your partner's primary love language is quality time; you can buy them expensive gifts, caress them passionately, bring them their favourite dish on a silver platter, and tell them everyday that they are the love of your life; but all these things mean nothing much if you do not spend your time with them. To them, your time is more important than your tries. You show them how much you love them by how much time you are willing to spend on them.

Physical Touch:

This love language is about expressing your love to your spouse by touching them physically. It involves kissing, caressing, cuddling, fondling, and patting. Nothing makes people whose primary love language is physical touch more loved than when you spend time on their body. It does not really matter where you touch them; what they really need is physical contact. They love it when their bodies are explored by the ones they love; and the more time spent on their body, there more loved and appreciated they feel. If they are not touched, they feel unloved. What makes them enjoy sex the most is that it involves the highest degree of physical contact. These are the people who are most likely to feel unloved if their partner does not have sex with them. I wouldn't be surprised if I were to discover that the primary love language of the person who came up with the word *'love making'* for *sex* is physical touch. When you touch their body, you touch their heart.

The only way you can accurately express your love to your spouse, whether he's a man or she's a woman, is by touching their bodies in various ways. To them, a thousand kisses from you is never too much; and they wouldn't mind spending a million days in your arms. No touch is ever too much for them. Even if you do not do all other things for them or with them, make sure that you never fail to touch them. The most effective way you can touch them deep within is by learning to touch them properly on their skin. If you won't take your hands off their body, they also won't take you out of their heart. If you touch them, you express your love for them and provoke their love for you.

Learning Your Partner's Love Language:

"How will I know what my partner's primary love language is?" That is probably the main question is your mind right now. Learning your partner's love language is not very easy; but it's fun. It is an adventure; like a search for the hidden treasure. There are a number of ways you can learn your partner's primary love language. The easiest way is to find a love language questionnaire for both of you and let each of you complete each form as honestly as possible. The findings can give you an indication of each one's primary love language. However, the accuracy of your findings will be determined by your honesty in completing the form. It is therefore advisable that you give honest answers; not 'desirable' responses.

The other way you can learn your partner's love language is through *mutual disclosure*. This involves you revealing your love language to your partner and your partner revealing theirs to you. The first thing you can do is learn your own love language by observing which one makes you feel loved the most. The next thing would be to communicate it to your partner. Your partner should do the same and then communicate theirs to you. Other way you can learn your partner's love language is by *observation*. People usually express their love using their primary love language; and in most cases they do it subconsciously. So, you can learn your partner's love language by observing the love language they use to communicate their messages of love to you.

If they show most interest in buying gifts for you, it could be that their primary love language is *gifts*. If they touch you physically most of the time, their primary love language could be *physical touch*. If they spend most of their time serving you, their primary love language could be *acts of service*. If most of the time you observe them leaving everything they are doing just to focus on you, their primary love language could be *quality time*; and if they keep on saying sweet words to you, their primary love language could be *words of affirmation*. Whatever love language your partner uses the most to communicate their messages of love to you, you may take it as a clue for their primary love language and begin to use it to express your love to them. The most important thing in learning each other's primary love language is *feedback*. As you try to express your love for each other using your primary love languages, make sure you give each other feedback to let each other know if you are on the right track.

The other way you can discover your primary language is by observing how you relate to children. Whoever we are, and whatever love language we communicate with, we have one thing in common: we love children. Generally, our interactions with children are mainly characterized by our expressions of love to them. People whose primary love language is *Words of Affirmation* would say all the nice things to children, telling them how beautiful or intelligent or smart they are. You seldom, if ever, hear them pass negative remarks to children. They love giving compliments to children telling them how much they love them. These are the kind of people who usually give children nicknames like 'Princess', 'My Angel', 'Honey', 'Darling', etc. Even when they address their partners, they call them with names that symbolize love.

People whose primary love language is *Gifts* seldom get out of the store without grabbing a toy or a candy for the child back at home. These are in my opinion the children's favourite because they never show up to them empty-handed. They always have something to give. They are usually the first ones to remember special days, and they would buy as many gifts as they can afford. They can hardly resist the urge to bring something home for the children; and they are usually the ones who buy clothes and other essentials for the children. All these actions are inspired by love and, at the same time, they are expressions of love. If they don't give something to the children, they tend to feel guilty for not loving them enough. It is also very easy for these people to suspect that the other parent hates the children if he (or she) takes too long before buying them something.

Those whose primary love language is *Acts of Service* always think about what they can do for the children. They delight in taking time to bath them, wash their clothes, cook for them, and groom them. They also love to assist them with homework or other projects. They are always watchful over the children to see that they are well dressed, and the hairs is well combed, the teeth are well brushed, the shoes are well polished, and the body is well groomed. They generally believe that if you leave the child to do things on his own, you do not really love him. These are the people who would carefully inspect their loved ones daily before they leave the house to ensure that they look their best.

People whose primary love language is *Quality Time* like spending time with the children. Very often you would see them playing with children or watching television programmes with them. They want to always be there for the children, and they tend to question the love for people who do not spend time with the children. These are of the kind that would not leave children alone at home. Almost everywhere they go, they take their children with them. They would go with their children to restaurants, movies, parks, vacations and other places of interest. They seldom, if ever, miss important events of the children; and they strongly disapprove those who do. They would just sit back and watch the children play or have fun, and at times they would join in and have fun with them.

Those whose love language is *Touch* can hardly keep their hands off the children without feeling guilty for not expressing their love enough. They love to carry children in their arms. Their relationship with children is mainly characterised by hugs, kisses and cuddles. They would not let children walk on their own when they are around; they would quickly pick them up and hold them, not because they think the children cannot walk by themselves, but simply because they subconsciously regard 'untouched' as 'unloved'. Even if you can buy your children candies or toys, they still think you do not really love them if you let them walk by themselves.

Take note that the reason all these categories of people do these things is not because they think children can't make it on their own; but because they associate such acts with love. For example, if your primary love language is Acts of Service and you double check your child everytime after he takes a bath, it does not necessarily mean you think they cannot bath themselves properly; that is just an expression of love from you to them. If your love language is Quality Time, and you don't want to leave your children alone, it does not mean you think they cannot survive on their own; it is simply because you subconsciously associate 'alone' as 'unloved'. As a couple, you can learn each other's love languages as well as your own by observing how you interact with children.

There is a terrible mistake some couple make in their marriages. They learn each other's love languages so that they can attack each other by deliberately keeping away from expressing their love for each other. Instead of using their knowledge of each other's primary love languages to communicate messages of love to each other, they use as a weapon against each other. They use love languages as hate languages to put each other down. They try 'sort each other out' by putting each other down. They try to construct their marriages by destroying each other; but no marriage can be build by tearing each other down. Love languages are meant to strengthen marriages; not to weaken the couples. If you hurt your partner, you hurt yourself, and you destroy your marriage.

If you can learn the skill of communicating your messages of love in your partner's primary love language, you will begin to see things move the right direction in your marriage. The warmth that seemed to have vanished from your marriage will return to stay. Loving each other as a couple is meaningless if you cannot communicate your love for each other. Communicating your love for each other is also meaningless if you communicate using the language you do not understand. Therefore, if you want a better marriage, learn your partner's primary love language and use it to communicate your love to them. Whether or not expression of love makes sense to you does not really matter; what really matters it makes perfect sense to your partner. Once if feel truly loved by your partner and your partner feels truly loved by you, you can rest assured that your marriage is heading upon the highway of ecstasy.

18

Temperament Issues

One of the most common questions couples ask themselves is "Why is my partner behaving this way?" More introspective ones may ask "Why do I behave this way?" If they were to get answers from their partners, those answers would most probably be "I have no idea". This is because all of us were *born* with a *combination* of *traits* that *subconsciously* influence our *behaviour*; those traits are called *temperaments* (*Tim LaHaye). Temperaments are not learnt, they are inherited from our ancestors. All of us have traits that we inherited from some people in our family trees. Those traits are the ones that make us unique; and they are the ones that influence us to behave the way we do.

Our temperaments influence every aspect of our lives. They influence our management styles, our parenting approaches, work performance, driving, studying and relationships. They also influence our interests and attractions subconsciously. We get attracted to our partners, marry them and then wonder "What in the world was I thinking to marry such a mismatch? Why didn't I discern it earlier?" We may even find ourselves asking "Why can't my partner just be like me?" We may find that our partners dislike what we like and like what we dislike and wonder "how come?" When we meet, we often think we have everything in common; but when we are married, we then think we have nothing in common. "What attracted us to each other being so different?" "How come something that annoys me so much excites my partner so much?" Well, the answer to all these and more related questions is one word – *temperaments.*

According to Tim LaHaye (the author of the book *"Why You Act the Way You Do"*), there is no influence in human life that is more powerful than our temperaments or combination of temperaments. This suggests the importance of knowing our own temperaments as well as our partners' if we are to succeed in our marital relationships. Just imagine this with me: *There is something in you that influences most of your behaviour as well as your partner's behaviour, and you don't know it.* Isn't that scary? The essential question is *do you know your temperament?* If you don't, then the above statement applies to you: There is something in you that influences most of your behaviour without you knowing it. Hence the question "Why do I behave this way?" Nevertheless, do not panic; I have the information that will surely help you. Just read on!

The idea of temperaments goes back a long way. It all started more than 400 years before Christ when Hippocrates, the brilliant Greek physician and philosopher, proposed the theory that there are four types of temperaments (Tim LaHaye). As we have discussed earlier, people differ in a number of ways. We have already discussed that some people are *introverted*, while others are *extroverted*; and some are *rational*, while others are *emotional*. Extroverts prefer to be with people more than to be alone or with few people. Introverts prefer their own space more than being with people. Rational people make more decisions with the head, while emotional people rather decide more with their heart. Each person in these four categories is equally important, and none is better than the other.

Among the four categories mentioned above, there are four main categories that are a blend of two of each trait. Some people are a combination of *rational and introvert*; some a combination of *rational and extrovert*; some *emotional and introvert*; and others *emotional and extrovert.* According to terminologies coined originally by Hippocrates, each of the above blends forms a dominant temperament category, forming four temperament categories, namely; Choleric, Phlegmatic, Sanguine and Melancholy. *Choleric* is the combination of rational and extrovert; *Phlegmatic* a combination of rational and introvert; *Sanguine* a combination of emotional and extrovert; and *Melancholy* a combination of emotional and introvert. These are the four basic temperament categories, and each one of us falls under one of these categories. Whatever category you fall under becomes your dominant or primary temperament.

All four temperaments categories are different but equally important; and all of them outline our strengths and weaknesses according to our primary temperament categories. With specific references to Tim LaHaye's book – *Why*

You Act the Way You Do – we will meet the four temperament mentioned above one by one. We will also outline their strengths and weaknesses and look at ways in which couples can get along despite their temperament differences. Please note that the reason for this information is not to give couples excuses for inappropriate behaviour; but to increase their self-knowledge so that they can understand each other, embrace their own and partners' strengths and work on their weaknesses so that they can become better individuals, and if better individuals, then better couples. This information also doesn't show you things to 'fix' in your partner; it instead shows you the things you should fix in you.

Sanguine

Sanguine is the most extroverted of all. He is a highly energetic individual who seems to be enjoying life the most. He is a fun loving and warm-hearted person. He is naturally a friendly and receptive person. Sanguine is never without a friend. His warm and receptive nature earns him favour with many people, and he takes great delight making new friends. Sanguine is known with his high level of enthusiasm, and his presence fills his surroundings with joy and laughter. He is highly compassionate, and is able to connect emotionally with people. His emotional character makes him emotionally unstable. He can cry with those who cry one minute and laugh with those who laugh the next. He is very talkative; and he loves to be the centre of attention wherever he is. Before you see his face, you have already heard his voice or whistle. He dominates every conversation, and he loves to dazzle people with his amazing personality.

Sanguine is the life of every gathering. A party is not really a party until Sanguine arrives. He is a now person; he is never troubled by the past or worried about the future. This adage applies to perfectly to him: "Yesterday is history, tomorrow is a mystery, and today is a gift; that is why they call it present". He leaves yesterday in the past, tomorrow in the future and lives in the moment. Whoever he meets matters the most for as long as he is with them; but as soon as they depart, he forgets them and focuses on the ones he meets next. His strong desire to impact people's emotions makes him an exaggerator. He narrates stories not to give information; but to impact the audience. To achieve this goal, he has a tendency to make things appear better or worse than they really are. To him, life is a song, and he is the singer. The ground he walks on is a stage, and the people around him are his audiences. His amazing ability to relive the events as he tells the stories makes him the darling of both adult and children when it comes to storytelling.

The worst thing that can happen to Sanguine is for him to be alone. His delight is to be where people are and steal their hearts with his heart-warming personality. He derives his energy from the crowds; and the more energy he obtains, the more energy fills the fill room because of his presence. He is great at making friend, but he is very bad at keeping them. This earns him lots of short-term friends. But that seldom bothers him; after all, how can he notice the friends he has lost when he's meeting so many new friends? Whatever is out of his sight is out of his mind. Even though he can forget you so fast, he has a way of making a mark in your life that will make it difficult for you to forget him. Just talking about him, you can already feel his energy.

Sanguine's Strengths

Sanguine's amazing ability to enjoy life shields him from boredom. He is seldom depressed or in a monotonous mood. His ever-present curiosity turns life into an adventure for him. He is seldom troubled by guilt or worries because of his natural ability to forget about the past and leave tomorrow until the next day. This makes it easy for him to forgive and let go of the grudges and pains from the past. All his energies are directed to the here and now, and that makes him a great impact maker in the lives of people around him. For as long as he is with you, he can make you feel like you are the most important person in the world; and while you are still left in wonder, another person is already feeling that way. His joyful mood is transmittable, and his personality can put a smile even on the saddest face.

His friendly character earns him favour with many people. He has a strong love for people and hates to see them upset. His affection for people works more like a boomerang; it always bounces back to him. His lively and confident appearance gives him an impressive presence, and his eloquence fuels his appearance and makes him the darling of the people he addresses. These features make him very good at making first impressions. This makes him a great public speaker, sales person, actor and storyteller. When is attends a job interview, his eloquence and impressive presence earn him good points before the panel of interviewers. His impressions last for a long time to people; but to him, their responses to those impressions are soon forgotten. He looks more confident than he really is; but what he has is what it takes to win the hearts and souls of his potential employers. His confident appearance and eloquence make him a charming personality.

Mr. Sanguine is an extremely optimistic person. He sees life from the positive light. If he fails today, he knows that tomorrow will be much better. He is not afraid to face today's challenges even if he failed yesterday; not that he has planned to approach things differently to prevent yesterday's failure from repeating itself. He's positive outlook to the world makes him a trusting and believing person. He is not afraid to take risks because in his mind he sees no possibility for failure. His optimistic personality also enables him to put people at ease. He is always looking forward to life and expects great things to happen. Though his emotional temperament makes it easy for him to be hurt, his positivity and 'live for today' attitude make it easy for him to forgive and forget. He expects the best in life; and if he experiences the opposite, his knowledge that things will be better keeps him going.

Mr. Sanguine is moved by compassion. Because of his inconsistence, people tend to think his acts of compassion are not genuine. But the truth is: the fact that he forgets quickly does not mean his compassionate responses are not real. He is very authentic; but only for as long as he is in the scene. As soon as he departs, he redirects all that energy to someone else. Sanguine loves for real, but not for long. According to Tim LaHaye, no one can love you more nor forget you faster than Mr. Sanguine.

Sanguine's Weaknesses

Mr. Sanguine lives in the moment; but he cannot stay in the moment. This makes him a very inconsistent person. Inconsistence also means unreliable. Mr. Sanguine's promises are valid until he meets another person and makes other promises. Ultimately, he has made more promises than he can carry out. His overwhelming compassion and burning desire to impact people earns him a weakness of biting more than he can chew. He makes more friends than he can afford to keep; and he makes more appointments than he can manage to keep. When he tells that he will be at your house in about two hours, you will be totally convinced that he will be there at that time. When he makes that promise, he really means it; and he intends to keep it. Until he meets another person on his way to your house; then he changes his destination completely. The last person he will meet will be the one in whose house he will be.

Of all the temperament categories, Sanguine is the most undisciplined one. He is the kind who would start reading a book and read another one before he finishes the first chapter of the previous book. He is easily distracted; thus he cannot stick to his plans. Today he can decide to be on a strict diet for some time, and tomorrow he indulges in every junk food he can get his hands on. Sanguine is an extremely weak-willed and disorganised person. His decisions are based on his convictions; but his convictions are based on his surroundings. He always starts things and never finishes them. He can wake up in the morning and take out garden tools to work on his garden; but soon after he started, he is already gone, and tools are left lying on the floor. By the time he comes back, he walks over the tools he left in the morning to do something else in the house; which of course he will not finish.

Mr. Sanguine is also emotionally unstable. He can cry bitterly in one minute and then forget completely about it the next minute; and then laugh like he never cried in ages. He can burst out in anger one moment and then repent the next moment. Sanguine seldom learns from his mistakes; and very often he finds himself sincerely apologising for the same thing over and over again; and soon after apologising, he's in it again. Because of his weak will, he has poor self-control. According to Tim LaHaye, because of his emotional receptiveness, Mr. Sanguine can be tempted more easily than other types, but he is also equipped with a weak will that finds him frequently giving in to this temptation. Because he is the person who lives in the present, he seldom anticipates the consequences of his actions and the damage they may cause in his family. He gives in to temptation based on how it feels rather than on the consequences thereof.

Mr. Sanguine is also a restless person, and because of this, he finds it extremely difficult to concentrate. His mind runs all over the place most of the time. This makes him a very unproductive person. His talkative nature makes him a poor listener. Usually, where there is a conversation, he is the one who does most or all of the talking. When you give vital information, his mind runs around to think about more exciting things; and he misses a large percentage of what you told him. He loves to be heard; but he hates to listen. This makes him an egotist. Every discourse is about what he has to say; and most often, he talks about the things that interest him, thinking others are likewise interested. This can be obnoxious to people around him; but before they get really irritated, he's already gone to dominate other conversations.

Choleric

Choleric, like Sanguine, is an extrovert; but unlike Sanguine, he is more stable and self-controlled. He is disciplined, and he possesses a strong will power. He is a workaholic type of a person, and he has a strong sense of achievement. He delights in getting things done; this is what drives him. Choleric is usually highly self-sufficient and very independent. What people think or say about him does nothing to him. *He does not need to be stimulated by his environment, but rather stimulates his environment with his endless ideas, plans and ambitions* (Tim LaHaye). He is more proactive than reactive; and he believes in planning and carrying out his plans. He is usually aggressive and domineering. He has strong confidence in his own abilities, and he usually prefers to do things his way or no way. He has good qualities to be a great leader, but he can be very controlling.

Mr. Choleric is a go-getter. Whatever he goes after, he will not rest until he gets it. He is the type that succeeds where few survive. Opposition does not put him down; it revs him up. He is not moved by the tears of other people; in fact, they disgust him. He is naturally unsympathetic to people around him. He is very good at manipulating people in order to achieve his goals. To him, 'the end justifies the means'. He goes for what he wants no matter how many people he hurts in the process. In fact, the more casualties he creates in the process, the more satisfied he becomes. Choleric is a table pounder and door slammer. He often uses aggression and intimidation to direct people towards his direction.

Mr. Choleric is one optimistic and practical person. He seldom, if ever, sees the possibility of failure. Obstacles seem invisible to him. The only thing he can see is an achieved goal, and don't you dare stand in his way! He sees people more as tools than co-workers; and he uses them to achieve his goals. His style of leadership is dictatorship. He is not a man of much detail; in fact, he finds details boring. Just tell him what needs to be done and leave the how part with him. Loafing is not part of Choleric's make up. Even if the rest can idle, he will still be pressing on. But people do not idle when Mr. Choleric is around; he will make sure they don't. He is a natural slave driver. It's either you help him or he uses you; but idling will only be in your wish list for as long as Mr. Choleric is around. This makes him a reliable and productive worker; but it also makes him people's number one enemy, not that it bothers him.

Mr. Choleric has an eye to spot an opportunity and find his way to it. He also has the ability to find the people he can use in order to grab that opportunity. He is a very decisive person. He never hesitates to make crucial decisions for himself and others; and if Choleric decides, the rest must follow – if they know what's good for them. Mr. Choleric is the kind of person who works a lot and never stops to love. He seems to value work more than he values relationships. For this reason, he is reputable to be a cold personality who is insensitive to people's feelings. He cares more about what he achieves through you than how he makes you feel. He is highly ambitious and never takes "no" for an answer.

Choleric's Strengths

Choleric is a highly productive individual. His strong will power makes him a man of his words. It makes him a consistent person who does not rest until he completes what he started. He is also highly disciplined and well organized. Wherever he is, things get done. His optimistic nature gives him confidence in the outcomes of his efforts. He has a strong ability to focus on the goal at hand without anticipating the possibility of failure. He is not afraid of adversities; once he sets his mind on something, nothing can stop him. He is relentless and resilient. Mr. Choleric is an independent thinker and a great decision maker; and he is able to react quickly in a crisis situation. He is stable in his thoughts and steady in his actions. He is a very reliable individual; and whatever he promises, you can rest assured that he will carry it out.

Mr. Choleric is a very practical person. Instead of placing his hands above his head to worry about the problem, he would rather roll up his sleeves and work on the problem until he gets the solution. He is more intuitive than analytic; that is what blinds him from obstacles and makes him more practical. But obstacles never bother him because he is highly confident in his ability to handle whatever difficulties that may crop up. He never sits back to wait for things to happen; instead, he always rises up to make them happen. His is a thick skinned person who is not easily offended. He is no man pleaser; he just does whatever needs to be done no matter how people feel about him. Choleric has strong leadership predisposition. Whenever there is a task to carry out, he will have volunteered to give direction and strategy, and before you know it, he's in charge. He takes over the responsibility and then runs over other people to achieve the desired outcomes. If Mr. Choleric can learn to deal with his controlling and domineering tendencies, he can make a great leader.

Choleric's Weaknesses

Mr. Choleric's relentless tendencies are strongly linked to his aggressiveness. He can be very hostile to people around him and feel no remorse about it. His hot temper brings people under his subjection out of fear of being attacked. His cruelty makes him a proud heart breaker. He cares less about the rights and feelings of other people. Sometimes he has fun putting people down. He is very sarcastic and inconsiderate. He never takes time to analyze his words before he utters them to see if they will not offend other people; but he doesn't care if they are offended. People tend to hate him; but that only encourages him to hurt them even more. He seems to love seeing people suffer because of him. Mr. Choleric is full of himself, and he always ensures that he intimidates people into carrying out his desires.

Choleric is a cold-hearted being. His attitude drives people away; but his domineering personality forces them to remain under his control. You are either in agreement with him or forced to cooperate with him. If you try to advise him, he makes fun of you and your 'ridiculous' advice. In short, Mr. Choleric is surrounded by casualties, and he is the culprit; and he loves it. His anger outbursts and aggressive attacks make him an undesirable person to be around; but the less people like him, the more he terrorizes them with his hostile personality. He is a violent person who takes what he wants by force. Unless Mr. Choleric learns to manage his weaknesses, he will remain a relationship disaster who inflicts pain wherever he goes.

Melancholy

According to Tim LaHaye, Melancholy has by far the richest and most sensitive nature of all the temperaments. He has a high level of intelligence, and he is exceedingly gifted. He is emotionally expressive and introspective; and he is also super-sensitive and thin-skinned. Mr. Melancholy is super-introverted. He enjoys his own company, and he does not stay long in the crowds. He is commonly known as the dark temperament because of his negative outlook towards life. He is very analytical and pessimistic; and these contribute to his tendency to find fault in everything, as if his mind was programmed to see what's wrong. His emotional nature contributes to his wavering moods. Sometimes he displays feelings of ecstasy, and this can make people confuse him for an extrovert; but other times he presents the feelings of doom and gloom, and these cause him to be withdrawn.

Melancholy, unlike Mr. Sanguine, does not make friends with ease, but he is a very faithful friend to the few friends he has. He seldom initiates friendships, but his loyalty to his friends is undeniable. He is a self-sacrificial person who could put himself in harm's way for the sake of his friends. This makes him the most dependable of all temperament categories. Mr. Melancholy has very strong perfectionist tendencies; and he has high standards of excellence and achievement. To him, excellent is not good enough; only perfect will do. At face value, his seems to be a highly unsociable person; but deep down he not only loves people, but he also has a profound longing to be loved.

Mr. Melancholy's thin-skinned personality makes him a self-protective person. Although he loves deeply, he also hurts easily; so, he doesn't trust easily. That could be one of the reasons why he finds it difficult to make new friends. Unlike the Choleric, Melancholy is more analytical than intuitive. *His exceptional analytical ability causes him to diagnose accurately the obstacles and dangers of any project he has a part in planning* (Tim LaHaye). This analytic ability enables him to plan ahead for the impediments and hazards that may occur in the process. He does not want to be caught unprepared; so, he diagnoses the problem before it occurs and prepares thoroughly for it. His successes are very high, but they are hardly ever celebrated because of his perfectionist tendencies making him think 'it was not good enough'.

Mr. Melancholy is a very detailed and determined person. He is the kind of person who never leaves a stone unturned. He is very neat and organized. He is also disciplined and dependable. He would never betray his friends; but he can be unforgiving and revengeful. He has good memory for the wrongs that were done against him; and he would make sure that he gives his wrongdoers a good dose of their own medicine. When provoked, Melancholy can be very aggressive. This is because he is emotionally sensitive and self-protective. Melancholy's emotional sensitivity also earns him a deep love for fine arts and nature. He is the kind of a person who would enjoy sitting alone outside to gaze at the sun going down.

Melancholy's Strengths

Mr. Melancholy is a highly intelligent being. In fact, it is believed that most geniuses are in this temperament category. He is also gifted and creative. His perfectionist tendencies turn him out to be a great achiever, bestowing upon him a very high performance standard. He is also highly introspective; and this enables him to evaluate his past performance and think of ways to improve next time. He never settles for less than the best. Mr. Melancholy is also a very organized person who puts everything where it should be and the way it should be. His perfectionist tendencies and analytical abilities enable him to recognize even the minutest detail that is not in order. He leaves no room for error.

Mr. Melancholy's exceptional analytical abilities enable him to perceive problems before they occur. It is not in his nature to think about the project without foreseeing the possibility for failure. This enables him to warn people about dangers before they occur. Mr. Melancholy is also a very faithful friend; one who would never disappoint those who trust him. He is a man of his word, and there is nothing he won't possibly do to see that his promises are carried out. He is also highly dependable; and when there is a division of work, his part will always be completed on time.

One of Melancholy's notable strengths is his exceptional ability to sacrifice himself for the betterment of his acquaintances. He is the kind of person who would lay down his life for his friends. He is a much disciplined person who is not easily distracted. He is highly industrious, and therefore, very productive. Mr. Melancholy is the most sensitive of all the temperament categories. He is emotionally responsive and deeply reflective in his thoughts. He does not play with words or talk for the sake of talking; instead, he weighs his words carefully before he speaks and communicates exactly what he means.

Melancholy's Weaknesses

Mr. Melancholy is a highly pessimistic individual. He is inclined to perceive problems to be solved instead of goals to be achieved. He most often has reasons why things will not work out. Because of his perfectionist tendencies and excessive pessimism, nothing is ever good enough for him. This makes him a very hard person to please. Even if you can do your best, he will always tell you what's wrong with you. He judges people not on what they are doing right; but on what they are doing wrong. His mind is seemingly programmed for negativity. When anything goes wrong, he would never fail to notice it. Even if things do go right, his strong analytical abilities will still help him locate wrongs. He would look beyond the exquisite decorations that give a face-lift to a house and locate the cracks and skewed wall pictures. Seemingly, the only time he notices that you have done something is when you have done something wrong. Unless Mr. Melancholy learns to train his mind to be appreciative, nothing will ever be good enough for him.

Melancholy is also self-centred. He lives his life on his toes, thinking that everybody is out to hurt him. This is probably because of his thin-skinned personality that easily takes offense. He is comfortable telling other people what's wrong with them, but he finds it offensive when people criticize him. He operates on two rules; rule number one: "When I say you are wrong, don't you dare argue with me"; rule number two: "Don't you dare tell me that I'm wrong". Mr. Melancholy sees the world as a planet of 'savages' that are looking for opportunities to destroy him; and he just won't let them. He takes correction as an attack, and he will retaliate. It seems like Mr. Melancholy's mind was programmed to think there's something wrong everybody else and nothing wrong with him. Sitting with him is like sitting on eggshell, and no matter how careful you are, the shells will break, and you will be in serious trouble.

Melancholy has a strong memory for the wrongs that were done against him; and he can be very unforgiving. He is like a filing cabinet for criminal records, and as long as he lives, no crime will be left unpunished. His unforgiving spirit is always screaming for revenge; and whatever wrong you do him, he will make sure it comes right back to you. Mr. Melancholy is the kind of person who would find it extremely difficult to follow the Biblical instruction that says *"love those who hate you and bless those who curse you".* He prefers repaying evil for evil, and *an eye for an eye* tends to be his favourite approach in dealing with those who wrong him. Whatever good you do to him will not be recognized; but whatever wrong you do to him will never be forgotten, and he will make sure he returns the favour. Of all temperament categories, none comes close to Melancholy in terms of holding a grudge and settling the score through revenge.

Mr. Melancholy is also a moody individual. You will never know how he will wake up the next day. One morning he wakes up excited, and the next morning he wakes up depressed. He can sleep on cloud nine at night and wake up in a whirlpool the next morning. His mood changes like weather, and there's no predicting how he might feel in the next minute. Mr. Melancholy's mood is like the wind; you need to continually study the direction to which it blows, and then adjust the sails accordingly, otherwise you will be in deep trouble. His mood swings make him an unsociable person because people never know the time he will switch off or strike back. Mr. Melancholy's emotional hypersensitivity, together with his perfectionist tendencies, tend to make him feel inadequate or worthless, thus making him vulnerable to depression. The highest rate of people who commit suicide for no comprehensive reasons is of those who belong to this temperament category.

Phlegmatic

Phlegmatic is the person of a well-balanced temperament. He is cool, calm, soft-spoken and easygoing. He is the kind of person who never reflects his feelings through his face. Whether is happy or sad, you cannot tell by looking at him. He never bursts out in anger or excitement. He is the kind of person who would receive the bad news and still retain the face he displayed when he received good news. If there ever be a person who is able to keep his emotions under control and remain consistent all the time, that would be Mr. Phlegmatic. Even his voice is consistent whether he is elated or degraded. It's not that he has no emotions; they just don't show in his face or voice.

Mr. Phlegmatic is not only a peace lover; he is also a peacemaker. He is not fond of tension, and he would do anything to avoid it. He enjoys people and loves to put the smile on people's faces, and he has an inborn sense of humour. *He is the type of individual that can have the crowd "in stitches" and never crack a smile. He has the unique ability of seeing something humorous in others and the things they do. He has a good, retentive mind and is often quite capable of being a good imitator* (Tim LaHaye). He is a natural man pleaser; but he never takes initiatives. He also never volunteers leadership, but when pushed, he can be a great leader. When there is a task to be carried out, he prefers to take the back seat and watch things happen; but when put on the spot, he can be very productive.

Phlegmatic seldom does beyond what is expected, and he always finds the quickest and easiest way to get things done. He tends to be a procrastinator; and he loves to put off important responsibilities until the 'right time', which almost never comes. Nevertheless, whatever he has being postponing until the eleventh hour, his special ability to excel under pressure enables him to see it to completion. He is the slow and sluggish individual, and he has a very weak sense of urgency; but his fear of disappointing people propels him to do whatever needs to be done. Mr. Phlegmatic has a serious trouble taking a decision. He can take forever before he makes a move. Once you ask Mr. Phlegmatic to do something, consider it done, but only after a while.

Phlegmatic's Strengths

Mr. Phlegmatic's easygoing personality and sense of humour make him the darling of many people. He has an incredible ability put a smile in people's faces and comfort in their hearts; and because of this he can make a very good counsellor. His fear of hurting people makes him a diplomatic person. He knows how to choose words carefully so that he does not start a fight when he communicates. His ability to sit back and observe enables him to learn more about people and find his way to their hearts. Mr. Phlegmatic is a person you can depend on. He is also very practical in his approach to life. He has the amazing ability to stay calm in crisis and excel under pressure. Because of his emotional stability, Mr. Phlegmatic never bursts out in anger or excitement. He is *swift to hear [but] slow to speak [and] slow to wrath* (James 1:19).

Phlegmatic's cool and calm personality enables him to appease anger in others by his gentle responses. He never yells at people, but the content of his utterances can be firm and weighty. Because of his ability to listen properly and choose his words carefully before he speaks, he is a good peacemaker and negotiator. Mr. Phlegmatic's emotional stability enables him to be objective. Unlike Mr. Sanguine, who is more sympathetic to those who are in pain, Phlegmatic his more empathic in his responses to people's hurts. He can understand your pain without having to cry with you. This is another trait that makes him a good counsellor. Mr. Phlegmatic, like Melancholy, is also a faithful friend who would never let the people who depend on him down. Although his loyalty is invisible in his face, it is always evident in his conduct.

Mr. Phlegmatic is a cheerful and friendly individual. He is also approachable and agreeable. People do not hesitate to break even the most sensitive conversations with him. Phlegmatic does not like doing things 'by the book'; he would rather think about his own practical ways of achieving the desired goals. He is capable of adjusting the methods without compromising the outcome. Mr. Phlegmatic's words and actions are always well thought of. This makes him an efficient person. Though he is a reluctant person, he is very good at what he is doing. What really works for him is that he never wastes his time trying to do the things he's not good at; he does only what he is good at and does it well. He is not a perfectionist like Mr. Melancholy, but he has high achievement standards which reveal high levels of accuracy.

He is also neat and organized. *The neatness of his desk top in the midst of a great project is always a source of amazement to the more active temperaments. But he has just found that putting everything in its exact spot is much easier and less time consuming in the long run, therefore, he is a man of orderly habits* (Tim LaHaye). Phlegmatic's personality is the envy of many people; but like all temperaments, he also has his weaknesses.

Phlegmatic's Weaknesses

Mr. Phlegmatic is very slow and sluggish, and it's not easy to know whether he's in or out. He is also a procrastinator. He is unmotivated and very reluctant; and he is the type of person who would fold his arms and wait for someone to do something. He is also very lazy, and most often you will find him dragging his feet in almost everything he does. When ordered or propelled to do things against his will, he would very often gear himself down on a go-slow. Mr. Phlegmatic is a spectator, and he always wants to do as little as possible. He never volunteers himself or make the first move in a project. He detests anything that may motivate him to 'get his hands dirty'. The lesser the work to be done, the better it is for him.

Despite his easygoing personality, Mr. Phlegmatic is very stubborn, and his stubbornness is always disguised in his humour and easygoing personality. He is also very selfish and egocentric. He is usually found opposing change, especially a drastic one, and he would not participate in anything he disagrees with. He always has a differing opinion, and if his views are rejected or ignored, he would pull out and 'watch things fall apart'. He has a strong need to be needed, and he gets very happy to have people begging for his assistance. When he perceives anything that seems like a personal attack directed to him, he would shut down like a tortoise pulling its head into its shell. Once he shuts down, it is almost, if not, impossible to get him to open up again.

Not only does he pull himself out; he also has a tendency to refrain from involving his resources into a course. This reveals the stingy side of him. He seldom participates in activities that may cost him something. Eventually, everything could be about how much will he lose into it. He is always the last one to dig his hand into his pocket. He is always on the lookout for great value at low cost; and he always puts in little and expects much in return. Unlike Melancholy, who can even sacrifice himself for the course, Phlegmatic would not get involved. He would rather watch the project collapse than engage himself in a 'failing project'.

Mr. Phlegmatic is also very indecisive. He can spend hours in a shop and come out with nothing. The cheap ones have 'poor quality', and ones with good quality are 'too expensive'; so, he would have trouble making a decision on which one to choose. Rather than taking a quick decision, Mr. Phlegmatic would decide not to decide and choose to leave things as they are. Because of this, he finds himself having to succumb to the decisions that were made for him while he was struggling to make up his mind. Usually he finds such decisions unfavourable to him, and he would not get involved. Although he is slow to decide, he is quick to criticize the decisions that are made and take the back seat to observe.

While he sits back and observes, he would tease everyone who seems to be making progress to try and discourage them. His goal is to have people come to him desperate for his intervention when the project fails. Even though he seems relaxed at face value, deep down Mr. Phlegmatic is a worrier. He is also fearful and insecure. He would worry about how people feel about him; and he usually fears that people might not like him, or that he is perhaps inadequate. He is the kind of a person who would enjoy the convenience while others carry the load.

How Our Temperaments Influence Our Marriages

How couples attract each other is very interesting. Very seldom, if ever, do people attract partners of the same temperament as theirs. Usually, friendships are formed based mainly on *similarities*, but marital relationships are form based more on *complementarities*. Attraction through similarities occurs mostly when people have similar goals, occupations, personalities, likes (or dislikes), gender, religion, political views, etc. People with similarities tend to like each other and establish friendships. Attraction through complementarities occurs mainly when one person sees something different in the other person that seems to complement him (or her). For example, men and women tend to like each other because they are different from each other, and they complement each other in many ways.

Friends with more complementarities than similarities tend to fall in love with each other and become lovers; but friends with more similarities than complementarities are most likely to remain friends without falling in love. So, marital relationships are usually established between couples who complement each other. Before we get married, all we see in our partners are people who will be our strength in our areas of weakness. We see in them people who have what we are lacking. It is only after getting married that we realize how different we are from each other. Then we start seeing people who lack what we have and are weak when we are strong. What we saw before marriage was that they will give us what we do not have; but marriage reveals that we also need to be their strength in the weakness as well. It's not only about them complementing us; but it's also about us complementing them.

Mr. Choleric is a domineering person, and Phlegmatic is a submissive type. The submissive trait of Phlegmatic attracts Choleric to him. Choleric is also pushy by nature, but Phlegmatic is more cooperative. One other trait that attracts Choleric to Phlegmatic is that Choleric is controlling, and Mr. Phlegmatic's inherent need to please everybody makes him controllable. Choleric is also impressed by Mr. Phlegmatic's calm voice tone because he never yells back at him. Mr. Phlegmatic's easygoing personality also excites Mr. Choleric because he feels he can always have his way; what more can Choleric ask for! One other thing that Choleric likes about Phlegmatic is that when they get married, Phlegmatic will be the softer version of him.

On the other hand, the indecisive Phlegmatic would fall in love with Mr. Choleric's amazing ability to make crucial decisions even in emergencies. At first, the reluctant Phlegmatic perceives Mr. Choleric's pushy nature as something that brings out the best in him; and that makes him fall for him. Mr. Phlegmatic is a procrastinator, and the fact that Mr. Choleric gets things done immediately captures his heart. While Phlegmatic worries about it, Choleric has already done it; and that makes Phlegmatic Mr. Choleric's big fan. Mr. Phlegmatic's overwhelming laziness also makes him see Choleric's workaholic tendencies as something that would give him a break. Mr. Phlegmatic's love for the 'back seat' also attracts him to Choleric's love for being on the forefront. Phlegmatic then assumes that when they get married, Choleric will be the tougher version of him.

Soon after the two get married, things begin to take another turn. The rough voice tone of Mr. Choleric provokes Phlegmatic's stubbornness. The more Choleric screams, the more stubborn Mr. Phlegmatic becomes; and the more stubborn Mr. Phlegmatic becomes, the louder Mr. Choleric roars. Choleric also begins to get annoyed by Phlegmatic's inability to take decisions; then he makes sarcastic utterances, from which Phlegmatic shuts down completely. Mr. Choleric loves to inflict pain in people and enjoys seeing them wail because of him; but Mr. Phlegmatic deprives him that joy with his facial display that never tells how he really feels. Phlegmatic's face and voice tone make him appear like he is numb; and this frustrates Choleric because it makes him feel like he is unable to hurt him. Instead of Mr. Phlegmatic breaking a tear at Choleric's offense, he would rather crack a joke or tease him, thus annoying him some more.

To bridge the gap between these two, Choleric should learn to deal with his anger outbursts, and Phlegmatic should learn to be more participative. Choleric should also try to slow down a little, and Phlegmatic should try to up his pace. If the wife is Choleric, it becomes more difficult for her to submit to her Phlegmatic husband than it is for a Phlegmatic wife to submit to her Choleric husband. The challenge for a Choleric wife would then be to train herself to submit to her husband according to Ephesians 5:22-24. It is also more difficult for a Choleric husband to be respectful and considerate to his wife. Therefore, Choleric should put more effort in loving his wife according to Ephesians 5:24-33. Mrs. Phlegmatic should also learn to deal with her stubbornness so that she can be fully submissive to her Phlegmatic husband, and Mr. Phlegmatic should also try to be more liberal and flexible when it comes to his Choleric wife.

Sanguine loves the centre stage, and Melancholy prefers to work behind the scenes. Melancholy also likes to be part of the audiences to be dazzled by the heart touching performances of Mr. Sanguine. Sanguine also loves the fact that Melancholy can actually be touched by his performances. This forms attraction between the two. Mr. Sanguine would also be able to adjust to Melancholy's mood swings and follow suit with his feelings. He would cry with Melancholy and laugh with him. This also draws Melancholy to Mr. Sanguine. Sanguine is also able to break though Melancholy's analytical abilities and appeal straight to his heart. Then Mr. Sanguine would leave Melancholy desperate for more and go on his way to impact many other people. But Sanguine wants to go where he is celebrated, and he knows just the person who does – Mr. Melancholy. Melancholy is also attracted to Sanguine's confident appearance, and Sanguine just loves the attention.

Then they get married, and Sanguine wants to go out and impact people as usual; but this time around Melancholy wants him all to himself. Then Mr. Sanguine would populate the house with people, which would make Melancholy uncomfortable. Melancholy would tell him what he is doing is wrong, and Mr. Sanguine will be quick to apologize; but after a short while, Sanguine is guilty of the same crime. After every apology, Sanguine thinks it's over, but how can Mr. Melancholy forget that Sanguine did him wrong? He would keep on bringing up to his face and make sure he pays for it; and the more he does that, the more frustrated Mr. Sanguine becomes by the person who fails to realize that 'tomorrow will be better than today'.

Before marriage, Sanguine's optimism and zest for life would amaze Mr. Melancholy; but in marriage it annoys him because it is 'based on illusions'.

On the other hand Mr. Sanguine is annoyed by Melancholy's negative attitude. Then Melancholy gets infuriated by the person who leave him alone every now and then as if he is the guard of the house, while on the other hand Sanguine wonders when will Melancholy 'get a life'. By the time Sanguine goes out, he would leave things haphazard in the house – dishes in the sink, dirty clothes lying around, garden tools abandoned on the drive way, etc; and Melancholy would make sure that he pays for every one of those offenses. Eventually their marriage becomes the battle of the absconder versus the avenger.

Sanguine should learn to keep his words and clean up after himself. He should also try to spend more time in his house and be consistent in his decisions. Furthermore, Sanguine should learn to keeps secrets because his blunt behaviour makes his Melancholy partner lose trust for him. Melancholy prefers keeping things to his himself, and he is not comfortable letting other people know his secrets. Melancholy can also make this better by training his mind to be more positive. He should also learn to accommodate Sanguine's people-centred personality. Sanguine should learn to be more disciplined, and Melancholy should learn to be more forgiving and less revengeful. Sanguine should also learn to practice what he preaches, and Melancholy should learn to be more appreciative and not expect too much from his Sanguine partner.

Mr. Melancholy is attracted to Choleric by his ability to get things done 'with ease'. He also falls in love with Choleric's positive attitude and his relentless tendency to go for what he wants until he gets it. Choleric's love for work makes him appear to Melancholy as someone who would bring his imaginative inventions into reality. While Melancholy argues about why 'it won't work', Choleric quickly shows him why 'it will work'; and that also draws Melancholy to Choleric. On the other hand Mr. Choleric falls in love with the self-sacrificing personality of Melancholy because that means he can manipulate him easily. Choleric knows that Melancholy would never let him down; so he would love to use that to achieve his goals. Melancholy also loves Choleric's sense of direction and achievement.

Then they get married, and Mr. Choleric starts being annoyed by Melancholy's negative attitude. He also gets bored by the details that Melancholy keeps on outlining. Then he begins with his violent attacks to Melancholy, and like boomerangs, Melancholy would send them right back to him. Whatever pain Mr. Choleric inflicts on him, Melancholy keeps it in a file and would not rest until Choleric has paid in full. When they take a trip, Choleric's main interest is to reach their destination; but Melancholy enjoys the views of nature along the way. When they take a bath, Melancholy wants to enjoy the water; but Choleric just wants to finish. Same applies in lovemaking. Melancholy would enjoy the kisses, caresses and the bond they build in the process; but Mr. Choleric's main goal is to reach orgasm and get it over and done with.

For these two to get along, they should learn to see the world from each other's perspective. Choleric should try to understand that the process is as important to his Melancholy partner as the product is to him; and Melancholy should also try to understand that the product is as important to his Choleric partner as the process is to him. Choleric should also learn to be kind and gentle to his Melancholy partner, and Melancholy should learn not to repay evil for evil. They say anger is just one letter away from danger, and these two should watch that they do not destroy each other in their anger. This is the couple that can really provoke each other; and unless they recognize their weaknesses and deal with them, they might inflict serious physical injuries and emotional damage on each other.

Phlegmatic can listen, and Melancholy loves it. He also loves Mr. Phlegmatic's amazing ability to put him at easy or make him smile when he feels gloomy. The gentleness of Mr. Phlegmatic makes Melancholy feel safe around him. Melancholy is confident that Mr. Phlegmatic's easygoing personality will not give him too much stress. On the other hand, Mr. Phlegmatic loves the ease that he enjoys out of Melancholy's hard work and commitment to his course. He is also confident that whatever Mr. Melancholy does, he does it well. Then Melancholy's perfectionism would make him feel he has not done well enough; but that's nothing Mr. Phlegmatic cannot talk him out of. The reassuring abilities of Mr. Phlegmatic help Melancholy discover positive things within himself and develop a more positive outlook towards life. Mr. Melancholy's loyalty also eases Mr. Phlegmatic's insecurities.

Phlegmatic's incredible ability to choose his words carefully before he speaks and think carefully before his acts earns him respect from Melancholy. Phlegmatic knows that when he's with Melancholy, he will not have to get involved or spend his money because of Melancholy's generosity to those he loves. Before Mr. Phlegmatic decides on how much he is willing to spend, Melancholy has already sacrificed his own money; and that seems to bail him out. Melancholy cannot rest until he completes the task, and that gives Phlegmatic a good opportunity to rest while Melancholy works himself to exhaustion. These are the things that attract Phlegmatic to Melancholy. Phlegmatic seems to know how to boost the emotions of Melancholy, and that also attracts Melancholy to him.

Because of their complementarities they may decide to get married. During preparations, Melancholy would spend most of his time drafting budgets, action plan and contingency plan. On the other hand Phlegmatic would be dragging his feet all the way. A day before the wedding, Phlegmatic has not decided what to wear. But lucky for him his Melancholy partner already saw that coming, and has already picked a good set of expensive clothes for him. Throughout the preparations, Melancholy has spent sleepless nights ensuring that their day becomes a great success, while Phlegmatic sits back and worries about this and that; eventually concluding that he will 'cross that bridge when he gets to it'. The day becomes a success; thanks to Melancholy's sacrifices and Phlegmatic's words of encouragement to his partner.

After the wedding, Melancholy continues to sacrifice his time and money to build their family; but Phlegmatic continues to sit back and relax, until Melancholy starts getting annoyed. Then Melancholy starts criticizing his Phlegmatic partner, to which Phlegmatic would just shut down and hide in his shell. Mr. Phlegmatic's humorous utterances then begin to be obnoxious to Melancholy. Melancholy then starts withdrawing, and Phlegmatic starts worrying; but his face makes his partner think he doesn't care. This can lead to serious tensions; and when it comes to tension, Melancholy is so much stronger than Phlegmatic. Desperate to put an end to the tension, Mr. Phlegmatic would try to initiate peace; to which Melancholy reacts aggressively. Melancholy's aggressive reactions would then provoke Phlegmatic's stubbornness, and this can become a cold war.

To tighten the loose ends in this marriage, Phlegmatic should learn to develop a sense of urgency in terms of deciding and acting. He should also try to be more generous with his resources and be more involved in the homebuilding activities. Melancholy on the other hand should learn to show appreciation for the efforts that Phlegmatic makes; this will encourage the men-pleasing Phlegmatic to do more. One of the things that Melancholy should avoid at all cost is to keep on judging and criticising his Phlegmatic partner for almost everything. This will push him into his shell, and he will be more reserved and reluctant. Melancholy should also try to ease up on his aggressive attacks against his Phlegmatic partner because they will trigger his stubbornness, and things might be worse than before.

Sanguine may be attracted to Choleric by his strong will and independence. This is complementary to his weak willed and dependent personality. Choleric's discipline also covers Mr. Sanguine's lack of discipline. Sanguine may also be drawn to Choleric's ability to relentlessly finish what he started; which is also something he lacks terribly. Wherever Mr. Sanguine is weak, Choleric becomes his strength; and that also attracts him. On the other hand, Sanguine's weakness of will becomes Mr. Choleric's manipulative tool on him. At face value, Mr. Sanguine appeals to Choleric as a very confident and competent person, and that influences his perception of him as a man he can 'do business with'. Sanguine's ability to magnify his statements also promises Mr. Choleric so much more, and it draws his deep interest towards him.

Not so long after the wedding, Mr. Choleric starts to get annoyed by Sanguine's empty words and inconsistencies. On the other hand Mr. Sanguine starts feeling bored by someone who is clearly not fascinated by his acts. Mr. Choleric would then be irritated by Sanguine's inability to finish what he started, and that would be followed by aggressive verbal attacks and acts of absolute cruelty. Then Mr. Sanguine, being a great storyteller as he is, would narrate his partner's atrocious brutality to everyone he meets, presenting it to be so much worse than it really is. Choleric, the 'slave driver', would push Mr. Sanguine beyond his limits and put so much pressure on him, and the more pressure he puts, the more Sanguine moves away to look for more exciting things to do.

Sanguine should learn to be more consistent and finish whatever he starts. He should also learn to speak with his mouth closed because action speaks louder than words. He should also learn to think about the negative impact of his phoney impressions and loafing tendencies on his general performance. Choleric should also learn to stop overworking himself and give himself time just to have fun with his Sanguine partner. There should also be a slogan between these two, and the slogan should be something like: "After the run comes the fun"; meaning you first get things done, then you go out and celebrate. This can have a bonding effect between these couple. It should not be an *all work, no fun* or *all fun, no work* relationship, but it must be mutually fulfilling to both temperaments.

Not only is Phlegmatic reserved in work; he is also reserved in speech. Not so with Sanguine. Phlegmatic loves to listen, and Sanguine likes to talk; and this is one of the complementary factors between these two. Phlegmatic would then enjoy sitting back and listening to Mr. Sanguine go on and on with his touching stories. Mr. Sanguine's outgoing and friendly nature also makes it easy for Phlegmatic to relate with him. Where Sanguine is, there is peace; and that's the place Mr. Phlegmatic would rather be. Mr. Phlegmatic understands that when he is with Mr. Sanguine, he does not have to deal with tension. Phlegmatic is very lazy, and that doesn't bother Mr. Sanguine at all. And he never criticizes him or belittle him as a person. Sanguine does not put pressure on Phlegmatic to perform, and that is one of the things Phlegmatic loves about Sanguine.

On other hand, Mr. Sanguine loves it that Phlegmatic seems not to ever get tired of listening to him when he speaks. He also loves the fact that Phlegmatic never screams at him even if he can make the same mistake over and over again. Mr. Sanguine is a man with many mistakes, but the peace-loving personality of Mr. Phlegmatic makes it easy from him to forgive him and move on. One other trait that Mr. Sanguine loves about Phlegmatic is his high tolerance and understanding. Of all temperament categories, none is more patient with Sanguine and forgiving to him than Mr. Phlegmatic; and that attracts Sanguine to Phlegmatic. Mr. Sanguine is also drawn to Phlegmatic by his amazingly approachable personality. No matter how many people he meets, Mr. Sanguine will always find a friend in Phlegmatic.

When these two are joined together in matrimony, they will also complement each other because of their differences. However, within the strengths that pulled them together are weaknesses that could drift them apart. Phlegmatic is always disappointed by Sanguine's inability to keep his promises because that leaves him to always clean up after his mistakes. He is also wearied by having to fake an excited face just to please his Sanguine partner who delights is seeing people in awe of his impressive words and deeds. The lazy Phlegmatic is also irritated by Sanguine's untidy and disorganised tendencies because that means he would always have to clean up where Sanguine messed up. Moreover, the stingy Phlegmatic hates using his money to pay the debts his Sanguine partner owes because of his impulsive nature.

Mr. Sanguine is not that 'happy' either. He finds the conservative nature of Phlegmatic and his slow and reserved personality quite boring and restrictive. He is also frustrated by Phlegmatic's seemingly non-responsive and uninvolved personality. Sanguine is a compulsive buyer, but Phlegmatic is a tight-fisted spender; and this can also be extremely frustrating to Sanguine. The more Sanguine spends, the more Phlegmatic spares; and this makes Sanguine feel like he is losing while his stingy Phlegmatic partner continues to gain. It also doesn't make sense to Sanguine why his Phlegmatic partner worries so much about almost everything when he could just take things one day at a time.

For these two to be well in their marital relationship, Phlegmatic should learn to loosen his hand in as far as money is concerned; and Sanguine should learn to be more disciplined and organised. Phlegmatic should also learn to be flexible, and Sanguine should try to be more factual than impulsive. For as long as Sanguine remains impulsive in his approaches, Phlegmatic will always be physically, emotionally and financially reserved. Sanguine can be highly frustrated by Phlegmatic's facial expressions that are seemingly incongruent with his verbal statements; but he can overcome his frustrations by learning to look beyond his 'silent' face and take him at his word.

The understanding of your partner's temperament as well as your own is highly essential in your marriage. Couples who do not understand their temperaments usually think they married wrong people. Others have no idea who in the world they are married to. Others wish they could have married partners who have similar temperaments with them. Well, first and foremost, you could not have married a better person than the one you've already married. All you need to do is try to understand that you have to be different if you are to fuse together. You need to understand your spouse the way they are and give them permission to be themselves, even if being themselves means being different from you.

You should also try to understand that people of similar temperaments seldom attract each other, and if they do, they will differ widely in their extremes. This means that if both of you are Choleric, one would be a more typical Choleric than the other, and still you will be different. People who are more like us are generally less attractive to us. Simply put, the person who is similar to you cannot be your spouse, and your spouse cannot be similar you. You have not married the wrong person; you have just married a different one, and the reason why you are different is so that you can be better together than you are alone. Therefore, our temperament differences should be accepted and embraced because they increase our fruitfulness as couples.

Now you know better why you and your spouse are so different; but this knowledge will not help you if you won't apply it in your situation. After acquiring this knowledge, you should be able to improve your life by working on your weaknesses and then improve your marriage by treating your spouse with grace while they work on their own weaknesses. Remember, once you discover your primary temperament, do not find excuses for your faults and shortfalls; rather find opportunities for your personal and marital growth. Once you learn about each other's temperaments, make sure you use that information to build each other and not to break each other. Also remember to try by all means to tolerate your partner's weaknesses as you deal with your own and celebrate their strengths as well as your own.

Your discovery of your primary temperament will help not only to achieve success in your marriage; it will also help you become a better person general. But change does not come as you know; it comes as you apply what you know. When you discover your temperament, you gain self-knowledge; it is only when you start embracing your strengths and dealing with your weaknesses that you begin to grow into a better person. I would like for you to take a moment and think about how this information can change your life if only you can get it into your system and start living by it. If you can just grasp this knowledge and commit yourselves to applying it into your marriage, then even your confessions could change from "Who in the world have I married?" or "What on earth was I thinking to marry you?" to "I'm so glad that I married you".

19

"Happily Ever After" – Happiness in Marriage

Everybody wants to be happy; but not everybody is. The difference between people who are happy and those who are not lies in their general attitude towards life. Happy people maintain a positive attitude and take responsibility for their own happiness; but unhappy people retain a negative attitude and make other people responsible for their happiness or lack thereof. Happiness and negative attitude can never co-exist. Therefore, you can't be happy and negative at the same time; you *choose* one and *lose* the other. Happiness is *intrinsic*; not *extrinsic*. It comes from *within*; not from *around*. It depends not on what happens to you; but on your attitude and reactions towards what happens to you. In other words, happiness depends not on happenings, and you can be happy no matter what happens to you. So, you know you are happy when nothing from the outside can disturb the peace you have on the inside.

People usually get married because they want to be happy. But being married or single or rich or poor has nothing to do with happiness; it's all up to you. You can be married and still be unhappy, and you can be single and still be happy. I know many people who are rich and are still unhappy; I also know people who are poor and are still happy. If money or marriage had anything to do with happiness, then all married or rich people would be happy; and all single or poor people would be unhappy. Happiness is not what you *find* in marriage; it is what you *bring* into marriage. No one can make you happy, not even your spouse; only you can.

No matter how hard you try, there is nothing you can do to make the person with negative attitude happy, and there is nothing you can do to make the person with positive attitude unhappy. The more you try to make the person with negative attitude happy, the more you will hurt yourself because their happiness is not your liability; it depends on them; not you. If you don't help them change their attitude, you can't make them happy. No matter how good you may try to be to them, they will always find fault in whatever you do. Happiness is like breathing. No one can breathe for you; only you can breathe for yourself. Similarly, no one can make you happy or be happy on your behalf; only you can make yourself happy. If you don't make yourself happy, you can't be happy. Your happiness is not your partner's responsibility; it all depends on you.

Let me make a simple illustration: In a certain community there was a man nicknamed "Mr. Blame-It-On-The-World". He got that nickname because he always blamed everybody for everything that went wrong in his life. Whatever he experienced, someone else was guilty. One day two naughty boys sneaked into his bedroom while he was asleep and smeared a little bit of human dung under his nose. When he woke up, he started noticing the unbearable smell of human dung. Furious as he could be, he yelled: "This room smells like dung. Let me go outside for some fresh air". But the smell followed him outside. Actually, as you can imagine, this smell followed him everywhere he went.

Every person he met smelt like human dung; none smelt better. Out of deep frustration he yelled: "This world is stinking, and so are all the people who live in it. Doesn't anyone know how to take care of themselves anymore?" The world then had become extremely terrible for him, and he spent that day totally unhappy. Then the two naughty boys came back to him and told him: "Actually, Sir, the problem you are having with the world is right under your nose. Try cleaning your nose; and the world will smell better for you". The man then, out of great fury, heeded the advice of the boys and cleaned his nose. Immediately after that, the world smelled better, and he was happy again. It was only then that he realized that all along he blamed the world for the problem that was in him.

Unhappy people usually do the same. They always blame other people for everything that goes wrong in their lives. They always look around to find out what's wrong with the world that makes them feel so miserable. They fully persuade themselves that if people can change their behaviour, then they would be much happier. But they are not aware that the problem lies not around, but within. It is not necessarily other people's behaviour that causes them to be miserable; it is their own attitude. They always expect the worst out of people; the very people upon whom their happiness relies. The truth is, you cannot be happy by trying to change other people; what really needs to change is your attitude.

If you find yourself praying to God frequently to change your spouse, it may be that the one who really needs to change is you. It could be that you have conditioned your mind to find faults in your spouse; and maybe also in all other people around you. Maybe it's about time you ask God to change you. Your world will never get better for you if you base your happiness on other people having to change. You can't control how people treat you, but you can choose how to react to their treatment towards you. If you find yourself continuously unhappy with your spouse, you need to realise that the problem could be with you. So, if you want the world around you to change, what you really need to change is your attitude towards it.

Do not be conformed to this world, but be transformed by the renewing of your mind... (Romans 12:2). In this portion of Scripture, the Apostle Paul beseeches us to not be *conformed* to what is on the outside (the world), but rather be *transformed* from within (the renewing of the mind). People with negative attitude are *conformers*; but people with positive attitude are *transformers.* People with negative attitude usually *conform* to how other people behave towards them by behaving likewise or worse; but people with positive attitude *transform* people around them by choosing to do the right thing no matter how others behave towards them. Conformers adopt other people's behaviour and lose their identity in the process, but transformers influence behaviour change in other people by their consistency of behaviour and firm maintenance of their identity regardless of how they are treated.

The statement "do not conform to this world" means you should not allow people around you to determine how you think, feel or behave. And the statement "be transformed by the renewing of your mind" means that the change you want to see should come from within. To renew your mind involves being able to treat each case differently according to its own merit. You do not have to punish the whole world for what one person or two did to you. If one person cheated on you in the past, it does not mean everyone will always cheat on you. So, to renew your mind is to make up your mind that you will not judge the present or the future based on the past. If you treat others the way you have been treated, you are conforming to the world. Conformers are most likely to be unhappy because they expect their happiness to come in from around; but transformers are happy because they generate their happiness from within.

Happiness is not an experience; it is a choice, a decision only you can make. It is more than just a feeling; it is an attitude, a positive attitude. People with negative attitude look for reasons to complain; but people with positive attitude find reasons to celebrate. A person with negative attitude complains that roses have thorns; but the person with positive attitude celebrates that thorns have roses. Same scenario, different attitudes; different perceptions; and different feelings. Unhappy people look for thorns in roses, but happy people find roses in thorns. It's all about attitude. Attitude then influences perceptions; perceptions influence feelings; and feelings influence actions. Actions then become habits; and habits ultimately form character. Therefore, attitude influences character.

Consider the wife of a noble character (See Proverbs 31:10-31). She does everything for her family; yet she never complains. This is the perfect display of positive attitude. Her husband praises her; and so do her children. All the days of her life she does good and not evil. Wherever she is, people are happy; because a happy attitude is transmittable. It spreads wide and affects people around. So is unhappy attitude; it infects whoever is around. But people with positive attitude are immune to it. People with positive attitude are always happy because they do good works without expecting anything in return. They continue to reach out with love even when it hurts because their happiness is based on them, and not on others. They don't blame others for how they feel.

Happiness does not turn people into robots. It does not mean you will not get hurt or disappointed. What happiness does is it helps you deal with your pain in a positive way. Happiness is not the absence of pain; it is the ability to maintain a positive attitude even in the midst of pain. Unhappy people tend to dwell in their pain; but happy people find a positive meaning for their pain, learn important lessons out of it and move on with positive mindset. Happiness is also the ability to find strength from within in order deal with whatever pain that might arise.

People who depend on others for their happiness are always disappointed because they are looking around for what they can only find within. They are waiting for what may never come to them because they are waiting for it on the wrong platform. They keep on telling themselves that if things could be better, they would be happier. Their general attitude is: "When I complete school I'll be a lot happier." Then they finish school, but still not happy. Then they say: "If I can just get a job, I'll be much happier." Then they get a job, but still unhappy. They then proceed to say: "I'll be happy if I can get my own house." Then they get their own house; but they are still not as happy as they anticipated. "Maybe I should get myself an automobile, then I'll be a lot happier", they say. Then they get it, and, you've guessed well; they are still unhappy.

"Now I know for sure that I will finally be happy when I get married", they think. They get married but remain unhappy. "Maybe I will be happy when I have children. After all they are 'bundles of joy'", they ponder. Then God blesses them with children, and then they say: "I will definitely be happy as soon as I retire from work. I'll have all the time I need to enjoy my surroundings and possessions." Then the time comes for them to retire from work; and then they would wait hopelessly for the time when they will depart from this 'miserable' world. They spend their precious lives hoping that something will come from outside and give them what they can only find inside. Even if they had achieved all they wanted, they would still remain unhappy because of their external *locus of control.*

People with negative attitude are happy 'only if'; but people with positive attitude are always happy 'no matter what'. The remedy for unhappiness is the change of attitude; not necessarily the change of the environment or friends or life partners. If you want to stop being unhappy and start being happy, you must stop looking around and start looking within. You need to stop blaming other people for what only you have power to control. If you don't take responsibility for your happiness, you will blame others for your unhappiness. Happiness is not what you *pursue*; it is what you *produce.* Trade your negative attitude for a positive one, and make up your mind that you will be happy 'no matter what'.

Another barrier to happiness is *worrying.* There's an old song that says: *Don't worry; be happy.* Even Jesus in the Bible said: *"Do not worry..."* (See Matthew 6: 25-34). Worrying does not uproot your problems; it uproots your peace of mind. Worrying is like swallowing poison with the hope that your problems will die. But the truth of the matter is: the one who dies is you. Worrying about your problems does not solve them; it dissolves your progress instead. In fact, no one ever changed anything by worrying about it. It is difficult, if not impossible, for worriers to be happy because worrying distracts their attention from positivity to negativity.

Most of the things we worry about never happen; so, worrying is really not worth it. Today is the tomorrow you worried about yesterday; but even today you still spent too much time worrying about tomorrow that you fail to realise that what you worried about yesterday did not affect you today. Even if everything we worried about happened to us, we still could not have prevented them from happening by worrying about them. It is not the things you worry about that affect you; what affects you is worrying. Worrying does not work on your problems; it works on your nerves.

Some people believe that not worrying is a sign of being careless or irresponsible. Thus they take pride in worrying as if to show that they care. To them, worrying is a heroic act because it 'shows that you are concerned'. But the opposite is actually true. Not worrying does not mean you are careless or irresponsible. In fact, worrying makes no difference; what makes a difference is to identify the problem, work out the solution and do something about it. People who take action to solve their problems are happier than those who only worry about them. A true hero is the person who takes the bold step to address the problem; not the one who sits back and worries about it. You can't worry and be happy at the same time. You embrace one and release the other.

Casting the whole of your care [all your anxieties, all your worries, all your concerns, once and for all] on Him, for he cares for you affectionately and cares about you watchfully (1 Peter 5:7 – AMP). Why worry when you have the God who cares so much about you? You can stop worrying about your cares, burdens, concerns and anxieties by casting them once and for all on Him. He will never ever let you down. If you find yourself worrying that your marriage might fail, cast it upon the most capable hands of the Almighty God. He is Alpha and Omega, and this means that He is able to sustain what He started until the end. When you know for sure that your problems are well taken care of, you will worry less if you trust more. Therefore, the more you trust God to take care of you or your marriage, the less you will worry about yourself or your marriage; and the less you worry, the happier you will be.

Rejoice in the Lord always. Again I will say, Rejoice! (Philippians 4:4). *Rejoice always* (1 Thessalonians 5:16). What the Apostle Paul is saying in these two Scriptures is: *Always be happy.* The fact that he puts it as an instruction means your happiness is totally up to you. It is your choice to be happy. It is your responsibility. You can choose either to worry or to be happy. But from the Bible you are encouraged to be happy. If your happiness depended on other people, these instructions would have been given to those people. But nowhere in the Bible are people instructed to make others happy. God can never instruct you to do what is supposed to be done by someone else. Jesus did warn us against *offending* other people (See Matthew 18:7); but He never instructed us to make them happy because their happiness is their sole responsibility; not ours. Therefore, you can avoid offending people without trying to burden yourself with the responsibility to make them happy. In other words, you can't *make* them happy, but you can *let* them be happy by keeping away from offending them.

Whether or not your partner offends you is up to them, but whether or not you take the offense is up to you. Therefore, you are responsible for how you allow your partner to 'make' you feel. You cannot control your partner's behaviour, but you can control how you react to it. If you let your happiness depend on your partner's behaviour, then you will only be as happy or as miserable as they make you; and that is too much power to give to someone else over your life. If how you feel depends on how you are treated, you cannot be happy. You need to take charge of your own happiness by being happy no matter how they treat you. The attitude of "I am because you are" or "I feel because you did" is the main repellent of happiness. You can't be happy in your marriage if you expect your happiness to be the product of your partner's doings.

As a husband, do not base the definition of your masculinity on how your wife treats you. You are the man whether your wife respects you or despises you. Your masculinity depends not on how your wife perceives or treats you; it depends on what God made when He made you. If she fails to treat you like the man that you are, that's her problem; not yours. How she treats you makes you no more or less of a man. Stop hurting yourself by trying to convince her how much of a man you are. Your masculinity is yours to celebrate; not hers to approve. Be happy with who you are; not who she thinks you are. Find happiness in your masculinity; not in her treatment of you.

In the same way, the wife's femininity should not be defined on the basis of her husband's conduct towards her. You are beautiful whether he tells you or not. God never creates ugly people; what makes people ugly is how they have allowed other people to make them see themselves. Your beauty depends not on what he thinks about you; it depends on what God created when He created you. You are beautiful, not because he tells you; but because God created you, and He saw that it was good (See Genesis 1). You are God's masterpiece; not somebody else's object of scorn. If he cannot see your beauty, the problem is with his eyes; not with your appearance. Therefore, do not take your husband's problem and make it yours by breaking down over how he perceives you. How he treats you is his problem; not yours. So, do not base your happiness on how he treats you; take charge over your life and be happy no matter how he treats you.

To be happy means to be contented; and to be contented means to be satisfied with who you are, where you are and what you have. Things don't have to be better for you to be happy; you just have to be contented where you are, with what you have. Statements such as "If I had a better job [or husband or wife or car or house], I would be much happier" are just antonyms of happiness. Happiness is not passive; it is active. Whether life treats you cruel or kind, you can decide in your heart to be happy. Worrying adds nothing to our lives; it only robs us off the joy that the Lord has ordained for us to experience. Therefore, no matter what life throws at you, you can dismiss every thought of worry and find reasons to be happy. Why worry when you can choose to be happy?

Happiness is enjoyed mostly by people who have *internal locus of control.* People with internal locus of control believe that their fate lies with them and not with other people. They do not depend on people or circumstances for their happiness; they find it within themselves. They are not arrogant or selfish; they just believe that deep *within* them they have great potential to fulfil their destiny. "If my father were here, I would not be suffering this much"; "If I were raised not by an alcoholic, I would not be this miserable"; such statements do not apply to people who have internal locus of control; they only apply to those with external locus of control. People with external locus of control are as happy or as miserable as other people or circumstances make them. They depend on their surroundings for their happiness. But people with internal locus of control are happy because they know that happiness depends on them and how they react to circumstances; not on circumstances themselves, and they often react to such circumstances with optimism.

You can spend your entire life miserable because things are not going your way, or you can change your attitude and be happy whether or not things go your way. There's more to life than moaning and groaning over how you would have felt if you had the things you could have had or were treated the way you should have been treated. Life is never progressive if it is lived looking behind; one needs to look ahead with a positive mindset to see the brighter future unfolding overtime. But you can't embrace a positive future with negative arms. You have to change your attitude. You need to come to a stage in your life where you start the habit of criticising less and appreciating more. You will be a lot happier if you start learning to *complain* less and *compliment* more.

Complaint and compliment are not mere words; they are attitudes, and they speak even when the mouth is closed. You can compliment your partner without saying it, and they still get the message. You can also tell your partner how much you appreciate them; and still they do not get the message. The difference is in the attitude. Attitude speaks louder than speech. It is possible to compliment with your lips and complain in your heart. A verbal expression of satisfaction from a negative attitude is just as good as the non-verbal communication of dissatisfaction. Appreciation and compliment are not merely lip services; they are matters of the heart. To be happy in your marriage, you need to learn to compliment and appreciate your partner from your heart and communicate to them with your lips what you feel in your heart.

One other thing that can help you to be happy in your marriage and every other area of your life is the *attitude of gratitude*. Grateful people tend to be happier than ungrateful ones because they have learnt to see the beauty of life and celebrate it; while ungrateful ones find faults in life and criticize it. People with grateful attitude are generally *appreciative*; but ungrateful people are mostly *apprehensive*. What makes grateful people happier is that they have learnt to count their *blessings* more than their *burdens*; but ungrateful people more often count their *burdens* more than their *blessings*. Ungrateful people always find reasons to complain, but grateful ones always find reasons to celebrate. Ungrateful people always look for more and are thus never satisfied, but grateful ones have learned to be satisfied with what they have and to never worry much about what they do not have. The more grateful we are, the more we attract the things that make us more grateful. The attitude of gratitude will give you the fortitude to reach your altitude.

Ungrateful people get irritated by the sound peacocks make, but grateful people get fascinated by the beauty of their feathers. Ungrateful people spend most of their time grumbling over crime and corruption in a country, but grateful people choose to marvel at the beauty of nature in the same country. Ungrateful people see their spouses as *trash*; but grateful people look beyond their spouses' trash to find *treasure* in them. The difference is in the attitude. What is important to know is that grumbling over it cannot change it if you do nothing about it; it only makes you unhappy. Rather focus on the brighter side and thus inject a positive energy within yourself. In everything there is a *burden* and a *blessing*; and whether you are happy or not depends on what you allow your mind to entertain. If all you see are burdens, you will be unhappy; but if you learn to look through the burdens and see the blessings, you will be happy.

It is extremely difficult, if at all possible, to satisfy the spouse who sees you as a burden. None of your efforts would ever be enough for them. The more you do, the more they want you to do. That is why you will most probably hear couples complaining: "I have tried every trick in the book to satisfy my partner, but none of my attempts seem to be working." But the problem here is not your attempts; it is their general attitude and their perception of you that is the problem. Once they perceive you as a burden, it becomes almost if not impossible for them to see how blessed they are to have you. Therefore, whether or not they are happy depends not so much on your efforts as it does on their attitude. Do not blame yourself if your partner remains unhappy despite your efforts; everyone is responsible for their own happiness. Just maintain a positive attitude and work your own happiness. In the meantime, be not weary in doing good to your partner; because one day your good efforts will pay off if you do not give up.

To be happy in your marriage, you need to develop the attitude of gratitude over your partner. Try to look over the things you hate about your partner and locate the things you love about them. The truth of the matter is: there is no way in this world your partner can make you happy; only you can. No matter how romantic or faithful or committed your partner is to you, they cannot satisfy you for as long as all you are looking for in them are flaws and frailties. You need to develop a new habit of looking beyond their faults and seeing their decency and integrity. No one is perfect; but no one is entirely imperfect. People who are happy in their marriages are those who have learnt to look beyond their partners' imperfections. In fact, they have learnt to love their partners perfectly despite their imperfections. So, the next time you feel you have married the worst person in the universe, ask yourself if the problem is your partner or your perception of or attitude towards them.

Well, you may be highly conscious of your partner's weaknesses, but do you ever take time to celebrate their strengths? Do you ever allow yourself a moment to appreciate your partner's goodness? Or have your partner's imperfections blinded you from their goodness? Would it make any difference if you changed the way you perceive them? It is unhealthy for your marriage for you to judge almost every other person of the opposite sex to be better or more valuable than your partner; and that is absolutely not true. The difference between your partner and the rest is that you are measuring your partner's weaknesses against their strengths, and this puts them at an unfair advantage over your partner. I know people who divorced their partners and married other people and wished they could go back to their partners. This usually happens because we fail to appreciate our partners because of our lack of gratitude.

Very often as married couples we want everything from our partners, and if we don't get everything, we think we got nothing. This is an indication that we have lost our attitude of gratitude. But people with the attitude of gratitude have learnt to understand that *not having everything* does not mean *having nothing*. If you focus too much on what you are not getting, you will ultimately be blinded from what you are getting; and *something* will begin to feel like *nothing*. But to people with the attitude of gratitude, *something* always feels like *everything* because they have learnt to focus more on what they have than on what they are not getting. So, instead of crying over what they are not getting, they rejoice over what they have. Instead of coveting to be with the one they love, they have learnt to love the one they are with because they understand that your love for other people depends not on what they do, but on who you are.

There are two sides to everything; the positive side and the negative side. This includes your partner. Let me make a simple example of a television. A television has many channels you can tune into. Some channels may be more interesting to you than others. But if you keep on tuning into the channels that you find boring, you will eventually conclude that television is boring. But the truth is; television is not boring, it's just that you keep on tuning into boring channels. Therefore, if you find television boring, don't change the television; change the channels. For as long as you keep on tuning into your partner's imperfections, you can never be happy in your marriage. The problem is not your partner; it is the channel you have tuned into. Therefore, if you are not happy in your marriage, do not change the partner; change your perception. Tune out of their weaknesses and tune into their strengths. Train your mind to perceive your partner's strengths more than their imperfections.

Everytime you lose sight to the value or attractiveness of your partner; sit them down and ask them how many people approach them daily telling them that they wish they were married to them. You will be shocked to find out that you might be the only one who fails to see how blessed you are to have married your partner. Yet your partner is faithful enough to give up all those people and continue to cling to you even though all they get from you are criticisms and hideous expressions of dissatisfaction. So, your partner has not lost their value; you just lost your attitude of gratitude. Open your eyes before it's too late to see your partner's beauty beyond their imperfections. If your partner refuses to give you a glass of water on a tray, don't let that blind you from all these other things they are so willingly doing for you. If you can train your mind to overlook the burdens and count the blessings, you will then be happy in your marriage. Rather than grumbling, be grateful; rather than complaining, compliment; and instead of apprehending, appreciate. Rather than worrying, be happy.

Happy people also have a *healthy self esteem*. They have a positive self-image. How you see yourself determines how you feel about yourself. If you see yourself as a worthless being, you will feel worthless; and you will be unhappy; but if you see yourself as valuable, you will feel valuable, and you will be happy. People with poor self esteem see themselves negatively. They give themselves less credit than they deserve; and they leave their worth to other people's opinions. Their feelings about themselves are determined by how people perceive them. They are as happy or as miserable as the feedback they receive from around. They judge themselves by the standards that are set for them by people around them. What happens within them depends on what happens around them.

But the truth of the matter is: you cannot be happy if you base your value on how people think or feel about you. Therefore, people with poor self-esteem cannot be happy unless they change how they see themselves.

As a married person, it is good to appreciate your partner's compliments; but it is unhealthy to derive your worth from them. You need to learn to value yourself whether your partner praises you or not. Whether people admire you or despise you should not be the determinant of your self-image or self-worth. You need to be stable from within and maintain a positive attitude no matter how people think or feel about you. Do not conform to the standards people set concerning how you should see yourself; rather set a standard for them concerning how they should treat you. You subconsciously attract what you think you deserve. Negative self-image subconsciously attracts criticism, which in turn worsens your self-esteem; but positive self-image subconsciously attracts compliments. Even if people with healthy self-esteem are not complimented, it doesn't really bother them because their happiness depends on how they see themselves and not on how others perceive them.

How you see the world around you is very important for your happiness, but more important than that is how you see yourself. Your outlook towards the world is not going to help you if you have a negative outlook towards yourself. In short, you cannot enjoy your surroundings if you cannot enjoy yourself. Do not allow how you look to determine how you feel; rather determine how you look by feeling great about yourself just as you are. Everything God has created is beautiful, and so are you. There is no need to change yourself; what really needs to change is how you see yourself. If your looks could attract your spouse to you, your self-image can keep them glued to you. Your beauty is not only about your looks; it is also about your outlook.

What you see when you look at the mirror is more important than what you hear when you listen to people talk about you. It is not what comes into you that makes you happy; it is what comes from within you. Instead of being discouraged by your weaknesses, rather be inspired by your strengths. Look for those positive traits within yourself and celebrate them. Whatever you permit, you perpetuate; and the thought you entertain in your mind is the one that grows. If you permit negative thoughts, you perpetuate negative experiences. If you concentrate more on your shortfalls than your accomplishments, you might end up believing that you are inadequate, and you will not be happy;

and if you are not happy, you cannot be happily married. Learn to focus less on your failures and more on your achievements, and you will start feeling better about yourself; and the better you feel about yourself, the happier you will be. A happy marriage is not a series of blissful events; it is a combination of two happy people. When each of you is happy, then your marriage will be a happy union.

Much has been said about finding happiness from within; but where do we draw this happiness from? Paul wrote in Philippians 4:4: *"Rejoice in the LORD always..."* This simply tells us that *God* is the Source and Sustainer of our happiness. He is the One who implants happiness in our hearts. He does not put it *around* us; He puts it *within* us. Blessed are those who find their happiness in the Lord, because He is the Well that never runs dry (See John 4:13-14). Everyone who trusts in the Lord and His faithfulness shall abide in peace under all circumstances. He is the Solid Foundation upon whom our happiness can be built. If we rejoice in the Lord, we can rest assured that our happiness is true and eternal. Actually, marriage is not the source of our happiness; neither are our spouses; God is.

The problem is that we keep on reaching out to people for our happiness, and we can never find it until we make a full turn towards the Great I am, the God and Creator of the universe. God will surely give us joy, and His joy is our strength (See Nehemiah 8:10). In fact, if you have God, you have joy; because *in [His] presence is fullness of joy* (Psalm 16:11). When you put your trust in the Lord, you worry less and rejoice more, because *God is our Refuge and Strength, an ever-present help in trouble* (Psalm 46:1 – NIV). So, even in trouble we know that God is always there to help us; therefore we continue to be happy in all circumstances because of our assurance of His consistent presence. Therefore, we do not draw our happiness from our marriages; we draw it from the Lord, who is within us through Christ Jesus and the Holy Spirit, and then we bring it into our marriages.

God does not change like shifting shadows. In fact, He is *the same yesterday, today and forever* (Hebrews 13:8). He even said it Himself: *"For I am the Lord, I do not change..."* (Malachi 3:6). This means if you depend on Him for your happiness, then you are guaranteed that it will remain forever and under all circumstances. Your happiness can never evaporate because the One upon whom it depends never changes. But people do change; so do circumstances.

Therefore, if your happiness depends on people or circumstances, it will soon vanish. Man-made things are temporal, but everything that comes from God is eternal. If you want to rest in your happiness, rest it in the ever-lasting arms of the Great God. He will surely keep what you commit to Him; and if you put your trust in Him alone, you will never be ashamed or disappointed.

If the Lord gives you joy, no one can take it from you. But if you surrender it into the hands of someone else and make it their responsibility, you will surely be unhappy. Love your partner and enjoy their love. But you cannot enjoy their love if you have made up your mind that they cannot love you. Stop stressing on what you do not have and start enjoying what you have. Your happiness in marriage depends not so much on what you have than on your ability to enjoy what you have. You can't have it all, but what you have is all you need. Therefore, instead of stressing about what is lacking in your partner, rather appreciate what is there and celebrate it in every way you can. You deserve to be happy in your marriage, but your happiness is your responsibility. If you are happy, then your marriage will be filled with happiness. So, make a positive decision for your marriage today, be happy.

20

Marriage Must be Managed

Falling in love usually happens by chance, but staying in love happens by choice; especially in a marital relationship. You cannot achieve marital success by letting things happen; you achieve it by taking control and making them happen. Achieving marital success is not about doing the things you feel like doing; it is about doing the things that will bring success to your marriage no matter how you feel. This involves having to do the things you do not feel like doing in order to get the results you want. You cannot build your marriage by 'going with the flow'; you need to determine the direction you want your marriage to take and then work out the systems that will help you reach your goal. Once you put the systems in place to help you achieve your marital goal, you need to make a commitment to stick to the practices that will help you contribute to the success of your marriage. In short, a successful marriage does not *just happen*; it must be managed.

The word *manage* means a number of things. It means to succeed in doing something; especially something difficult, or to be able to solve problems and deal with difficult situations, or to be able to survive with limited resources, or to use resources in a sensible way, or to be able to do something at a particular time, or to control or be in charge, or to keep something under control. The first part of the definition describes the word manage as succeeding in doing something. In other words, management brings success; even in difficult situations. If management brings success, then mismanagement brings failure; and lack of management is just as bad as mismanagement. One of the main reasons why marriages fail is mismanagement or lack of management. Marriages fail because couples do not consciously work on bettering their marital relationships. They accept everything as it is instead of doing something to make it better.

I once heard the story of a man who worked for a construction company. Each and every day he came to work with baloney sandwiches. But his problem was that he did not like baloney sandwiches; so, everyday he requested his fellow workers to exchange their lunchboxes with him. Some agreed, and others refused. This went on and on until no one was willing to exchange with him anymore; yet he kept on coming with baloney sandwiches and requesting them to exchange with him. One day they asked him: "Sir, why don't you request your wife to give you something else?" To which he responded: "Gentlemen, there are two problems I think you should know; one, I am not married; and two, I prepare my own lunchbox." His fellows then replied: "If you do not like it, then change it."

Well, you might be laughing your lungs out at this man. Perhaps you think he's a 'moron'. But if you can take a closer look, you will be shocked to find out that we are also guilty of the same 'crime'. Most often we are the main cause of many problems we are experiencing in our marriages. For example, you beat your wife every week; then you wonder why she is not responding to your touches anymore. The truth is, she no longer sees love in your hands; all she sees in those hands are weapons. Maybe you are a wife and you insult your husband almost everyday; then you wonder why he's not kissing you anymore. The problem is that he has come to see your lips as weapons; and to him, kissing you is like rubbing his lips against the mouth of a loaded firearm. You may wonder why your partner does not trust you or believe you anymore; but it could be that your partner no longer trusts you because you've been unfaithful, and that you are the one who broke their trust.

I am of the opinion that the man chose to take baloney sandwiches not because he wanted them, but because they were easier to make. The same is true for many of us. We do some things in our marriages not because we want the results we may get, but because they are easier and more convenient. We are reluctant to inconvenience ourselves in order to get the results we want. Words like "I love you", "please", "thank you", "I'm sorry" and "I need you" are very difficult to say; but the results thereof are responses of love, help, kindness, forgiveness and commitment. Yet we'd rather experience the opposite of these simply because we find it too difficult to communicate our deepest needs and feelings in humility. If we are to succeed in our marriages, we need to be courageous enough to do the things that are not easy so that we can get the results that are pleasing.

The principle of *sowing and reaping* applies perfectly in marriage. Whatever you reap presently is what you sowed previously. When you sow one seed, you reap the harvest of whatever you sowed. Many couples are currently reaping the harvest of the mean words they once spoke to each other. You cannot reap what you have not sowed, and you cannot sow weed and get wheat in return. Furthermore, you do not sow thistles when you find the ground full of thorns; instead, you uproot the thorns and sow the seed of whatever you want. Same applies in marriage. You should not disrespect your partner when they disrespect you; instead, you should choose to sow the seed of respect by respecting them even when they disrespect you. You cannot put out evil with evil; you can only extinguish it with good. If you keep on sowing the seed of respect to your spouse, you will eventually enjoy good returns of respect from the very person who once disrespected you.

If you want a great harvest, sow a great seed. Whatever you *give will come back to you; a good measure, pressed down, shaken together and running over will be put into your bosom. For with the same measure that you use, it will be measured back to you* (Luke 6:38). You can't sow a bad seed and expect a good harvest. If you don't like the reactions, change your actions. This is where the law of *cause and effect* applies. If you hate the *effect*, change the *cause*. If you want to be trusted, be faithful. If you want to be forgiven, forgive. If you want to be loved, love; and if you want to be respected, respect. You should not wonder why your partner does not talk to you if you keep on yelling at them whenever they raise an issue. As Zig Ziglar once said, *do not be upset by the results you did not get with the work you did not do*. Sometimes you need to do what you don't want to do in order to get want you want to get. So, if you frequently fear that your partner might leave, check if you're doing enough to make them stay.

You cannot choose how your partner treats you; but you can choose how you respond to your partner's treatment, and your response has the power to either aggravate or alleviate the treatment. Just because they treated you wrong does not mean you should also treat them wrong. You should be the one to take a stand and break the cycle of pain and strife in your marriage by sowing good seeds. Do not wait for your partner to be nice to you before you start being nice to them. This is how you manage your marriage; you do not leave anything to chance, but you make efforts to make your marriage succeed. Whenever you go through a situation that you cannot control, at least don't let it control you. Remain steadfast in your principles, and your marital success will be solid despite your surroundings. If you as a couple can learn to manage your marriage together, you will stand a better chance of staying together till the end.

Whatever is not managed will be damaged. Think about any business or organisation that has no management; where things are left to chance. No one takes responsibility to see that anything happens. If there is a crisis, everybody just sit back to see what will become of the situation; hoping that someone does something about it. What is the probability of that organisation succeeding? Well, success for such organisation is almost, if not, impossible. Same applies in marriage. If couples leave things to chance and hope someone else will do something about their situation, things will only get worse, and the marriage might not survive. Couples who take control and manage their marriages are most likely to achieve marital success despite all difficulties they may come across.

To manage also means to solve difficult problems and keep things under control. Sadly, an increasing number of couples resort for divorce when they encounter problems in their marriages. They are always looking for problem-free marriages. But the only way to avoid marital problems is to remain single. A problem-free marriage does not exist. In fact, as long as life endures, problems will never cease to exist. So, couples abandon their marriages to look for something they will never find. Successful marriages are not problem-free marriages; they are marriages under control. Marriages fail not because of the presence of problems; but because of the absence of management. Couples who manage their marriages do not end their marriages because of the problems; instead, they sustain their marriages by solving the problems.

Success is not only about having; it is also about managing what you have. So, if you can't manage it, you can't sustain it. There are two essential outcomes in managing, namely, *survival* and *progress*. Survival means to continue to exist despite difficulty or danger. Survival is also linked to longevity. Any institution that is managed properly will continue to exist for a long time, even in the midst of threats or adversities. Same applies with marriage. With proper management, marriage will survive; but marriages that are not managed will be short-lived. Management of marriage also ensures progress. To progress means to improve or develop over a period of time. It means to draw nearer to achieving the desired goals. Management not only ensures that marriages exist for a long time; it also ensures that they get better with time.

To manage your marriage effectively as a couple, you need to have a joint *vision. Where there is no vision, the people perish...* (Proverbs 29:18 – KJV). A vision is the ability to think about or plan the future with great imagination and intelligence. It is a mental picture you have today about where you will be in future. Vision provides direction. If you know where you are going, you will know which direction you will take and what resources you will need. If you do not know where you are going, you will die in the middle of nowhere. A marriage without vision is a marriage without direction; and a marriage without direction is a marriage without success. In short, a marriage without vision will neither progress nor survive.

Married couples should have a mental picture of where they see their marriage in future. Once they have a vision, they should set goals that will help them progress towards their vision. For example, if your vision is to build a consummate love relationship between yourselves as married couple, you need to determine what it takes to build such relationship. Whatever it takes to realize your vision, you need to turn it into an achievable goal. A consummate love involves three elements, namely, passion, intimacy and commitment. These elements can be turned into goals. Then you can determine the means to achieve those goals and commit yourselves to the process regardless of how you feel or how the situation may be.

If the means of achieving intimacy is spending time together, you need to make sure you adjust your busy schedule to make time to spend together. It's not about waiting for the perfect time; it's about allocating time to spend together. If you wait for the perfect time, you leave things to chance; but if you make time, you manage your relationship. Perfect time is not something you wait for; it is something you create. You don't have to wait hoping for it; you need to make a deliberate decision and take deliberate action to make it happen. If you don't allocate time for your marital relationship, you are simply wasting each other's time because without the two of you, there will be no marriage.

Once you anticipate your future and get excited about it, you will not be put down by anything you go through. In fact, if you can be thrilled by where you are going, you will be able to put up with whatever you come across along the way. If you can *see* it, you can *seize* it, and what you *perceive*, you *receive*; hence the adage *"when you visualize, you materialize"*. All successful people have been there before in their minds, and they worked their way to where they have already been to make it a reality. In the same way, a successful marriage does not happen by chance; you have to be there before in your mind and purpose in your heart that you will work your way until you make it a reality.

There are two essential things, amongst others, that you need to manage in your marriage, namely, your *actions* and your *reactions*. The only person you can control in a relationship is you. You can control your actions towards your spouse, but you cannot control your spouse's reactions towards you; and you cannot control your spouse's actions towards you, but you can control your reactions towards your spouse. Sometimes you may feel like acting spitefully against your partner or reacting out of anger towards them, but you can manage how you act or react regardless of how you feel. You might not be able to control how you feel, but you can sure manage your actions and reactions. Feelings are experiences, but actions and reactions are decisions. A feeling is what happens to you, but a reaction is how you choose to handle the feeling. So, if you cannot control the feeling, neither should you let it control you.

Be angry, and do not sin: do not let the sun go down on your wrath, nor give place to the devil (Ephesians 4:26-27). Anger is in itself not wrong, but it is your reaction that determines whether you are right or wrong. We all get angry at some point in our lives, but that does not mean we should hurt others. There are times in your marriage when your partner will really annoy you, and that you cannot control; what you can control is to react in such a way that you do not sin, and that you do not let the sun set on your anger. In other words, you can choose to do right even when they did you wrong, and you can determine the duration of stay for your anger. This is how we manage our actions and reactions.

In your marriage, you can control everything but your spouse. This is the mistake many couples do in their marriages: they take full responsibility over their partner's behaviour. Some even blame themselves for what their partners are doing. The husband might think that his wife disrespects him because he is not man enough, and the wife might think her husband ignores her because she is not attractive enough. This is what I call *unfair self-torture*. You are being unfair to yourself to attribute your partner's behaviour to your personality or features. Your wife disrespects you because she chooses to disrespect you, not because you are not man enough; and your husband ignores you because he chooses to ignore you, not because you are not attractive enough. Do not blame yourself for what your partner is doing or failing to do; not even to you. You are not responsible for your partner's behaviour, but your partner is responsible for his (or her) own behaviour; and you are responsible for your own. Therefore, do your part and leave your partner's part to your partner.

Proper marriage management is achieved when both partners are involved, and each of them should play their part diligently and faithfully. Marriage cannot be successful if one person carries all the weight while the other enjoys all the ease. Both of them should carry the weight together. It takes one partner to make the marriage durable; but it takes both of them to make it enjoyable. In other words, marriage can still *survive* with the efforts of one person; but it cannot *progress*. It will be a tedious lifetime experience. Marriage should not be about one always giving and never receiving while the other is always receiving and never giving. There should be a plain balance; and such balance does not happen spontaneously, it is a deliberate effort by both partners. As I have already mentioned, "I love you too" is good, but it can never be as powerful as "I love you". "I love you too" is based on your partner's expression of their love to you, but "I love you" is based on your own love for your partner.

Marriage is not for toddlers; it is for adults. I say this because some adults handle their marriages with *toddlers' mentality*. Toddlers want everything ready for them; but adults understand that it won't be ready if you don't prepare it. Toddlers want to enjoy the food, but they can't endure the cooking; but adults understand that to enjoy the eating, you must first endure the cooking. You keep on complaining that your spouse is boring and lacks adventure; yet you are the one who keeps on rebuking them everytime they express their authenticity. That is a toddler's mentality. No one can be exciting to you if you won't let them be themselves around you. If you keep on complaining about the water bill that is too high, then you have no right to complain about the grass that is not green and the flowers that are not blooming. If you keep on kicking your spouse painfully, don't expect them to kiss you passionately. That is also toddlers' mentality. Toddlers make everything wrong and then wonder why everything is so wrong; but adult couples never expect anything out of their marriage that they have not put into it.

Couples who manage their marriages together are always in control. Nothing happens by chance in their marriages. They anticipate everything before it happens and prepare for it. They expect nothing out of marriage that they did not put into it. They take full responsibility for their own behaviour and let their partner take responsibility for their own behaviour. Instead of wondering what happened, they take the initiative to make things happen. They are driven more by their vision than they are by their feelings. You can be one of those few couples and start managing your own marriage. Do not allow things to go their way in your marriage; take control and direct the currents toward your direction. Do not leave things to chance in your marriage; roll up the sleeves and create the change you want to see. When you manage your marriage, you maximize your marital success.

21

"In Sickness and in Health" – Illnesses in Marriage

"*In sickness and in health...*" These are the words we never hesitate to say when we exchange our vows to be joined together as husband and wife. Even though we mean ever word at that time, deep down we can't help wishing no one gets sick. We say these words in anticipation for health and no sickness. At this stage all we see are better days before for us; as if we have reached the beginning of the end to all our sorrows. We say those vows believing that we are entering into the world that is so much better than the world we come from. At this moment our minds are caught in the high of love, and as we see it, we had rather be sick together than healthy apart. We are both confident that our chance has finally come to build the life that most couples have clearly failed to build, and we know that we are going to make it better than all those couples who failed.

After the wedding celebration the reality of marriage strikes; and the couple is living happily as expected. They are having a good time together with lots of time to spare. They spend each night in each other's arms and greet each other with a goodnight kiss. As time goes on the reality of marriage sinks in, and they are starting to have break ups and make ups here and there; but that's nothing their love cannot bring them through. As they sail through their honeymoon stage, their bond gets stronger each day; and with no children to disturb, lovemaking is always spontaneous. Even though the harsh realities of marriage keep on intruding into their newly established relationship, they still seem to be having greater days ahead.

And then sugar diabetes invades the happy marriage and grabs hold of the husband. This then brings us to a question: will things still be the same in sickness as they were in health? Sickness is not something we invite into our lives. It comes in as it pleases and stays as long as it so desires. Yes, some sicknesses we invite ignorantly through our life style; but some are hereditary, and some are environmental. Some can be avoided, but others cannot; and for some there is a cure, but for others there isn't. Some are acute, and others are chronic. Some are physiological, and others are psychological. But one thing is common among them all: they impair the functioning of your system and affect your general performance.

When people are sick, the fail to do what they are able to do when they are healthy. They become less effective than they are when they are well. Something in them no longer functions the way it used to. These are the times when the words are tested that say *"in sickness and in health"*. Can you still love her when she is weak to stand up and cook for you? Will you still be affectionate to him even when his illness has robbed him off his sexual drive? You have been together in health, but can you stay together in sickness? Will you respect him when he is sick the way you respected him when he is healthy? Will you love her when she is disfigured by sickness the way you loved her when she was well? Will you endure the burden of his illness the same way you enjoyed the benefits of his wellness? Will you hold her throughout the night now that she is too sick to hold you back like you used to when she was strong enough to embrace you?

Sickness is the test of true love. It is the state of being where the person is weak and vulnerable. Sickness infects one person and affects the rest of the people in the house. It inflicts pain in the husband and thus afflicts the wife. Some sicknesses are life-threatening, and this makes things worse for the loved ones. Some people go so far as to pray for their partners to just die so that they can be free from the pain. From headache to heart attack, sicknesses can be fatal; they can shatter dreams and break hearts. The burden of taking care of the sick person can be overwhelming; it is stressful enough to make one sick. Sickness can also produce feelings of resentment towards the ailing for putting the partner through so much trouble. The caring partner can even suspect the ailing partner for 'faking' some of the symptoms. They may think the ailing partner is just a 'lazy attention seeker' who is playing on their sympathy. This could lead to the caring partner abandoning the ailing one; and that could worsen the situation.

Only psychotic people can fake their illnesses to seek attention. Faking an illness is another sign of sickness. How sick must you be to put the lives of the people you love on hold so that they may focus on your faked sickness? If you are physically ill, you need medical help; but if you fake your illness, you need serious psychiatric intervention. Either way, you are sick; and you need help. Have you ever considered that faking your illness could lead to your partner ignoring you next time when you are really sick and in need of help? If you really want your partner's attention, why not organize a romantic treat instead? If that fails, try something else, just don't fake an illness.

That being said, if your spouse happens to be the one that falls ill, do not underestimate it or think it's a fake. Ignoring your partner's illness with an assumption that it is made up could be a fatal mistake. I know people who had to bury their loved ones having thought they were faking their illnesses. It is not your part to determine whether or not the illness is made up, unless you are a competent medical practitioner. If your partner is really faking an illness, that conclusion is better left to the doctor. Sometimes you suspect that your partner is exaggerating, but remember that you cannot really measure the intensity of the illness to determine whether it is exaggerated or not. All you can do is be there for your spouse and show them that you really care, and that you will be glad to see them well again.

There is something about been ill that affects one's self esteem; and how you treat your ailing partner can either help or hurt them. It can make one feel worthless or inadequate, and this feeling can be worse if you make your partner feel they have 'allowed it'. But an illness is not a deliberate experience; and it is extremely unfair to judge your illness or blame yourself when you are ill. All your ailing partner needs from you is your full support, continuous encouragements and frequent reassurances of love. Love has a way of making sick people heal faster. Some people confuse sickness with a 'weakness' or being 'pathetic'. They think you are sick because you are weak. Yes, this is true, but the other way round: you are not sick because you are weak; instead, you are weak because you are sick. Illness can happen to your spouse as much as it can happen to you. The worst case would be for both of you to get ill at the same time. That would be the time to enjoy the benefit of relatives and true friends.

Some illnesses and medications affect the sexual functioning of the ailing. This can damage the ego of the ailing, especially if that one is a man. A man's ego is closely linked to his sexuality. Therefore, being unable to perform sexually can make him feel he has lost his manhood. He may even feel miserable for not being 'man enough' to please his wife sexually. This goes with strong feelings of insecurity because he may fear that his wife might leave him for a 'real man'. This can also be frustrating for the wife, especially if she is in her sexual peak. Even though sexual dysfunctions affect men the most, women can also be victims; and this can have the same effect on them as it has on men. It can also be frustrating for a sexually active husband. This is a true test of love, faithfulness and trust in a marital relationship.

Sexual dysfunctions can cause couples to disengage completely from sex and romance; and this can turn a happy marriage into a cold war. However, things do not have to turn sour in marriage because of a partner suffering from sexual dysfunctions. After all, love is not only about sex, and sex is not only about penetration. You can still enjoy each other's love and sexuality even when you cannot have a penetrative intercourse. Now more than ever, there are many creative ways to celebrate your love without penetration. Sex is now called love making, not necessarily because of the penetration, but because of the touches, kisses, caresses and whispers of love messages. Such bond can still be achieved without penetrative intercourse. Couples can also reach orgasm without penetration; all you have to do is be creative and *think out of bed*.

Most illnesses are curable; some naturally, and others with treatment. But there are sicknesses that are incurable; they can only be managed with medication so that they do not reach the point of fatality. Even though there are incurable diseases, the Word of God still gives us hope for healing, even for incurable diseases. The Bible is full of promises for healing and stories about incurable diseases being healed by the supernatural power of God. *But He was wounded for our transgressions, He was bruised for our iniquities; the chastisement of our peace was upon Him, and by His stripes we are healed* (Isaiah 53:5). Jesus Christ paid a full price for our complete healing. He suffered so that we can enjoy the benefits of good health. If you cry out to Him in your trouble, He will save you out of your distresses. He will send His Word and heal you, and also deliver you from your [sickness] (See Psalm 107:19-20).

Jesus Christ is the same, yesterday, today and forever (Hebrews 13:8). If He ever healed people before, He can still heal you even today. He does not change with the times, but He can change your situation at any time. If He managed to create you (See Genesis 1:26-28), can He fail to heal you? *"I am the Lord, the God of all mankind. Is anything too hard for Me?"* (Jeremiah 32:27 – NIV). The answer to this question is in Jeremiah 32:17: *"Ah, Sovereign Lord, you have made the heavens and the earth by your great power and outstretched arm. NOTHING is too hard for You"* (Jeremiah 32:17 – NIV). *Nothing* is too hard for God. Whatever sickness you are suffering from, it will not be hard for God to heal you. Not only can He heal you, He is willing to heal you, and He has promised: *"Nevertheless, I will bring health and healing to it; I will heal my people and will let them enjoy abundant peace and security"* (Jeremiah 33:6 – NIV).

Your healing is just as sure as your sickness. There is no sickness that God cannot heal. According to Psalm 103:3-4 (NIV); He *forgives ALL your sins and heals ALL your diseases,* He *redeems your life from the pit and crown you with love and compassion.* As long as you have Christ, you have hope; for Christ is *the Hope of Glory* (See Colossians 1:27). *In Him we live and move and have our being* (Acts 17:28). He can still heal you even if the best doctors in the world have given up on you; *For with God nothing will be impossible* (Luke 1:37). God will never withhold healing from you if you believe in Him; *For the Scripture says, "Whoever believes on Him will not be put to shame"* (Romans 10:11). You can die hopeless in your 'incurable' sickness, or you trust God for your complete healing. He's done it for others, and He can do it for you.

Is anyone among you suffering? Let him pray (James 5:13). *And the prayer of faith will save the sick, and the Lord will raise him up* (James 5: 15). Sickness is not your portion; for Jesus was wounded for you to be healed. Just pray and believe, and the Lord will do to you according to your faith. God promised that if you call unto Him, He will answer you and show you great and mighty things (See Jeremiah 33:3). Why worry about your sickness or your spouse's sickness when you can pray to God for healing? As a believer, God is aware of your sickness; and He will never leave you without healing if you ask Him. If your spouse is sick and doctors have nothing left to do, you can worry yourself to death; or you can pray and watch God perform a miracle over your spouse's life.

Sickness happens not only to wicked people; it can happen to anyone. Consider the story of Job (See the Book of Job in the Bible); he was blameless and upright, and he feared God and shunned evil (See Job 1:1). Even so, he was afflicted by a terrible sickness; so much that his wife encouraged him to curse God so that he can die (See Job 2:9). His wife was so troubled by his sickness that she even wanted him to die. But Job seemingly understood that *many are the afflictions of the righteous, but the Lord delivers him out of them all* (Psalm 34:19). Clearly Job's wife could not take it anymore, and many of us Christians spend most of our time talking about how she tried to separate Job from God. But none of us seem to have noticed that throughout Job's difficulties, his wife never left him. She remained with him until God finally restored him and gave him double for all his trouble (See Job 42:10).

Not only is it unfair to ill-treat or abandon your spouse because of an illness; it is also ungodly. You made a vow to love and to cherish your spouse in sickness and in health; but now that your spouse is sick you decide to turn away from your vow. Sickness was just part of the vow as health was. According to the Bible, it is foolish to make a vow and not fulfil it. *When you make a vow to God, do not delay to pay it; for He does not take pleasure in fools. Pay what you have vowed. Better not to vow than to vow and not pay. Do not let your mouth lead you to sin, nor say before the messenger of God that it was an error. Why should God be angry at your excuse and destroy the work of your hands?* (Ecclesiastes 5:4-6). This is the greatest excuse people make when they break their vows: "It was a mistake." Breaking your marriage vow because of an illness is not only foolish; it also provokes God's anger against you and destroys your success.

For as long as you remain committed to the vow you made to God concerning your spouse, God will always be by your side and bless the work of your hands. The love that stands the test of time is one that continues to burn the same way in sickness as it does in health. That is what we call *unconditional love.* In fact, the most powerful way to win your partner's love is to remain with them even when they expect you to leave them; to love them even if you might never get anything in return. If you give your spouse more love than they think they deserve, they will be provoked to love you just the same way. Even if your partner shows no gratitude for what you are doing; just take pleasure in the knowledge that you are being faithful to God by keeping your vow to love and cherish your spouse in sickness and in health.

22

Marriage Killers

Marriage was built to last. It is not just a temporary union that will soon fade away; it is a lifetime commitment, an institution that was established by God to stand the test of time. Marriage was built to end only when life ends; but there are common habits and traits that can choke the life out of it. In this chapter we will highlight ten marriage killers that married couples should always guard against. Those ten marriage killers are: Infidelity, Confinement, Domestic Violence, Addictions, Selfishness, Destructive Criticisms, Sarcasm, External Interferences, Pride, and Excessive Jealousy and Insecurities.

22.1 Infidelity

Unfaithfulness to one's partner is highly toxic for marriage. Few marriages survive it. Not only does it destroy the marriage; it also destroys the very people involved in it, including innocent people who have remained faithful in their marriages. People are acquiring sexually transmitted infections outside and bring them into their marriages; making innocent people suffer because of the diseases that were brought in by the person they trusted with their lives. Others find themselves having to raise the children that are not theirs; and each time they see those children, they are continually reminded of what their trusted partners did to them.

Cheaters are liars; and lies are the offspring of the devil. In fact, Jesus calls the devil the father of lies (John 8:44). A marriage cannot be built on lies; it is built on the truth because the truth is of God. Actually, Christ Himself referred to Himself as the Truth (See John 14:6). Therefore, you can't build your marriage with Satan's brick and expect it to succeed. Satan is on a mission to try and destroy anything that is of God. Marriage is of God, and he uses lying and cheating to destroy it. Faithfulness to one's partner is one of God's ways to establish marriage; but infidelity is Satan's way to destroy it. You can protect your marriage from the devil by being faithful to your partner.

Remember, the thief comes only to steal, to kill and to destroy; but Jesus came so that we may have life, and have it more abundantly (See John 10:10). Satan is a thief, and he uses infidelity to kill marriages; but God uses faithfulness to make it prosper. Therefore, if you yield to Satan by being unfaithful to your partner, your marriage will be destroyed; but if you yield to God by being faithful to your partner, your marriage will be established until the end of time. Infidelity defames one's partner. It insults their worth and intelligence. It makes them feel stupid for trusting the person who has been playing them all along. But if you cheat on your partner even though they trust you, it does not mean they are stupid, it simply means they are giving you more credit than you deserve. Eventually, that trust will be shuttered, and so will your marriage.

People who have extramarital affairs cannot be fully committed to their marriage. They think about someone else while they are with their partners. They belong to their partners, but their love belongs to someone else. When problems arise in their marriages, they just take off to see their lovers. They do not feel the need to work on their marriages because they know that even if they do not get love at home, they will get it somewhere else. Many people have left the good partners to pursue worthless relationships. They have left eighty percent of what they were getting in their marriages to run after the twenty percent they were not getting. They have given up eighty percent, but now they are left with only twenty percent, and they do not know what to do with their lives because they traded their marriages for misery.

If you do not learn to appreciate your partner while they are still around, one day you will regret having misused the treasure you should have cherished. Do not worry yourself to death about what you are not getting from your partner; rather celebrate what you are getting and remain faithful to one partner for as long as you live. The restlessness you feel when your phone rings and the sparkle in your eyes when you are texting are giving you away. If you are a man and you are unfaithful to your wife, she will know. She may not confront you about it, but that does not mean she knows nothing. She may ask you questions, and you may tell her lies; but before she asks you a question, she already knows what is going on. When you lie to her, not only does she think you are stupid; she also gets shocked at how stupid you think she is.

The more you lie to your partner, the deeper your marriage will drown. Even if you are a woman and you cheat on your husband, you won't get far with it. You are practically killing your marriage with your own hands. If you have been unfaithful to your partner, make a sharp turn towards God and make things right with your partner. God is still able to forgive you and restore your marriage if you repent and forsake infidelity. He can also give you power to overcome the temptation to act unfaithfully in your marriage. Be faithful to each other as a couple, and your marriage will stand a better chance of succeeding; but if you fail to be faithful, you will soon be single.

22.2 Confinement

Marriage requires full commitment; but *commitment* is not *confinement*. When you were pronounced husband and wife, you were not given a life sentence in solitary confinement. Therefore, you should by all means avoid making yourselves feel like you are confined to each other. Both of you still have a life; and you have different likes and interests. Some of the things you really like may be the things your partner hates, and you may not be able to do those things together. This should not hinder you from enjoying the things you like simply because the other partner does not like them. You need to give each other freedom to stay committed to each other and still enjoy the things you like. Marriage is not house arrest. Therefore, your marriage should not make you feel you are confined to your partner for the rest of your life.

You are *married*; not *buried*. So, there is a need for you to give each other space so that both of you can be free to explore the areas of your life that the other partner is not interested in. Sometimes you may want to go out only with your friends who are the same gender as you; and you should be able to give each other freedom to do so. Even though you are spending the rest of your lives together, you can't always be together; you still need to do things separately. A lifetime is way too long to spend it in solitary confinement with each other. As a couple, you need to learn to trust each other enough to give each other the freedom to enjoy your lives in every possible way; even if it means you should spend some time apart. This should not be used as an excuse not to spend time with your partner; it should rather be taken as a suggestion for you to allow each other to participate in different social activities.

There are people who always want to be everywhere their partners are, even if the situation does not allow for them to go together. If they can't go with them, they won't let them go. This can make their partners wish they were never married, and it might affect their peace as a couple. Some marriages feel more like cages than homes, and some people feel like they are prisoners to their own partners. No sooner than the moment they get out of the house do they receive the call from their spouses demanding that they should 'come home'. This can be very frustrating, and it can make one feel hopelessly miserable in marriage. It can make the person feel that they would rather be alone than stay in a marriage that feels like prison.

Marital commitment is not about *force*; it's about *choice*. It is voluntary; not coercive. Forced commitment is confinement. If the wife wants to go and spend time with other ladies, the husband should trust her enough to let her go; and if the husband want to spend some time with other men, his wife should love him enough to release him. Successful couples have learnt the art of balancing their family life with their social life. They have also learnt to give each other the freedom to enjoy their lives apart for a while without breaking their commitment to each other. If you keep each other in marital confinement, you will most probably miss out on the true beauty of marriage; and you might end up killing the very marriage you are trying to preserve.

22.3 Domestic Violence

There are people who literally use violence to try and solve their marital problems. Well, this is more like using petrol to put out the fire. No marriage was ever strengthened by violence, and no marriage ever will. The outcome of domestic violence is broken trust, hatred, injuries, divorce, imprisonment and death. Not only does it destroy the marriage, it also destroys the couples involved. Its effect on children is more harmful than words can express. It crushes their self esteem and distorts their understanding of relationship, love, marriage and family. When violence breaks out in a marital relationship, one wins and the other loses; and if one loses, both have lost. Domestic violence turns a warm home into a warzone; and where there is war, there is no peace.

Violence is a behaviour that is intended to hurt or kill somebody, using physical or emotional force and energy. If the intention of violence is to hurt and kill a person, then it sure can't be used to build a marriage. You cannot strengthen your marriage by hurting or killing your partner. Violence happens always as a result of fear or hatred and never out of love or care. Very often you will hear people who abuse their spouses claiming that it is because they love them. That's a pure lie! You cannot hurt or kill the person you love; you can only do so to the one you hate. Violence and love never go together. Where there is violence, there is no love; and where there is love, there is no violence. Violence is meant for destruction, and it is impossible to destroy the one you love.

The general understanding is that violence is a physical act; so if there are no physical attacks, the situation is not violence. This cannot be further from the truth. Violence is not only physical. It also involves emotional abuse, sexual abuse and verbal attacks. Emotional abuse involves deliberate acts that are intended to hurt the feelings of the other person. It violates the things the person holds dear and promotes the things the person hates. Some people go as far as hurting or neglecting their children with an intention to hurt their partner's feelings. Others would have extramarital affairs just to hurt their partners. Emotional abuse also involves stalking, threatening and emotional blackmails. Unfortunately, emotional abuse happens all the time in marriages, and it is as harmful as physical abuse; it just cannot be proved in the court of law because its scars are invisible.

Sexual abuse involves deliberate sexual acts that are intended to hurt the other person. When a person forces another person to do sexual acts that are harmful or uncomfortable, that act is also regarded as sexual abuse. Sexual abuse also involves neglecting the other person's sexual needs deliberately with an intention to hurt him (or her). It also involves forcing one's partner to watch sexually explicit materials against his (or her) will. This also includes forcing one's partner to watch one have sex with another person. Rape and sexual deprivation are also components of sexual abuse. Rape is the act forcing the other person to have sex with you against his (or her) will. It usually leaves permanent emotional scars within the people to whom it was performed. The effects of rape continue to haunt the victim even long after the person who did it has forgotten.

Sexual deprivation involves neglecting one's partner's sexual needs deliberately to hurt him (or her). In this case, one's partner gets to see one naked everyday but still be deprived sex. One can go so far as to pleasure oneself sexually in front of one's partner to seduce him (or her); but still no sex will take place. The victim can only see but not touch. This can be a serious torture to a person, especially if that person loves or values sex. As a result, some people resort to having sexual relationships outside marriage, and things get even worse instead of getting better. Sexual abuse, whatever shape or form, is part of domestic violence, and it can destroy marriage.

Verbal attacks involve insulting, cursing, name calling and any other word that is uttered with an intention to hurt the other person. Violent utterances can make the person feel humiliated and degraded. They can also shutter the self esteem of the person to whom they are directed. They can also destroy the person emotionally. The debilitating effects of verbal attacks, like emotional abuse, are also as harmful as physical abuse; but sadly there are no visible scars to produce as prove in the court of law. Physical wounds heal naturally after a short time, all it takes are few stitches; but wounds caused by emotional abuse, sexual abuse and verbal attacks take more effort and time to heal. Actually, no medical practitioner can put stitches on a broken heart or a crushed spirit.

Generally, when the word domestic violence is mentioned, the first thing that comes into mind is that a man is abusing his wife. Very seldom, if ever, do we think about the possibility of a woman abusing her husband. In every violent relationship, according to general understanding, the wife is 'innocent', and the husband is 'guilty'. But honestly speaking, as long as we believe this fallacy, we will never overcome domestic violence. The truth is: if you can go deeper into the problem, you may discover that both of them are guilty. As I explained in the earlier chapters, generally, men are physically stronger but emotionally weaker; and women are physically weaker and emotionally stronger. I also mentioned that marriage will become chaotic if both can use their strengths against each other. Women also have verbal power over men. Very few men can exchange violent words with women and win.

Yes, statistics do reveal that in most violent cases men are perpetrators and women are victims; but remember that those statistics were gathered from reported cases which can be proven, and emotional scars and effects of verbal attacks are invisible. From my daily interventions with people, I come across more and more cases of men who endure serious emotional abuse and verbal attacks by their wives. A number of men who are emotionally damaged as a result of domestic violence is increasing at an alarming rate, but very few people realize that because such cases are not reported at police stations. If such cases were to be reported, there would not be sufficient evidence because the victims have no bruises to show for it. They also have no way to prove that they are being hurt by way of sexual neglect. Hard as it may be to believe, the verbal attacks that husbands endure in their marriages are just as excruciating as the physical attacks that are inflicted upon wives.

In most cases of domestic violence, husbands and wives are both guilty; it's just that wives can prove it with cuts and bruises on their bodies, but husbands have no evidence to show for their damaged egos and broken spirits. The first step to overcoming domestic violence is to acknowledge the possibility that both the husband and wife could be equally guilty. We cannot defeat this monster as long as we keep on reducing it to physical abuse against women. We need to tackle it holistically from both parties. Unless husbands stop using their physical strength against their wives and wives stop using their emotional and verbal strength against their husbands, domestic violence will never be defeated. God empowered us differently according to our sexes not so that we can attack each other; but to protect each other.

These things I do not say to justify the abuse of women by men. I strongly condemn such acts, and I will always keep my voice raised against the abuse of women and children. The point I am trying to make is that domestic violence (whether by men to women or by women to men) must come to an end. Whether the husband abuses the wife or the wife abuses the husband, domestic violence is still a marriage killer, and it still damages both the innocent and the guilty. Violence by women against men is still violence, and it happens all the time in the areas that human eye cannot see. As we strive to stop the abuse of women by men, let us also remember to tackle the abuse of men by women.

Intense episodes of domestic violence are usually followed by unusual acts of romance. As a result people are deceived to believe that violence improves marriage. But that is not true. That is what we call the *cycle of domestic violence.* In this cycle, what was will always be unless the cycle is broken. Every romantic episode will be followed by another episode of violence, which will be followed by another flower, then another slap, then another chocolate, then another stab, and so on and so forth. This can only get worse and occur more frequently. If not broken, this will go on and on until imprisonment, or hospitalization, or divorce, or death. The cycle of violence has four phases, namely: Tension Building, Incident, Reconciliation, and Calm.

The *tension building stage* is characterized by the increase of tension and the breakdown of communication. The victim becomes terrified and feels the need to appease the abuser or attacker. However, at this stage there seems to be nothing the victim can do to talk the abuser out. This then leads to the *incident stage*, which is characterized by the verbal, emotional and physical (or even sexual) abuse. This is the stage where the attacker inflicts pain upon the victim, and this could lead to severe injuries and emotional damages. The incident would then be followed by the *reconciliation stage*. This is where the attacker apologises and gives excuses for the violence that just happened.

The apology would be something like "I'm sorry I hurt you. It was not intentional"; and the excuse would be "If you had not done that, I would not have done this." This goes with the shift of the blame to the victim, where the victim will hear words like "You made me do this". The attacker may even deny that the abuse occurred or just diminish it by saying that it was not as bad as the victim claims it was, even though there are clear signs that the victim is badly injured. After this comes the *stage of calm*. The stage of calm is in simple terms the 'honeymoon' stage, where the incident is 'forgotten'. No violence is taking place, and the couple seem happy and in love again. Soon after that the cycle repeats itself, and each time it is repeated, the incident phase increases, and the calm stage decreases; until it becomes a full-blown violence which could be fatal.

Violence can never solve a marital problem; it can only make things much worse. Eventually people make a wrong conclusion that 'love hurts'. But I have already mentioned that where there is love there is no violence, and where there is violence there is no love. So, this has nothing to do with love in the first place. Love does not hurt; people do. It is impossible to deliberately hurt the person you love. Hurt goes with hatred. Therefore, people who use violence to hurt each other hate each other. Hatred hurts, but love heals and protects. It forgives, tolerates and endures. Couples who really love each other do not go out of their way to hurt each other. Therefore, violence is not an expression of love; it is an indication of the absence thereof. Domestic violence should be eradicated in any form; but if you fail to root it out, it will kill your marriage.

22.4 Addictions

It is so shocking how marriages fall apart because of addictions. There are many people who take refuge in substances to hide from their problems. This goes on until it becomes a habit; and before they know it, it has become an addiction. Once they get addicted to substances, they come to a point where they cannot live without them. This usually causes too much strain in their relationships; especially their marriages. Not only do such addictions strain their relationships; they also cause much harm to the addicted. People get addicted to many things; but there are two most common addictions that are known to destroy marriages throughout the world; namely: alcohol and drugs, as well as pornography.

Every addiction to drugs and alcohol started with one drink and one 'fix'; and every addiction to pornography started with one video clip. Drugs and alcohol can influence you to do the things you would not normally do. They can turn the most reserved person into the most outgoing. People who are normally quiet and reserved become extremely talkative. Drugs and alcohol can also make users experience the high feelings of ecstasy. They can also make problems appear less than they really are. Therefore, people resort to them for feelings of excitement despite the problems at hand. This is how people come to use them as the hiding place from life's realities.

Unfortunately, alcohol cannot solve problems; neither can drugs and the feelings they produce. So, as soon as users sober up, they wake up to find that their realities have not changed; then they would reach for another class or needle to make themselves feel better. As they continue to drink alcohol or take drugs, their bodies gradually develop *tolerance*; and it can no longer respond to certain amounts of substances. At this stage, the body needs more in order to give the desired 'fix'. This goes on and on, until the body develops *dependence.* This is where the user can no longer survive without drugs or alcohol; and this is the beginning of addiction.

Once a person gets addicted to drugs or alcohol, he (or she) loses the ability to stop using them. This is where people empty their coffers and begin to sell their assets so that they may be able to buy more drugs or alcohol. On top of that, they start taking cashing loans everywhere so that they can have a drink or a 'fix'. Meanwhile, their families are suffering, and their marriages are sinking.

The problems they are trying to hide from continue to increase; and the more their problems increase, the more they drink. This becomes a vicious cycle of serious trouble for them; which they deal with by indulging all the more in harmful substances. Like an ostrich, which hides its head in the sand to try and escape from danger, they hide their heads in glasses full of alcohol, hoping that their problems will disappear.

Drugs and alcohol do not solve problems; all they do is make things worse while they destroy the user. Some people use alcohol to 'drink their marital frustrations away'; but with every drink they seem to be swallowing more frustrations into their marriages. If you ask them why they are drinking their lives to death, they would probably respond by saying, "I drink this way because I have too many problems'; as if their drinking flushes their problems away. Even today, people are still drinking their way to divorce. They use drugs and alcohol to kill the very marriages they are hoping to save. Some end up having done the things they should not have done and having said the things they should not have said. Eventually, they end up alone and desperate with an empty glass they cannot afford to fill with the substances that destroyed the marriages.

Other people are losing their marriages because of addiction to pornography. They started using it as way to 'spice up' their sex lives; and initially, it seemed to be working perfectly. But what they did not realise was that their bodies were gradually depending on pornography for sexual arousal. Just as your body gradually develops tolerance for alcohol and drugs; it also develops tolerance for pornography. Therefore, the more you watch pornography, the more you struggle to achieve sexual arousal without it. At this stage your body requires more pornography with more explicit sexual scenes in order to reach sexual arousal. Eventually, you can no longer be aroused sexually by your own partner; and you can no longer have sex without watching pornography.

One other dangerous thing about pornography is that it creates unrealistic expectations when it comes to sex. The wife may expect her husband to make her scream the way the man he saw in the movie made her sexual co-actor. On the other hand, the husband may expect his wife to perform all the sexual moves he saw a woman performing in the movie, and he may expect her to 'enjoy' those moves the same way that woman does. What couples who watch pornography seem not to notice is that what they see in those videos is not real.

Those people are acting; and even if they feel extremely uncomfortable, they act as if they are enjoying so that they can keep you entertained.

I know that there are sex 'experts' who encourage couples to watch pornography because they believe it can serve as a cure for sexual boredom. But I totally differ with this. Pornography is not the cure for sexual boredom; it is one of the main causes of sexual frustration in marital relationships. Always keep this in mind: Pornography was not created to improve sex; neither was it designed to strengthen marriages. It was created to make money by playing with people's sexual *fantasies*. Fantasies are experiences that exist only in the mind. In other words, fantasies are not real. So, pornography plays with your mind and causes you to run after unrealistic pleasures. It diminishes the sanctity of marital sex by making casual sex, group sex, one night stands and all other forms of sexual immorality appear extremely pleasurable. What they are not showing you is the debilitating experiences of pain, guilt, shame, emptiness and misery that the actors and actresses are going through.

Most of the actors and actresses in pornographic movies hate what they are doing, yet they feel they have no choice but to keep on doing it because they get paid for it. Some are manipulated with drugs and threats to keep on acting and pretending to enjoy the experiences that are literally tearing them apart. When the producers and directors feel that their actors are 'wasted', they make them act in scenes wherein they would perform group sex and pretend to enjoy dreadful experiences with complete strangers. The poor actors, especially actresses, also have to pretend to be aroused by the insults they have to endure during those sexual scenes that actually feel like hell. Some must pretend to enjoy anal sex and having the semen of complete strangers being shot into their faces. They are forced to respond to pain as if they are experiencing pleasure. Deep down they wish they could break free from that pain; but they feel like they are already in too deep to ever come out again.

Back in your room you are watching lustfully with the hope that your partner would give it to you exactly the way you saw her give it to him. If she doesn't, you get frustrated; until you go out to find someone who can give it to you. But the more you search, the more frustrated you get because you are looking for something you will never find, and the reason you will never find it is because it is not real. You are actually trading the real thing for fake. Even if you can try the very character who played on that scene, you will be shocked to find out that even the character that you watched doing it in the video would not do it in real life. Pornography diminishes the value of sex; and moreover, it destroys the marriage. It causes people to lose interest in their partners and fall in love with their own palms and fingers as they replace real sex with masturbation. Even if it can appear to be solving your sexual problems for a while, it gradually destroys your marriage – permanently.

Addictions make people absent even when they are around. They break trust and destroy marriages. They rob us off the people we love and turn them into our worst enemies. Yet people keep on flirting with them by indulging in harmful practices. If you are reading this book and you are suffering from any kind of addiction, I advise you to seek help immediately. You know you are addicted when you are no longer able to stop or hold back. It's never too late to regain your personal power and reclaim your dignity. If you can make up your mind to fight your addiction and totally commit yourself to the course, no level of addiction will be too strong for you to overcome. With God on your side and professionals to help you, you can make it. Even if it feels like you are down and out, you can still rise up and turn your life around for better; and you can start today.

22.5 Selfishness

If you carefully study human temperaments, you will find out that all of us have some elements of selfishness within us. Phlegmatic wants everybody to like him, Melancholy thinks everybody wants to hurt him, Choleric wants everybody to do everything his way, and Sanguine wants everybody to listen to him. We all have those moments when we feel that everything is all about "me"; and that's quite normal. But this becomes a problem when it happens all or most of the time. Selfish people want every good thing to happen to them only, and they want every bad to happen to anybody else except them. This is very harmful to human relationships. It is much worse in marital relationships. Your marriage cannot succeed if everything is all about you.

Sometimes we behave selfishly in our marriages, and we don't even realise it. We get furious at our partners for the things we ourselves are doing. We accuse them for not involving us in their decision, yet we also don't involve them in our decisions. We complain to them that they hurt our feeling, yet we ourselves also hurt their feelings. We easily recognise the offense when we are the victims, but we hardly recognise it when we are the culprits. This makes it clear that selfishness is one of the harmful attributes that are lying in our blind areas. So, everytime you think what your spouse is doing is wrong, ask yourself if you are not by any chance doing the same thing.

If you keep on placing concern with yourself or your own interests above the well-being or interests of your partner; or if you care only about yourself and never about your partner, this suggests that you are selfish. Your partner is as important as you are in your marriage; therefore, his (or her) interests and well-being are just as important as yours. Your marriage can never succeed if it's all about you. You want your wife to listen to you when you tell her to exchange her skirt that is 'too short' with the longer one, but you would not listen to her when she tells you to exchange the shirt you have just put on for the one that matches your trousers. That's being selfish; and this attitude can destroy your marriage.

Almost every sinful action ever committed can be traced back to a selfish motive. It is a trait we hate in other people but justify in ourselves (Stephen Kendrick). As I interact with couples in marriage counselling or relationship programmes, I meet a lot of people who complain about what their partners are doing or failing to do to them. They would say something like: "My partner is disrespectful to me"; "My partner thinks only about himself (or herself)"; "He does not tell me he loves me"; "She does not iron my clothes"; etc. It's all about what their partners are doing or saying to them and never about what they themselves are saying or doing to their partners. In most cases, I have discovered that the ones who complained about their partners 'victimizing' them are the main culprits. They happen to be the ones who are more selfish in their marital relationships.

The fact that you think your partner is selfish could serve as an indication that you yourself are selfish, because the main reason why we think people are selfish is because they 'fail' to meet our selfish needs and interest. As I have mentioned earlier, you judge people not as they are; but as you are. So, what you see in other people is usually a reflection of what is happening within you. They say "it takes one to see one"; and within the context of selfishness I strongly agree. It is very easy for selfish people to recognise selfishness in other people. Therefore, the selfishness you see in your partner could be a reflection of the selfishness in you. So, the next time you think or say your partner is selfish; take that as a clue and look within yourself, because the selfish one in that relationship could be you.

In marriage, you succeed when you treat your partner exactly the way you want them to treat you. You don't expect respect from your partner if you won't respect them. The output you expect from your spouse should be determined by the input you exerted in them. Do not expect the harvest where you have not planted a seed; neither should you expect the vine when you have planted thorns. Your spouse has needs as much as you do, and they also have bad days like you. Your marriage will not succeed if you feel you are winning while your partner feels they are losing. You cannot be truly happy if you make yourself happy by hurting your partner. So, as much as you want to be understood by your spouse, be understanding of them, and your marriage will become a successful union wherein both of you feel you are winning.

22.6 Destructive Criticisms

Criticisms are good when they are meant for construction. They serve as a way of providing feedback to a person to help them improve their performance. Criticisms will always be there because no one is perfect. In a relationship, inappropriate behaviour will always be criticized. But now that everybody behaves inappropriately at any given time, everybody needs to learn how to handle criticism. Not only should people learn how to handle criticisms; they should also learn how to criticise considerately. As mentioned above, criticism should be *constructive*; not *destructive.* Constructive criticism brings growth because it is *corrective*; but destructive criticism blocks growth because it is *punitive*, and it provides no alternatives.

Constructive criticism reveals the strengths of the person being criticized; but destructive criticism majors on weaknesses. Constructive criticism clearly differentiates people from their actions; but destructive criticism does not distinguish between *who you are* and *what you do.* In other words, when you make a mistake, constructive criticism will say "change your approach"; but destructive attitude will say "you need to change or let someone else do it". Constructive criticism says "you have failed, but you can make it better if you try doing it differently"; but destructive criticism says "you are a failure". However, in reality, failing does not make you a failure because *doing* is not *becoming.*

The word *failure* is a noun describing the *verb* and not the *name*. Therefore, failure is *what you did*; not *who you are*; and it takes a constructive attitude to understand this truth. Destructive criticism defines who you are by what you do; but constructive criticism tells action and person apart. Constructive criticism makes you see a mistake as an opportunity for growth; but destructive criticism makes you see it as the end of the road.

Criticism is *vital* when constructive but *fatal* when destructive. The aim of criticism in marriage should be to build and not to destroy. Marriage suffers a great deal of harm because of destructive criticisms. Destructive criticisms are like verdicts; they are mostly characterised by words such as 'always' and 'never'. A practical example for this is couples telling each other statements like "You *always* disappoint me"; "You *never* do anything right"; "You *always* come home late from work"; "You are never at home" and many more you can think of. *Always* and *never* are eternal words. They suggest no possibility for change or growth. They also disregard ones attempts to improve.

If you say your partner is *never* at home, are you implying that there is not even a single night or day he or she ever spent at home? What about those days and nights when your partner does spend time at home? Are they also part of *never*? For destructive criticisms to be alleviated in marriages, words like 'always' and 'never' should under no circumstance be used when one is criticising the other. These words can make a mistake appear worse than it really is. They eternalize the wrongs of the other person, leaving no room for improvement. Instead of encouraging, they discourage; and instead of correcting, they condemn. If you want to save your marriage from error or divorce, the primary aim of your criticism should be not so much to ventilate your feelings, but to correct your partner's behaviour if necessary.

It is better not to criticise at all than to criticise destructively. Constructive criticism makes the relationship better, but destructive one makes it worse. Destructive criticisms can make you win the argument and lose the relationship. It does not solve the problem; rather, it hurts the person. One other thing that can help you improve your marital relationship is to keep the criticisms as minimal as possible. Even if it is constructive criticism; too much of it can also be harmful to the marriage. It can demoralise your partner. It can also crush their confidence; and everywhere they go they will need you to approve or disapprove whatever they do. Sometimes too much of a good thing is not good anymore.

Even the Bible confirms it: *If you find honey, eat just enough – too much of it, and you will vomit. Seldom set foot in your neighbour's house – too much of you, and he will hate you* (Proverbs 25:16 - NIV). Excessive criticism can make your partner reject you. Even too much praise can be irritating; how much more infuriating can excessive criticism be? Too much of constructive criticism can be destructive. How much more, then, can destructive criticism damage the marriage if used excessively? When you criticise, make sure you criticise the behaviour; not the person. If you criticise the person instead of the behaviour, you may end up having lost *them* permanent over *what they did.* For marriage to be safe from demolition, criticism should always be for construction and never for destruction; and it should always be used moderately and never excessively.

22.7 Sarcasm

The original meaning of the word *sarcasm* is to tear the flesh, bite the lip in rage, or to sneer. It involves making fun of another person's efforts or features. Sarcasm is basically one's way of making oneself laugh by making the other person feel upset. Sarcastic people do not laugh *with* people, they laugh *at* them. They usually ridicule other people and make them feel stupid; and for some reason they think it's funny. While their sarcastic behaviour cheers them up, it tears others apart; and at the same time, it pushes them away. No one wants to be with the person who treats them like a joke.

Sarcasm has a damaging effect upon the one to whom it is directed. It does not correct; it humiliates. It breaks trust and destroys confidence. It hurts the very person it was intended to help. It also destroys the relationship between the one practicing it and the one experiencing it. If you keep on making sarcastic remarks at your spouse, they may not leave you entirely, but they will shut down completely from you. You will have their body; but not their heart. Eventually, you will end up all alone. It is better to keep quiet if you have nothing constructive to say, than to say something that could make you laugh your way out of your marriage.

Sarcasm is usually mistaken for humour; but there is a huge difference between these two. Sarcasm laughs *at* the person, but humour laughs *with* the person. Humour laughs at the joke, but sarcasm turns the person into a 'joke'. Humour cheers people up, but sarcasm tears them down. Humour carefully considers the feelings of other people, but sarcasm does not care how other people feel. Humour breaks the tension, but sarcasm builds it up. Humour reduces the pain, but sarcasm induces it. Humour strengthens marriage, but sarcasm weakens it. It's not funny if it hurts the other person; and it cannot build your marriage if it breaks your spouse's heart. No matter how funny you think it is, if your remark offends your spouse, it's not a joke; it's sarcasm – a marriage killer.

22.8 External Interferences

Every couple is fully responsible for the success or failure of their marriage. However, sometimes the toxin that kills marriages comes from outside. We all have those people who 'care' so much about us; who have deployed themselves as 'guardian angels' over our marriages. These people observe our every move and act as our partners' eyes to watch us when they are not around; then they bring back the report of whatever they saw as it appeared to them. They would keep them updated on everything they saw us do, and they would add their own stories to give more weight to their reports. Such people will always be there, and they will always tell stories; but they cannot affect our marriages in any way unless we allow them by entertaining their stories.

Although they mean well, people who keep us updated on our partners' behaviour when we are not around are like poison to our marriages; but the poison cannot hurt you if you don't swallow it. So, if we keep on swallowing whatever stories they feed us regarding our partners, our marriages will eventually die because of their poison. Do not believe anything that anyone says to you about your partner, because you don't really know if they really want your marriage to succeed. If they really want to help your marriage succeed, they would confront your partner regarding whatever they observed instead of reporting them to you. The person who truly wants to see your marriage succeed will turn your focus away from the bad things about your spouse and direct it towards the good ones.

The light of the eyes rejoices the heart, and a good report makes the bones healthy (Proverbs 15:30). If they really care about you, they will give you a good report; and if you accept bad report from them, it will make you sick. If they have a problem with your partner's behaviour, and they want to build your marriage, let them talk to your partner; not to you. *The soothing tongue is a tree of life, but a perverse tongue crushes the spirit* (Proverbs 15:4 – NIV). No one can build your marriage by crushing your spirit; they can only do so by telling you the things that will comfort you. So, it's totally up to you whether you will accept their report or not. If you accept a bad report concerning your spouse, it will crush your spirit and break your marriage; but if you accept a good report, it will become to you a tree of life.

22.9 Pride

Some people ended up having lost their marital relationships because they put their pride before their marriages. They would not say "sorry" or 'thank you" or "please" to their spouses. They seemed to have forgotten that *pride goes before destruction, and a haughty spirit before a fall* (Proverbs 16:18). They esteemed themselves more highly than their partners. In their marriages, it was their way or no way. They would not 'stoop down' to their partners' level. They tried to teach their partners everything, but they were too arrogant to learn anything from them. Their general attitude in their marriages was "I do not need you..." and "I don't care". They held on to their pride and let go of their marriages in the process.

When proud people go through problems in their marriages, they arrogantly disconnect themselves from their partners and act like they are not affected at all; even though in actual fact they are. Even if they can be aware that things are falling apart in their marriages, they won't take the initiative to solve their problems. They usually think they are too smart for that. They like to make their partners feel like they are at their mercy; and that they did them a great favour by marrying them. They have a false attitude that shouts "I can live without you, but you can't live without me". They are too proud to ask for forgiveness when they are wrong. In their opinion, their partners are always wrong, and they are always right. They never acknowledge their weaknesses before their partners because they like to portray the wrong impression that they are perfect and self-sufficient.

Pride and marriage can never co-exist. Pride is of the devil. In fact, it was pride that caused Satan to forfeit his place in heaven (See Ezekiel 28 and Isaiah 14). It was his pride that led to his fall. But marriage is of the Lord. It was established by God, and it can never be sustained by Satan's traits. Pride is one of Satan's main traits, and even today he still uses it to bring many of God's people down. Where there is pride, there is a fall. Therefore, the marriage that has pride in it cannot stand; it will fall apart. Trying to make your partner feel inferior does not make you superior to them; it only destroys your precious marriage. You can't be proud and happily married at the same time. If you hold on to your pride, you will ultimately forfeit your marriage.

If you want your marriage to stand a better chance of succeeding, you need to swallow your pride and humble yourself. *...All of you be submissive to one another, and be clothed with humility, for God resists the proud, but gives grace to the humble* (1 Peter 5;5-6). God is on the side of the humble and against the proud. As a couple, you need to learn to be submissive to each other; and if you do, God will give you grace to make your marriage succeed. You can't sustain your pride and your marriage at the same time. To sustain your marriage, you must kill your pride; but if you sustain your pride, it will kill your marriage.

22.10 Excessive Jealousy and Insecurities

Jealousy is very common in human relationships. We experience it very early in our lives. We get jealous over our parents, our siblings, our toys, our friends, and our partners. Jealousy usually occurs when we anticipate the loss of the things we hold dear to our hearts. It is usually characterised by feelings of anger, doubt, anxiety, fear and insecurities. It also leads to the feelings of resentment, helplessness and disgust. We usually feel extremely unsettled when we experience the feelings of jealousy. We all experience jealousy when we anticipate that someone is trying to take away something that rightfully belongs to us. This happens mainly in human relationships, especially marital relationships.

We all feel jealous when we perceive that someone is 'stealing' our partners' attention; and we very often feel resentful not only to the person stealing our partners' attention; but also to our partners for 'allowing' them to do so. The main reason why we feel jealous in our marriages is that we and our partners belong together, and we have a need to feel that our marital relationships are exclusive to us and not inclusive of other people; especially the people of the opposite sex. Every man has a need to feel that he is the only man in his wife's life, and every woman has a need to feel that she is the only woman in her husband's life. If we perceive that our partners seem to be 'too comfortable' with the person of the opposite sex, we feel jealous, and that is normal.

Jealousy is often used synonymously with envy; but these two are different. Envy is when you experience the feelings of jealousy over something that is not yours. You are envious when you resent people for what belongs to them; but if you experience similar feelings over what belongs to you, you are being jealous. If you feel jealous over someone else's partner, you are being envious; but if that partner is yours, that becomes jealousy. Therefore, jealousy, as opposed to envy, is legitimate, because it has to do with what belongs to you. But jealousy can be very irrational, and thus, unhealthy for relationships. There are people whose jealousy is irrational. They feel jealous over their partners in almost everything. This usually stems from excessive insecurities. As a result, they restrict their partners' interactions and monitor their every conversation. They expect their partners to be rude to every person of the opposite sex, and if not so, they start feeling jealous, and that often leads to quarrels.

People feel insecure in their marriages for a number of reasons; some of which are: Experiences from previous relationships, experiences from current relationship, and self-esteem. People who have been hurt, betrayed or disappointed before are most likely to experience the feelings of excessive jealousy and insecurity. They usually relate whatever is happening in their current relationships with what happened in previous ones. This can lead to conclusions that are totally inaccurate. The fact that the previous partner was unfaithful does not mean the current one is also unfaithful. This kind of jealousy punishes the latter for the mistakes of the former. If your former partner used a phone to cheat on you, that does not necessarily mean your current partner is cheating on your when he (or she) is on the phone. There is therefore a need to train our minds to distinguish between what the previous partner did and what the current one is doing.

If you judge your current partner based on your previous partner's mistake, you might end up losing a good person who is in your life because of mistakes of the bad person was in your life. Not only because of our previous relationships do we feel jealous in our marriages; it is also because of our experiences in our current relationships. Generally, people feel insecure when their partners show more interest on other people of the opposite sex than they do on them.

This can make you feel like you are losing your partner to someone else. This also happens when you compliment other people of the opposite sex more than your own partner. People also feel insecure when their partners behave in ways that make them suspicious. This usually occurs when their partners show unusual kindness to other people of the opposite sex; or when they make too many secret calls or carry their cell phones wherever they go, even if there is no reason to do so.

People also get suspicious when they feel their partners are hiding something; and this can also cause jealousy and insecurity. Another reason why people feel insecure in their marriage is low self-esteem. If you feel that you are not doing enough to 'keep your partner interested' on you, you might fear that someone else might steal them from you by doing for them what you are 'failing' to do. If you have low self-esteem, you are always afraid that someone might take better care your spouse than you do; and you might find yourself trying very hard to keep him (or her) away from them. This is where you find couples restricting each other to ensure that they stay away from people of the opposite sex. If you know you are not doing your best in your marriage, you will experience insecurity because you will always be afraid that someone might outdo you and take over your family; but if you know that you are doing your best, you will be more confident that your partner can find no one better than you.

If you know that you are playing your part excellently in your marriage, it will be easier for you to overcome insecurity. If you know you are the best, you seldom worry about the rest. Let's take the example of employment. The employer who knows he is underpaying his employees feels insecure because he knows they might leave him to find better-paying jobs; and they use threats to keep their employees grounded so that they are restricted only to those jobs. They don't even let them interact with employees of other companies that are in similar business because they are afraid that they may find out that they are being underpaid. On the other hand, well-paying employees are more confident. They are not afraid to let their employees interact with other employees; in fact, they love it because they are confident that they will find no better paying job than the one they are in.

Same applies in marriage. You are more likely to keep your partner restricted to you if you know you are not doing enough to keep them glued to you. But if you know that you are playing your part to the best of your ability, you will be more confident that your partner can find no one better than you. You will be less afraid to let them interact with other people because you want them to see for themselves that you are the best. You will also be less insecure when you know that there is nothing your partner will find from others that they are not getting from you. The question is: are you doing your best for your spouse? One of the lessons that successful couples have learnt is *self-confidence*. Self-confidence is an antidote for insecurity. Self-confident people base their confidence in their own excellence, but insecure people base their fears on their partners' potential to betray them. You can overcome insecurity and excessive jealousy in your marriage by developing confidence in your ability to handle whatever your partner might do.

Several marriages are broken because of excessive jealousy and insecurity. Today we have an increasing number of divorcees who pushed their partners away from their marriages while they were trying to keep them in; all because they were too jealous and insecure to let them live their lives without restraint. They built borders for them in terms of who to talk to, how to talk to them, when to talk to them, and what they should talk about; and they monitor them very closely. They 'caged' them in so much that they ended up losing them. Their fear of losing their partners caused them to behave in such a manner that they subconsciously attracted the very thing they feared. Their obsession over the possible loss of their partners eventually costed them their marriages. Jealousy in marriage is not a bad thing, but too much of it can destroy marriage. Couples should learn to overcome their insecurities. They should also help each other by doing away with any kind of behaviour that triggers each other's insecurities.

23

Marital Conflict

Conflict is normal in every human relationship. It is part of our daily interactions. In fact, it is abnormal to not have conflict in a relationship. It would mean that the two of you are identical in your values, interests, thoughts, feelings, wishes, believes, personalities, temperaments and every other aspect of your being; which is totally impossible. Every human being is unique; no two humans are totally identical, not even twins. The natural differences between people are the main causes of conflict in relationships. Conflict occurs when there are opposing ideas, opinions, feelings or wishes, and this happens most of the time in relationships.

It is impossible for people who stay together to not experience conflict, especially in marriage. The wife may want to watch a soap opera in one television channel, and at the same time the husband may want to watch a football game in another channel. Or the wife may want to use an automobile to go to a women's club meeting, while at the same time the husband wants to go to the stadium to watch a soccer match using the same automobile. The above scenarios are a clear illustration of *conflict*. Married couples experience conflict in a number of ways, starting from trivial issues such as deciding which television channel to watch to more serious issues such as deciding which house to buy. Conflict is just as real as the relationship itself, and if it is not managed properly, it may lead to serious disputes and tragic endings.

Conflict can yield results that are either positive or negative, depending on how it is addressed. How conflict is dealt with can make or break the relationship. If addressed violently, it can lead to disintegration; but if addressed peacefully, it can lead to growth. It is therefore important to learn healthy ways of dealing with conflict if you are to succeed in your relationships. To a large extend, the difference between successful marriages and unsuccessful ones lies in the manner in which couples handle their conflicts. Couples who cannot handle conflict properly are at a very high risk of experiencing unhealthy marriages. They end up dealing with serious episodes of domestic violence, divorce, injuries, or even death. On the other hand, couples who have learnt healthy ways of dealing with conflict experience growth in their marriages. The more the conflict, the stronger their relationships grow.

People use different styles to deal with conflict, and those styles are mainly influenced by their temperaments (there are also other factors that influence the styles of dealing with conflict). Some use *force* or intimidation to get their way, others just *yield* to the demands of the other party. Some choose to *withdraw*, others just *compromise*, and others use *joint problem solving* or *joint decision making* to address their conflict. People who use *force* to deal with conflict direct their energies towards getting what they want and making other people change. They are usually domineering and controlling, and they like threatening people and ordering them around to get things done their way. They manipulate other people's consciences and try to make them feel guilty for not complying with their demands.

Forceful people are generally table-pounders and door-slammers. They behave that way to strike fear in the hearts of those in 'opposition'. If they cannot threaten you physically, they will terrorize you emotionally. They apply a *survival of the fittest* approach when dealing with conflict. Their eyes are very sharp to see the blunders of other people, but they are blinded from their own errors. They are aggressive in their approach, and they are happy to get what they want regardless of how other people end up feeling. They help themselves by hurting others. Eventually, they *win*, and others *lose*. But remember, if only one person wins in a relationship, both of them lose. True victory in a relationship is if both of you win. This is therefore not a healthy way of dealing with conflict in a relationship, especially a marital relationship. People using this style of handling conflict usually win the argument and lose the relationship; they gain what they want at the expense of what they need.

People who use *yielding* as a way of dealing with conflict are more submissive. They direct their energies towards changing themselves for the benefit of others. They are cooperative and agreeable, and they often give in for the sake of peace. They inconvenience themselves for the benefit of others, and they make others feel better while they themselves continue to feel worse. They deprive themselves from their wishes so that they can grant the wishes of their counterparts in a conflict situation. Such people are seldom happy because they get nothing they want as they give others everything they want. They respect the interests of others more than their own. Ultimately, they *lose*, and others *win*; and this too is a loss for both of them. They end up feeling resentful towards their partners and start withdrawing from the relationship; thus losing the very relationship they were trying to save.

People who use *withdrawal* as a style of dealing with conflict prefer not to be involved. Their energies are directed towards avoiding confrontation and controversy. They usually disengage or change the subject when the issue is raised. Instead of playing an active role in dealing with conflict, they just sit back and let things be. They do not *act*; they just *wish*. They'd rather leave things as they are than risk making them 'worse'. Withdrawal is an act that seems to make one innocent, but it can cause serious damages to families. For example, a girl may disclose to her mother that her stepfather is abusing her sexually. If the mother chooses to withdraw and avoid confrontation with her husband, the abuse will continue to happen. To avoid confronting in this situation is to actually let the abuse carry on, and *letting* it happen is just as bad as *making* it happen. Eventually the mother will resent her husband for abusing her daughter sexually, and the daughter will hate her mother for letting it happen by failing to address it.

You can avoid dealing with the problem, but you cannot avoid the consequences of avoiding the problem. If you avoid confronting a problem for fear of rejection or embarrassment, the consequences of avoiding that problem might be much worse than the possible rejection or embarrassment you might have experienced had you confronted the problem. People who withdraw when there is conflict are like tortoises, which hide their heads in their shells hoping that the problem will be gone by the time they come out. But conflict stays longer where it is avoided; and the longer it stays, the stronger it becomes. You cannot avert conflict if you cannot address it; and if you don't address it, it will attack your marriage. It is better to risk embarrassment than to risk losing your marriage; after all, unresolved conflicts often lead to unsuccessful marriages.

People who use *compromise* as their style of dealing with conflict are bargainers. They address conflict by negotiating deals in which each one loses some and gains some. They are willing to sacrifice some, but only if the other party is also willing to sacrifice some. For example, if the couple experience a conflict situation whereby both of them are hungry, but they have only one apple, the *compromiser* will handle this situation differently for the *intimidator* (forceful) and the *submissive* (yielding). The intimidator will force the partner to give up the apple and hand it over to him (or her). The submissive will simply give up the apple to the partner. But the compromiser will have the apple cut into two equal pieces so that both of them may eat half each. None of the compromisers got the full apple, but at least both of them had equal shares.

Much as compromise caters for both parties, it cannot be applied in all situations. For example, if the couple have conflicting views on which school they should enrol their child into, they cannot possibly decide for the child to be enrolled for half a year in one school and the other half in another school. Neither can they tear the child into two pieces so that each half can attend the school of each partner's choice. Compromise cannot be applied in this situation; the couple has to agree on one school for the child. This suggests that compromise is a limited approach to dealing with conflict. There has to be a more effective style for handling conflict, and that style is *joint decision making* or *joint problem solving.*

People who use *joint decision making* or *joint problem solving* to handle conflict direct their energies towards solving the problem together. They see conflict not as an argument to be won by one party; but as a problem to be solved by both parties. Their aim is mutual gain. They commit to sharing ideas and communicating further about the desired outcomes for both of them. They are both involved to see that each one of them plays an active role in ensuring that the desired outcomes are reached. They are responsive to each other's needs and sensitive to each other's feelings. They see conflict as an opportunity for growth and deal with it together. They constructively give each other feedback where necessary. They use problem solving and decision making skills to ensure that they address conflict effectively and efficiently. At the end, both of them win, and their relationship grows stronger and more intimate.

There are other general approaches to dealing with conflict, namely: conflict prevention, conflict management, and conflict resolution. *Conflict prevention* includes actions that can be taken to prevent conflict from prevailing or escalating into a violent outbreak. It involves acting proactively to ensure that conflict does not repeat itself in the same form. It applies mainly in situations where the couple knows the things that are likely to cause conflict and addresses those things before conflict breaks out. For example, the couple who once had conflict over whether to watch a soap opera or a soccer match can decide to buy two television sets and put them in separate rooms so that they can both watch their favourite programmes at the same time. This decision is one way of preventing conflict relating to television programmes.

Couples can prevent conflict by addressing issues that caused it previously so that they do not cause it again. Marriages in which couples experience the same conflict over and over again cannot grow unless the couples learn to master the skill of conflict prevention. It will be helpful for couples to communicate their needs, values, beliefs and interests to each other and decide on common goals that will benefit both of them. It can also be helpful for couples to acknowledge each other's differences and learn to harness them towards achieving the mutually fulfilling results. Remember, your differences as a couple were meant to build you; not to break you. If you find yourself quarrelling frequently because of your differences, it might be a good time to start learning how to make your differences work for you and not against you. Differences were designed to help you achieve more together than you could apart. It is your differences that brought you together, but it is your skills to handle those differences that will keep you together.

Conflict management aims to manage or control an existing conflict in order to prevent it from worsening or spreading to other areas within the relationship. It does not necessarily resolve conflict; it just keeps it under control so that things do not get out of hand. Conflict management ensures that the clash of interests does not lead to the crash of the relationship. Conflict managers direct their energies towards maintaining the relationship despite the existing conflict. They do not lose sight to the value of their relationships because of conflict; and they try by all means to keep the peace for the sake of the relationship. Conflict management puts conflict under control, but it does not resolve it.

Conflict resolution aims to resolve conflict by addressing the root causes thereof. Conflict resolvers direct their energies towards the solution to the problem that led to conflict. They do not waste their time trying to point fingers at each other; instead they point towards the problem and work together until they find a common solution. Healthy communication is highly essential for conflict to be resolved effectively. Blaming and shifting responsibilities cannot resolve conflict; it can only evolve it. Successful resolution of conflict involves the sharing of responsibilities and joint decision making or joint problem solving.

How conflict is viewed determines how it is dealt with. If you are to resolve conflict effectively, you need to see it not as a battle to be won by either of you; but as a problem to be solved together. If you see it as a battle to be won, you will treat each other as enemies, and you may win the battle and lose the marriage. But if you see it as a problem to be solved, you will be able to work together to solve it. Basically, there are six steps to be followed in the problem solving process. The first step is to *jointly acknowledge that there is a problem*. You cannot amend what you do not acknowledge. Denying that you have a problem will keep you longer in it. People tend to believe that acknowledging that they have a problem is a sign of weakness. But the opposite is true. If you act like you are okay when you are not, it can be interpreted as insanity. You can hide your problem, but you cannot hide from it. The sooner you acknowledge it, the earlier you can resolve it.

As soon as you carry out the first step, you are then ready for the next, which is to *define the problem* together. How you define the problem the problem determines how you will go about solving it. For example, if you and your spouse experience a conflicting situation whereby you find yourselves having to be in two different places at the same time having only one car, you can define it either as a problem of *clashing times* or as a problem of *shortage of cars*. If you define it as problem of clashing times, you will try to look at ways in which you can adjust your schedules such that there will be no clashes. But if you define that problem as shortage of cars, you may consider the possibility of buying another car. Therefore, the definition of the problem gives direction towards the solution.

The third step is to *suggest possible solutions and explore each one of them*. At this stage you work together to identify the means of solving the problem at hand. This allows for open discussion between the two of you. The first part of this stage is more like a brainstorming session. No suggestion should be blocked or rejected until both of you feel that you have suggested all possible solutions you could identify. The second part would then be to explore the each of the suggested solutions to identify the best possible solution. When you explore the possible solutions, you look at the advantages, disadvantages and possible consequences of each proposed solution. The one with the most advantages and the least disadvantages, with the prospects of bringing the most desirable results, would be chosen as the best possible solution.

The fourth step would be to *draw an action plan* together. The action plan will give both of you an indication of what needs to be done, when, by whom and with what. It helps you turn the proposed solution into a workable plan by breaking it down into a sequence of smaller activities. It also allows the couple to share responsibilities and assign time and resources to every activity that will be carried out. But the plan is not important if it is not implemented; which brings us to the fifth step. The fifth step is to *implement the action plan* together, ensuring that both of you play your roles as planned. Planning makes the change possible, but implementing the plan makes it happen.

The sixth step, which is the last one, would be to *jointly conduct an evaluation* to check whether or not your problem solving process has been successful. If it fails, you can go back to the third step and choose another possible solution, repeating the process until you succeed. If it succeeds, you can celebrate it together as victory for both of you; then work on ways to prevent such conflict from repeating itself in future.

To sum up the approaches discussed above, let us consider as an illustration the scenario of the house on fire. Conflict in a relationship is like fire burning a house. Conflict management would be the means to manage the existing fire so that it does not spread into other areas in a house. Conflict resolution would be to put out the fire by first dealing with the cause and then using the fire extinguisher to put out the fire. The fire extinguisher in this case would be the six steps of solving a problem. Conflict prevention would then be the actions that are taken to prevent the fire from burning the house again. Conflict prevention also involves changing the behaviour that led to the rise of conflict. In the case of the burning house, it would involve putting away anything that could set the house on fire.

Couples often face serious marital problems because they are too quick to decide who is wrong and who is right. They see conflict more as a battle to be won than as a problem to be solved. This approach is like pouring petrol into the fire trying to put it out. Many couples wonder why they keep on fighting all the time; and they seem to be blinded from their unhealthy ways of dealing with conflict. Eventually they learn to accept their marriages as 'warzones'. Thereafter they would convince other couples that married couples are bound to fight. They mistake conflict for combat. Conflict is inevitable, but combat is; and you can avoid combat between you and your spouse by learning skills to handle conflict properly. Remember, you don't have to be alike to get along; you just need to learn how to deal with your differences such that they work for you and not against you.

24

"To Have and to Hold... Till Death Do Us Part" – The Truth About Divorce

"*To have and to hold... till death do us part*" are some of the most common words people pronounce in their exchange of vows on their wedding day. But in the world today, weddings seem to be more successful than marriages. This suggests that more couples are more able to *have* than to *hold*. They are more able to *get* married than to *stay* married. But staying married is more important than getting married. Marriage is not a short-term contract; it is a lifetime covenant. Therefore, married people should be able to stay together until one or both of them die; just as they declared on their wedding day.

In the modern society, the rate of divorce is increasing at an alarming rate. Divorce no longer comes as a shock like it used to. In fact, it has become so common and socially acceptable that societies regard it as normal. "My ex husband" or "my ex wife" seem to have become some of the fancy words in societies. Staying in marriage for five to ten years is now regarded as a great achievement; and if it's more than ten years, it is considered to be weird or abnormal because seemingly societies no longer expect couples to stay that long in marriage. When you confide in a friend about your marital problems, the first advice you get would most probably be "file for divorce". It seems like marriage is gradually losing its sense of permanence.

That divorce has become so common in societies does not make it less painful. Though the fusion process is painful, it is not half as excruciating as the pain of divorce. When couples get married, they become one flesh; and once they become one flesh, it becomes impossible to separate them. Divorce is amputation with no anaesthetics. It tears you apart without sedating you. By divorcing your spouse, you are practically dismembering yourself. You are cutting yourself into pieces. You are killing yourself alive. That is why it is called a *break up*. It *breaks* each of you apart along with your marriage. Remember that the Bible says the husband is the head of his wife (See Ephesians 5:23). Therefore, if you divorce, you are practically cutting your head off. If the husband hurts his wife, he is actually hurting his own body, and he will have heartache; and if the wife hurts her husband, she is hurting her own head, and she will have a headache. Even if you do divorce, you will carry a part your former partner's being with you for as long as you both live.

And this is the second thing you do: You cover the altar of the Lord with tears, with weeping and crying; so He does not regard the offering anymore, nor receive it with goodwill from your hands. Yet you say, "For what reason?" Because the Lord has been witness between you and the wife of your youth, with whom you have dealt treacherously; yet she is your companion and your wife by covenant. But did He not make them one, having a remnant of the Spirit? And why one? He seeks godly offspring. "Therefore take heed to your spirit, and let none deal treacherously with the wife of his youth. For the God of Israel says that He hates divorce, for it covers one's garment with violence," says the Lord of hosts. Therefore take heed in your spirit that you do not deal treacherously (Malachi 2:13-16).

It is so unfortunate how people nowadays enter into a marriage covenant just to test the waters and break the covenant as soon as they feel that the waters are not as 'sweet' as they expected. People tend to get married because they want the wedding celebration; not the marriage commitment. After the wedding, they are ready to go separate ways. They fail to understand the meaning of the vows they took before God and men that they will be together till death separates them. They treat marriage like a short-term contract that can be terminated at any time; and they are too quick to break their covenant when adversities occur. This happens most probably because they lack understanding of marriage as a life covenant.

Of all the things that God hates, there is nothing that He hates more than the breaking of the covenant. He literally ignores the cries of the covenant breaker and disregards his offerings. In his first epistle, the Apostle Peter commanded husbands to dwell with their wives with understanding and give honour to them, *so that their prayers may not be hindered* (See 1Peter 3:7). You cannot impress God by depressing your spouse; rather, God will be pleased when you honour each other as a couple and keep your marriage covenant. One of God's main ideas of marriage is that He seeks a godly offspring, and divorce opposes that idea. It compels parents to raise their children separately and fail to agree on how to raise them. Believe it or not, divorce inflicts severe damages on the children's concept of life and love. It imposes unnecessary hatred and bitterness in their hearts, and it frustrates God's original idea of marriage and family.

Divorce is not the will of God; in fact, He hates it (See Malachi 2:16). It rips apart what God Himself has joined together. It breaks the covenant that was established before God and witnesses. *And He answered and said to them, "Have you not read that He who made them in the beginning 'made them male and female,' and said, 'For this reason a man shall leave his father and mother and be joined to his wife, and the two shall become one flesh'? So then, they are no longer two but one flesh. Therefore what God has joined together, let not man separate* (Matthew 19:4-6). This is the decree from above: No one can separate what God has joined together.

Legally, marriage is just a contract; but spiritually, it is a lifelong covenant. A contract can be annulled, but the covenant is for a lifetime. A contract is signed and authorized before the marriage commissioner, but the covenant is sealed before God and approved by Him. Marriage is more than a contract; it is a covenant. Therefore, divorce ends the contract; not the marriage. In front of the law, you are divorced; but in front of God, you are still married until one or both of you die. The legal framework that regulates the law of divorce is man-made. Therefore, it cannot annul what God has established nor separate what He has joined together.

Divorce *cannot* end marriage because marriage is bigger and more significant in God's eyes than divorce. Therefore, if you divorce your spouse, the contract ends, but the covenant goes on. The only godly way by which marriage can be ended is if one or both of you die; as your vows testify: *"...Till death do us part." For the woman who has a husband is bound by law to her husband as long as he lives. But if the husband dies, she is released from the law of her husband. So then if, while her husband lives, she marries another man, she will be called an adulteress; but if her husband dies, she is free from that law, so that she is no adulteress, though she has married another man* (Romans 7:2-3). This Scripture implies that divorce cannot put an end to marriage. You are bound to your spouse until he or she dies.

A wife is bound by law as long as her husband lives; but if her husband dies, she is at liberty to be married to whom she wishes, only in the Lord (1 Corinthians 7:39). If your partner dies, you are then free to marry whoever you wish; but only within the parameters of your religion. In this case a believer should not marry an unbeliever; but the two should share the same faith. However, it is not wrong if you choose to remain single after your partner dies (See 1 Corinthians 7:40). But if you divorce your partner and marry another one while he or she is still alive, your second marriage then becomes an adulterous relationship. Each time you get into bed with your current partner while your former partner still lives, you are actually committing adultery. Even if the law of your country declares you divorced, you are still married in the eyes of God because you are bound to your partner for as long as he or she lives.

Jesus testifies to the above Scripture: *"And I say to you, whoever divorces his wife, except for sexual immorality, and marries another, commits adultery; and whoever marries her who is divorced commits adultery"* (Matthew 19:9). Jesus in this text gives one exception to divorce and remarriage: *sexual immorality.* In other words, you may divorce your spouse if they committed sexual immorality. However, this is permissive; not mandatory. It is not wrong to continue in marriage with your partner even after the act of sexual immorality. Whether you end it or continue with it is up to you. After all, marriage is worth fighting for.

Sexual immorality dishonours marriage and defiles the bed thereof; but *fornicators and adulterers God will judge* (Refer to Hebrews 13:4). When you commit adultery or any form of sexual immorality, you become a *profane person like Esau, who for one morsel of food sold his birthright* (See Hebrews 12:16). In other words, if you commit sexual immorality, you are practically selling your marriage away with one act of sexual indulgence. You are trading your lifelong relationship in exchange for a five minute pleasure.

There is another exception in as far as divorce and remarriage is concerned. *But if the unbeliever departs, let him depart; a brother or a sister is not under bondage in such cases* (1 Corinthians 7:15). In the above text, the Apostle Paul addresses the situation in a marital relationship where one partner becomes a believer in Christ and the other does not. The emphasis here is in the importance of our relationship with Christ more than our relationship with our spouses. In fact, without relationship with Christ, it would be impossible to have a healthy relationship with our spouses. However, the believing partner should not be the one who takes the initiative of separation. But if your unbelieving spouse decides to divorce you because of your relationship with Christ, you become free from your commitment. You may get married to whoever you please; but still within the parameters of your faith. However, you will still retain your right to remain single after divorce if you so choose.

If you divorce your spouse for any other reason except for these that were mentioned above, you are not allowed to remarry. You must remain unmarried. But if you want to remarry, you must go back to your former partner. Any other marriage is an adulterous relationship for you. *Now to the married I command...: A wife is not to depart from her husband. But even if she does depart, let her remain unmarried or be reconciled to her husband. And a husband is not to divorce his wife* (1 Corinthians 7:10-11).

Marriage should not be taken for granted. It is a serious relationship, and it requires lifelong commitment between husband and wife. You do not marry and divorce as you please. You must remain committed to your partner for as long as you both shall live. There's no turning back in marriage. Once the covenant is sealed, you are bound to your partner for a lifetime. A bound person does not go in and out as he pleases. *Are you bound to a wife? Do not seek to be loosed* (1 Corinthians 7:27). Marriage is binding; and everyone who is *bound* in marriage to their partners should not seek to be *loosed*. Simply put, you are confined to your partner for as long as you live (See 1 Corinthians 7:4).

It is better to remain single than to marry and divorce (See Matthew 19:10). When you are single, you are complete *alone*; but when you are married, you are complete *together*. Fusion is irreversible. Therefore, divorce makes you incomplete because it tears one flesh into two pieces. Even if you divorce under Biblically permissible reasons, it becomes no less painful. Divorce can be more agonizing than staying married. But sexual immorality is just as painful as divorce. So is being deserted by your partner for your faith in Christ. But nothing is less painful than divorce. Even if the reason for divorce is Biblically acceptable, it is advisable that you do everything in your power to save your marriage. Do not be too quick to break away. If you reach the conclusion to divorce, make sure you have tried everything, and there's nothing more you can do. Divorce should be your ultimate resort; not an immediate alternative.

Divorce is even more excruciating when there are children involved. You lose your privilege to raise your children together under one roof. Sometimes one partner loses legal custody of their children over to the other. This limits their interaction with their own flesh and blood. Having to live without both parents is much more agonizing for children. Sometimes children are used as weapons by the divorced couples to hurt each other. But the truth is that if you deprive your partner the privilege of seeing his child, you are also depriving your child the privilege of seeing his father; and the poor child does not deserve this. Couples usually divorce each other and leave their children under severe emotional damage. No child wants their parents to live apart; let alone being raised by a step father or step mother; especially when both their parents are still alive. Divorce paralyzes the future of humanity by tearing the hearts of children apart. Before you finalize your divorce, think about the children.

Divorce also causes severe economic setback for the couple; especially if they were married in community of property. They lose half of everything they own and have to sell the other half to cover the legal costs of divorce. Then they are left with almost nothing; at the same time experiencing the overwhelming feelings of emptiness. Divorce causes too much emotional strain. The pain of having to go to the house that used to be your own to see your children, whose mother used to be your wife; is not to be underrated. It could be much worse to find that your ex wife is raising your children with another man; who is raising them contrary to how you wanted them to be raised. This can torture you for as long as you live.

For many broken marriages, divorce could not have taken place had they taken time to understand marital truths and learn skills to navigate in marriage. Many couples are divorced but are still in love with each other. They broke up too soon over normal marital experiences that were actually meant to strengthen their marriages. They failed to appreciate each other because they were caught up in their apprehensive attitude towards each other. They could not handle their differences, and they focused too much on each other's imperfections that they failed to recognize how blessed they were to have each other. Even they themselves cannot provide valid reasons why they divorced; thus they exaggerate their stories in trying to validate their reasons before other people. But if you take a closer look, you will see that the problem they had was not *fatal* for their marriage; but it was *vital* for their marital growth.

Divorce never happens in isolation, it most often occurs as a result of breaking the smaller vows that were made on the wedding day – vows like "I will love, cherish and respect you under all circumstances for as long as I live". If you break those smaller vows, you are basically breaking the bigger covenant of marriage. Divorce, therefore, is not always the breaking of the covenant; it is sometimes the act of acknowledging that the covenant has already been broken. Divorce can also be the result of the broken covenant caused by the breaking of the vows that were taken before God and men. For example, if you vow before God and men that you will respect your spouse, you will be breaking the covenant if you disrespect them anytime afterwards. Divorce would be reduced tremendously (if not ended completely) if all the marriage vows could be kept at all times. As a matter of fact, divorce is not the death of a marriage; it is the burial of the marriage that is already dead. If you insist on keeping what you should bury, you are actually leaving the situation to get worse because your whole life will be filled with the stench of a decayed marriage. Therefore, much as you don't want divorce, make sure that you do not try to resuscitate what is already dead.

If you have been through this painful breakup called divorce, you don't have to condemn yourself. God hates divorce, but He still loves divorcees because Christ died for them as well. Your excruciating experience of divorce does not make Him love you less. He is the God of second chances; the Healer of every broken soul. The end of your marriage is not the end of your world. With the all-sufficient grace of God your Father, you can start over and be completely restored. There is no sin God cannot forgive through Christ Jesus His Precious Son, and there is no pain He cannot heal. Jesus has died for you, and through Him you can live and be victorious; even though your divorce experience practically took your life away. Submit your broken life at once to Him; He will give you a fresh start and forgive you like you've never sinned and heal you like you've never been hurt. Forgive and move on. Look ahead and not behind. God is more than able to give you a future that is far greater than your past and renew your life like an eagle.

Finally, my brethren, be strong in the Lord and in the power of His might (Ephesians 6:10). God can rewrite your life and give you a brighter future. You are never too broken for Him to restore you. He is the God of all flesh, and nothing is too hard for Him (See Jeremiah 32:27). Your heart may be overwhelmed with pain and grief, and inside you may be deeply hurt more than words can express. You may be living the life that is covered with total darkness and depression, and your heart may be filled with sorrow. Nevertheless, your purpose is more powerful than your pain, your hope is higher than your hurt, your dreams are dominant over your darkness and depression; your Saviour is stronger than your sorrow, and your God is greater than your grief. *Weeping may endure for a night, but joy comes in the morning* (Psalm 30:5).

Do not rejoice over me, my enemy; when I fall, I will rise; when I sit in darkness, the Lord will be a light to me (Micah 7:8). You may be down, but you are not out; and you may be covered with darkness, but the Lord is your Light. People may write you off, or maybe you may write yourself off because of your experience; but in God's eyes you are still precious. He loves you just the way you are, and He will cleanse you from within and give you beauty for ashes and the garment of praise for the spirit of heaviness (See Isaiah 61:3). Cry your last tear drop; but afterwards you should rise up, remove the ashes, shake off the dust and march on. God's strength is perfect when yours is gone, and He is always there to carry you when you cannot carry on.

No one marries with an intention to divorce. We all want our marriages to be successful; but without learning how to apply godly principles in our marriages, we may not succeed. Some marriages fail not because they do not know the principles of marital success; but because they do not practice those principles in their own marriages. Understanding without application is futile. You need to apply the Word of God and the principles you have learnt in your marriage. It is not enough to learn if you are not going to apply it into your situation. If all couples applied what they knew in their marriages, the rate of divorce would have been reduced enormously, and married couples would stay *together till the end.*

25

Count Yourself In

"...*You shall love your neighbour as yourself...*" (Leviticus 19:18). This is one of the greatest commandments God ever gave to us. It also forms part of the *Golden Rule* (or *Ethic of Reciprocity*); which encourages us to treat others as we expect to be treated. Mutual love begins with self-love. Actually, self-love is the benchmark for mutual love. You cannot have a healthy relationship with other people if you cannot have one with yourself. In fact, you will never know how to love other people if you do not know how to love yourself. In several cases as I do marriage counselling and relationship empowerment programmes, I have met people who struggle to love others; and I could trace their problem to their inability to love themselves.

You cannot love your spouse if you do not love yourself. In fact, your love for your spouse is an overflow of your love for yourself. Many a times I have seen people give their all to their loved ones and then give nothing to themselves. Such behaviour is commonly referred to as *altruism*. Altruistic people focus only on others and never on themselves. Their practices are always self-sacrificial. They are totally selfless; and they put the interests and welfare of other people before their own without expecting anything in return. The world is benefitting a lot from such people. However, altruistic behaviour neglects the most important person – the very person who always performs self-sacrificial acts. If you keep on helping other people while you neglect yourself, you might end up not having enough energy to carry on; and they might end up having no one to help them.

Consider the transactions that are taking place in the bank. You cannot make withdrawals from your bank if you made no deposits into it; unless if you have made an arrangement with the bank that you will withdraw on an overdraft, which occurs when money is drawn and the available balance is below zero. But even overdrafts have limit; and interest is charged with every withdrawal. When you exceed the limit, more interest is being charged; until you cannot afford to pay back to the bank what you owe them. This can also prohibit you from making further withdrawals not only from the bank you owe; but also from all other financial institutions. Eventually, you will be not only broke; but also disqualified to borrow money from anywhere. This can lead to severe episodes of depression and nervous breakdown. The best way you can manage your bank account is by ensuring that you never withdraw more than you have deposited.

Your life is a *personal bank.* If you keep on giving out to other people more than you are depositing into yourself, you will soon start withdrawing on overdraft – operating with the energy you do not have. Even if it feels like you are going strong, the truth is that you are gradually wearing out. As time goes on, you will start experiencing debilitating feelings of emptiness, because you will be left with nothing to give. Eventually you will start burning out like the fire that was never refuelled. Once you burn out, you will lose the strength not only to help others; but also to help yourself. This can also lead to severe episodes of depression and nervous breakdown; and the very people you were trying to help will be left wanting you. As much as it is important to love and serve other people, it is more significant that you make sure you never leave yourself behind.

In my observation, I have noticed that women tend to be more altruistic than men in relationships. This could be as a result of their tendency to be emotionally attached to their surroundings. Several times I have observed significant quantities of women focusing so much on being mothers and wives that they forgot to be themselves. They devotedly take care of their children and husbands; but they forget to take care of themselves. Very often they allow their loved ones to make withdrawals from them, but very seldom, if ever, do they take time to make deposits into their own lives. In the process they feel angry and miserable because their wells are starting to run dry; and the less they are able to give, the more demands their loved ones make on them. All their loved ones keep getting better, but they themselves keep getting worse. Then they start hating their lives and blaming themselves for failing to play their role as mothers and wives. Some end up suffering heartbreaking experiences of being left by their husbands and being disowned by their own children because they gave themselves so much that they were no longer able to perform. Now they have to deal with the pain of being deserted by the very people they always sacrifice themselves for.

It is good to love and cherish your spouse; but it is bad to neglect yourself in the process. If you love them like you profess that you do, then why don't you take care of yourself for their sake? If you keep on neglecting yourself while trying to serve them, they will ultimately be without the one to serve them when you eventually experience nervous breakdown. You cannot survive if you keep on exhaling; you also need to inhale. Whatever is used without being reloaded will be used up. This goes for you as well. If you keep on filling up other people without taking time to fill yourself up, you will soon be empty; and so will the people you were trying to fill up. As you help your spouse realise their dreams, also pursue your own. Learn to invest in yourself so that you may have a large capacity to impact your spouse and children. As you teach your children to pray; also make time to pray. As you minister to them, give God time to minister to you. As you encourage them to read, also take time to read.

You cannot give what you do not have. So, before you give, take time to acquire. If the axe is not sharpened, it will become dull; so will you if you keep on pleasing people at the expense of your wellbeing. You can't perform well if you are not well. Your spouse needs you happy and strong; and it does not help them if they are happy and you are not, because your misery will rub off on them in one way or the other. This is not about anybody having to do anything for you; it's about you having to do something for yourself. If you don't take care of yourself, there are major chances that nobody will. As a matter of fact, how you treat yourself teaches other people how to treat you. Even if you treat them well, and they are willing to return the favour, it will be hard for them to treat you differently from the way you treat yourself. You can't afford to be a hero to them and yet be a zero to yourself. That is not healthy for you; and your marriage cannot be healthy if you are not.

If you read through the four Gospels in the New Testament, you will notice that even though Jesus devoted Himself to helping people, He also took time to be alone and pray. He not only gave Himself for people to withdraw from Him; but He also withdrew Himself from the people to allow God to make deposits into Him. When He was tired, He rested. When He was hungry,

He ate. When He was thirsty, He drank. When He was troubled, He prayed. When He was sad, He wept. Although He kept in touch with the people, He never lost touch with Himself. Even though He was needed everywhere, He did not try to please everybody by sacrificing His prayer time to be with them. When they came to hear His sermon on the mount, He understood that they were hungry, because He felt it in Himself. He could relate with people and be sympathetic to them because he knew not only how it felt to be in their situation; but also how to deal with it. As He healed the sick, He also trusted God for His health. That is why He was never affected by the sicknesses He was healing and the problems He was solving.

You can take after Jesus today and start learning to take care of yourself as much you want to take care of others. When you are hungry, eat. When you are tired, rest. If you have questions, ask. When you feel sad, take time to cry. Do not let yourself sink into the problems you are trying to solve and needs you are trying to meet. Before you help them, strengthen your helping hands; and before you love them, fortify your loving heart. As you try to please them, see that you do not lose yourself in the process. As you try to save your loved ones from drowning, watch out that you do not sink into the same water from which you are trying to save them. As you help them reach the top, be careful not to get stuck at the bottom; and as you get out of your way to make them happy, count yourself in.

26

Marriage: A Type for Eternity

The main reason why marriage is under so much attack is because Satan hates it, and the reason why he hates is because it brings honour and glory to God its Creator. Marriage brings godly order into families. If families are in order, communities will be healthy, and if communities are healthy, the world will be healthy. Satan hates godly order in the world, so he works hard to attack marriages by introducing ungodly practices such as divorce, casual sex and cohabitation. As a result, children grow up without their fathers, and this contaminates godly order in families. God wants to be known to us as the Father, and we cannot understand Him that way if families have no fathers. What Satan hates the most about marriage is that it is God's model for our salvation in Christ Jesus our Lord. It reveals the loving and forgiving heart of Christ for us His bride.

Marriage is the ultimate expression of our relationship with Christ. It is through our marriage to Christ that we are adopted as sons by God our Father. That is why Jesus said *"No one comes to the Father except through Me"* (John 14:6). *For you are all sons of God through faith in Christ Jesus* (Galatians 3:26). Our relationship with God as our Father begins with our marriage to Jesus Christ His Son. This marriage makes us children of God and *joint* heirs with Christ our Lover (See Romans 8:15-17). In other words, by being *joined* with Christ the Son, we are heirs of God the Father. Christ did not just take us at no cost as His own; He paid the ultimate price by shedding His own blood for us. His precious blood was our bride price. It is through His blood that He took our sins and gave us His righteousness. *For He made Him who knew no sin to be sin for us, that we might become the righteousness of God in Him* (2 Corinthians 5:21).

Marriage is not just a legal contract; it is a divine union that typifies the life that we will finally live with Christ in eternity. It is a revelation of how Christ relates with His church. His great love for us is typified by the husband's love for his wife, and our submission to Him is typified by the wife's submission to her husband. Our relationship with Christ is the ultimate pattern for marriage, and marriage is a type for our adoption as sons by God the Father through our marriage to Christ Jesus His only begotten Son. Like I already mentioned earlier, the husband cannot truly love his wife if he does not understand how much Christ loves him; and the wife cannot submit to her husband if she cannot submit to Christ. Furthermore, the husband cannot say he loves Christ if he fails to love his own wife; and the wife cannot claim to submit to Christ if she fails to submit to her own husband.

Marriage is a type for eternity. It is an anthropomorphic way of revealing the eternal life to which we are entitled through Christ Jesus our Lord. *And this is the testimony: that God has given us eternal life, and this life is in His Son. He who has the Son has life; he who does not have the Son of God does not have life. These things I have written to you who believe in the name of the Son of God, that you may know that you have eternal life, and that you may continue to believe in the name of the Son of God* (1 John 5:11-13). There is no eternal life for those who do not believe in the Son of God; but for those who believe in Him, who are *joined* to Him, there is eternal life; and that eternal life is in Him. This Christ is the Head of the church, and it is this same Christ who made the husband the head of his wife; and just as He made the church His body, so has He made the wife to be her husband's body. The wife is *joined* to her husband just as the church is *joined* to Him.

As soon as the wife is *joined* to her husband, they become one flesh. The father of the husband then becomes the father of the wife also. In the same way, as soon as we believed in Christ and accepted Him as our Saviour and Lord, we became one with Him; and His Father became our Father. That is why the Bible says we shall reign with Him (See 2 Timothy 2:12). Christ's Kingdom is our Kingdom because we are joined to Him; and being joined to Him, we are one with Him. Therefore, whatever is His is also ours. Whatever we lack, He has; and we have it in Him. Since we believed in Him, we are in Him, and He became for us wisdom from God, and righteousness and sanctification and redemption (See 1 Corinthians 1:30). In Him we have everything, and without Him we have nothing. Even though we are not perfect as humans, we are perfected in Him. All the curses we deserve, He took away; and all the blessings we do not deserve, He gave freely to us.

We are weak, but we find our strength in Him. Without Him we are poor, but in Him we are rich. We are sinful, but in Him we are righteous. We are in the dark, but He is our Light. Without Him we are foolish, but in Him we are wise. *In Him we live and move and have our being* (Acts 17:28). He is the Vine, and we are His branches (See John 15:1-8). We are crafted in Him to bear fruit. Without Him, we are nothing, and we can do nothing. On the other hand, He is invisible; but we are visible, and He manifests Himself on earth through us. Because of our union with Him, we have become the visible image of the invisible God. Our imperfections are complemented by His perfection, and His invisibility is complemented by our visibility. He also uses our visible relationships with our spouses to reveal His invisible relationship with us. He represents us in Heaven, and we represent Him on earth.

Marriage operates with the same principle. Usually, we have what our spouses lack, and they have what we lack; but because of our marriage to them, whatever we lack in ourselves, we have it in them, and whatever they lack in themselves, they have it in us. Husbands are male versions of their wives, and wives are the female versions of their husbands. Whatever the husband lacks in himself as a man, he has it in his wife; and whatever the wife lacks in herself as a woman, she has it in her husband. Similarly, we are the mortal version of the immortal God, and He is the immortal version of the mortal humans. His supernatural power is manifested on earth through our natural beings.

Christ never leaves nor forsakes us; neither does He ever give up on us. He even said in His Word: *"... I am with you always, even to the end of age"* (Matthew 28:20). He never walks out on us no matter how many times we fail Him; and still He never fails us. Even when we are unfaithful to Him, He remains faithful to us because He cannot deny Himself (See 2 Timothy 2:13). Take note that Christ remains faithful even if we are not because *He cannot deny Himself.* This means that His faithfulness to us is based not on who we are or what we do; but on who He is. This is how couples should treat each other in marriage. We should learn to be faithful to our spouses not because of what they do, but because of who we are. We should love them not because they love us, but because we are loving in nature, and we cannot deny ourselves. As couples, we should be to each other as Christ is to us His church. We should never walk out on each other; but we should be faithful and totally committed to each other so that we may live successfully *together till the end.*

References

LaHaye, T. 1988. Why You Act the Way You Do. Tyndale Momentum (first published January 1st 1987)

Masters, WH & Johnson, VE *Human Sexual Response*, Bantam, 1981 ISBN 978-0-553-20429-2; 1st ed. 1966

Phillips, RS. 2008. http://www.medicinenet.com/sexual_response_cycle_phases_of_sexual_response/page3.htm

Printed in the United States
By Bookmasters